THE WRITER'S FUGUE

Also by Ruth Skilbeck

Australian Fugue novels
The Antipode Room
Missing

THE WRITER'S FUGUE

Musicalization, Trauma and Subjectivity in the Literature of Modernity

RUTH SKILBECK

POSTMISTRESS PRESS

NEWCASTLE

Copyright © Ruth Skilbeck 2017

First published by PostMistress Press
The Old Post Office, Adamstown, Newcastle
www.postmistresspress.com

The right of Ruth Skilbeck to be identified as the author of this work has been asserted by her in accordance with the Copyright, Designs and Patents Act 1988.

All rights reserved. No part of this publication may be reproduced, stored in a retrieval system, or transmitted, in any form or by any means, electronic, mechanical, photocopying, recording or otherwise, except in the case of brief quotations embodied in critical articles, or reviews, without written permission from the copyright holder.

National Library of Australia
Cataloguing-in-Publication data:

Skilbeck, Ruth, author.

The writer's fugue: musicalization, trauma and subjectivity in the literature of modernity/Ruth Skilbeck

ISBN: 9780992277949 (paperback)

Includes bibliographical references

Fugue.
Fugue in Literature.
Literature—Adaptations.

784.1872

Contents

PART 1

Preface   1

INTRODUCTION   3

1 EXILED WRITERS' HUMAN RIGHTS & SOCIAL ADVOCACY
MOVEMENTS IN AUSTRALIA: A CRITICAL FUGAL ANALYSIS   14
Action Writing—Writing Action: the Post-Kantian Subject—
Journey into Exile—Fugal Approach—Cases of Exiled Writers
and International Human Rights Law—Deconstructing
Dehumanization and Deviancy—Refugee Writers: Beyond
Detention—Changing Policies—Islands of Despair: Pacific
Solution v2—Sydney Biennale Boycott Protest Background—
Sydney Biennale Boycott Protest—Official Audit Criticizes
Department of Immigration and Border Protection—Arts
Funding Cuts—Behrouz Boochani Posts—Christopher Barnett—
Fugal Analysis

2 TAKING FLIGHT INTO WRITING   86
Methodological Issues: Intentionality and Phenomenology—
Psychoanalytical Themes: Mimesis, Trauma, Affect

3 FUGUE VARIATIONS: POLYPHONIC CONVERSATIONS   114
Structural Form and Techniques—Variations in Interpretation:
Modality to Tonality—History and Development of Fugue—
Canon—Polyphony—Variations, Texture and New Contexts—
Rousseau, Rameau, and the Dispute over Harmony: Querelle des
Bouffons

4 IDENTITY SHIFTS, FUGAL RECURSION   138
Fugal Journeys—Musico-Literary Terms—Fugue Narratives—
New Limits of Representation—Fugal Paradox: The Dichotomy
of Writing—Fugal Recursion: A Perceptual Function of Memory

5 STATELESS. THE DISSOCIATIVE FUGUE   157
Early Definitions of Psychogenic Fugue—Fin de Siècle and
the Emergence of Fugue—Cornelia Rau: a Case of Mistaken
Identity—Medical Conclusions—Objects of Love and Hate—The
Writer's Fugue: Paradox of Modern Subjectivity

PART 2

6 LITERARY FUGUE STUDIES — 199

7 THOMAS DE QUINCEY'S *DREAM-FUGUE* — 202
The English Mail-Coach—'Into my dreams forever'—De Quincey's 'Literature of Power'—The Young Romantic and Romantic Withdrawal—Re/connecting Life, Work and Art Involutes—Emotional Avoidance, Trauma and Fugue—'Author's Postscript' to the *Dream-Fugue*—Post-Traumatic Stress Disorder—Musicalization in *Dream-Fugue*—Writing Accidents—Cracking the Puzzle-Canon of the 'Dream-Fugue'—Interpretations of 'Dream-Fugue'—Musicalized Readings—Reverberation and 'Impassioned Prose'—'Dreadful resurrections that are in dreams'—Rapture and Ravishment—Postmodern Readings of *Dream-Fugue*

8 MARCEL PROUST'S FUGUE OF *LOST TIME* — 242
Through the 'I's of Lost Time—Shifting Perspectives—Proust in Time: La Belle Èpoque—Memory/Modernist Métier—Proust and Bergson—Élan Vital and Memory Binding—Metaphor, Motif and Metonymy in Proust—I-Spy: How Many I's am 'I'?—'Invisible Music' of 'Unknown Pleasures'—The Importance of Being Affective—Musicalized Sign Language—Metaphors in Metaphors: the Art of the Infinitely Expanding (self-generative, associative) Metaphor—Metonymy: Coded Associations-Discreet Language of Text—Motif/Motive: Objectifying Others, The Writer's Bliss—Motion and Motive Energy: Musical Analogies to Temps Durée and Temps Espace—Chora—The Proustian Writing Machine: What Makes *À la recherche du temps perdu* a Performative Fugal Text—The Antilogos and the Fugal Modality of Writing

9 JAMES JOYCE *SIRENS'* FUGUE — 293
Homecoming: *Ulysses*, a Strategy of Invention—Protagonists on a Mock Epic Journey—The Mystery of Joyce's *Fuga per Canonem* Revisited—Fugue Devices and the *Fuga per Canonem*—Double Meanings of Joyce's Double Counterpoint—Sirens' Setting and 'Technic'—Fugal Texture—Fugal Variation on A Theme—Songs of Seduction and Rebellion—Comparative Interpretations—Figures of Speech Sound—Joyce's Fugal 'Quintet' of 'Master Singers'

10 PAUL CELAN AFTER THE *DEATHFUGUE* — 346
Black Milk—'Death is a Meister from Germany'—*Deathfugue*'s Structure—'Poetry after Auschwitz is Barbaric'—Music after Auschwitz: Klezma Chronotope

11 SYLVIA PLATH *LITTLE FUGUE*   370

12 THE WRITERS' FUGUE IN REVIEW   380
Crab Canon—Writing Subjectivity—Invention—Arrangement—
Trauma: Style—Delivery—Modern Fugal Modality of Writing

Notes   393
Works Consulted   414

PART ONE

Preface

Fugue is derived from the Latin word, fuga, which refers to 'flight', 'fleeing', and 'to chase'. The source of fuga, originally stood for what musicologists call 'canon'. The word 'canon' originated in Pythagorean philosophy. Pythagorean inquiries were predominantly mathematical:

> arithmetic construed as an investigation into the patterns of numbers, geometry construed as an investigation into metrical patterning of shapes, and harmony construed as an investigation into the patterning of musical intervals.¹

Pythagorean harmony was based on properties of musical intervals, it could be related to mathematics and geometry because relations between various musical intervals could be discovered by comparison to lengths of strings which, when plucked, produced the different tones, writes David Hamlyn in his History of Western Philosophy. *From this mathematical analogue developed a mystical belief by some Pythagoreans that similarities between mathematical principles—likenesses—could be seen in many different things. Pythagoreans entertained the mystical belief that as the planets moved through the heavens they made a divine music of too high a frequency for human ears to hear. From this application of commensurability, developed the theory that the universe was ordered entirely according to rational (mathematical) principles that articulated divine order or will to a 'perfect' plan. The Pythagoreans' discovery of incommensurables (irrational numbers, such as root two, which cannot be expressed in terms of a rational fraction) was considered to be dangerous to society. There is a story of Hippasus of Tarentum discovering incommensurability, being rowed out to sea and drowned for revealing Pythagorean secrets.²*

The word 'canon' in Pythagoras's usage referred specifically to the template that was used for marking off the harmonic divisions in the monochord. The Pythagoreans believed that the study of geometry and harmony (by analogy) would lead to gnosis (wisdom), and that mathematical patterns in the natural world reflect profound archetypal laws that all phenomena are based upon.³

2 THE WRITER'S FUGUE

The conceptualization of canon (as rule) influenced Greek Rhetoric, as codified by the Roman author Quintilian, wherein there are five canons evoking harmonic principles of invention, arrangement, style, memory, and delivery. They evoke harmonic principles of ordering by intervals and in musical composition. They stipulate the 'rules', the social conventions or laws of language use for discourse in political and forensic oratory, and to some extent for criticism of the arts and poetry.

Resurrecting this beginning-etymology of the word 'canon' there have been parallels and interrelationships between the development of musical language, and the uses and functions of language as social, political, philosophical and critical discourse in western culture. The issue for modern artistic literary uses of musical concepts is not only how but why creative literary artists have used fugal musicalization in significant literary narratives and texts of Romanticism and Modernism, and in postwar literature.

Stories of exiled writers are discussed in Chapter 1. This essay is an updated version of 'Exiled Writers, Human Rights and Social Advocacy Movements in Australia: A Critical Fugal Analysis' which is published in the book *Cultural Studies of Rights: Critical Articulations* (Routledge 2014), which first appeared as a special issue of the journal *Communication and Critical/Cultural Studies* (2010). The essay includes studies of two writers, journalist Chiekh Kone, and poet Mohsen Soltany Zand, who were held in immigration detention centres without trial for years in Australia. The updated essay includes three new studies, the first on the boycott of the Biennale of Sydney in 2014 that occurred in protest against the ties of the Founding Sponsor, and the then Biennale Board chairman, to the infrastructure company that was in process of being awarded the ongoing multi-billion dollar contract for management of the garrison and welfare services in the offshore processing centres, of the detention centres. As a result of the boycott the Biennale board severed the ties. Most artists returned to the Biennale and in 2014, new sponsorship by the inaugural Principal Sponsor, the Neilson Foundation, began. This study is followed by a brief study on exiled journalist, Behrouz Boochani, currently in limbo in the 'Manus offshore processing centre'; and a dialogic study of the work of émigré Australian poet Christopher Barnett.

INTRODUCTION

This book addresses the fugue in music, psychology and literature, and is perhaps the first to do so. In Part I the etymological development of fugue in music and psychology is traced, with case studies that focus on the psychological and musical meanings of fugue. Part II comprises in depth and finely grained musico-literary analyses of the adaptation of musical fugue forms and techniques in the inventive musicalized fugue works of Romantic, Modernist, and Contemporary authors and poets. Authors discussed herein, who use the musical form of fugue, in their works include Thomas de Quincey, James Joyce, Marcel Proust, Paul Celan, Sylvia Plath, and Christopher Barnett. In this literary investigation, from the perspective of the multivalent figure of 'fugue', I discuss selected literary fugue compositions of modernism, and contemporary writing. The analysis is grounded on theories of how literary processes relate to articulation and consciousness of individual subjects and subjectivity in innovative intermedial uses of language.

The literary figure of fugue is used as a heuristic device to approach and investigate concepts of authorship, and to examine contradictions inherent in concepts of representation, imitative mimesis, and the construction of the 'subject' in language, as identified in contemporary discourse. The inquiry aims to deploy an array of established analytic strategies, and to further advance understanding of the cultural figure of fugue and its applications. This endeavour is expressed in the concept 'the writer's fugue'.

In the focus on the style of musicalized fugal writing, the investigation is informed by Mikhail Bakhtin's approach to *stylistics*, which he wrote has been 'deprived of an authentic philosophical and sociological approach'. He wrote:

> More often than not, stylistics defines itself as a stylistics of "private craftsmanship" and ignores the social life of discourse outside the

artist's study, discourse in the open spaces of public squares, streets, cities and villages, of social groups, generations and epochs.[1]

The social life of discourse now exists in the online public squares of social media. In Part 1, the inquiry draws on a range of genres, not only of literary writings of fugue narratives and poetry, but also professional writing of government reports, medical articles, media articles, and musical articles, and interviews, from research into fugue writing; and in the case studies in Chapter 1, draws on open letters, and articles in online media and on blogs. This approach is informed by another idea put forward by Bakhtin about *heteroglossia* or the living formation of meaning (in discourses) and genres in languages, that occurs in a play of dynamics created by what he terms the centripetal forces (of centralization and unification) and centrifugal forces (of decentralization and disunification), which is a continual process in living language:

> At the time when poetry was accomplishing the task of cultural, national and political centralization of the verbal-ideological world in the higher official socio-ideological levels, on the lower levels, on the stages of local fairs, and at buffoon spectacles, the heteroglossia of the clown sounded forth, ridiculing all "languages" and dialects; there developed the literature of the *fabliaux* and *Schwänke* of street songs, folksayings, anecdotes, where there was no language-centre at all, where there was to be found a lively play with the "languages" of poets, scholars, monks, knights and others, where all "languages" were masks and where no language could claim to be an authentic, incontestable face.[2]

Some of the authors of the literary works discussed herein, for instance Joyce, do use parody, in the creation of new forms of musicalized language, and each of the fugue authors discussed creates new forms of language in literary language, including new words and terms. In the earlier part of the book which discusses the dissociative fugue, a range of sources are drawn on. As is shown in differing ways throughout the book, one voice or point of view, may not define the 'truth' of a historical event, but through listening to many voices, on the themes, a fuller and more accurate account is created from which the reader is able to gain a broader and deeper understanding. This holds true, too, in individual works of literary narration, the interweaving of many 'voices', in polyphonic literature echoes the form of the fugue in music. This is discussed in various ways and forms in the book.

'Every utterance participates in the "unitary language" (in its centripetal forces and tendencies) and at the same time partakes of social and historical heteroglossia (the centrifugal, stratifying forces), wrote Bahktin in his essay *Discourse in the Novel*.[3] In my literary investigation I focus not only on the morphology, and use and forms of fugue, in literature, and different discourses, but primarily on the authors, and why they used fugue. It is my focus on the author, in social and cultural contexts of their lives, that makes this study. The focus on the authors in the contexts of their lives, shows that despite the possible use of carnivalesque or parodic forms of language, that what was driving them deeply were traumatic experiences, and that many authors who write deeply from traumatic contexts and experience, with political engagement use polyphonic and fugal forms of writing, and in different ways. In this book, I do not use the term 'centrifugal', I refer to the term I develop, *fugal modality*, in relation to musical form, which I then apply to literary writing, and criticism.

I do refer to the term *dialogism* that was coined by Bahktin. Michael Holquist, translator and editor of *The Dialogic Imagination*, gives a succinct definition:

> Dialogism is the characteristic epistemological mode of a world dominated by heteroglossia. Everything means, is understood as part of a greater whole- there is a constant interaction between meanings, all of which have the potential of conditioning others.[4]

In this living process:

> A word, discourse or language or culture undergoes "dialogization" when it becomes relativized, de-privileged, aware of competing definitions of the same thing. Undialogized language is authoritative or absolute.[5]

Holquist identifies two ways in which Bakhtin uses the term dialogism, and these are, too, the ways in which I use the term throughout this book. 'Dialogue may be external [between two different people] or it may be 'internal [between an earlier and a later self]'.[6]

These two types of dialogue have been distinguished and described as respectively spatial and temporal communication acts.

In my analysis of literary works, specifically of Proust's *In Search of Lost Time*, which is an excellent example, I suggest another dimension: of space-time, a virtual dimension, which is entered in the reading of the work. How this dimension, or space-time, is activated and entered in the writer's process of writing, is an underlying theme of the *Writer's*

Fugue. Bakhtin referred to space-time in the novel, as a chronotope. I do not specifically refer to this in this book, but I do explore in depth the dynamics and dimensions of the fugal writing process, and relate this to the musical form of fugue, which gives such a concept as space-time a more grounded context, of analogy and comparison in the time and space of musical performance.

As I have been researching fugue for twenty years I show here some ways in which its uses have changed over that time. A new interest in fugue and fugal writing in literature is developing around the world in Europe, Australia, America, and Asia, and more widely.

Fugue is a potentially enigmatic (and thereby instructive) example of linguistic duality in itself. Its dual, apparently dichotomous, meanings potentially render it a performative example of rhetorical and symbolic linguistic contradiction. Derived from the Latin *fuga* or flight, the fugue presents as an apposite device to indicate and explore recent attempts to 'ground' or 'anchor' allusive definitions of the elusive and divided subject in language.

As an enigmatic literary figure, fugue has various applications, uses, and functions, to do with different interpretations and constructions of the 'subject' in musical, psychological, and literary language.

In its musical meaning, the fugue is a many 'voiced' musical form that develops from the *subject,* a short melody, initially presented by a 'voice' which is met by an *'answer'* another voice that replays or imitates the notes of the melody in a different way; all the voices play the notes of the *subject* line, and there may then be a *countersubject* that is introduced and answered and played by the voices. In baroque fugue, the voices play the subject themes in variations of counterpoint, and with 'ornaments' (accidentals) adding interest and variation, to the theme and/or countersubject theme. There may be a *codetta*, a cadence at the end of the playing of the first exposition, and a *coda* a longer cadence that signifies the close of the fugue. It is a form of invention, the 'rules' of which are determined by the notes of the subject melody-line and how many ways in which they can be played, and varied. It is dialogic, as the voices 'talk' to each other. The voices are not 'artificially' harmonized, but naturally harmonize in the playing or singing. 'Voices' (or 'parts') are instruments or singing voices. The instruments typically used to play eighteenth-century fugues are violins, cellos, violas, harpsichord, and recorders. It emerged in pre-modernity to reach an apex in the complex intellectual music of composers such as Bach. Fugue is exemplary of polyphony, imitative counterpoint, and invention in musical language, and remains in extant use as a texture, rather than a form. The fugue in music and the development of ideas of the modern subject are discussed in Chapter 2. A free form, it is disciplined by the 'rules' emerging from the notes, and the latter forms of fugue reached extraordinary enactions of infinity in Bach's mirror fugues.

In striking contrast, in its psychological meaning, fugue is a condition of dissociation involving an individual subject losing awareness of her or his self, and wandering away, or metaphorically taking flight from their usual surroundings, on a journey in which they are in a state of self-amnesia. This definition emerged in 1887 in France. Dissociative fugue is increasingly described as a 'flight' response to emotional trauma. The fugue in psychology is a term for a condition of self-loss, dissociation and alienation felt by the 'subject', which was identified by Baudelaire in his writing on the 'shock' of modernity, experienced by the individual.

This psychological diagnostic meaning which emerged in the late nineteenth century serves as a metaphor for the post-Kantian divided subject. Prior to the German philosopher's *Critique of Pure Reason* (1787) the prevailing view was that everyone had a soul, and that the individual subject was unified. The divided subject has become a prevailing metaphorical concept in industrialized capitalist modernity.

Through focusing on authors' use of musicalization in their literary poetic writings, in the historical, social, cultural and biographical contexts of their lives, in which, and of which, the works were written, the studies in this book produce a different perspective on the 'subject' and aesthetic representation which moves beyond the Kantian 'divided subject', discussed in Chapter 1, to produce a conceptual understanding of the subject as comprising different parts, that are conscious and unconscious, intentional and unintentional, yet which are not incompatible with the idea of a different kind of 'unified' self of many parts a self that in the right conditions feels and apprehends itself as 'unified' or in natural harmony and well-being (no matter how rare such conditions may be).

This eighteenth-century philosophy of the divided subject, coincided with the new form of harmony spreading in European and western music. Kant's theory of the 'divided' subject echoes the structure of a particular form of chord in the more complex chordal harmony that Rameau advanced, that enabled tonality, and which is used today. The 'seventh' chords have a missing 'tonic' note, which has to be compensated for by other instruments, and which enabled the development of tonal chord progression of the classical style, in symphonic music, and the sonata. A form which musicologist Susan McClary, in *Feminine Endings* (1991) suggests reflects relations of the domination in patriarchal colonial societies. In contrast, the musical fugue is of melody, its contrapuntal polyphony creates a natural harmony, yet it was turned into the later development of tonality and chordal harmony, that led to the classical style. It was thereby the vessel of the changing articulations and styles in music.

Rousseau who was a composer of natural melody was against more complex forms of harmony and was highly critical of fugue and its contrapuntal polyphony even though fugue is based on melody. The distinction between melody and new harmony was considered to be of great political significance in pre-Revolutionary France in 1752. When a melody-based comic *opera buffa* troupe was booked to perform in the intervals of the (harmonic) operas at the Paris Opera, this caused a long controversy, known as the Querelle des Bouffons (Quarrel of the comedians) and the Guerre de Coins (War of the Corners), as supporters of new French harmony met each day under the King's cornerbox at the Opera, and the supporters of Italian melody under the Queen's cornerbox. As Paris became absorbed in the politicized quarrel over aristocrats' and peoples' tastes, this was later said to have prolonged the Ancien Regime by years (discussed in Chapter 3).

Meanwhile in Germany, Kant proposed that 'The effect of an object upon the faculty of representation, so far as we are affected by it, is sensation.'[7] The idea that affect is part of the process of intuition, and that the effect of an object upon the faculty of our representation is in sensation, is an idea that was taken up by literary authors and poets of romanticism, and also in modernism. It is also of significance in the concept of the fugal modality of literary writing in which the impacts of trauma are transformed into musicalized literary language, where the shaking of the subject, who might have received a shock so severe that he or she has an out-of-the-body experience, or loses awareness of self, is transferred into phonematic devices (speech sounds in words) that in musicalized writing conjure up: reverberations, vibrations, and involutions, in the narratives and poetry of the authors discussed in this book. This process of musicalization in writing is not (necessarily) conscious, or consciously chosen as such by authors, but it can be, and in the chapters on the works discussed I show how each of the authors uses these modes. However the significance of using musicalization, is that music is what is sometimes termed *non-representational*. Music is sometimes described as *non-objective*, as it is not attached to objects in a representational way, yet it is the mode by which feeling is authentically expressed, which translates into musicalized writing; how fugue musicalization is used by the authors is discussed in this book.

Gathering these diverse meanings together, fugue has become a rhetorical, symbolical, and above all a creative figure in the literature of modernity. As such, it emerged in Thomas De Quincey's *The English Mail Coach*, in the third part *Dream-Fugue* (1897a). Variants of the fugue form have been used by authors composing original works using the phonematic devices of musicalization; articulations and utterances of fugue form, inflected by meanings from music and psychology are to be found in many literary texts of Romanticism and Modernism and contemporary writing.

The self-evidence of altered consciousness or intoxicated sensibility articulated by De Quincey in *Dream-Fugue* has led some to suggest that we can interpret and understand the 'subjectivity' of modernity according to De Quincey's foreshadowing of 'intoxication' in modernist writing. But my study shows the salient premise in this articulation of subjectivity in these modernist works is not 'intoxication', which is an effect, but the experience of trauma, that is the driver underpinning the articulation of the subjectivity inscribed in these examples of the literature of modernity, in the works of De Quincey, Proust, Joyce, Celan, Plath, and Barnett. A close reading of this literature, when read in biographical, social and cultural contexts shows that articulation of traumatic affect takes the form of transfer into musicalized language form. Forms of intentionality operate simultaneously in the writing of these fugue narratives, which can be read as more politically engaged than has been said of modernist literature, for instance by Lukács.[8]

Within the last decade, there has been and continues to be a resurgence of reporting on the psychogenic fugue, that has been re-termed the dissociative fugue, that is congruent with increasing incidences of dissociation in the twenty-first century, an era which is characterized by the largest displacement of people since the Second World War due to the wars in Europe and the Middle East. Since this thesis was first written, dissociative fugue has been redefined as an anxiety disorder in the *Diagnostic and Statistical Manual-13;* and in literature, there is a new movement of fugue literary writings; the book-length poem *when they came for you/elegies of resistance* (2013), a fugal literary work by Australian poet Christopher Barnett, in France, is discussed, in Chapter 1.

Chapter 1 includes discussions and interviews with writers in exile, who fled from homelands where their lives were in danger due to the repressive regimes that they wrote in, and critiqued in their writings. This does not only apply to the writers who were in Australian immigration indefinite detention centres (one of whom is marooned in the 'offshore processing centre' on Manus). It also applies to poet Christopher Barnett who left Australia permanently following several attacks, being badly beaten, due to his political protesting in the anti-Vietnam War movement, as a teenager, and his poetry and theatre writing and production in the late 1970s and 1980s. He fled to France where he has lived since in Nantes, where he is widely appreciated for his work as a poet and dramaturg and as co-founder of Le Derniere Spectateur for the disenfranchised, where he runs writing workshops for the marginalized. He has been commended by Jean-Marc Ayrault, French Prime Minister; his work included giving workshops in prisons, hospitals and asylums, and collaborating as writer and dramaturg for many years with the anti-fascist filmmaker Thomas Harlan, who translated Christopher's first book of poetry *bateu bleu/blue boat* (1994).[9]

The background to the present study is a disturbing change in Australian society and culture.

At the same time that new stricter oppressive immigration restrictions and jailing of asylum seekers without trial in indefinite detention began in Australia, accompanied by an increasing movement to silence opposition to this regime by the introduction of new laws that prohibit any who work in the asylum seeker detention "offshore processing centres", including medical staff, teachers, social workers, from speaking out about what they see there, including horrific abuses, with the threat of a two-year jail sentence to any who do, concurrently research shows an epidemic of 'psychosis' amongst young people in Australia. Yet many do not accept that psychosis exists, and reject the model, but it has been largely taken as 'real' in Australia, without question.[10]

Not only have these cruel policies of detention discussed in chapter one, impacted on the mental health of the asylum seekers, as revealed by the Amnesty reports, and government inquiries, this has apparently had a severe impact on the mental health of young people growing up in Australia who are taught a very different view at home and school, about the values of Australian society as caring, humane and multicultural. Yet what they see as they leave school, and enter society as young people, is that the reality of Australia is different, as is shown in these policies, which form a constant and dark background to public life, as they are discussed in the media and politics and have been and still are the major election issues that politicians rely on to win elections through appealing to inhumanity of the electorate; young people are losing touch with reality. They are lost, in the disjuncture between the values they are taught of what it is to be "Australian", and the political reality of how Australia is treating asylum seekers, and also Indigenous peoples. It seems these policies might be traumatizing and damaging young people in Australia; increasing racism and alienating migrants; and there is an increasing epidemic of Indigenous suicides.[11]

The 'colonizers' and descendants are damaged too by this practice of inhumanity.[12] This is critiqued in many ways in Australian culture, and in literary movements. For instance in recent movements to bring forgotten and unknown women into wider awareness; and, in different ways, in Charlie Bunt's candid memoir of her mother: *A Blossoming: A Memoir of Australian Artist Joan A. Holt* (2015).[13] Australian/Filipino poet Ramon Loyola explores his anxiety in *The Heaving Pavement: Epistles on an Anxious Life* (2016). I explore themes of personal identity, loss of awareness of identity, and the borderline between memoir and fiction in fugue novels.[14] There is a strong, growing movement of Indigenous authors, for example, Alexis Wright, author of *Carpentaria* (2006).

There has been a strong counter-movement to the new restrictive 'gagging' policies, of the Australian Border Force Act 2015-Section 42, which prohibits professionals who work at or visit, the "offshore processing centres" or work with refugees from the centres, from speaking out about what they see; with the penalty of a two-year jail term.[15]

Opposition to this law has united people from all walks of life across Australia. Doctors and health professionals consistently defied the law designed to silence them, and have protested publicly and effectively, the law is contrary to their professional oath, as well as their personal ethics.[16] Teachers, of the hundreds of children imprisoned for years in the "Nauru processing centre", are subject to this law; teachers are collectively publicly protesting against it, and have been criticized by the prime minister,[17] who denies the evidence of the Amnesty report, *Island of Despair* (2016), on inhumane conditions on Nauru.[18] Australian journalists required to apply for visas with $8,000 non-refundable visa applications that are selectively awarded, are effectively prevented from visiting and reporting.[19] Some church ministers actively oppose the policies.[20]

Author, playwright, teacher, and former Uniting Church minister, John Queripel, has published a book of relevance to the post-Kantian question of obedience to immoral laws versus ethical action, this is the question of Queripel's play, *Bonhoeffer: Prophet and Martyr* (2016)[21] on Dieter Bonhoeffer, Lutheran minister, in Nazi Germany, who was part of a conspiracy to assassinate Hitler. If more people had resisted the laws implementing the persecution of Jews and 'others' in Germany in the 1930s, there would not have been the Holocaust. Instead it was a small circle of well-educated, highly cultured, free thinking, and intelligent people who opposed and undermined the Nazi regime and took action from within. This ethical dilemma has renewed importance, as there are discernible moves in the new 'global' world by the totalitarian forces of multinational corporations, which, remarkably, appear to have had influence, if not power, over government policies, in an effort to silence protest, and works by writers and artists that do not support them who must remain beyond and outside their control, for the sake of freedom of expression and free speech, for all.

I discuss cases of real-life fugueurs documented in recent medical journals, in government reports, and in the media in Australia, including the story of young German-Australian woman, Cornelia Rau, who escaped a cult only to be then diagnosed as schizophrenic, and medicated, and hospitalized. After escaping a psychiatric hospital, she was held without trial in prison and immigration detention centres for ten months unlawfully. Previously she had been a flight attendant on Australia's leading airline. It was due to asylum seekers in the detention centre in the desert where she was incarcerated, alerting advocates, to her plight, that her story was written about in the Fairfax newspaper, *The Age*. Friends who saw this, alerted her family, and she was found. This was before a new law was passed, the Border Force Protection Act recently implemented in Australia to prevent whistleblowers writing about what is happening in immigration detention centres. I wrote in a journalism article on the potential effects of this stifling of freedom:

> With medical professionals who've worked in detention centres demonstrating their concerns at being gagged by the Border Force Protection Act, Cornelia Rau's case is a timely reminder of the value of doctors, and others, in prisons and detention camps reporting on what they see: there might be missing persons in fugues held in cases of mistaken identity.[22]

The use of fugue musicalization by each of the authors whose works I examine also shares a striking characteristic. In each of these, fugue musicalization is used to bring back a lost time and place, a lost object. Of relevance to this is the concept of musicalization to access a dimension of space-time, through the process of writing, and reading these works, this is relevant to the authors discussed who, in different ways, use techniques of musicalization as a modality of writing to write of lost objects (people and things). In doing so, unintentionally or unconsciously they created a dimension of virtual reality, of space-time, in literary writing, which remains accessible, long after the death of the author.

Themes that emerged in this research include the relation between the individual and the state in modernity, and the theme of expatriation and the patriot, or immigration, migration, exile, and nationalism. This theme has arisen in the research as it was part of the context of all the writers who use musicalized fugue as a form in their writing; each of the authors discussed is affected by this major theme of modernity, they are exiles, migrants, refugee; and they write in contexts in which patriotism and nationalism are rising and prevalent forces. States of ultranationalism, fascism and totalitarianism, played a significant part (and constitute real threats) in the context of their lives and work. How to negotiate the dichotomy of the state and the individual in language, when language is the mode that was, and is now, constantly surveilled by the state? To write as individuals who have to first find their authentic voices and ways in which they write, without being oppressed by the state directly, or by internalized oppression; how to write authentically of what one witnesses in one's life. This is a major challenge and ongoing struggle for writers and 'subjects' in modernity.

1

EXILED WRITERS' HUMAN RIGHTS AND SOCIAL ADVOCACY MOVEMENTS IN AUSTRALIA: A CRITICAL FUGAL ANALYSIS

Whereas much work in literary cultural and communication studies of "the subject" and subjectivity in language has focused on deconstructive theory and critique disconnected from actual practice and people, this essay applies an innovative cultural studies approach to a journalism reflective practice research project, conducted by the author, into human rights advocacy for cases of exiled writers in immigration detention centers in Australia. In the intellectual context of "counter-hegemonic" theories that use music as an analogy for affective social relations, the paper applies what is herein termed a "fugal critical analysis," by drawing on both musical and psychological meanings of fugue (as musical counterpoint and psychological loss of awareness of self-identity following trauma) to discuss a human rights research project. The project includes conducting interviews with an exiled Ivory Coast journalist, and an Iranian poet-musician, held in indefinite detention for refugees that has since been deemed illegal for breaching human rights laws; second is on the exiled journalist Behrouz Boochani incarcerated in the Manus "offshore processing centre" with a couple of his recent Facebook reportage posts; followed by a brief study and my email interview with exiled Australian poet Christopher Barnett in Nantes, France.

A shorter version of this essay was published as 'Exiled Writers, Human Rights, and Social Advocacy Movements in Australia: A Critical Fugal Analysis', in a special issue of *Communication and Critical/Cultural Studies*, Vol. 7, No. 3, September 2010. It is republished in a book, *Cultural Studies of Rights: Critical Articulations*, ed. John Nguyet Erni, London: Routledge, 2011 (hardback); 2014 (paperback and ebook). Here, it is updated and expanded with recent and current cases.

'Christopher Barnett. Interview with Ruth Skilbeck', was first published on the Arts Features International website, 01/02/2013.

ACTION WRITING

> The need to detain an unlawful non-citizen should be assessed on a case-by-case basis, taking into consideration the circumstances of the individual concerned, rather than mandating detention for all individuals who fall within certain broad groups. (Migration Amendment (Immigration Detention Reform) Bill 2009. Submitted by the Australian Human Rights Commission, to the Senate, 31 July 2009.[1]

Shifting modalities, from the 'reader' to 'action writer,' produces a dis-position to social agency and action in cultural and critical studies research. Demonstrating such a shift, this paper reflexively deploys an innovative creative practice methodology—herein termed *fugal critical analysis*—to discuss a case study of journalism reflexive practice into cases of exiled writers in immigration detention centers in Australia; and since 2012 in the "offshore processing centres" on the islands of Nauru and Manus (Papua New Guinea). The methodology is situated within the intellectual historical context and terminology of counter-hegemonic, or contrapuntal, approaches that allude analogously to the social relations and affect enacted in the form of musical counterpoint;[2] in studies of writers where human rights laws of freedom of opinion and expression, intersect with the rights of refugees and asylum seekers. The argument is developed through a critically reflective account of research into contemporary cases of a number of exiled writer, political refugees, who were held for years in immigration detention, and advocacy movements in Australia including PEN Australia, International PEN (an acronym for Poets, Essayists, Novelists), non-government organizations (NGOs), and grassroots activist movements whose sustained case-by-case lobbying—of government and at the Refugee Tribunal—eventually helped secure release of the writers. This was prior to 2008; since then, as this essay discusses, new centres of "offshore processing" have been implemented along with laws which prohibit reporting and pose a threat to free speech.[3]

The studies are taken from a research project the author undertook into media representation of refugee writers between 2007 and 2009, and in addition, with updated research from a case study of the Biennale Boycott of 2014, which I covered as an art writer, and followed by the current cases of exiled writers (2013-2017).

The research for this project involved the reflective practice of writing interview-based media articles on writers who were exiled due to their writings that exposed official corruption, putting their lives in danger in their undemocratic homelands. On arrival in Australia during the years of the 'Pacific Solution' version 1, and met with mandatory indefinite detention and temporary protection visas, the two writers in the first two cases, were each held for years without trial in detention centers. The interviewed writers included a former Ivory Coast political journalist, and now high ranking public servant Cheikh Kone, and Iranian poet and musician, Mohsen Soltany Zand, both of whom are now permanent residents of Australia. This paper discusses articles published from this research in *Homepage Daily*, 'Make Art Not War' (a 750-word experimental mixed-media piece and 'Refugee Writers Beyond Detention' (a 2,500-word factual reportage story).[4]

The third study is of the Sydney Biennale boycott and the current uncertain future of "offshore processing centres". I attended meetings, and lectures, and interviewed several artists in the Sydney Biennale boycott. The study discusses a series of open letters that were posted by the #19BoS Working Group (Biennale artists), and articles posted on *The Daily Fugue*.[5] The fourth study discusses exiled Kurdish journalist Behrouz Boochani held on Manus island, whose case has been taken up by international PEN and Reporters Without Borders. The fifth study includes a discussion and interview with émigré Australian poet Christopher Barnett (This was conducted in 2013, and published by Arts Features International, in 2013). The first two studies discuss PEN interventions, including starting the Writers in Detention Committee and publication of *Another Country: Writers in Detention* in 2004 edited by novelists Rosie Scott (author of *Faith Singer*) and Thomas Keneally (author of *Schindler's List*), which helped secure release of all the writers in the anthology. In 2004, PEN was awarded a Human Rights Community Award for its work in advocating for exiled writers helping to raise public awareness of asylum-seeker issues in Australia. As part of the research the author made contact with founding members of the committee and interviewed Dr Rosie Scott.[6] In critically exploring and developing this theme, the paper analyses discourses of advocacy for exiled writers and imprisoned writers, and the policies of the Pacific Solution versions 1 and 2,[7] mandatory indefinite detention, and temporary protection visas. There have been two incarnations of the 'Pacific Solution' concerning 'irregular arrivals' of asylum seekers.

I interviewed advocates and activists on their practices of advocacy including involvement in tribunal cases. Field research included attending events with advocates and activists, visiting poetry readings, writers' festivals, and Villawood detention center. Taking this methodology one step further, the chapter suggests that such dialogic practice might effectively focus on particular cases and might play an active part in resistance to unfair hegemonic structures, through active resistance occurring in the advocacy of democratic freedom of expression in a range of media, thereby playing an active role in advocacy that may intervene in particular cases and at the same time reasserting the active social and cultural role of the public intellectual. Since the first publication of this article, the 'Pacific Solution' has been revived in the new, more severe, current form.

The broader context in which this methodology is developed and deployed is the (re)turn to both distributive and recognition justice, discussed here in reference to politics of social inclusion and calls for conceptual frameworks and more attention to what Hurriyet Babacan identifies: 'culture, ethnicity, and other diversity signifiers as a causal factor of disadvantage'.[8] However I suggest we must also guard against applying a perhaps simplistic, naive and reactive even revanchist and irrendentist policy of reverse racism. The context is complex. The significance of considering musical analogies beyond literary criticism to contexts of the 'subject' and writers in exile in social theory is that music constitutes an expression of social relations, whether in actual or analogous form;[9] as it is through relationships that people are products of society and a part of it. As the fugue prefigured contemporary digital electronic musical forms of mixing and remix, it is particularly relevant to discussion of 'mixing', in current social theory and policy on migration in European policies, for the future of European society.

The fugue (from the Latin *fuga* for flight), is the exemplary contrapuntal polyphonic and thereby relational musical form as it proceeds by way of counterpoint, or interweaving voices (an instrument can be a voice), in relational response to each other. In its dialogic application, the fugal methodology is informed by music and methods including Said's contrapuntal reading across cultures;[10] Bakhtin's dialogism and heteroglossia;[11] Bhabha's cultural hybridity;[12] or the mixing and interweaving of cross-cultural references in the production and writing of texts; and the 1970s movement of women's writing and art in women's voices.[18] This suggests the 'remixing' analogy for expanding cross-cultural conversations for multiculturalism in the 'globalized' world. The term 'remixing' is currently being applied to European social policy (2015).[14] This includes a focus on political impacts of collective memories surfacing in discussions on the 'politics of remixing' in ongoing social, migration, and geo-economic policies.

The word fugue also has a more recent 'psychogenic' meaning of dissociation: as a post-traumatic response of 'flight' and loss of awareness of self-identity. As dissociative disorders are increasing in this era of globalization (as discussed in Chapter 5), this is used not only as a cultural metaphor but for the practical purpose of developing knowledge for advocating for the rights of exiled writers in relation to effects of cultural and psychological trauma. This aspect of the fugal methodology is informed by post-Freudian feminist psychoanalytical theories that explore the unconscious function of writing as a form of restitution of a 'lost object'. This is a field for cross-disciplinary inquiry in relation to contradictory, mediated impacts of globalization, and further informed by contemporary trauma theories, including recent work on cultural trauma following the September 11, 2001, and literary trauma theory.[15] This is referred to in relation to cultural trauma and collective identity formation, and practices of social inclusion and exclusion through memory and amnesia. Foucauldian discourse analysis of institutional power informs the research framework.[16] Together, these interpretations inform the comparative literary cultural studies methodology deployed in the media practice theorized here.

WRITING ACTION: THE POST-KANTIAN SUBJECT

Fugal critical analysis relates to a new research field of multimodality that constructs meaning as an assemblage of perceptual, conceptual, and material elements; the methodology is phenomenological, i.e., based on experience. This essay develops a concept herein termed *contrapuntal writing*. In constituting a relationally based critical/cultural theory of social inclusion, the paper argues for and re-positions a focus from the contrapuntal reader to a contrapuntal author who is an active social agent. Several functional shifts occur in the transposition of focus from the reader to the writer. This, crucially, includes a shift from a *de dicto* (about) to a *de re* (of) relation of modality of intentionality (relation to objects of thought) of the researcher to the objects of research. A *de dicto* relation is one of about-ness, about an object of thought. It is a relation of second-hand 'knowledge' or information, and received ideas. A *de re* relation is a phenomenological relation of the 'subject' (researcher/active writer) to objects based on a phenomenological experience gained directly through (multi-modal) sense perception. This adapts Brentano's theory of intentionality (discussed in the next chapter).

Part of a 'modal' shift from reading *about* to one of active writing *of*, basing on the researcher's experience, is a shift away from a theory based on metaphor to one that is empirically based on experience of phenomena through sensory perception. This modal shift produces, for example, a shift from the term 'exiled writers' used as a metaphor such as the 'death of the author' or 'dissolution of the unified subject'. Kant's theory of the 'dissolution of the unified subject' follows.

These are terms which have been widely used in critical theory as a kind of shorthand for theories that were first postulated, in the case of 'death of the author' by Barthes, in 1968; and in the case of the dissolution of the unified subject by Kant, in *Critique of Pure Reason*, first published in 1781. Barthes' theory is well known now, and is discussed in the final chapter of this book, so I will not elaborate on it here, save to reiterate its metaphorical aspect, and that it refers to the 'textuality' of literary writing, the idea that all 'texts' and writings are the product of language and interweave traces of other texts that have in various degrees inspired or influenced their writing, which has resonance with Bakhtin's ideas of heteroglossia in language.

Kant's theory of the Subject (Soul)

A digression on Kant's theory of the 'dissolution of the unified subject', and discussion of its significance, follows. Here I draw on David Hamlyn's discussion in his *History of Western Philosophy*.[17]

Kant's theory of the split subject had a foundational impact on ideas of the subject in industrialized modernity. Whilst his observation may be correct in its identification of the 'split' between what is in effect consciousness and the unconscious, terms that later were developed in the nineteenth century, it is limited, and based on a false premise: that the self or subject is solely equivalent to the 'thinking 'I''. A theory of the 'divided self' or subject is not necessarily incompatible with the idea of a different kind of self that encompasses ways of thinking and knowing, that are consciously known, and parts that are unconscious, I argue below.

Kant's theory developed from thinking of the two types of knowledge that western philosophers have since classical times categorized: *a priori* (Latin for what comes before) and *a posteriori* (or what comes after).

An *a priori* proposition is one that can be known to be true or false without direct reference to experience, except in so far as the experience which is necessary for understanding its terms, for Kant space and time are *a priori*; whereas an *a posteriori* proposition can be known to be true or false only by reference to how as a matter of contingency, things have been, or are, or, based on this are likely to be, such propositions are verifiable only by recourse to evidence, which will be only obtained in the first instance through the senses.

Kant's idea of the self is based on his reflection on how it is we come to have knowledge of the world around us (a posteriori knowledge). He proposed that all this kind of knowledge is based on representations from sensory perceptions, which the subject receives through his or her senses, represented as 'objects' (of thought), in acts of intuition and judgement. (He proposed some properties that we observe in objects might be due to the observer rather than the objects themselves). He used the term 'apperceptions', better associated with Leibniz, meaning self-consciousness or inner perception. Through apperceptions Kant proposed one represents to oneself a synthesis (of a manifold) based on the representations which appears to us in 'absolute unity', this does not imply a unity of the soul, or a soul on the traditional idea of having a 'simple' substance, but only that there is an illusion of having a unified soul; when all there is, is a (seeming) unity of one's apperceptions.

> We can say of the thinking 'I' (the soul) which regards itself as a substance, as simple, as numerically identical at all times, and as the correlate of all existence, from which all other existence must be inferred, that it does not know itself through the categories, but knows the categories, and through them all objects, in the absolute unity of apperception and so through itself. (A. 402)

The observer is not able to be at the same time observing or thinking and aware of the self observing or thinking about the representations:

> Now it is indeed very evident that I cannot know as an object that which I must presuppose in order to know any object and that the determining self (the thought) is distinguished from the self that is to be determined (the thinking subject) in the same way as knowledge is distinguished from its object.

Kant adds:

> Nevertheless there is nothing more natural and more misleading than the illusion which leads us to regard the unity in the synthesis of thoughts as a perceived unity in the subject of these thoughts (A. 402).

Hamlyn remarks on the significance of Kant's thinking on the subject: 'It is important however that Kant thinks he can show why we are naturally inclined to think that way, even if it is wrong.'[18]

A main significance is that Kant was the first philosopher to say, in this way, that the soul, or subject, is not a unity or a simple substance. This also implies that self-deception is not only possible but is natural for us, and it implies a more complex concept of the subject that was to radically prefigure and profoundly shape thinking on the subject, or self, in industrialized modernity.

In the section of the *Critique* known as the 'Dialectic', Kant shows the fallacies that occur when reason (thinking) attempts to go beyond the bounds of experience and make claims to metaphysical truths about reality, and his first example, and primary concern, is about the Transcendental Idea of the soul, which he claims to show to be an illusion.

He conceives of the Ideas of Reason, as Transcendental, pure concepts of reason, and holds that (although they are illusory) it is 'natural' that we should have such Ideas, which arise when we attempt to think of or about an absolute unity that is not conditioned by actual experience or relative to such experience. He claims all argument is conditioned by premises, which are the only conditions under which conclusions can be asserted. Yet reason wishes to speculate (as it were be free and fly beyond these conditions and speculate on what might be), to arrive at premises unconditioned by argument or further premises (this tendency has flowered in the genres of science fiction and most recently speculative realism in literature).

Kant believed that Transcendental Ideas are systematically derived from a consideration of the traditional logic of syllogistic argument and he conceived of a system based on categorical, hypothetical and disjunctive syllogisms as a basis for a tripartite division between Transcendental Ideas. These would (hypothetically) govern and regulate ways in which we think when we go beyond the realm of possible experience. However such ways of thinking are, to Kant, an illusion and so the tripartite division between Transcendental Ideals corresponds only to a classification of what he thinks are the illusions of speculative metaphysics (which had been concerned with ideas of God, freedom, and immortality); Kant claimed the classes of Transcendental Ideas can be arranged in order:

> the first containing the absolute (unconditioned) unity of the thinking subject, the second the absolute unity of the series of conditions of appearance, the third the absolute unity of the condition of all objects of thought in general. (B391)

When the Transcendental Idea of the unity of the thinking subject is applied, as in this way, outside or beyond the bounds of possible and conditioned experience they give rise to the pseudo-rational defective inferences, or dialectical syllogisms, which Kant claims are, 'defects of reason'.[19]

In relation to the thinking 'I' and the illusions of speculative psychology he calls these: Paralogisms; in relation to the world as totality of appearance and the illusions of speculative cosmology: Antinomies; and in relation to God and the illusions of speculative theology: Ideals, of pure reason.

Kant identified four Paralogisms of defective reasoning concerning the unity of the 'thinking 'I'', which are concerned to identify as a simple substance the subject which has (only) the unity (or illusion of unity) given or afforded it by apperceptions; a simple identity which holds through time, and which is related to objects in space, primarily the subject's own material body. He identifies the four paralogisms of the self as: *substance*; as *simple*; as *having a unity or identity through time*; and as having *relations to bodies in space*.

Kant claims that all of rational psychology is summed up in a fallacious syllogism:

> That which cannot be thought otherwise than as subject does not exist otherwise than as subject, and is therefore substance; A thinking being, considered merely as such, cannot be thought otherwise than as subject; Therefore it exists also only as subject, that is, as substance.

This Kant says is fallacious as 'thought' is used in the two premises in different ways. In the first premise, in relation to what can be thought in general and in the second: how a subject can think of it.

Hamlyn points out that Kant is also taking the word 'subject' in two different senses, in the first it means subject as opposed to predicate; in the second it means the subject who thinks.[20]

In relation to the second sense, Kant considers soul to be equivalent to the "thinking subject". This, I maintain is a false premise.

Kant claims that the Transcendental Idea of the unity of the subject is based on defective reasoning, and is an illusion, and he claims the tendency to identify the thinking I, or subject, with a simple substance, such as the unified soul produces a fallacy. The only legitimate conception of the subject or self, or the I, is that of the 'I think' or the 'unity of apperception'. As Kant reiterates the subject cannot know itself, as an object as such, his views on the inability of the subject to know itself is expressed thus: 'In thinking my existence I cannot employ myself, save as subject of the judgement' (B411). He claims that 'rational psychology owes its origin simply to a misunderstanding' (B 422).

> The unity of consciousness, which underlies the categories, in here mistaken for an intuition of the subject as object [a soul], and the category of substance is then applied to it. But this unity is only unity in *thought*...Consequently this subject [soul/self] cannot be known. The subject of the categories cannot by thinking the categories acquire a concept of itself as an object of the categories. For in order to think them, its pure self-consciousness, which is what was to be explained is pre-supposed. Similarly, the subject, in which the representations of time has its original ground, cannot thereby determine its own existence in time. And if this latter is impossible, the former, as a determination of the self (as a thinking being in general) by means of the categories is equally so. (B 422)

Kant was seeking to refute Leibniz's idea of the monad (that each person is a monad). Hamlyn adds that this was expressed in another, relevant, way by Locke on personal identity, that the 'self is the only truly simple substance.'[21] This was what Kant was attempting to refute and seeking to move beyond. He seems to say that as a thinking subject, one cannot as it were step outside of self to a meta-level where one can be as it were an object to oneself.

Yet, my observation is, in moments of extreme trauma, some people have out-of-the-body experiences. This subject is not the 'thinking 'I' and these are not Transcendental Ideas of reason but extreme shock, which can later, in some cases, give insight into how the mind works, and insights into the fragility of the illusory 'unity' of apperceptions, of the thinking I and 'self-consciousness' which is a sign of well-being that eludes a person who is traumatized, for some time, and for whom self healing, attempting to heal, and perhaps to regain a lost sense of former self, and make sense of the world, is writing. Self-based writing and story-telling (narrating the story) can be a modality of restitution of the shocked self. In this way the most traumatic experiences can (with work by the writer) afford the deepest insights into the subject (self), in contexts of lives, as living beings in (a) time and (a) space, that some authors of modernity have been able to capture and narrate in their literary writings. Thomas de Quincey's writing and life, illustrating this, is discussed in Chapter 7. Charlie Bunt in her memoir of her artist mother, *A Blossoming*, describes this when she was with her mother in her last hours: 'I felt outside of my body.'[22]

Kant identifies the thinking "I" with the soul and believes, on this basis, that the 'unity' of the soul is an illusion. If we take the 'soul', or self or subject, to comprise more than self-consciousness of the 'thinking I', and to encompass its unconscious parts which effect and affect one's apperceptions (and) how one perceives objects a different idea of a soul/self/subject comprising many parts emerges.

Kant argues that the soul is not a substance, and is not simple.

I would suggest that the self is not a substance of matter but more akin to music, a non-representational emanation from the play of the functions of our material bodies activated through our senses, which provide the representations and impressions of perception for our apperceptions.

The self-consciousness of the thinking 'I' is constituted through 'apperceptions' yet apperceptions are of, or about, objects of thought derived from the perceptions (representations) of objects, therefore which are not a part of the thinking subject (the Kantian 'thinking 'I''), (although one can say now they are in that they are apart of it).

This revised concept of the subject or self includes the unconscious, nothingness, forgetting and amnesia as well as memories and remembering. In this way it might also include our own death, and our life; as if all the experiences we have of 'unconsciousness' are little deaths, or preparations for death. Does it include what comes after death; does the 'soul' survive after death? We do not know, as that is by definition impossible to know. Does the self or subject or soul contain traces of past lives in cellular memory of our ancestry in our DNA? Can we ever be conscious of this? To what extent does this (unconsciously) affect our 'decisions' and actions (and ideas of who we are)? Does ancestral cellular memory slip into our dreams, and guide us? Some Indigenous people believe that the spirits of our ancestors remain with us, within us guiding us, for seven retrospective generations, and then they disappear. Such questions have a renewed significance in the contemporary field of robotics and artificial intelligence, where science fiction has come to actual life or virtual reality, and there is a new effort to create immortality of the soul through merging of digital technologies with the human, in the 'posthuman' era, which some scaremongers are now saying poses real dangers to the human race.

Whereas philosophers before Kant had taken it as a given that the soul exists and that the soul is a unity, the conclusion Kant made from his insight was that the soul or subject is thereby divided, or that the idea of the unified soul, is based on an illusion. This led to the modern ideas of a 'non-unified subject', or the 'dissolution of the subject', that later led to theories of dissociation; it prefigured experimentation in the nineteenth century into dissociation, and later to the theories of the 'unconscious' which Freud is credited with 'discovering' although he was not by any means the only psychologist and researcher to be working in this field, and his writings and discoveries were a development of work by the groups now known as the early psychodynamic researchers (Pierre Janet was one; who were grouped around what has been termed 'Charcot's Axis'), in the late nineteenth century.[23] There was a focus in the early nineteenth century research into dissociation, on immortality, and trying to discover if the soul survived after death, which was connected to ideas of *metempsychosis*, the transmigration of souls; all of which ideas had a strong presence in the literature of the nineteenth century, and also twentieth century modernity (the word is even mentioned, in Joyce's *Ulysses*). What psychologists have recently discovered is a truth that echoes throughout storytelling, of all times, which is that what is called 'trauma' and shock, for instance of a sudden accident, can cause people to have out-of-the-body experiences, and temporarily lose awareness of being themselves. The phrase 'shocked out of himself', is not a metaphor, but has a literal meaning for those unfortunate people who have out-of-the-body experiences following accidents, profound shocks, encountering 'sudden death', for example in a car accident or a terrorist attack, or finding a loved one who has died. (This is discussed in detail in the chapter on Thomas de Quincey, and is also relevant to Christopher Barnett). Asylum seekers and exiles discussed in this book have written of the trauma of such accidents and traumatic contexts, of war and conflicts, and loss of loved ones.

In literary critical theory since the late 1960's, the terms 'death of the author' and 'dissolution of the unified subject' have been used in a metaphorical way. In this essay I take these terms used as metaphors and show that they have a very different meaning when used in relation to people who have been exiled due to their writing, who will be jailed, tortured or executed for writing that political groups or governments in their home countries prohibit. The terms 'dissolution of the unified subject' is herein used to describe effects of trauma; this calls for a new appreciation of the unified subject, and an understanding that the self or subject is divided but that this does not preclude a 'unified subject' overall, but instead admits of a subject that is comprised of different parts, that are conscious and unconscious. It is only when in harmony in the natural harmony of health balance, that the 'subject' or person is able to feel fully 'unified' without dissonance; as the studies in this book will show; cognitive dissonance, is a tactic used by those in power to make people feel uncomfortable; and in the cases discussed here, in Australia it has been and continues to be used as a political strategy to encourage the population to reject asylum seekers who have no other way of seeking asylum but 'irregularly'. This also is a case study in the construction of the subject as 'deviant' and 'irregular' and 'unlawful' in the societies of modernity, in this case in Australia.

An encounter with the asylum seekers, and refugees, the seafaring travellers and storytellers, leads to a phenomenologically-based connection with cases of exiled writers—based on face-to-face interviews with writers in exile. This shift produces not only an awareness but also in varying degrees, an engagement with the social and cultural contexts of the writers' exiles. But it is also an awareness of their situation as human beings who may still be suffering the after-effects of the trauma of exile and detention. This produces a different kind of research process and knowledge than the one based only on 'reading'. First hand phenomenological experience impacts upon the writer and causes reflexive affects which can be profound and motivate a deeper level of engagement. Such direct involvement turns the 'objects' of research into actual living 'subjects' with subjectivity and human identities, and stories, and leads to taking up and advocating for individual cases, as with the exiled writers.

There is a strong movement of support and advocacy for asylum seekers in Australia, which has paralleled the increasingly draconian policies implemented by the Australian government which recently, on 1 July 2015, includes the passing of a law as part of the new Border Force Act 287-Section 42 that prohibits doctors, nurses, teachers, child welfare professionals, and lawyers, who work at the Australian-run 'offshore processing centres,'[24] or with asylum seekers and refugees, from speaking about human rights abuses in immigration detention, with the threat of prosecution and a two-year jail term. This turned up the volume of the ethical debate. The law has been condemned and defied by Australian Medical Association doctors; health, legal, and teaching professionals have protested widely, and reported abuses. Opposition to these alarmingly undemocratic policies that seek to stifle and penalize free speech and allow abuses to be perpetrated by those profiting from the centres financially (discussed in detail soon) has united many groups and individuals across Australia, medical, welfare, psychiatric, legal, and teaching professionals, and many who work in churches of different denominations, as well as writers and artists. A recently published work by author, musician, teacher, and former Uniting Church minister, John Queripel, explores related ethical issues of relevance in contemporary Australia, and indeed the rest of the world.

His play *Bonhoeffer Prophet and Martyr* (2016) focuses on the central moral question that was interrogated by Lutheran minister and theologian Dieter Bonhoeffer who was part of a conspiracy to assassinate Hitler, in the second world war. That was the question of moral purity versus ethical action. Should one always tell the truth? And should one be obedient to what is not serving the good? Should you obey a law if the law is immoral? Bonhoeffer answered emphatically no. He urged his fellows to rise above the absolutism that paralyzed many Christians from taking moral action that could have prevented the rise of Hitler, and the Nazis, and stopped the Holocaust.

> **Bonhoeffer**: Duplicity even has its place. Telling the truth is not absolute. The philosopher Immanuel Kant gives us the example of a murderer seeking out someone who has taken refuge in your house.

> He asks, is that person here? To that question Kant says we must tell the truth and turn then the refugee over. This is because for him the truth is an absolute. But how does the truth serve the good in such a situation? I profoundly disagree with Kant. There are no absolutes in ethics, but rather the seeking out in each situation the best of imperfect options. (Act 3, p. 72)

This is of great relevance to the new law in Australia which is applied to all who have been or are an 'entrusted person'. This law is disturbingly reminiscent of laws passed in Hitler's Third Reich which similarly stifled the professions and institutions: the law, teaching, the medical professions, enabling the spread of hatred and fear and deportation of Jews to concentration camps that once would have been criminalized. It was an offence in Australia until recently to *not* report human rights abuses witnessed in workplaces; now those who do report can be jailed for two years. In Australia the large movement of concerned citizens is intuitively following the moral principles that Bonhoeffer advocated:

> **Bonhoeffer:** No one has the right to demand that you pledge obedience to that which is immoral. That is immoral in itself. (Act 3, p. 73).

In Australia many in the medical, teaching and social work professions have defied the law and spoken out. Yet the policy has not changed. An amendment has recently been made for doctors and medical workers, due to the protests of doctors and medical staff. Teachers, lawyers, and social workers, are pushing for a similar amendment, on the grounds that despite years of filing reports through the official channels, nothing has been done, the reports of abuse and trauma have been ignored. In an article in the *Guardian*, a teacher who worked on Nauru, said:

> Myself and colleagues lodged literally hundreds of information reports and we had an issues register, which was forwarded to Canberra, and there were issues like family separation, severe health risks, mental health....Beyond that I have written to senators, helped file official complaints to UN special rapporteur, I have tried everything before this very public avenue. It's not something I take lightly but it has fallen on deaf ears. (October 21, 2016)[25]

JOURNEY INTO EXILE

In terms of psychological aspects of the fugue, analogously the form relates to origins of language formation in the body, in the unconscious that Julia Kristeva referred to as the 'pre-semiotic chora'.[26] Reference to the non-representational, fugal, musicalized language of literary art is relevant to the origins of the case studies of the exiled writers. The journey described in the next part of this paper is an active development and application of research into the writer's fugue, later in this book, which discovered a link between uses of fugue form in musicalized writing and authors' experience of trauma—including the experience of exile.

Some of modernity's most innovative and profound poets, writers and artists were propelled by traumatic experiences of loss to create musico-literary fugues including De Quincey (*Dream-Fugue*), Proust (*À la recherche du temps perdu*), Joyce ('Sirens' in *Ulysses*), Celan (*Todesfuge*, Plath (*Little Fugue*), Barnett (*when they came/ for you/elegies of resistance*) This related to a phenomenon observed in research into ways that individuals and communities may recover from trauma through the practice of innovation. Writers may symbolically and literally re-make themselves, and create or join new communities in the process of writing. The fugal modality of writing involves a paradoxical loss of awareness of self-identity: a temporary experience of dissociation and yet at the same time, a process that may constitute re-membering or re-construction of a fragmented self.

This occurs in the telling of stories, and writing. In world literary history there is a tradition of seafarer stories, a new tradition of storytelling is emerging now of seafaring tales of asylum seekers, and their long and dangerous sea voyages which are as fraught with obstacles as was Ulysses' nineteen year homecoming journey by boat.

FUGAL APPROACH

Fugue serves not only as a multi-modal analogy, but also suggests a number of critical style terms transposed from music, as outlined below and applied to a fugal analysis of the cases:

Fugal Modality: In the fugal modality of writing, two theories of modality are brought together. The first derives from the philosophical concept of modality and modal logic, and is related to the concept of *de re* thought as articulated in linguistic propositions. The second is derived from modal music and is related to re-writing language as creative art. How it works can be conceptualized imaginatively. It is the modality of creative psycho-linguistic re-invention in any medium of language and (potentially) infinite variation on a theme.

Fugal Recursion: A concept of reflexivity, which 'puts on hold' one voice, whilst another picks up and plays the theme.

Polyphony: Many voices.

Counterpoint: Interweaving of 'voices' (not necessarily verbal, a visual image or effect can be a 'voice').

Variation: The fugue develops in variations on the theme including elaboration, embellishment, distortion, inversion, mirroring, repetition, diminishment.

Double Counterpoint: A relational aspect is implied, as in musical fugue; carnivalesque, parodic satirical discourse or dialogue, in which a dominant voice switches place with a sub-dominant, and vice versa.

Dialogism: Bakhtin's term for the interplay and intertextuality of voices in cultural productions.

Recurring Motifs: An image, a shape, a sound: that may be a signifier of un/conscious subliminal or subtextual psychological or cultural motive.

Memory Involuntary: Memory and loss of awareness of self identity that constitutes an a-semantic link in the creative processes of composition, particularly in the 'inspirational' mode of compulsion to make art. Paradoxically this process of invention from memory also involves forgetting in a form of fugal recursion. This may be applied to the phenomena of cultural memory and cultural amnesia.

CASES OF EXILED WRITERS AND INTERNATIONAL HUMAN RIGHTS LAW (PACIFIC SOLUTION VI).

Article 1 (A2) of the UN Declaration of Human Rights defines a refugee as being 'a person who ... owing to a well-founded fear of being persecuted for reasons of race, religion, nationality, membership of a particular social group or political opinion, is outside the country of his nationality and is unable or, owing to such fear, is unwilling to avail himself of the protection of that country.' It is this definition that has been incorporated into Australia's 1958 Migration Act.[27] Australia is a signatory to the 1951 Refugee Convention relating to the Status of Refugees and its 1967 Protocol.[28] This has recently been amended by the Australian Government and will be discussed soon. The Australian

Human Rights Commission has contested the mandatory detention system that is aimed at 'deterring' asylum seekers from approaching the country, implemented by the Pacific Solution v1 between 1999 and February 2008:

> The Commission has consistently called for an end to the mandatory detention system because it places Australia in breach of its obligations under the International Covenant on Civil and Political Rights (ICCPR) (1966) and the Conventions on the Rights of the Child (CRC) (1989) to ensure that no one is arbitrarily detained. (8.48 Migration Amendment (Immigration Detention Reform) Bill 2009)[29]

> Australia maintains one of the most restrictive immigration detention systems in the world. It is mandatory, not time limited, and people are not able to challenge the need for detention in a court of law. The Commission has for many years called for an end to this system because it leads to breaches of human rights obligations under treaties to which Australia is a party. (AHRC. *Asylum seekers, refugees and human rights, snapshot report*, 2013).[30]

The policies of the 'Pacific Solution' (v1) created migration 'zones of excision' excising coastal borders and waters from Australia's 'migration zone' to prevent arrivals of asylum seekers by boat. Those in the excision zone could not access Australia's migration determination system, and have been transferred to Papua New Guinea's Manus Province or the Pacific island of Nauru. This followed what is known as 'the Tampa incident:' when a Norwegian ship that had rescued asylum seekers from a sinking boat brought them to Australia, as the nearest country, and was refused permission to land. At the same time, policies were implemented of mandatory indefinite detention and Temporary Protection Visas (TPVs).[31] In 2014 the Migration and Maritime Powers Legislation Amendment was passed making significant changes to the Migration Act and removing most references to the Refugee Convention. (Since 2013, all boats with asylum seekers have been intercepted and towed to Nauru and Manus Island detention centres).[32]

Asylum seekers arriving without a visa including accompanied and unaccompanied children were classified as 'non-legal non-citizens,' and held in mandatory indefinite detention. This included those who arrived by plane or by ship at a city port, in the first two case studies.

If they were granted refugee status, 'non-legal non-citizens' were granted only three-year Temporary Protection Visas, in contrast with 'legal non-citizens' arriving in Australia with visas, who were granted Permanent Protection Visas.[33]

'Temporary Protection' meant a state of chronic indeterminacy. In detention, political exiles and asylum seekers are homeless and stateless in a zone of psychological and physical limbo. This state of limbo produces psychological trauma and has serious effects for the mental health of exiles and detainees. Detention Centers are located in isolated areas, in Pacific Solution v1, in deserts surrounded by razor wire, e.g., the notorious Woomera Immigration Reception and Processing Centre in the South Australian desert (closed in 2003). Now in Pacific Solution v2, they are located on tiny remote islands. Suicide attempts, self harm, and desperate acts such as lip sewing were everyday occurrences and still are. Suicides occur, as do fires, protests, hunger strikes, and occasional break outs. As a sign of their official dehumanization the detainees are numbered, and in some places and times are called by their numbers for head counts every few hours throughout each day and night.[34] The following extracts are from articles, AHRC reports, and my face-to-face conversations with exiled writers and advocates in PEN, in Sydney, in 2007 and 2008.

> As far as history goes in Australia, it was one of the worst periods ... It was the complete abnegation of their human rights. They weren't even allowed a trial. (Dr Rosie Scott, interview with the author).[35]
>
> in Woomera ... 400 people shared two toilets. (Steven Biddulph, psychologist, 2007).[36]
>
> A child attempts to hang himself with a bed sheet on playground equipment. A child on hunger strike.
>
> A child found in razor wire again.[37]
>
> If you want to close your eyes, to not see what happen in the world, you become blind. (Mohsen, interview with the author, 2007)[38]

The impacts of the indefinite detention environment on mental and physical health are extensively documented in *A Last Resort, National Inquiry into Children in Immigration Detention* (2004) by the Australian Human Rights Commission (formerly Human Rights and Equal Opportunity Commission). Impacts are documented in advocates' reports in books, articles, and also on websites through NGOs, and many groups and individuals that make up the social movement of refugee advocacy in Australia.

> If you close your eyes you cannot see. You cannot close your heart. You cannot close your ears. If you want to close your mouth, ear, heart. If you are heartless, you have no emotion. You are going to be a robot. And not be human. (Mohsen, in interview with author, 2007)

"How important was poetry to you in detention?"

"It was like breathing" (Mohsen).

> *(Writer 1)—The way they treated us was disgusting ... The way they practice their interview techniques like no respect at all. And not that: we know that you come from a difficult situation, we can help you now, but we need to find out what really happened. There was nothing like that. It was like: why the hell did you come here in the first place, you know? Yeah, I think that was one of the main things that people felt that they were so, you know, unwelcome. That no matter what they did ... Yeah that was really key to the whole story.*

"And so the opposite kind of reaction from other people on the outside helped to counter-act that?" (R.S.)

> *(Writer 1)—Yes. That attitude of hey, we believe you, you know we want to hear your story. Tell us what happened and how you are feeling. What can we do. Yeah, not much we can do about it, but what do you think we can do, and just people saying, I'll send you a phone card so you can contact your family. Things like that. And that's when PEN, they did start helping. Wanted to find out what was happening. And from then on the story was more public.*[39]

It was in this zone of indeterminacy and uncertainty in 2001 when PEN heard about the exiled writers, who had begun to send out messages from detention, including Cheikh Kone's newspaper called *Freedom*. Kone, a political journalist from the Ivory Coast, produced this newspaper with a group of detainees on a computer in Port Hedland Immigration Reception and Processing Centre (detention centre) and faxed it to Amnesty International.

DECONSTRUCTING DEHUMANIZATION AND DEVIANCY

Foucault drew attention to the kind of foreclosure of technical instrumental rationality that operates in 'rational' systems such as prisons. On his account we can be seen to be living in an 'episteme',[40] where the immigration detention center is an institution where the power/knowledge intersection is enacted in an authoritarian practice in which exiles are routinely 'dehumanized' as a matter of implementation of policy. Their individual cases not considered, and they were left in limbo for years before their cases were brought to the Refugee Tribunal (where over eighty percent of detainees were found to be refugees, and given TPVs).[41] These have been proven to prolong the psychological trauma of uncertainty for refugees.

Such institutional responses of the episteme of postindustrial late modernity constructed a response that has had an affective dimension that generated fear, paranoia—and resistance. Sharon Pickering analyzes media discourses on asylum seekers and refugees, concluding that in Australia they are routinely constructed not only as a 'problem' population but as a 'deviant' population in relation to the nation state, race, and disease. She argues that this is systematic and endemic to the construction of 'normalcy in prevailing social orders and the reproduction of hegemony.' She concludes that 'frameworks of deviancy help us to unpack the way asylum seekers can be put on trial by the media without the power to narrate their own stories'.[42]

The power to tell stories about oneself is intrinsically related to a sense of self-identity. It is in many respects what makes us human. Yet, negative stereotyping and misinformation about 'illegal immigrants' relayed through the media caused a counter response in the form of strong refugee advocacy movements that spread across Australia.

The cases of the first two exiled writers in the studies were taken up by PEN, a group that lobbied tirelessly for their release. 'Poets, Essayists, Novelists' is an international humanitarian organization of writers that started in London in the early twentieth century to lobby for the rights of imprisoned writers around the world. In 2001, Sydney PEN formed the first Writers in Detention committee after members had found out that there were exiled writers held in immigration detention centers in Australia. PEN's influential author members, including novelist Thomas Keneally, Rosie Scott, and some journalists including David Marr, put out strong messages in the media through articles, broadcasts, and books that drew attention to their plight.

In (striving for) the international return to recognition justice, the Australian Human Rights Commission in 2009 called for case by case assessment of those detained as an 'unlawful non-citizen.' The Commission states: 'While the initial detention of unauthorized arrivals might be legitimate on these grounds, this must be for a minimal period, and be proportional [to legal and safety concerns].[43]

The focus on the individual is very significant. The humanity and success of the PEN campaign for the writers in detention was that the writers were humanized as individual cases. They were exiled for the very reason of expressing their views as individual authors: practicing the right to freedom of expression and free speech with the aim of exposing corruption for the benefit of their communities.

REFUGEE WRITERS: BEYOND DETENTION

Mohsen Soltany Zand

Mohsen Soltany Zand is an Iranian poet and musician who fled Tehran after he wrote pieces that tried to expose corruption. In Australia he was detained in Port Hedland, and Villawood, mandatory detention centers for four years. When in Villawood, Mohsen met advocates who took up his case, including Rosie Scott and Tom Keneally. He has since made CDs, *Mohsen* and *Australian Dream* with many prominent writers, and performers such as Bryan Brown, John Bell, Tom Keneally, Geoffrey Datson, Annette Hughes, Claudia Karvan, and politician Senator Kerry Nettle, reciting Mohsen's spoken word poetry, accompanied by Mohsen's music. All the proceeds from the CD sales went to Chilout, the organization that lobbied to end the detention of children.[44]

In two interviews at his home in Sydney, Mohsen talked about the trauma that he had experienced and how this had affected him.[45] Even though he had been released three years before under medical advice, he still could not work full time. He was finishing a surveying course at a Sydney college of Technical and Further Education (TAFE). He had fled Iran after exposing corruption: 'For my political activism I became endangered. I came to Australia by plane to Perth.' He had thought that he was going to Perth in Scotland. When he arrived he was put into Port Hedland Detention Centre and moved to Baxter Detention Centre. He said: 'There were five people to a [small] room with two beds...if the door opened [it] banged you on the head.' Following a protest, detainees were sent to prison for a few months. In comparison, he said: 'when I went to prison it was wonderful. Everything was good. The doctor—we could see. In 18 months I hadn't seen any doctor, any specialists. I was in a very, very bad condition.' After three years he was transferred to Villawood Detention Centre in Western

Sydney. In total he spent four years in immigration detention.

The article, written after speaking with Mohsen, entitled 'Make Art Not War' is experimental art writing. It is written in the 'voice' of Rosa Viereck, art critic and abstract expressionist artwork, in a column entitled Pink Oblong (Rosa Viereck is the title of a painting by Vasily Kandinsky). Yet the story was clearly ascribed to the author (myself) in a copyright attribution at the end of the story. The story also included my photograph of Mohsen reciting poetry at the poetry reading. The story began:

> Australia, or Invasion Day, makes me think of geometric shapes. Black squares. White cubes. Me. In a gallery. A pink oblong. My own shape. Rosa Viereck: pleased to meet you.

The abstract, fragmented voice continues:

> I'm secure in my identity. But sometimes just the sound of the word Australia, let alone its abstraction, can make me question who I am. "Where do we come from? What are we? Where are we going?" was modernist artist Paul Gauguin's heartfelt cry in "French" Tahiti. His painting's plea becomes an epithet to colonial identity confusion.

Interweaving in a multimodal fugue:

> ...I am looking at the symbolic shape of what is known as an icon of Australian identity art. Sidney Nolan's outlaw: Ned Kelly. Riding through a desert. Gun in hand. In reverse. A symbol of quixotic alienation: human form reduced to a black abstraction in the red heart. White settler alienation in a black helmet. What are we? What does it mean to be Australian? It's a familiar refrain. Can we find ourselves through Art? I am here to tell you, yes, and lose ourselves as well. Look at me! And look at Nolan ...

The voice of Rosa Viereck, abstraction personified, drew a connection between unsettled Australian artists, indigenous women activists and exiles in detention in the desert:

> Looks like he found out a thing or two as he lost himself in a hallucinogenic landscape of his own perception. About the shifting shapes of "settler" identity. The outlaw. The colonial law enforcers.

The voice stops and starts, breaks and continues:

> But things have changed since Nolan painted his Kelly series in the late 1940s. The modern era has shifted to postmodernism. Multiplicity abounds. Polyphony rocks. In the new era of protest, outlaws are replaced by activists. Fighting for social justice for outsiders 'othered'

by the ex-colonial law makers. Refugees in detention.
Indigenous communities. Stranded in 21st century deserts. Deprived of health and education services settler society calls basic. When activists faced charges—later dropped—of helping refugees escape the country to a third country of refuge, writer and refugee supporter Tom Keneally wrote to those facing court: "The better angels of Australia are singing with you."

The story was intertextual, quoting from an artwork and from: *Another Country, writers in detention,* edited by Tom Keneally and Rosie Scott. I open the book, and read lines from Mohsen's poem, *Drought,* that he wrote when incarcerated in Baxter Detention Centre, where Cornelia Rau was also imprisoned (her story is discussed in Chapter 3).

> In the midst of parched desert
> No one can come with us
> We cannot journey hand in hand
> There is no green place to rest the eye
> And the scorching wind of destiny lashes at our backs
> A call to DIMIA is a like the smell of rain in the desert
> Hope, like black clouds, building in our thirsty hearts
> Turns quickly to grief... ('Drought', *Another Country*, p. 114)

The deconstructed narrative ended with an exhortation:

> In the great southern land we are all at heart dislocated, invaded and invaders. Together, we can reshape the future. Through mutual acceptance of many colours and shapes. Reconciliation. Make Art not War.[46]

Why take this approach? Much affected by Mohsen's story and by the anguish of his poetry, this drove an attempt to inhabit more deeply the imaginative and affective space that Mohsen described in his poetry, his music, and his conversation. Visualizing this space—of trauma, isolation, and displacement—in the paintings of Sydney Nolan in a retrospective of his works at the Art Gallery of New South Wales at that time. Hearing it in the words of indigenous speakers on Human Rights Day; weaving together these threads in an abstract piece on cultural trauma and identity on Australia or Invasion Day. The article was published with photographs of Mohsen, Aunty Shirley an indigenous rights activist radio broadcaster ('Aunty' being the term for respected elder), and an image of Nolan's Ned Kelly painting.

Cheikh Kone

Cheikh Kone was a young journalist in the Ivory Coast, working for *Le Patriot*, when his life became endangered after he wrote articles critical of government elections. He was forced to flee. Concealed under a blanket in a four-wheel drive car driven by a friend of his father, over the border to Ghana, and then to Benin, where he was given berth on a ship. And after a long and dangerous journey via South Africa, he stowed away on another ship (and, as he says, believing it was bound for Europe), then he arrived in Australia.

Whilst in detention, Cheikh was adopted as International PEN's first 'writer at risk' from policies of Australia and was the first asylum seeker in Australia to have his case 'internationalized by PEN.' [47] Taking up his case when he was under consideration of deportation by Australia to the Ivory Coast, PEN centers around the world contacted the government. The PEN Submission to the Human Rights and Equal Opportunity Commission for the Community Services Award (2004) states: 'Eventually, through the work of many groups and individuals, including the PEN Australia centers and International PEN and their network of associated writers and human rights advocacy groups, Cheikh was released this year after spending three years in detention.'[48] He was released in 2004; and after gaining his Law degree, he is working as a field officer in a union, 'looking after public servants,' and is married with a child.

In the asylum seeker detention centre, Cheikh continued to actively write. At Port Hedland Detention Centre he and some other inmates started up a newspaper. He said:

> We had a committee management that said we could have a newsletter. We were allowed to have a computer at least a couple of hours every day so we started a little newspaper called *Freedom*. We did only three issues, once a month ... People who got their visas were leaving and I smuggled a copy out so people could read it on the outside. I faxed a couple of copies to Amnesty International overseas ... Some Australian people [from outside] got involved knowing what we are doing* and I asked for and I got my own computer, and so then I started to write, a story... [49]

The journalism story was written in a factual reportage style designed to give maximum opportunity for Cheikh to tell his story in his own voice. He said that the catalyst for his still being sane, after almost four years in detention centers, was communication with people outside:

> I really made sure that I was in contact with people as much as possible. I spent *hours* on the phone and also talking with people in that environment with people that showed me that I wasn't worthless. Because being in detention give you this sense of being worthless. You're not at home. You're not where you want to go. You're not in prison. See, it's just, it's the middle of nowhere, that feeling. So just being in touch with people, talking to people in the community was really, really important, just that verbal communication with people and their letters. And then people, like saying, yeah we know how you feel, even though we're not there, and we believe your story. In any case [if] not true, we just want to make sure that it's given ...we want to hear your story. (Cheikh Kone, interview with the author, 2008)[50]

PEN submission to the 2004 Human Rights Community Award stated: 'While Cheikh's case ignobly signalled the first time Australia was included in International PEN's infamous *Writers In Prison* publication, because of the manner and scope of refugee detention in Australia and the advocacy of the PEN Australia centres, the Australian Government has come under more sustained international pressure than any other country over this issue'.[51]

CHANGING POLICIES

Changes have been made several times to refugee and asylum policy in Australia since 2004. The Rudd Labor government disbanded the Pacific Solution v1 in February 2008. In 2008, Temporary Protections Visas were replaced with Permanent Protection Visas, and detention was recommended only as a 'last resort' and for the minimum time for processing asylum seekers (rather than as a punitive 'deterrent'). The Australian Human Rights Commission—which was called the Human Rights and Equal Opportunities Commission until August 9, 2009—has a public website where Submissions and Reports are accessible, as is a detailed account of the recent history of changing refugee human rights policies.[52] Temporary Protection Visas were reintroduced under Pacific Solution v2, in 2013, dismissed, and accepted again in 2014, with the commencement of Operation Sovereign Borders. On 1 July 2015 a law was introduced that gives the government the power to prosecute and impose two year jail sentences on medical, teaching, and child welfare professionals, and any who work in the camps who speak out about violations of human rights, and anything, they witness in the 'processing" camps; this is a deterrent to 'whistleblowers' from speaking to the media.(Journalists have to apply for a visa which costs $8000 per application, which is not refunded if the application is not accepted, the approvals are opaque and selective, which effectively means journalists are prevented from visiting and reporting first-hand what is happening).[53]

On September 8th, 2009, The Migration Amendment (Abolishing Detention Debt) Bill was passed through the Australian Senate. Australia was the only country in the world where asylum seekers were charged for the cost of their mandatory detention; a policy introduced by the Labor government in 1992, which 'had proven to be highly ineffective and heartless.'[54] On their release, refugees were given huge bills. For some families it was over $200,000. 'Those unable to pay their debts were left with a debt to the Australian Government which saw them included on a Movement Alert List. This prevented them from traveling or from applying to be reunited with family members overseas'.[55] For Mr Kone, this had unforeseen negative effects when, in 2004, after his release he was invited to speak at International PEN's Congress in Barcelona. He was refused a visa by the Department of Immigration at the last minute, as he had a detention debt of $89,000 dollars.[56] Although nothing could be done, this is further evidence of the importance of a case by case approach, for the carriage of social justice for the individual.

Meanwhile this has been harder under Pacific Solution v2. Amnesty International has recently published their report: *Island of Despair: Australia's "processing" of refugees on Nauru* (2016). The executive summary includes the statement:

> The report exposes how the Government of Australia has flouted the Refugee Convention, undermining its purpose and values for which it stands by subjecting children, men and women who have sought protection in Australia to egregious abuse, as part of the Government's policy of offshore "processing" of people seeking protection.[57]

ISLANDS OF DESPAIR: PACIFIC SOLUTION v2

> 'Only in the Lager was the restraint from below non-existent and the power of those small satraps absolute.' Primo Levi.[58]

The offshore processing centres filled with people who are 'stateless' and therefore utterly vulnerable, are run in the same way with no possibility of any control from 'underneath'. By locating these on islands and largely prohibiting the media from inspecting these, this created a 'black site', where the total control from the top prevented any access or monitoring whatsoever.

It was only after the 26 April 2016 PNG Supreme Court ruling that Manus Island offshore processing centre is illegal, in breach of human and constitutional rights,[59] that there has been a more open communication between people about what is happening. In 2016 Amnesty International published a report, *Island of Despair* on the torture of the harsh regime which 'deters' people from seeking asylum in Australia, by punishing and abusing those who have tried, and who are now held in the 'offshore processing' detention centres on the islands of Nauru and Manus. The Amnesty report explains:

> The Government of Australia's approach to people seeking asylum is focused on deterrence–that is: discouraging anyone who cannot travel to Australia without a visa from attempting to enter the territory irregularly. The vast majority of people who come from countries from which refugees flee–such as Afghanistan, Iraq, Somalia, Sri Lanka, and Syria–would fall within that category.[60]

The report continues:

> The Australian authorities attempt to achieve deterrence through two principal means. One is a practice called "pushbacks' or "turnbacks", which is a military-led operation during which Australian officials intercept and repel asylum-seekers arriving by boat. The second is the policy of "offshore processing," which involves taking people who do reach Australia by boat to offshore places of detention.[61]

The supposed justification for this policy is that it prevents deaths at sea, and is 'necessary to save lives'. Yet instead it is 'warehousing' hundreds of asylum seekers in a perpetual limbo, where they are subjected to dehumanizing treatment, and abuse, they are not given any information on what will happen to them, or how long they will have to stay; they are treated like 'criminals', and their hope and dignity as human beings is systematically and deliberately eroded, as a 'deterrent'. The 'offshore processing centres' of Nauru and Manus reopened in 2012, refugees have been held in limbo for almost six years, waiting to have their refugee status determined, and allocated a safe place to live.

This is classified as a form of torture.[62]

An Amnesty researcher interviewed asylum seekers, refugees and service providers on Nauru. The conclusions reveal the extent of the horrors:

> The humanitarian justification for the policy is a gross and cynical misrepresentation...in an effort to prevent people arriving by boat, the Australian Government has set up a deliberate system of abuse, which has caused irreparable harm to thousands of people. Offshore processing and detention have also resulted in numerous preventable deaths, as a result of poor medical treatment, horrific cases of self-harm resulting from mental anguish, as well as murder.[63]

Amnesty comments:

> The idea that one group of people can be subjected to horrendous abuse in order to prevent another group from putting themselves in harms' way is the flawed foundation of Australia's policy towards asylum-seekers.

It is a fallacious argument, which produces inhumane results. Yet, this is also a profitable big business. Those running the camps are making a vast amount of money which is paid to them by the Government from the money of taxpayers, who meanwhile have been kept in the dark as to the expense and the processes, that is until a recent audit has revealed the scale of profit being made.[64] The Australian engineering and construction company, Transfield now known as Broadspectrum, that runs these camps, providing "garrison and welfare services" receives 1.5 million Australian dollars a day; a three year contract worth 1.5 billion has been renewed and has trebled to $3.045 billion, as revealed in audit by the Australian National Audit Office: *Offshore Processing Centres in Nauru and Papua New Guinea: Procurement of Garrison Support and Welfare Services* (September 13, 2016), this is viewable online, has no page numbers, and will be referred to throughout this essay.[65] Transfield is given $578,000 per annum, per asylum seeker in the 'offshore processing centres', a figure that has more than doubled since 2014, as, at the same time, the mental and physical health of the asylum seekers in their care has declined. This is an amount (apparently decided by the Transfield entity) based on higher numbers of asylum seekers and refugees than have ever been held, as reports discussed below show. The 2016 audit concludes that the Department of Immigration and Border Protection has failed taxpayers and government in Australia, let alone the asylum seekers who are amongst the most vulnerable people in the world and in their care. The audit criticizes the Department's deficiencies: 'amongst departmental personnel at all levels,' concluding: 'the deficiencies have resulted in a higher than necessary expense to taxpayers and significant reputational risks for the Australian Government and DIBP' (ANAO audit 2016).[66] This has been seen in numerous ways, for example the effective boycott of the international Biennale of Sydney 2014 by artists and writers in ethical protest at the sponsorship ties with Transfield, that resulted in a philanthropic sponsor taking over, the Neilson Foundation in 2014, which has renewed as Principal Sponsor for the Biennale of Sydney editions, of 2018 and 2020.[67]

SYDNEY BIENNALE BOYCOTT PROTEST BACKGROUND

Transfield, the engineering and construction infrastructure corporation that took up the lucrative contracts for running Nauru and Manus Island 'offshore processing' camps, was in 2014 the 'founding partner' of the Biennale and its major sponsor.[68] Luca Belgiorno-Nettis who was in 2014 chairman of the Sydney Biennale is one of three sons of the founder of Transfield, Franco Belgiorno-Nettis, In 2006, he founded his political 'newDemocracy Foundation' group to influence opinion. "refashioning our governing institutions through the newDemocracy Foundation, a broad group of eminent former politicians, academics and civic leaders."[69] Franco Belgiorno-Nettis founded the Biennale in 1973, and there was a belief in Sydney that the Biennale could not exist without Transfield. According to an interview on *Australian Biography* website Franco Belgiorno-Nettis (1915-2006), who in World War II was an officer in Mussolini's fascist army, was imprisoned in Africa, and India in British Prisoner-of-War camps for years, he immigrated to Australia in 1951 then married by proxy his girlfriend, Amina Cerino-Zegna, who was from a well-to-do northern Italy family (his brother stood in for him and his wife joined him in Australia). He was a patron of the arts, Sydney Biennale founding patron and chairman of the Biennale board, three sons succeeded him.[70] Belgiorno-Nettis came to Australia after Australia adopted the 1951 Refugee Convention which was developed to help 'displaced persons' and refugees, the victims of German, Italian and related fascism following World War II, and this enabled a postwar wave of migration.[69]

But not all those who migrated from postwar Europe were refugees. Many Nazis, collaborators and war criminals posing as legitimate refugees escaped by being given cover, Red Cross passports, and jobs in destination countries, as Mark Aarons and John Loftus show in *Unholy Trinity: The Vatican, the Nazis, and the Swiss Banks* (1991),[72] Aarons in *War Criminals Welcome*. Fascists, collaborators and war criminals were able to make new lives in Australia.[73] After the Ustasha genocide of Jews, Serbs and Roma in Jasenovac, Ustasha (also spelled Ustaše) fascists in Croatia, who ran the Jasenovac extermination camps in the former Yugoslavia, came to Australia,[74] Barry Lituchy at the Jasenovac Research Institute too suggests that fascists were recruited by intelligence agencies. There were expatriations into Australia, Canada, Austria, South America, the United States, and Germany. Known fascists were recruited by ASIO in Australia if they were actively anti-communist.[75] There has never been a successful trial of a war criminal in Australia.[76]

B.A. Santamaria (1915-1998) was a Catholic anti-communist political activist and journalist, the son of an immigrant Italian grocer, who was educated by Christian Brothers in Melbourne and wrote his MA thesis on *Changing Shirts: The Origins of Italian Fascism*. He formed the Catholic Social Studies Movement (the Groupers) in 1941, and played a part in the 'anti-communist movement', that infiltrated the Unions.[77] In 1954 he was instrumental in the bringing in of a controversial Land Bill to allow Crown land to be sold to "Italians with foreign capital".[78] This was the year of the 'Petrov affair' when Vladimir Petrov, a soviet diplomat in Canberra and his MVD officer wife defected after being offered political asylum in return for giving evidence of Soviet espionage and documents which they provided. Petrov had been befriended by a Michael Bialoguski, a Polish musician, doctor, and ASIO agent.[79]

Notorious war criminals were recruited by ASIO (Australian Security Intelligence Organization) where they joined agents spying not only on suspected communists and communist sympathizers but also on any 'writers and intellectuals' as shown in the miniseries *Persons of Interest* (2014) where the declassified files of prominent writers were read by their subjects, including the file of author Frank Hardy whose novels include *But the Dead Are Many* (1975) on the disappearance and death of communist John Morel (Hardy's granddaughter, Marieke Hardy, read his file).[80] This history is verified by David Horner in *The

Spy Catchers: The Official History of ASIO Vol 1, 1949-1963 (2014). Horner commends Aarons research in this field, and he confirms that 'ASIO turned a blind eye to war criminals once they reached Australia as long as they were strongly anti-communist'.[81] War historian, Peter Edwards, wrote, 'Monitoring the CPA and extending this to surveillance of often mildly left-wing writers and intellectuals became an obsession.' Horner describes this as a 'massive waste of time and resources'.[82]

For many writers and artists this has had severe and cruel repercussions. Their publications, which in a democracy should ensure their success, caused them to become targets of ASIO—profitable targets as secret agents are paid to watch them, and this is paid for through taxpayers money. It is a form of bureaucratic control, which rewards administrators and bureaucrats for 'managing', watching and keeping under surveillance, writers and 'casual' academics, who are oppressed.

Persons of Interest reveals that wives and women are also spied on by ASIO. Roger Milliss's wife, Suse, had her tapped phone calls recorded including a sensitive conversation about a potential abortion.

Many writers and artists with PhDs have had their careers blocked or prevented by the 'casualization' of universities leading to massive reduction of full-time employment in universities, and due to lack of payment and income, writers, artists and intellectuals are often forced to go onto inadequate social security payments, where they are under surveillance.[83] There is a fascist, anti-intellectual propagandist misinformed anti-media and far-right view along the lines of: *the radical left mentality of the 1960s, 70s, that,* according to this propaganda, *despises the West and its values has turned mainstream and been institutionalized inside organizations such as the ABC, the universities, the Greens and sections of the Australia Labor Party.*

This led to the spying on and blacklisting of untold of authors and artists and intellectuals in Australia; and lack of employment resulting in poverty, isolation, and oppression which leads to suicide.[84] Horner's volume is "well timed" as recent changes to laws governing ASIO have reinvigorated debates on the 'balance between national security and civil liberties.'[85]

This is a system which is easily manipulated by persons in power, who might watch and destroy the careers and lives of people they wish to: that can include personal vendettas and wishing to get revenge on a partner, or hobbling a professional or business rival, in a way that is hidden, simply by someone deeming the person a suspected 'security threat'.[86] Horner reveals that not only does ASIO conduct 'counter-espionage (fair enough) but it devotes enormous resources and money to 'counter-subversion' which his history shows, meant that they must have spied on most academics, artists and writers in Australia since the 1940s. As Mark McKenna writes: 'ASIO displayed a catch-all approach to intelligence: cast the net wide, and if we happen to burn some reputations and careers along the way, it's the price we pay'. He adds, the 'entrenched suspicion of intellectuals, writers, artists'[87] in Australian security and politics, which persists as shown in new restrictive laws, is attributable to and can be traced back to the start of ASIO after WWI.[88]

There is a surveillance economy which targets writers and artists, for profit. This must raise the question why was the word 'subversion' introduced into art theory in the 1960s/70s as a concept that students were required to apply in assignments? This is still the case, students at New South Wales universities are encouraged to use the terms 'subversive' to indicate a work is relevant and 'critical'. I speak as a former lecturer. What this means is that unknown to lecturers and students they will become lucrative targets of ASIO spying for profit: suspected of 'state subversion'. This may seem extreme and frankly ridiculous but the history of ASIO reveals a lack of understanding of the context of the youth movements of the 1960s and 70s; of art and literary cultures (let alone intellectual discourse). Imagine: an ASIO agent saying: "They are all talking (or writing) about subversion". One might imagine it was an easy way for the agents to make money, spying on students, writers and artists; it was and is a form of intimidation by the state.

Tom Shepherd, who worked for twenty-four years as an ASIO spy, spoke in the *Persons of Interest* documentary. He explained that "agents would gild the lily just to make themselves interesting." They saw conspiracies where there were none. Shepherd also says that ASIO agents were under "constant pressure" to discover "something else", about the one/s (e.g. writers and artists) they were spying on, even when the evidence was non-existent. Shepherd confesses that for this he still feels "duplicitous": "I still don't know whether I'm lying or telling the truth".

Agents were under pressure to 'gild the lily' for bosses and concoct 'threats' and suspects to justify their work and ongoing pay. Meanwhile the careers and lives of writers and artists were destroyed, or aborted.

The question that emerges from this Australian context is: How can writers and artists whose work is made from freedom of thought, and expression, in the inner space of thought, live and work in these conditions of surveillance, and persecution? This by the way is where the current government proposed to reduce author copyright to five years after date of first publication, then to 15-20 years and still has not made on any decisions on how it will effect its proposed amendments to copyright laws, keeping Australian authors in anxious limbo whilst the government stalls on this for years now. As an author and publisher, in July 2016, I presented my views to the Productivity Commission hearings in Sydney in defense of copyright, as I am British with dual Australian nationality, my works are covered by British copyright law. This is an inequitable situation where a preferred nationality overrides the Australian citizenship; it is unfair to, and disadvantages many Australian authors in Australia, where people expect that the government would enthusiastically seek to protect the rights of writers and artists; instead the rights and the livelihoods of authors have been threatened by the proposed changes by the government, and creative innovative citizens and residents are being treated with callous lack of feeling and disrespect.[89]

Belgiorno-Nettis arrived in Australia in 1951, an engineer employee of the multinational engineering firm Electric Power Transmission, a branch of the Milan-based Societa' Anonima Elettrificazione, which was constructing transmission lines around the world, and in Australia. In 1956, he started up with three others the Transfield Group of Companies. One of Transfield's contracts, the Snowy River Hydro-Electric power scheme was in 2016 listed as a World Heritage Site renowned for employing thousands of postwar European migrants. This is officially held to be the basis of 'multiculturalism' as explained in a Government website, *Anti-Racism Education for Australian Schools*: 'Snowy Mountains Scheme: Birthplace of multiculturalism in Australia.'

> The Snowy Mountains Scheme is not just a great feat of engineering, it is also a great social achievement. When the Snowy Mountains Hydro-electric Authority was established in 1949, there was a serious national shortage of skilled personnel, equipment and construction materials as a legacy of World War II....Overall 10,000 people worked on the Scheme's construction between 1949-1974 two-thirds of them migrant workers. The workforce reached a peak of 7, 300 in 1959.[90]

Immigrants were encouraged to migrate, and assisted in their passages. The Scheme is written of in *Il Globo* as a 'symbol of Australia's multicultural identity'; and it received world heritage listing in 2016.[91] One of the post war Nazi war criminals who was selected for immigration to Australia was Lyenko Urbanchich (also spelt Urbančič), wartime Nazi propagandist. The Allies policy was to return war criminals, and collaborators to Tito's government. Aaron writes in his obituary of Urbančič[92] that collaborators classified as 'blacks' or 'greys', were not allowed to migrate. Only 'whites', Nazi victims, were permitted entry to Australia. Despite being on an Allies final list of 44 Nazi collaborators (and not allowed into Australia), he was selected to migrate arriving in 1951, and worked on the Snowy Mountains Scheme. According to his obituary in the *Sydney Morning Herald*, 'Ardent Nazi took Liberal to extremes' (March 4, 2006) Urbanchich infiltrated politics, where he had a decades-long career and influence.

> The passing of Lyenko Urbanchich ends the almost 70-year long political career of the man who invented ethnic branch stacking in Australia. He was also the last, and most powerful, of the central and eastern European Nazi collaborators and war criminal who infiltrated the Liberal Party from the 1950s and coalesced with Australian rightest to form the "Uglies" faction'

Urbanchich, a 'Nazi propagandist and political powerbroker', built up a faction in New South Wales which he helped form in the 1970s.[93]

> The peak of Urbanchich's success came in 1977 with the formation of the Liberal Ethnic Council. As council president, he automatically had a seat on the state executive. Other council executive members included his close ally, David Clarke, who learnt ethnic branch stacking techniques from his mentor and today leads the "Uglies" faction established by Urbanchich 40 years ago.

Urbanchich stacked the branches of electorates in Sydney and Newcastle writes Aarons,[94] in the early 1960's Urbanchich was under surveillance by ASIO and the police, 'Nazi collaborators and war criminals had infiltrated the Liberal's Migrant Advisory Council, whose leaders included a former Hungarian mayor responsible for deporting 18,000 Jews to Auschwitz'.[95] Urbanchich emerged as a 'key organizer of fascist groups', he recruited 'fellow Nazi collaborators and supporters of far-right campaigns', and stacked branches.[96] All of this helped to shape today's environment of oppression of writers, artists and academics, resulting in lack of creative career structures; and in poverty for writers and artists, in teaching, research and small business and the media; structures which have been attacked and dismantled by governmental forces that have 'casualized' and reduced grants for writers and artists, and which in subliminal ways mirror the cruel policies of asylum seeker 'non-processing'. In Australia; only a very small percentage of artists and writers make a living from their creative works alone, and work is hard to come by.

The Cornall Review quotes a 'security risk assessment' description of the 'transferees' at Manus Island Offshore Processing Centre as:

> predominantly physically fit, and physically strong, with a large percentage under 35. They have a variety of backgrounds ranging from military personnel to professors. Many are highly educated, articulate and bi-lingual.[97]

The passage cited is in the Australian Government inquiry *Review into the events of 16-18 February 2014 at the Manus Regional Processing Centre* [Cornall Review]. They are held in detention for many years in Manus province (men); and Nauru Island (families and unaccompanied children). Transfield/Broadspectrum (the audit shows) is being paid AU 3.045 billion dollars per year and a half contract, to manage the 'processing centres'. Thousands of cases of abuse in the 'offshore processing centres' have been reported.[98] This shows a striking change in attitudes, practices and policies. The company that employed immigrants and offered them a life is now being paid billions of dollars per year to keep in indefinite detention people who are like the displaced persons and migrants they employed. People whose identities are displaced by wars and conflicts in Europe, like the 'stateless' who are waiting, on Manus; and Nauru: families, women and children. The abuse of asylum seekers for private profit, and the revelations that war criminals were given a sanctuary in Australia, the only country in which not one Nazi war criminal was successfully tried,[99] and evidence from the current Royal Commission into Institutional Responses to Child Sexual Abuse[100] shows that giving sanctuary to sadistic war criminals, has had barbaric repercussions of horrifying abuse of children involving churches, schools, sporting groups, residential care, among other institutions, which makes Australia's self-congratulatory reputation for successful multiculturalism look like an artificial halo.[101]

In Australia there is a major problem with sexual abuse and physical abuse of children in institutions. The ongoing *Royal Commission into Institutional Responses to Child Sexual Abuse*, established in 2013[102] is investigating responses of institutions, primarily the Catholic church, and Cardinal George Pell, Treasurer of the Vatican, former Archbishop of Melbourne, and Sydney, who is being investigated by Victorian Police for allegations of abuse of boys and 'failing to exercise proper care of children in a Melbourne parish'.[103] In 2014, Pell was appointed to the new Secretariat for the Economy at the Vatican, in Rome, with responsibility for economic control of the agencies of the Holy See. When called to the Royal Commission on Institutional Responses to Sexual Abuse of Children questioning, Pell could not return to Australia on grounds of ill-health, he has been interviewed via video-linkup and by Australian police who travelled to Rome to interview him, Pell is being questioned on being part of, and concealing, a network ring of paedophile priests in the state of Victoria when he was working in the church up the ladder from a priest to Archbishop of Melbourne.[104] This ongoing Royal Commission shows the horrific scale of organized institutional abuse in the Catholic Church, of helpless children in Australia, which was reported from 1950-2010.

Canon law with its rules of secrecy enables child abuse to be perpetrated and covered up. In 1974, the pope gave an instruction called *Secreta Continere*, the 'pontifical secret' which imposes strict secrecy on 'investigation' of child sexual abuse allegations.[105] This puts the church above the law. Not one paedophile priest was reported to police by the church authorities in seven decades yet there were thousands of complaints of abuse, and it was widely known about. The church flaunts it.

The first published report by the Royal Commission into abuse in the Catholic Church, reveals the staggering scale of the abuse, and this is just those who reported, many victims remain silent, many commit suicide.[106] The compensation payments made to survivors testifies to the magnitude of the abuse and the cover up.

The report documents facts: average age of survivors at age of first abuses: 10.5 years of age for girls; and 11.6 years of age for boys.[107]

> Overall, 3, 066 claims of child sexual abuse resulted in a payment being made following a claim for redress. Catholic Church authorities made total payments of $276.1 million in response to claims of child sexual abuse received between 1 January 1980 and 28 February 2015, including monetary compensation, treatment, legal and other costs.[108]

The paid claims averaged $91,000. 2,854 claims of child sexual abuse resulted in monetary compensation. The Christian Brothers had both the highest total payment ['total' means for multiple assaults] and the largest number of payments. The Jesuits (the Society of Jesus) had the highest average payment. Between 1950-2010, 7 per cent of Australia's Catholic priests were accused of abusing children;[109] a staggering 40.4 per cent in St John of God Brothers, based in Rome, which first came to Australia in 1947 and has orders around the world.[110] Many of the children were in residential care. This reflects on the worldwide mistreatment of children which is connected to the atrocities of the second world war, and the genocides where children were murdered on a massive scale. A horrific example is Miroslav Filipović, Croatian Nazi collaborator, and Franciscan Friar, known as 'The Devil of Jasenovac' and 'Brother Satan'. There is one account of his massacre of a class of school children related by their teacher who survived which is available online.[111] The methods of the Ustasha fascists were 'medieval' involving things like gouging out eyes of the living, slaughtering thousands with knives and axes, slashing throats from ear to ear, and were so bloodthirsty and barbaric it was reported that German Nazis and Italian fascists recoiled.[112] The Ustasha fascist regime was initiated with the foundation of Independent State of Croatia (NDH) on 10th April 1941, a short-lived puppet state of the German and Italian axis, that annexed Yugoslavia. The Ustasha fascists massacred 30,000 Jews; 40,000 Gypsies, and 300,000-700,000 Serbs in the new state of Croatia. A detailed history by the Jasenovac Research Centre in New York describes the Ustasha regime: convert one third of Serbs to Catholicism; deport one third of Serbs; and kill one third of Serbs.[113] This was undertaken quickly with depraved relish in bloodthirsty days and weeks of locals massacring locals in villages and towns, and Jasenovac extermination camps covering 150 square miles, the biggest extermination camp system outside the Third Reich:

> operated not by the Germans, but by the Croatian state authorities of the time...in which hundreds of innocent men, women and children were put to death in the most brutal way.[114]

It is inexplicable, unless it is through sheer ignorance of history, that for years right-wing Liberal Australian politicians have been attending the annual celebrations at the Sydney Croatian Club commemorating the 10th of April, the date of the illegal founding of the Independent

State of Croatia, an extreme ultrafascist state, which was set up under Axis rule (Italian fascists and German Nazis), after Yugoslavia was attacked and invaded by Germany on 10th April, 1941 and the Kingdom of Yugoslavia monarchy went into exile. (The royal family returned in 2001).[115] In 2007, Howard's Communications Minister, Helen Coonan, Liberal Senator Concetta Fierravanti-Wells (Minister for International Development and the Pacific since 2016) and NSW Liberal MP David Clarke were reported attending these celebrations in *The Jewish News*, and *Crikey*.[116] In his obituary for Urbanchich, Aarons wrote:

> Clarke helped organise the numbers to narrowly save Urbanchich from the Liberal Party after a 1979 ABC radio documentary (which I [Arrons] produced) exposed him as a Nazi propagandist...despite the evidence, the 1980 vote to expel him fell just short of the 60 per cent required.[117]

Clarke was reported in *The Jewish News*, by Vic Alhadeff, executive of the Jewish Board of Deputies, as attending 2005 and 2007 commemorations at the Sydney Croatian Club of 10 April, the foundation of the neo-Nazi Ustasha state.[118] *Crikey* wrote: 'In 2005, he feigned surprise at being connected to the Ustaše...after he was caught out celebrating the exact same event at an Ustasi function'.[119] Alhadeff's article was later referred by Dr John Kaye in the *J-Wire* (digital Jewish news) transcript of a debate in the NSW Legislative Council on BDS (boycott, divestment, sanctions), published on September 16, 2011.[120] Dr Kaye supported the motion, arguing for Israel to follow and not break international law.

Dr John Kaye, in countering points made by Clarke, said:

> David Clarke who twice—once in April 2005 and then in April 2007—attended a commemoration of the rise of the fascist Ustasha Government into power in Croatia in April 1941. He is the same David Clarke who was reprimanded by the chief executive officer of the Jewish Board of Deputies, Mr Vic Alhadeff, who I acknowledge is present in the gallery today. In the Jewish News of 26 April 2007, Mr Alhadeff said of the Hon. David Clarke:
>
> o   The function—
> that is, the function attended by Mr Clarke—
> o   celebrated Hitler's establishment of the Nazi state of Croatia ... This is a state that supported the Jasenovac extermination camp,
> o   where hundreds of thousands of people were murdered, including 60,000 Jews ... It is very troubling that such a brutal regime still finds support in democratic Australia.[121]

The 2007 attendance of NSW and federal Liberal Party members at the commemoration of the foundation of the Ustasha Nazi state was reported in *Crikey*, and the *Jewish News:*

> The Howard Government has been embarrassed by the appearance of a cabinet minister at a Croatian independence function linked to a murderous neo-Nazi regime....NSW Jewish Board of Deputies (NSWJBD) CEO Vic Alhadeff described the celebration as "offensive" to Australians, while it is understood Croatian embassy officials are also angered at the involvement of a senior government minister.[122]

In 2014, shortly after the artists Sydney Biennale boycott protest, Australian Prime Minister Tony Abbott was alleged to have sent his 'good wishes' via his envoy Craig Kelly MP (Member for Hughes):

> On behalf of the PM, who is in Japan, I'm conveying his greetings and good wishes on the occasion of the celebration of the 10th of April to you and all Croats in Australia and those in Croatia.[123]

This message was published in *InSerbia News* citing the Croatian weekly *Boca CroPress*, that reported:

> The celebration was organized on April 13th, in the presence of some 200 Croats, many Australian politicians and a Ukrainian diplomat.
>
> The Independent State of Croatia, often referred to simply by the abbreviation NDH, was a World War II puppet state of Nazi Germany and Italy established in part of Axis-occupied Yugoslavia.[124]

This incident was reported in *CounterPunch* by Cambridge Commonwealth Scholar, Dr. Binoy Kampmark.[125] According to all these reports, Liberal Prime Minister Tony Abbott, sent a message of good wishes to an ethnic group in Australia celebrating the founding of an extreme, murderous neo-Nazi fascist state. Dr Kampmark clarified, 10th April is not the national day of its present state.[126] I should clarify too this is not a racist slur on the Croatian state or people now.

This became an international incident, SBS TV news reported that 'also in attendance at the event were NSW Liberal MP for Riverstone Kevin Conolly, The Hills Shire Councillor Robyn Preston, Penrith City Councillor Marcus Cornish and Ms Nadia Namuren of the Ukrainian Council of New South Wales.'[127] And:

> Mr Kelly reportedly attended the event on behalf of the Parliamentary Secretary for Multicultural Affairs, Senator Concetta Fierravanti-Welles.[128]

The Croatian Ministry of Foreign and European Affairs issued a statement including the following words, to SBS:

> "We have summoned Her Excellency Susan Cox to express our protest because it is absolutely unacceptable to commemorate 10th April and so-called NDH, or Independent State of Croatia.[129]

A spokesman for Australia's Department of Foreign Affairs and Trade issued a statement to SBS that included the following:

> Mr Kelly attended a Croatian community event in Sydney last week in good faith...Mr Kelly was not representing the Prime Minister at the event.[130]

There is a wider current significance to this which is of ongoing relevance. To what extent is such political support of neo-fascism, and/or ignorance of cultural significance, and history, effecting the policies which are shaping the employment prospects, and small businesses of writers and intellectuals in Australia? Irredendist and revanchist tendencies of diaspora groups of fascist war criminals who were allowed to migrate to Australia, and a 'religious right' fundamentalism which eventuated, is linked to the confection of causes for continuing attacks and fundamentalist discrimination against 'Islam'; proven to be based on a false claim (non existent 'weapons of mass destruction') and unlawful, and continues to be the basis for policies, for excluding legitimate migrants and asylum seekers; what about those who have written about exiled writers for instance? Am I excluded from an income and a viable life in Australia despite being a citizen; albeit secretly, accidentally or as collateral damage? [131]

In terms of the economy of global security, the so-called 'War on Terror' has replaced The Cold War. Announced less than two decades later, it works too on a level of intimidation and paranoia, surveillance of 'suspects', presumably still including writers and artists, and guaranteeing employment for 'security agents'. To what extent is this at the expense of the arts writers and intellectuals who might hold different views, as the research books by the respected historians Mark Aarons and official war historian David Horner shows was happening during the Cold War?[132] What if this is happening even to writers, intellectuals, and artists who are: democratic, pacifist, anti-violence, anti-fascist and not-communist? What I would like to know is, what is an author living in abject poverty in Australia to do, highly qualified and experienced, unable to gain a position at an Australian university, or support oneself through one's writing despite years of lecturing and research and publishing as an oxymoronic 'casual academic'? Some internalize oppression and commit suicide. For many, it is a fight not to [133]

Shortly before the April 2014 political incident at the Sydney Croatian Club, many international artists selected to participate and exhibit their works in Australia as representatives of their countries at the 19th Biennale of Sydney, boycotted in protest, in protest against the Biennale's board chairman sponsorship ties to his company profiting from mandatory indefinite detention of asylum seekers, including children, in the Australian-run 'offshore processing centres'.

BIENNALE OF SYDNEY 2014 ARTIST BOYCOTT PROTEST

In February 2014, as ninety-two international artists flew into Sydney from over thirty countries around the world they were greeted by the news that Biennale founding sponsor, Transfield, one of whose directors was Biennale chairman, was about to be awarded the contract to run the controversial refugee 'offshore processing centres' managed by Australia on the islands of Nauru and Manus. The news circulated on Facebook, blogs and art media. A boycott was organized by Biennale artists calling to cut ties with a corporation profiting in mandatory indefinite detention of asylum seekers, including children. As a freelance art journalist and media writer, I had written about the Biennale since 2003. And in 2014, I wrote on the unfolding events on *The Daily Fugue* site.

On February 16th 2014 there was news of protests and a barbaric attack on the asylum seekers at the Manus 'offshore processing centre'. Over a period of two days from 16th-18th, Papua New Guinea nationals broke through and jumped fences into the processing centre and with security guards, both locals and expats, severely beat many men and murdered Reza Barati, 23. This is described, and referred to, in the investigation into this attack *Report to the Secretary Department of Immigration and Border Protection Review into the events of 16-18 February 2014 at the Manus Regional Processing Centre* by Robert Cornall AO, 23 May 2014 (hereafter referred to as the 'Cornall Review'). Mr Cornall went to the Manus centre to investigate and interviewed asylum seekers about what happened. This section is based on his report.

> The worst injury was sustained by Reza Barati. Mr Barati suffered a severe brain injury caused by a brutal beating by several assailants and died a few hours later.[134]

At least sixty-nine 'transferees' (as the refugees are termed in the report) were treated with over ten being taken to hospital in Papua New A victim has his throat slit from side to side from an assailant attacking him from behind, 'causing a 10-12 cm' 'gaping wound'; one 'lost his right eye as a result of the bashing he received', one was shot 'with the bullet lodging in his right hip'. There were many injuries of broken bones and lacerations. A significant number did not report their injuries for a variety of reasons including fear of reprisals.[135] Many had psychological injuries and an extra nine mental health care staff were assigned to the centre. All this is detailed in the Cornall Review.

> In the days following the incidents under investigation other persons came forward for treatment, particularly for post-traumatic stress disorder.[136]

The Review found the murderous attacks had occurred in response to fairly small protests by a small group (25%) of men in one of the four compounds. In summary, the context was this. The centre has been reopened in 2012 (as part of Pacific Solution v2) as a supposedly 'temporary low security offshore processing centre' which was initially for men, women and children. (Due to the high levels of abuses against children this changed later). The contract between the Australian government and the garrison service provider stipulated that 50% of its security officers had to be Papua New Guinea nationals, or engaged through a local business; and 75% had to be locals for all other services (cleaning, cooking, gardening). Initially the refugees were going to be resettled to Australia. But on 19 July 2013 then PM Labor's Kevin Rudd announced a significant policy change: refugees would be resettled in PNG not Australia. PNG is an emerging nation, and has not enough resources for its own peoples, as its Ministers have since pointed out. This created hostility in some people who were working in the asylum seeker processing centre. There was confusion around the implementation of the policy and the asylum seekers (not one claim had been processed) were left in the dark, not knowing what was going to happen to them, many had relatives or direct family already in Australia and were facing permanent separation. According to the Cornall Report this was an environment of frustration, misinformation and lack of communication, and what happened was 'eminently foreseeable'.

A rumour was spread that there was going to be an 'amnesty,' and they were being transferred to Australia, at Christmas, Cornall reports; frustrated, the men asked for information; in January 2014 a meeting was scheduled with management and officials, at this meeting, Cornall reports, the setting was chaotic, it was hard to hear, all their questions remained unanswered (pp. 30-31) There was a protest. 70-75% of the men were not involved in protest.[187] About 30-35 men tried to escape, they were caught and attacked violently by 'mobile unit' police who broke fences into the 'processing centre', and 'gave a beating' to scores of refugees and Mr Barati who was killed by guards from Papua New Guinea and Australia who kicked his head and dropped a rock on his head.[188]

Reza Barati, a 23-year old architecture graduate was murdered by a group of expat and local guards, eye witnesses said in taped interviews with Cornall, who wrote: 'His friends at Mike [residential compound] told me he was a very gentle person.'[139]

None of the men in the compound where Mr Barati was murdered were involved in the protests. One of the witnesses was a friend of Mr Barati and they had come together from Indonesia on the same boat. He said to Cornall 'I don't feel safe. I feel they want to kill me.'[140]

A group of witnesses to Mr Barati's murder saw it through the open door of a room many were hiding in. They could see outside to a staircase with a landing external to the building which is where the murder took place.

> I saw the scene of killing my friend... I saw how he was killed brutally. From that night on, I'm not in good mental conditions. I can't sleep, I'm always distressed, see nightmares, always scared.[141]

Another said '....because I saw the killing of [Reza Barati] I am mentally tortured'.

> I saw in front of me Reza Barati was murdered they 'MOBO Squad' and G4S (the security guards) hit them on head with stones and sticks and we could not save our friend.[142]

Cornall reports:

> Mr T3 says that when the riot happened, Mr Barati was in the internet room at first and then, after gunshots were fired in Mike compound he observed Reza Barati coming up the stairs towards his room. Mr

Barati was being followed by a PNG national known to him as [redacted] who worked for the Salvation Army. [Redacted] has been identified as [redacted] and the Salvation Army has confirmed it employed him.[143]

The eyewitness said:

> when he (Mr Barati) was trying to come upstairs, he hit him twice with a very long stick... when he fell down, more than 10 officer passed him and all of them, they kicked him in his head...it was including the PNG locals, PNG guards and Australian expats....Then, at the end, when he was down, all of those officers, they had the riot gear...When he fall, all of the guards who were passing, they kick him in the head and the last one, one of the PNG locals... he put a very big stone on his head.[144]

Mr Barati was taken to the emergency triage centre, nearby. The medical officer's record states:

> When he was brought in Mr Barati was alive but the medical staff knew from his injuries he was not going to survive.

> Mr Barati's head was shattered by a crack to the left side of his skull.... He also had facial abrasions and knocks indicating he has received a general beating (not just the blow to the skull).[145]

Reza Barati died soon afterwards from heart failure caused by severe brain injury.

The man who lost his right eye

Robert Cornall was not able to interview the asylum seeker whose eye was lost in the attacks. 'He has been taken away from the Manus Centre for expert medical treatment elsewhere'.[146] There were records of interview notes with a medical officer, and the treating doctor. The medical officer's record of interview notes revealed:

> The man who lost his right eye was brought to the triage centre. He said that, just observing him, it appeared the victim had been beaten with a stick or an iron bar. His face was incredibly swollen, red and bloodied.[147]

The treating doctor's record of interview added more detail:

> On arrival, she observed that the right side of the patient's face was very swollen to the extent that his skin was tight as a drum and he was bruised black and blue. His right eye was enclosed by the swell-

ing. The patient was in huge pain and very distressed. On examination, the doctor was more concerned about the man's eye than severe brain damage.

The doctor was concerned that his level of pain could mean he had suffered a retro orbital haemotoma which can squash the optic nerve and cause loss of sight in that eye. If so, she would have to make a slit in the canthus lateral to the eye to relieve the pressure.

When the doctor prised the eye open, blood and pigmented matter flowed out suggesting the patient had a global rupture [his eye burst]. This meant that making the lateral slit was no longer a clinical priority.

They treated the patient for pain and he was sent to the hospital in Lorengau. The treating doctor went with him.

The doctor said it was clear that his injuries had been caused by a severe beating with a blunt object.[148]

Artists' responses and ethical protest

In Sydney, many artists were shocked that the Biennale's sponsor was running the offshore processing centres. It was morally reprehensible to many from outside Australia, as well as many people from Australia. Furthermore, several international artists had exhibits in the Biennale on broad issues of displaced peoples, and that involved refugees.

Biennale artists found it unacceptable that they had been offered a platform for critique that was implicated with what they were critiquing: 'that Transfield provides via the Biennale'.[149] In order to provide an authentic and meaningful response, they had to do this independently. Some formed the *#19 BoS Working Group* blog, and published *Statement of our withdrawal from the 19th Biennale of Sydney*:

> We have revoked our works, cancelled our public events and relinquished our artists' fees. While we have sought ways to address our strong opposition to Australia's mandatory detention policy as participants of the Biennale, we have decided that withdrawal is our most constructive choice. We do not accept the platform that Transfield provides via the Biennale for critique. We see our participation in the Biennale as an active link in a chain of associations that leads to the abuse of human rights. For us, this is undeniable and indefensible.
>
> ...We withdraw to send a message to the Biennale urging them, again, to act ethically and transparently. To send a message to Transfield

that we will not add value to their brand and its inhumane enterprise. Finally, and most importantly, we withdraw to send a message to the Australian Government that we do not accept their unethical policy against asylum seekers.

We ask that the Biennale of Sydney acknowledge the absence of our work from the exhibition. As the Biennale has offered to provide a platform and support for our dissent, we request that our withdrawal be registered on the Biennale website and signposted at the physical site of our projects. In the pervasive silence that the Government enforces around this issue, we will not let this action be unnoticed.[150]

More than half the 19th Biennale of Sydney artists boycotted the Biennale and organized in their response, writing and publishing letters. They called for the severing of the sponsorship from Transfield.[151]

We make this statement in light of Transfield's expanding management of Manus Island and Nauru immigration detention centres. We act in the wake of the death of Reza Berati from inside Manus Island detention centre on February 17. We are in urgent political circumstances with a government that is stepping up their warfare on the world's most vulnerable people daily....

...We have received indications from the Board of the Biennale and Transfield that there will be no movement on their involvement in this issue. In our letter to the Board we asked for action and engagement, but we are told that the issue is too complex...[152]

The announcement of the international artists boycott sent the management of the Biennale into crisis. The opening was just days away, artists were publishing open letters stating their position, and moral concerns. Open letters were published calling to sever ties with Biennale sponsor, and Board chairman's multinational, Transfield that was expanding its contract to run Manus and Nauru mandatory detention 'processing centres'. The response from the artists was swift, focused, and powerful. Throughout this protest there was little involvement by spokespeople in the media. The Artists ruled. The letters were posted on artist websites. The shock for many of the suddenly revealed sponsorship of the Biennale, from profits of mandatory detention of exiles (many of whom are writers and artists), disrupted the cherished image of Sydney's Biennale as epitomizing freedom of expression and international exchange, in the Sydney artworld this created a moral lacuna that jarred the status quo; countered by the determined action of brave artists who cared, knew how to organize. Change was starting to stir.[153]

The boycott grew. As the number reached fifty Biennale artist signatures, Board chairman Luca Belgiorno-Nettis resigned. A statement was issued that the Biennale was severing it ties with Transfield.

> "We have listened to the artists who are the heart of the Biennale and have decided to end our partnership with Transfield effective immediately," organizers said in a statement.[154]

Most artists then returned to the Biennale, and allowed their works to be exhibited. Only two artists did not, on moral grounds.[155] It is worth noting that of the core group of first boycotters, all had young children or babies; parents of infants are keenly aware of the value of life, and the need to make a better world for children.

It is a feature of the Australian discourse on how asylum seekers are treated and written about that writers and journalists who write in any ways other than uncritical endorsement, about the policy in Australia and 'offshore', risk being criticized from 'above'. There is criticism and surveillance of writers and journalists who cover these very significant issues. There is a false rhetoric that it is due to ones who are supportive of and sympathetic to refugees, that the marooned refugees are suffering.[156] Following the Boycott, the most draconian cuts and attacks on the arts in Australia ever, were made by Arts Minister George Brandis, who condemned the international artists for, as Malcolm Turnbull put it: "vicious ingratitude", discussed later in this essay. And meanwhile, the abuse of the innocent children in the 'offshore processing centres' has continued, and worsened.

In 2014, the Australian Human Rights Commission conducted an inquiry into children in the detention camps which found thousands of incidents of abuse of children at Nauru offshore processing centre, and recommended that all children be removed from detention, in the Review: *The Forgotten Children: National Inquiry into Children in Immigration Detention* (2014). Philip Moss conducted an independent review *Review into recent allegations relating to conditions and circumstances at the Regional Processing Centre in Nauru* (February 2015).[157] This investigated a list of damages to the children: 'Sexual exploitation in exchange for access to showers and others amenities'; 'Rape and physical threats'; 'Indecent assault and sexual harassment'; 'Trading of cigarettes and marijuana for sexual favours'; 'Physical assault of transferees by contract service provider staff members'; 'Lip-stitching and self-harm by minors'; 'Sexual and other physical assault of minors'. These types of allegations were all substantiated except 'access to cigarettes for sexual favours' that was said to relate to the time before cigarettes were available in the camp.[158] In Nauru there are families, young single women, and children, housed in tents. The Moss Review reports there is much apprehension about personal safety and the legitimate concerns about privacy arise from their accommodation in non-air-conditioned, soft walled tents in a tropical climate. Anecdotes were included of incidents that heighten apprehensions about personal safety, privacy and the 'contract service providers staff members'.

> One night I was going back to my room. I went to the bathroom and on the way back, I noticed one of the Nauruan officers was standing right in front of our tent. He called me and summoned me to get closer to him and it was absolutely clear that he was even drunk or on drugs because he could not keep his balance properly. Then he suddenly grabbed my arm and he said, "You are so sexy, and you're so beautiful." Then I was so petrified that I just pulled my arm and I ran into my tent. Then ever since, whenever he sees me he addresses me as Sexy Lady."

> During the day, it was so hot in the tent that we were almost naked. We just had our underwear. I was lying on the bed studying some English, and there was a blue curtain I had tucked under the fans to secure it, but after sometime I noticed that someone was looking at me and watching me. I noticed that the curtain was drawn and two of the officers were looking at me and watching me.[159]

The Review investigated allegations that were made against Save the Children contract workers that they had 'orchestrated and facilitated protest activity' and that they had 'coached and encouraged self-harm' amongst the asylum seekers. These allegations were dismissed as lacking of any evidence.

> The transferees who spoke to the Review were very clear that they received no encouragement to self-harm from any contract service provider staff member.[160]

There have been cases of desperate asylum seekers losing hope, suiciding through self immolation, dousing themselves with flammable liquid and setting fire to themselves. There have been sexual and physical abuses of children and young women. These have been condemned, internationally and in Australia. The 'processing centres' were not supposed to be punitive imprisonment but short term 'processing centre' where asylum seekers' claims were processed. Yet the political rhetoric continues that the policy is a 'deterrent'. This combined with the policy of 'stopping the boats' (a slogan in Australian elections) has had politicians paying 'people smugglers' to take the asylum seekers back to Indonesia.[161] In addition to the murder of Reza Barati, and other assaults there have been alleged crimes committed by 'expat' employees at the 'processing centres' a robbery, and drugging and assault of a Manussian employee, where the expats have been flown off the island before police could question them. In September 2015, the ABC news reported that this has:

> caused local police to threaten to arrest the centre managers...Police want Australian company Transfield, which runs the centre, to change the policy of removing staff before they can be questioned.

Two men were charged with the murder of Reza Barati and received five-year suspended sentences. Judge Kirriwom, said this was:

> "because there were other people involved in the killing who had not been charged...."

The main witness to Mr Barati's murder:

> said there were many people involved in the killing, as well as other acts of violence during the riot which had not been charged..

> ..police told the court they had not received any cooperation in bringing the men back to PNG [162]

This is creating and increasing tensions between PNG locals, 'processing centre' staff and refugees. *The Undesirables*, a book by Mark Isaacs, a former Salvation Army employee at Nauru offshore processing centre, discusses the policies from the perspective of one who was there and witnessed what is happening.

> Since 13 June 2013, 17 people have died... These people have been subjected to horror upon horror, and yet our politicians continue to justify human rights abuses as humanitarian and essential to protecting our borders...The inexcusable continues to be excused because "We are stopping the boats." [163]

The Australian government continues to reiterate that no one who has been interned in the camps will ever be allowed to come to Australia regardless of whether they have family already here. Isaacs writes:

> This accounts for everyone on Manus Island and Nauru. Many of

these people have family in Australia. Just why they deem this necessary is unclear. By their own admission, the boats have stopped and the policy has been a success. What purpose does this cruelty have than to punish people further?[164]

This is increasingly relevant, as the asylum seekers still have not been resettled. Instead, in 2015, the Department of Immigration legislated the Australian Border Force Act 2015 Section 42, making it a crime punishable by two years imprisonment for all people working in the 'offshore' detention camps to report trauma and abuse.[165] Yet this has not stopped doctors, lawyers, teachers from speaking out and protesting against this law. The Facebook accounts of 'activists' who have been accused of giving 'hope' to asylum seekers are patrolled by 'immigration spies' and under surveillance, an article in the online newspaper *Crikey*, 'Immigration spies on Facebook pages to weed out 'false hope' for asylum seekers' (2016) by Josh Taylor, shows that pages and posts are screenshot, and recorded and published. Behrouz Boochani, journalist and refugee, reports from Manus regularly in the mainstream media, and social media, on news from Manus.[166]

In August 2016, *The Guardian* put online 'the largest cache of documents to be leaked from within Australia's asylum seeker detention regime': *Nauru Files: cache of 2000 leaked incident reports of sexual and physical abuse of children at the Nauru Processing Centre*, with the database of leaked files. The 2000 incident reports on Transfield letterheaded forms, record the daily assaults, sexual assaults and self harm.[167] In the same month, there was a ten-hour performance of readings of the files in a vigil outside Australia House, in London.

In 2016 the International PEN Congress in Spain adopted a 'Resolution on Australia' calling on the Australian Government to:

> Repeal these unnecessary and draconian laws
> Support journalists and their sources by amending the data surveillance laws to remove restrictions placed on journalists to allow them to undertake research and gather information from whistleblowers;
> ...end the offshore processing of asylum seekers in Nauru and Manus, and ensure that asylum seekers and those in immigration detention in offshore processing centres, including Behrouz Boochani, are provided with adequate legal protection in line with Australia's commitments under international law.[168]

OFFICIAL AUDIT CRITICIZES DEPARTMENT OF IMMIGRATION AND BORDER PROTECTION

Meanwhile, the Australian National Audit Office audit of *Offshore processing centres in Nauru and Papua New Guinea: Procurement of Garrison Support and Welfare Services* (September 13, 2016)[169] focused on Transfield, as it has been the main provider of all services since 2014, showed that Transfield is receiving from taxpayer moneys $1.5 million AU dollars *per day* for its running of the two offshore processing centres, with no records of required authorization. Transfield's contract has been extended to October 2017, and the company was given the contract for services in 2012, the current contract is triple: $3.045 billion. Transfield is now being paid $573,111 per asylum seeker in the processing centres each year, from tax payers' money. This is more than twice as much than the AU$201,000 prior to the consolidation of service providers, from the previous combination of GS4 and the Salvation Army. The purpose of giving the tender to Transfield was due to the expectation they would provide 'innovations and cost reductions' but neither have eventuated according to the critical audit. The objective of the audit was to find out: 'whether the Department of Immigration and Border Protection had appropriately managed the procurement of garrison support and welfare services at offshore processing centres in Nauru and Papua New Guinea (Manus Island); and whether the processes adopted met the requirements of the Commonwealth Procurement Rules including consideration and achievement of value for money.' The audit noted: 'Due to the shortcomings in DIBP's record keeping system DIBP was not able to provide the ANAO with assurance that it provided all departmental records relevant to its audit.' The missing documents were to do with conflict of interest and due diligence:

> Department of Immigration and Border Protection's management of procurement activity for garrison support and welfare services at the offshore processing centres...has fallen well short of effective procurement practice. [ANAO audit online: www.anao.gov.au][170]

The audit identified serious and persistent deficiencies in all the three phases of procurement activity undertaken since 2012 to: establish the centres; consolidate contracts; and achieve savings through an open tender process.

Of most concern is the department's management of processes for contract consolidation and the open tender.

The audit excoriates the department *at all levels*, for inefficiency:

> The conduct and outcomes of the tender processes reviewed highlight procurement skills and capability gaps amongst departmental personnel at all levels....the deficiencies have resulted in a higher than necessary expense to taxpayers and significant reputational risks for the Australian Government and DIBP. [ANAO audit]

The award of the tender was not based on competitive submission of a proposal specifying services and prices, there was no proposal made available to the auditor, which is highly unorthodox:

> The department did not require Transfield to provide a proposal specifying services to be delivered and a price. As a result it was very difficult for the department to demonstrate that it had conducted a robust value for money assessment which considered the financial and the non-financial benefits of the proposal. Transfield was instead assessed on its ability to respond in a short time frame. [ANAO audit]

The award of the tender was made on the basis of bogus grounds and claims of 'urgent circumstances' for which there was no evidence:, the audit concluded:

> The department again relied on paragraph 10.3 (b) of the CPR's (rules) to conduct a limited tender, on the basis of urgent and unforeseen circumstances to engage Transfield... as part of a consolidated process... At the time, consolidation was considered an interim measure pending an open tender process in 2014. The available record does not indicate that urgent or unforeseen circumstances existed but suggests that the department first selected the provider [Transfield] and then commenced a process to determine the exact nature, scope, and price of the services to be delivered. [ANAO audit]

Whereas Transfield is given $573.111 per asylum seeker in indefinite detention per annum, this is not calculated on actual number of asylum seekers and refugees, writes the auditor, but on the estimate of increasing figures that was made in 2013, in the month when asylum seeker 'arrivals' were at the highest point recorded, which was 1,648. Yet in March 2014 when Transfield took up the consolidated contract there were 'zero' arrivals. And since then the Government has had an ongoing (military) campaign to 'stop the boats' which the Government has said is effective. This suggests that Transfield is paid an enormous amount of taxpayers' money, millions, every week, for literally as well as symbolically 'non-existent' asylum seekers. The hidden number of refugees on the islands is thought to be between 1250 and 2500.[1]

> while the department based the negotiated contract price on a high capacity scenario, there was a steady drop off in new asylum seeker arrivals from a high of 1648 in August 2013 to zero in March 2014. On this basis it was increasingly unlikely that the high capacity levels would eventuate. The resulting contract was volume driven with significant economies of scale expected at high capacity levels. This contract exposed the Commonwealth to the risk of locking-in a higher price for services delivered at lower capacity levels. [ANAO audit]

What concerns the auditor is the lack of evidence of conflict of interest declarations, and due diligence in the award of the lucrative tender.

> 20. There is no available record of specific conflict of interest declarations having been made by departmental officers who were responsible for the procurement. There is also no available documentation to indicate whether the department performed due diligence checks on the successful tenderer or is subcontractors as part of the contract consolidation. [ANAO audit]

At the same time that Transfield was taking up their contract, ministers were scathing of the Biennale Boycott. Communications Minister Malcolm Turnbull, now Prime Minister, spoke of the artists 'vicious ingratitude', and the then Arts Minister Senator George Brandis wrote to Rupert Myers, Chair of the Australia Council, public funding body of the arts in Australia expressing his outrage at the artists' 'insult' and insisting that he alter wording of artist grant contracts.[171] Misinformation spread in the mainstream media.

The Biennale management wrote in an open letter:

> Firstly, let us say that we truly empathize with the artists in this situation. Like them, we are inadvertently caught somewhere between ideology and principle.'[172]

The Board announced it was severing sponsor ties with Transfield, and invited the artists to draft a corporate social responsibility policy, which they did. The key point that emerged from the boycott of the Biennale of Sydney by Australian and international artists who were representing their countries in the Biennale is ethical sponsorship.[173]

---

[1] This is reported (2 February 2017) in Australian media articles and broadcasts on the US President Donald Trump's response by tweet of the deal made by Obama at the end of his presidency to take the refugees, after his telephone conversation with the Australian PM Malcolm Turnbull..

As the Biennale severed ties with Transfield, the artists returned to exhibit their works in the Biennale. Misinformation continued to circulate on social media sites and in mainstream media articles, which the artists countered:

> MEDIA RELEASE FROM THE ARTISTS
> Transfield & Biennale - responses and clarification of key points
> FOR IMMEDIATE RELEASE
> Wednesday 19 March
> Biennale artists' Working Group clarifies and responds to key points
> "9 pesky artists"
> 51 participating artists signed the letter to the Board of the Biennale requesting that they end their funding arrangement with Transfield.
> Following the Board's response, 9 participating artists withdrew from the Biennale of Sydney by the time Luca Belgiorno-Nettis resigned from his position as chairman of the Board.
> Pressure from international funding agencies (government and non-government) who were withdrawing their sponsorship due to the Board's decision to remain loyal to Transfield was cited by Luca Belgiorno-Nettis and the Biennale as a factor in his resignation....
> ...Employees of the Museum of Contemporary Art have resigned over Transfield's sponsorship of the organisation, and artists are beginning to question future involvement in organisations sponsored by profits of mandatory detention.[174]

Later in 2014 the Neilson Foundation was announced as the Biennale's Principal Patron for the 2016 Biennale, extended to 2018 and 2020.

In this same time, since 2014, the Government has given $55 million dollars to Cambodia to resettle, so far, one refugee. $40 million in aid to the government; $15.5 million to resettlement agencies.[175]

ARTS FUNDING CUTS FOLLOWING BOYCOTT

The biggest cuts to arts funding in Australia were announced in 2014. Prime Minister Tony Abbott slashed $100,000 from public arts grant funding, $28 million of this from the Australia Council of the Arts. In 2015 Arts Minister George Brandis seized $104.8 million from Australia Council public arts grant funding, for his program known as Catalyst, which is under ministerial control. In 2013 the Labor government had pledged an additional $75.3 million for arts grants but the cuts more than erased this. These cuts have seen the decimation of dozens of established arts enterprises and groups, and the loss of hundreds of jobs in the arts. In the 2016 cuts, on May 13, a day known as Black Friday, 53 of 147 organizations that had previously been regularly awarded multi-year 'key organization' funding were defunded. Australia Council grants to individual artists and writers and projects fell 70 percent from 2013-14.[176] The experimental arts theatre group All Out Ensemble lost its federal funding (after forty years in existence and in this time employing hundreds of painters, sculptors, musicians and artists); it was co-founded by poet, Christopher Barnett, subject of *These Heathen Dreams* (2014).

BEHROUZ BOOCHANI

Behrouz Boochani is a Kurdish-Iranian writer and freelance journalist, who fled Iran where he faced arrest, imprisonment, and death. He has been incarcerated on Manus for more than two years, throughout all this time he has been reporting, and the *Guardian* and independent publishing houses have been publishing his writings. Boochani is 32, and is an ethnic Kurd from Ilam city. The Kurdish people are stateless and form the biggest ethnic group of stateless people in the world.

He began his career as a writer and journalist writing for the student newspaper when he was studying geopolitics at Tarbiat Modares University in Tehran. He freelanced for newspapers and the Iranian Sports Agency. When Boochani and others started a newspaper devoted to Kurdish language and culture which he edited, *Werya* (or *Varia*) a political and social magazine, he became known to the authorities.

He said in an interview that they started it because: "The new generation are talking with their children in Farsi language and the Kurdish language and culture will be destroyed in the near future."[177]

Boochani was a member of the Kurdish Democratic Party which is outlawed in Iran. For several years he was under surveillance. Then in 2011 he was arrested and interrogated by the paramilitary intelligence agency Sepah, or the Army of the Guardians of the Islamic Revolution. They warned him to stop writing or he would be shut in detention for years. They wanted to stop him promoting Kurdish culture. The magazine and his work as a writer and editor continued. In 2013 the offices of *Werya* were raided by Sepah who arrested eleven of his colleagues. Boochani escaped arrest as he was in Tehran that day. He published a report on his colleagues arrest on the website *Iranian Reporters* which gained global attention. This put him at risk of arrest and he had to go into hiding. When two of his colleagues were released, they told him the article he wrote saved their lives, Sepah had asked questions about him, and that they wanted to arrest him.

That was when Boochani realized he must flee to escape arrest. He was under the belief that Australia was a free country where he would be able to keep working, and publish his ideas which would benefit his own Kurdish culture. Little did he know that the regime confronting asylum seekers who 'come by boat' is little different to the opposition he had faced as a Kurd in Iran: he was put into detention for years by Australia. He had travelled through southeast Asia and taken a boat to Christmas Island, which is Australian; from there he was transferred to Manus Island offshore processing centre on 27 August 2013, month of the highest asylum seeker capture. Since his arrival he had continued to write, and he is writing a book with publisher contract. He has been accepted as a refugee, but does not want to stay in a place where there are no facilities for locals let alone refugees; and ever since Reza Barati was murdered, he fears for his safety.

Boochani is an honorary member of Pen International Melbourne.

Recent Facebook news reports by Behrouz are published here, with his permission. Note: Lombrum Naval Base is the site of the Manus Offshore Refugee Processing Centre, also referred to below as RPC- or Refugee Processing Centre. IHMS stands for International Health and Medical Services, the contractor at the processing centres. In his post of 4 March, 2017, he reports 'two days ago it was announced that IHMS has been working on Manus Island illegally over the past four years'.

11 January 2017 15:19

> Some comments about H, the refugee who has psychiatric problems who we published a story about in the Guardian today... First when he was in Lombrum detention centre (RPC) he had an argument with a local officer from Wilson [Security-RS].. I remember police beat him in SAA (VSRA) - the confinement room for sick people - and the Guardian published a story about that. He was sent to the police station for a few days and then sent back to the detention centre. They gave him a tranquilliser injection. He then had another argument with a VIHICKEY officer (a branch of Wilson). The officer was trying to force him to bed by pushing him into a room, but he resisted and pushed the officer back and they sent him to court. The court sentenced him to 36 days of prison because IHMS refused to confirm

he had psychiatric problems even though they know he does. So he was again in CIS jail (the Manus jail in Lorengau) and after that they wanted to send him back to the detention centre but they could not find room for him and transferred him to East Lorengau camp. In East Lorengau he started to bother other refugees there and assaulted them. He was a big problem in East Lorengau and the refugees were angry with him because he talked a lot and did not allow the refugees to sleep. He also bothered local people and was making trouble for them. He sometimes was naked and only wearing boxer shorts in Lorengau street and most of the time he was hungry and homeless. The small children made fun of him and disturbed him. The refugees, local people and police beat him because he was mentally ill and he used to disturb people. Everyone would run away from him because of his behaviour. On another recent occasion he pushed a Wilson guard and that guard made a complaint against him. They took him to police lockup for about a week and then again put him in CIS prison. It's been a month now that he has been in prison and he has to be there for about three months. When he was in RPC in Lombrum he had requested to be returned to his country. I talked with one of his friends and he said that he had helped him to fill in the request form to go back to Iran. His family have also requested that he goes back to Iran, and have made all the necessary arrangements for this at their end, but Australia is not preparing the documents for him to be returned to Iran. The main issue is that the Australian gov is not cooperating and not putting things in place for him to be able to go back to Iran. *Behrouz Boochani*

11 January 2017 9:34

Australia is trying to shift its problems to PNG. They are doing it in a systematic way. The refugees in Manus prison have been under systematic torture for a long time and they need medical treatment and specialist psychological treatment, but instead of protecting them Australia has released them in Lorengau town without any psychological treatment. We know that there are not any facilities in Manus for psychological care and refugees are left in an island with local people who are not satisfied with having them there. It's obvious that this situation will make trouble both for the refugees and the local people. Also the police, as a security structure with a duty to make the society safe, have problems with the existence of refugees in the town. The system puts people in conflict and this is a big problem at this moment. Hamed, as a refugee who is need of psychological care, is an example of how Australia does not care about what local people want or about refugees. Instead of providing medical treatment for him Australia has abandoned him in Manus society where it makes trouble for locals, police, the court and refugees. In other words after causing so much psychological harm they have left a man with a lot of mental problems in a strange society without any protection and put him in danger. They have left him in hunger and homelessness.[178] *Behrouz Boochani*

CHRISTOPHER BARNETT

Whereas the writers in the first three studies went into exile as asylum seekers, Christopher Barnett, the émigré Australian poet and dramaturg, went into self-imposed exile, from the inhospitable climate of Australia disappearing to France in the 1980s where he has lived and worked, since the early 1990s, as a poet and dramaturg at Le Derniere Spectateur, the experimental company he co-founded. He runs writing workshops for communities in trouble. Among his many dramatic productions are *Selling Ourselves for Dinner,* with All Out Ensemble in Adelaide 1982, *Last Days of the World* with All Out Ensemble, Sydney 1985; *Ulrike Meinhof Sang* performed in Stockholm in 2003 and Copenhagen in 2005. Barnett's books are *Last days of the world and other texts* (1984), poetry *bateau bleu/blue boat bilingue* (1994) and *When they came/for you elegies/of resistance* (2013). The latter was shared on Facebook, when he was writing it, where it attracted many readers, which is an illustration of Barnett's belief in taking poetry to the people.

In the tradition of storytelling in poetry, it tells the story of Furkan Doğan, the student who was murdered by Israeli gunfire, as he was on the boat in a flotilla in which he and his comrades were attempting to break the Gaza blockade and draw attention to the Palestinian plight in 2010; this story is interwoven with memories of the unwell ageing poet, as he looks back on his youth, the loves and political convictions that shaped his life. It is a passionate political critique of the destructive forces of capitalism, the devastation of the ancient world, the cradle of civilization, by military attacks on the Middle East. Interwoven into it is his threnody for Thomas Harlan, the German filmmaker and novelist, who translated Barnett's *Blue Boat*. In its tender, steely, sometimes searingly painful reiterations, bravery of bearing witness and affective power, *when they came/for you* recalls fugue writings one does not want to end; it is written more like a diary with dates, than separate poems, set in double columns. Its fugal techniques include recurring motifs, of waves and vulnerable bodies. Barnett is likened to Mayakovsky, and for him, too, the motif of waves, endlessly repeated, provides rhythm.

juin 10

when they came for you fugue 2

fugue 2
it is now
so they say
time though
feels as if
centuries
pass
from you
to us
today injustice
bhopal union carbide
whomever
they've become
freed in courts
and countries
they own
down
to last minister
holding out hand
in this
moment
i want
to hold
your hand
furkan dogan
for you
never
to be forgotten
as another
fact you are
for me
19 year old
teenager with heart
and head

(*when they came for you*, pp 22-23)

In *When they came for you* the autobiographical narrator identifies with and mourns humanitarian heroic youth of action and ideals, Furken Doğan (also spelt Dogan), who is gunned down at point blank range, shot by five bullets. He mourns his own body that was beaten (his teeth were knocked out by police), when he was vulnerable. After his father died when he was twelve Christopher found him, dead in bed. He had TB and a window was left open. After this terrible shock, for a while he had to live in an orphanage as his mother struggled; this was when he was a young poet in Adelaide. After building a reputation of notoriety in Australia, he moved to Nantes, France, where, in contrast, he found a very different and welcoming civil society. He is now working on his next book. In recent years Barnett has discovered lost family origins, roots had been severed when parents migrated to Australia, including Russian Jewish. His parents were migrants, in a land where he found he could not live.

I met Christopher in 2013 on Facebook, and interviewed him.[179]

Ruth Skilbeck: I am particularly interested in your work with marginalized and disregarded groups of people and in how your own life experiences and background have shaped your vision and choice to work as artist in these ways through which you have achieved so much. You were born and brought up in Adelaide, with émigré parents. How did that experience affect you, and shape your perspective as a writer, how did you feel as a child of émigré parents growing up in Adelaide, did you feel as if you fitted in to the local life and can you say how did this shape you as a young poet and artist as you grew up?

Christopher Barnett: The primary impact of my childhood and adolescence was poverty. Profound poverty. I witnessed in a rich country the vast inequalities of opportunity in housing health and education—these affected me quite literally. The *patrimoine* of my parents less so. My father was in a tuberculosis sanatorium except for the last nine months of his 44 years. The youngest boys were placed in a orphanage for a short time because my mother could not sustain our care for a moment. This abandonment, even short, was enough to seek another family. That family was the Worker-Student Alliance—W.S.A and then to the communist party of Australia (Marxist-Leninist) a clandestine organization which involved both clandestine activity and voyages in the seven years I was in it. I saw myself as Vietnamese and did all in my power to aid the Viet Cong and North Vietnamese in their struggle. That was the formative moment in the making of me as a writer. I wrote early, eight years old, under my father's instruction, it was an organic and natural voice that then articulated itself in the struggle against war and imperialism. It also supplied me with frameworks and models that are still resonant in my practice today.

Skilbeck: You began writing poetry at an early age and also, I believe, publishing and performing your poetry. What inspired you to begin writing poetry? Who were you influenced by? How and where did you first encounter poetry? Can you remember the first poem you wrote? What was your first published poem? What and who are your influences and inspirations now as a poet?

Barnett: I began writing with my father who though exceptionally ill was an accomplished writer, the first real poem at 8, the first published poem at 14 in a school magazine and in pamphlets. I also wrote street theatre and polemic during this same moment. I understood I was gifted because the reaction by the public was instantaneous and I felt a real humility in front of the complexity of my work even at this young age. I surrendered to it if you like and I always listened and listened and listen. Writing is about listening at a very deep level, because it is polyphony, a multiplicity of voices. The influences were Michael Dransfield and Charles Buckmaster but really the major influence was and remain Vladimir Mayakovsky and Nâzım Hikmet. I read poetry today in 3 languages and though that circle of influence now includes other people like Pier Paolo Pasolini and especially the Greek poets of that time especially Odysseus Elytis and Yiannis Ritsos but the central influences remain the same.

Skilbeck: At the age of twenty, you had a media write-up, was it your first? when you started up a poetry reading venue, because you considered there not to be enough opportunities to encounter poetry in Adelaide. You were with a group that included writers who went on to become well-known Australian authors including Larry Buttrose. What gave you the idea to do this, to bring performance to poetry and make it performative; and could you talk a little about that experience. What was important to you about the physical performance of poetry?

Barnett: I was covered by the media much earlier than that as much for my politics as my poetry, I identified with very few contemporaries but I had people who were talented as musicians, for example, and that created an organic need to create venues which I did and I created a group—Action for People's Art— to perform in parks. I have never ever considered myself a 'performance poet' but saw that I was continuing a tradition of Mayakovsky and Hikmet to read to people publicly—to confront people more than to console them. I think I was the first person to do readings at a systematic level in high schools and do what were writing workshops, with very very tough schools of which I have good memories.

Skilbeck: Earlier than this, at age thirteen, you were "recruited to a Maoist division of the Communist Party" according to the information on *These Heathen Dreams* Facebook page. Could you say something about this, how this happened and what it involved, and the effects on your later beliefs and work as an artist?

Barnett: It was and remains important for me even if that organization was flawed. Deeply flawed. Many of the comrades I began with especially the women were very influential and only consolidated the thoughts that were already nascent within me. It provided analysis with which I largely agreed—dissent came much later and that was essentially because I have a deep relationship with Latin Americans — and the Chines reaction to Chile 1973 made me want to leave, there were necessary lies within the part but for me it was a lie too far and too obscene to be complicit with. At the same moment I was supporting Chilean exiles in public concerts. Other than this, you must understand that as I was doing my schooling I was participating fully in political work, while other teenagers were doing 'normal' things, sport, chasing girls etc. I was involved in both legal and illegal actions on a fairly vast level and for a long time. The women in the party were extraordinary—they were so strong yet very human, they contextualized the struggle for me in the most human terms and this was to have a long-term affect in both my cultural work/political practice. Study applied study, what would be now called close reading was trained into me and I still use these tools today. I read 12 books a week in three languages and my ability to do so was born in that moment in the Party. I still regard myself as a communist and am regarded, I do not regret that appellation and hope I will be remembered on that political level I have never ever compromised, on the contrary I have fought when it was a very lonely act. Given the conditions of capital, of late capitalism, of its complete collapse essentially—I find myself very close to that 14-year-old boy, with the same engagement and same will to wonder.

Skilbeck: As documented in the media reviews from the time, when you were working in Adelaide in theatre you gave performances in carparks—could you say something about that, what did you perform and who were your audience, what kinds of reaction did you get?

Barnett: I performed everywhere under different conditions. I performed work and had a close relationship with the Experimental Art Foundation. I founded the All Out Ensemble with Nicholas Tsoutas and Peggy Wallach and I think we were known as much for our excellence as for our violence. Contrary to myth I am not a violent man but the work certainly is, it is something I live with and am proud of its passion and energy. The audience reaction was always in extremes and we worked with those extremes—successfully I think. We worked towards transmutations, rapid, volatile, but considered.

Skilbeck: Did you go to university or art school, and if so where?

Barnett: No, I went to a teacher college and participated in the lectures and tutorials of Dr Neale Hunter's honors class on China at Adelaide University and the lectures of Brian Medlin, Ian Hunt and Greg O'Hair at Flinders University. Like many of us, though, the real schooling was in the streets and formed also in the Party.

Skilbeck: When did you first become involved in theatre?

Barnett: 1980 with Nick Tsoutas and Peggy Wallach.

Skilbeck: Who were your main influences?

Barnett: Meyerhold and Piscator, Brecht, Artaud.

Skilbeck: Experimental Arts. In the 1980s you were a driving force in the underground art scene in Australia. Can you talk more about All Out Ensemble. Could you say something about this experience?

Barnett: The All Out Ensemble included many people, mostly painters, sculptors but included musicians and actors. It was a very dynamic and politicized group. And I think we were all concerned by excellence within the experimental. It was brutal in its deconstruction but it was also familial, Nick and Peggy helped to make that so—and we worked densely and dynamically, and we worked across forms all the time. Mayakovsky was close to all of us so it is no accident that my *Selling Ourselves for Dinner* should become a central work. It was not without problems, but how could it be otherwise with so many people at such a dynamic level and in great intensity? We also engaged many other people who were not 'in' the ensemble but saw what we were doing.

As a formation we received considerable support. Theatre was dead in Australia even if Melbourne had tried to fight the good fight against imperial culture, and in Sydney The Performance Syndicate under Rex Cramphorn was doing important work—but we were all connected in one way or another and in fact I would go on to work with the central members of The Performance Syndicate, Nicholas Lathouris and Margaret Cameron whom I considered and still consider amongst the most impressive theatre workers Australia has ever produced. I am very very proud of the people who I have had as collaborators. I have been honored by their work with my texts and with me as a human being.

Skilbeck: Working in the mode of collaboration, you worked in Melbourne with artists Nicolas Lathouris, Margaret Cameron and Alison Davey and I believe with many others in Sydney, specifically people including The Central, Art Unit, founded by former Adelaide artists Juilee Pryor and Robert McDonald, Performance Space. Could you talk about these performances and works? And the importance of collaboration to your mode of working?

Barnett: When I moved to Melbourne, began a collaboration with Nicolas Lathouris and Margaret Cameron, which in a spiritual sense, still exists today, these two were the most gifted practitioners in Australia, as actors, as thinkers, as collaborators, as initiators. It is a special relationship, for each page of text I wrote, Nicholas wrote four meditating on the questions. It was a very very close collaboration which also included many people, actors like Ramesh Ayyar, John F. Howard and many others. Again it included artists across all forms—musicians and painters. I also wrote on these painters, or text for the musicians. I did radio work, texts for radio, and I also wrote text for film with such people as John Hughes and Daryl Dellora. Melbourne was a very rich time in the sense of the depth of collaboration and the prolific nature of our work, many, many performances in Melbourne, Sydney and Adelaide. Collaboration has remained central to my work. When I came to France I worked with people from MC93 the most prestigious company in France at the time where Heiner Müller, Robert Wilson, Peter Sellars introduced their work. Évelyne Didi the great actress (also seen in much of the work of the Finnish film maker Aki Kaurismaki) was important here but in many ways Évelyne and her group were French versions of Nicholas and Marg, exactly the same background. Great classical actors who primarily worked experimentally. I have collaborated with many people in France, when I first came a colloquium on the *centenaire* of Vladimir Mayakovsky held at the Pompidou Centre and universities in Paris chose me—as the contemporary version of Mayakovsky. I performed a text for theatre for them, it was a great honour to be recognized by the experts in Mayakovsky from around the world including Russia who thought I represented what Mayakovsky would be today. It was one of the most important moments in an already rich history that has maintained its resonances today.

Skilbeck: According to your biography on *These Heathen Dreams* Facebook page, when you left Australia you were battling a drug or alcohol addiction. Could you talk a little about this? How did you overcome this? Is part of your work in theatre to help others also to overcome addictions?

Barnett: This is a myth really. I was never an addict of any kind. I was just messy. It didn't take a great deal to derange me, so I never had to use what other might have been obliged to—what was dangerous, in a life with many calculated risks, I took risks that were close to suicidal, there was also a great risk of an unhappy accident. I stopped all that in the mid-eighties and never returned to it, never wanted to. It was not an important aspect of what I was, what I was doing, in fact it risked that work. I drank and took drugs because I could not bear the Australian reality, it was a barbarism coated in culture. It was and remains a culture that is complicit in the crimes of its political classes. I was born in a very dark place, I have worked within a very dark place, I have searched within such darkness I thought there would never be light—so intoxication had as much to do with the pain of that. Or the boredom of living in a dying culture.

Skilbeck: Many artists, of course, have taken drugs or drank and there is a discourse that sees a connection between intoxications and artistic creativity, as there also is with madness and artistic genius. What do you think of these ideas? Is there a symbiotic relation between intoxication and poetry that it may inspire greater visionary works and or flight of creative insights? Or would these be delusions? Or does this go beyond either/or binaries?

Barnett: As I said that aspect was not important to me. At all. I drank to stop the hurting and ennui that a culture like Australia reproduces.

However, I worked as a writer in the community from very young and I worked in many psychiatric hospitals and foundations. The question of madness, of barbarity was important to me then, it remains important now.

Skilbeck: When and why did you decide to leave Australia? Could you say something about that decision to go into self-imposed exile?

Barnett: I started leaving in 1987—to work in France, Italy, Holland Sweden and Montreal but I would come back but not for very long. I consider I left finally in 1990—I had had enough. There was nothing within Australia culture that I recognized, it was foreign to me at almost every level. There was no risk. My work has always embraced risk.

Skilbeck: Would you return to live in Australia and what are your thoughts on this? Have you returned to visit and/or work?

Barnett: Only twice, very early, in 92 and 93 to work on a French film *Brûlure*s which John Cumming filmed for and I wrote a text for the Splinter Theatre Group in Canberra under the direction of Nicholas Lathouris.

Skilbeck: Can you talk a little on your views on the Australian political scene and arts and cultural scenes now?

Barnett: In real terms I have not 'lived' in Australia for 25 years so I can say little but from what I read and in communications with colleagues—it appears very very ugly. Certainly I do not recognize myself in that culture. Since 1975 the political class and the public had accepted a servitude to U.S. imperialism and a complicity in the crimes of that empire. It disgusted me. That disgust turned to fury with what Howard transformed that country back into the one I was born in— the Menzies meanness towards others, towards the 'other'— in this moment I spoke out against Australia long and often in Europe, I spoke of it as a filtered apartheid South Africa. That situation has worsened but given that I gave medical aid to the Viet Cong directly when they were fighting Australian soldiers, my critique of that culture has been there since I was very very young. And I regret nothing about that critique.

Skilbeck: You moved to France, to the western Brittany city of Nantes on the river Loire, which is widely regarded as the Breton cultural capital. What made you choose Nantes?

Barnett: Alchemy. The town's willingness to support what was a very risky proposition; great collaborators. I knew the city from 1977/8—I fell in love with the city and the people.

Skilbeck: How did you come to start up the experimental arts laboratory and theatre company? What was the purpose and mission of Le Dernier Spectateur Theatre?

Barnett: I was invited to but I was going to work with actors, which I did. In 1997 I worked with the greatest Cuban actors of this era on a version of *Macbeth—El Macbeth*, they taught me so much and I hope I taught them but from this moment I decided I wanted to pursue my work with the dispossessed, which I was already doing in Nantes in parallel. LDS was about the transformative nature of creation, about the richness of interiority that only the poor possess, it was about polyphonies and multitudes, it was not accidentally a search for excellence in the very people dominant culture ignored. LDS has done writing and theatre workshops every week, ten séances a week for over 20 years now, we have made a singular contribution to French culture. Our thirty books prove without exception that this population is capable of the most profound gifts and articulation of those gifts. All the political apparatus here accept that and certainly all the scholars, hospitals, doctors, institutions are aware of our work.

Skilbeck: Looking back, what have been the most significant achievements in your work at Le Dernier Spectateur?

Barnett: To survive. To create. To prove my proposition. To see people who have been ignored, create extraordinary things, for them to continue their education.

Skilbeck: One of your poems [in progress] that I know through following its developments and reiterations on Facebook is 'Furkan', and I've seen you perform the poem to the accompaniment of a saxophonist to a group of peoples in Nantes, in a video by Georgia Wallace-Crabbe. It's a very moving poem. Could you say something about how you came to write it and what it is about? And the particular significance of this subject to you?

Barnett: It is a poem that pays homage to the young Turkish medical student Furkan Doğan who was murdered by Israeli commandos. It is a requiem for all those who struggle. It is a magnificent poem that has benefited directly from my service to the community. The poem and the workshops are one. It continues with the improvisations *pour le memorial.*

Skilbeck: Looking back on your life's work so far, what have been the most memorable achievements? What are you most proud of?

Barnett: All. I regret not one moment. But for the world's experts, people whom I respect to denote me as this epoch's Mayakovsky touched me deeply, very deeply, because that connection remains. I write almost impossibly epic poems, I work amongst the people at a level which does not reduce them but demands that they explore their interiority with the precision of scholars. And I have succeeded.

Skilbeck: What has been the biggest influence on you in your life and work as a socially engaged artist?

Barnett: Tran Duc Thao and Louis Althusser. And my late collaborator film maker and novelist Thomas Harlan which requires a book.

Skilbeck: What drives you to make art in all the ways that you do and to work with others?

Barnett: I believe in serving the people.

Skilbeck: What have been your greatest joys and happinesses?

Barnett: To be alive in dangerous times.

Skilbeck: Do you have any regrets?

Barnett: No regrets, none at all.

The documentary *These Heathen Dreams: Journey of a Cultural Bolshevik* written and directed by Anne Tsoulis, with cinematography by Georgia Wallace-Crabbe, has been released into international distribution. Tsoulis was at Teacher Training College with Christopher in Adelaide and they were friends. He disappeared from Australia in the 1980s and they had lost touch before that. After they reconnected on Facebook in 2010, she visited him in France and made the film, in collaboration with Film Projects (Australia) and Les Films du Balibari (France).

FUGAL ANALYSIS

Throughout this discussion, terms have been referred to in accounts of the dialogic, polyphonic exchanges between the exiled writers and their advocates, in relation to the communication of the advocacy movements, and the phenomenological practice of the research project. Fugal concepts are deployed in analysis of the communication—between the advocates and the exiled writers and in the wider context of Australian society in a process of ongoing social, cultural, and institutional change. To draw out terms, specifically the fugal aspects in the studies include:

- *Make Art Not War—Rosa Viereck*. The voice is dissociated. The story is carnivalesque, exhibiting modes of parody and satire driven by a deeper sense of social injustice, and clearly articulated affect of trauma. Interwoven through the written text [of the media article] are striking modes or 'voices' of visual communication: images of artwork and photographic portraits. Recursion occurs in 'putting on hold' one voice (written text) whilst another voice (visual communication) interprets a theme in a different way. This creates a counterpoint of voices. The double counterpoint occurs in the parodic subversive intertextual modality of inter-discourse. The story's dialogism operates on multiple levels of cultural, social, political, historical and art historical discourse.

In the second story, *Refugee Writers*, the dialogism of the polyphonic fugue may be interpreted to include elements of non-verbal communication in the dialogic performative encounter of the interview.

The performative dialogic exchange comprises the look in Cheikh Kone's eyes, the tone of his voice, certain hesitations and accelerations, when he says: 'It is a long time since I have spoken of such things' or 'I never usually talk of this.' An intensity of wordless gestures. A poignancy and strength. And grace of spirit, expressed through the language of the body, in the time of the interview.

- **Dialogism**: The broader fugue is the dialogic communication between advocates and exiles, the polyphonic communication that occurred in the multiple forms and modes of exchange and interaction including letters, faxes, emails, phone calls, visits, non verbal, and empathetic communication between advocates, writers and exiles.
- **Counterpoint**: Occurs in the interweaving of the voices in this fugue, the exiled writers, the advocates and activists (and adversaries) it occurred through dialogue, performance, writing, telling stories.
- **Double counterpoint**: Occurs in the communication between dominant voices and marginalized voices, of the exiles and supporters or advocates, that throughout the process of the 'exiled writer's fugue' changed places as the writers were freed and gained permanent residency (and the policies of mandatory detention and TPVs have now been rescinded), at least in the first two cases. Behrouz Boochani

remains in the limbo of indefinite detention.

- **Cultural memory and amnesia:** Many have commented on the anomaly of Australian refugee policy that, in effect, repeats in a distorted form the origins of the colony as an off-shore prison for convicts and 'undesirables' that was settled by incoming boat people. To interweave a Foucauldian influenced trauma theory, this may be understood as the systematic return of the repressed. The 'processing centre', literally and symbolically articulating a (non)'processing' of trauma. Cultural trauma theory suggests that such trauma may be caused by guilt. A Freudian analysis in 'Remembering, Repeating and Working Through'[180] would suggest that automatic forms of repetition may only be resolved if the traumatic 'memory' is worked through or processed consciously in the culture. Eerie echoes of the origins of the colony, and its inhabitants, return—such as a traumatic repressed memory, a recurring nightmare—in the shape of the detention 'processing centre' in the desert...or a prison island. Many comment on the surreal irony, and denial, of the almost hysterical obsession with 'stopping the boats' by politicians, and the fact that Australia was settled by 'boat people'. The migrants came mainly by boat. Meanwhile, cultures, languages, and societies of the Aboriginal people were shattered, and Aboriginal people continue to be discriminated against in many ways, reflected in mortality rates, age of mortality: twenty years lower than for non-Aboriginal people, and one of the highest suicide rates in the world. There is now a recognized 'epidemic' of Aboriginal suicide which is linked to cultural poverty and disadvantage. In Australia, eight out of ten suicides under the age of twelve are of Indigenous children, and the number of children committing suicide is increasing, reflecting the depths of the despair Aboriginal people are suffering.[181]

- This in effect is a continuation of the hidden policies of cultural and racial genocide, which underlie white Australia, and which many see in the impacts of the policy of the 'Northern Territory Intervention'. In order to introduce this policy of racial discrimination in 2007, the Government had to suspend the racial discrimination law. It discriminates against unemployed Aboriginal people by quarantining welfare payments and issuing a 'Basics Card' for all purchases.[182] Kylie Sambo talks about this from the perspective of young people, as 'hurtful'.[183] 'It's degrading, humiliating, and pride-sapping emotional whipping of the highest order,' Bev Manton ('Shopping with the Basics

Card is Utterly Useless).[184] So far in a familiar pattern, $88 million has been spent on paying bureaucrats to 'manage' the Intervention, and pay for services. Poet, Ali Cobby Eckerman, has said: 'the doctors were on $5000 a week'. Consultants were paid $300,000 to consult with 12 communities but their results were not used in any way'.[185] Aboriginal girls under the age of seventeen now have the highest reported suicide level in the western world yet in 1980 according to researchers there were no reported suicides in this group.[186] There is a call for a Basic Income to be implemented instead of the Card.[187]

- This results in a government-created economy of oppression (and creation) of the vulnerable for the profit of 'service providers' and administrators on a neo-colonial model as in the asylum seeker detention regime. Taking an active writing approach gives the opportunity to investigate and write on cases of writers, as individuals. This investigation followed British and Australian journalism ethical guidelines for reporting, on the vulnerable, and refugees.[188]

A main conclusion to emerge from this research is the vital importance of restoring a sense of the human value of the subject and the author, in theory as in practice. For this research shows what happens when a 'subject' is under threat of erasure through 'dissolution'—when even a name is replaced by a number. Without a sense of the worth of individual personal identity, the subject does dissolve. But that occurs as the result of trauma, the taking away of human rights of freedom of expression and free speech. Self-based narratives and story telling are components to building a strong sense of self identity that is necessary to write actively and effectively albeit that may be in disguise or through an alter ego, in contrapuntal, parodic, or carnivalesque forms.

Replacing a 'model' of the passive reader or viewer with an active writer produces different effects, and an ethic of experiential engagement, including experimentation, invention, and discovery. This may lead to writing: a book, an article, a film, a documentary, creating an event, an alternative event, or work in the public sphere, transforming and processing trauma in creative cultural production.

2

TAKING FLIGHT INTO WRITING

In recent years, a new interdisciplinary area of studies has emerged. Defining this field involves terms such as: intermedial studies, interarts, musico-literary analysis, and melopoetic research, as outlined by one of the recognized founders of intermedial studies, Steven Paul Scher.[1] Bringing together these developments gives rise to the idea that certain feelings and thoughts may be more readily communicated through the a-semantic, semiotic form of music, in contrast to the symbolic form of words alone. The focus on musical structures translated into rhetorical and symbolic form in literature extends the scope of musicological analysis from music to literature and through literary cultural studies into a wider cultural and political context. This is, also, part of a movement of global postcolonial cultural studies suggested by Edward Said (1994) in his theories of *contrapuntal reading*, and Homi Bhabha (1994) in his writings on *cultural hybridity*. The value of developments in intermedial studies and postcolonial studies inheres in the interlinking and comparison of the technical aspects of intermedial musicalization and the socio-cultural, and political contexts in which these literary innovations have been produced. Its further value is in consideration of how such innovative symbolic and rhetorical literary structures symbolize, represent, and stand as tokens for the wider cultural and political realities of the societies that their authors write from, of, and about. A form of cultural and social analysis that began with Plato, using musical structure and form as a polemical measure of social and cultural formation has a long and controversial history. In the twentieth century, this strategy of analyzing social uses and functions of music in cultural and political analysis was revived most notably by Max Weber (1921), and Theodor Adorno (1947; 1991).

Techniques of musico-literary, melopoetic analysis form part of a methodology of interpreting and theorizing literary narratives that are 'intermedial' in the sense that their authors have intentionally set out to adapt and apply musical techniques from one artistic medium, musical composition, into literary composition. Werner Wolf (1999) develops the term 'musicalization' in reference to authors' intentional translation of musical effects into literary form. In this investigation, I adapt and apply musicalization to authors' intentional (and perhaps unintentional) uses of fugue forms, such as contrapuntal polyphony, in their writing of literary fugue narratives.

The original contribution of this to the contemporary intermedial field is in development and application of the psychological together with musical meanings of 'fugue' in relation to the individual subject/writer's construction of subjectivity in his, or her, literary writing. In adapting the generic (musical) term 'fugal analysis' to literary fugal analysis, I address three central aspects, constituents and perspectives that I derived from the theoretical literature and phenomenological evidence of the literary fugue studies themselves:

(1) The writer's fugue
(2) The fugal modality of writing
(3) The textual/literary fugue.

Writer's fugue relates to the discursive, generative, and inscriptive phenomenological process, writing that draws intentionally or otherwise on more generalized techniques and affects of musicalization. The *fugal modality of writing* refers to symbolic and rhetorical altered or obscured states of consciousness in which the writing self 'processes' language into writing through an existential inner 'flight'—the writer's creative process. The *textual/literary fugue* refers to the written fugue as articulated and inscribed in the musicalized literary text. It is the specific, paradoxical, symbolic and rhetorical form, which manifests (and figuratively 'takes flight') in 'compulsive' subjective writing of the writer's fugue articulated in objective formalized, musicalized poetic-prose written using fugue techniques.

Contradictions in poststructuralist theory, linguistic theory and thinking in psychoanalytical approaches to mimesis may be perceived in a different light in an intermedial musico-literary analysis. Musicalized fugal writing exceeds the subject, in the text, whilst also coming from the subject (the author of literary textual compositions) via their post-traumatic memories and a compulsion to write. This Romantic,

Modernist (and perhaps 'post' modernist) pattern of individual self-based writing is further illuminated when set within the social and political context of modernity from whence it has arisen.

METHODOLOGICAL ISSUES: INTENTIONALITY AND PHENOMENOLOGY

Interdisciplinary studies have rapidly increased in our age of cultural studies.[2] The potential scope for this kind of contemporary inquiry was indicated by Edward Said (in 1991) who called for the wider use and interpretation of music beyond the conservatorium and in relation to culture and society: 'the study of music can be more, and not less, interesting if we situate music as taking place, so to speak, in a social and cultural setting'.[3] This musically based cultural inquiry can be further extended into a setting that is primarily literary. But there are issues to address.

One of the criticisms to arise in interarts studies is of the tendency for musico-literary analysis to be overly impressionistic and lacking in intellectual rigour.[4] This can apply to a literary-musical analysis where the literary text takes precedence when the musical text is analyzed using literary techniques such as narratology.

Roger Fowler recognized a methodological flaw for interdisciplinary studies: 'Interdisciplinarity in practice often founders on the fact that two disciplines are merely juxtaposed; work at their interface, which should be most exciting, can become embarrassingly vague'.[5]

In addressing these methodological issues, it is useful to look further into the strategy of self-investigation that Edmund Husserl termed 'bracketing'. Husserl set out his method of *epoché* in *Ideen zu einer reinen Phänomenologie und phänomenologischen Philosophie* (Ideas Pertaining to a Pure Phenomenology and a Phenomenological Philosophy) (1913). The conceptual term epoché derives from the Greek Skeptics' notion of the suspension of belief. Husserl adapts this idea as 'bracketing off'. He uses it as the first stage of philosophical investigation in which investigators approach any object of inquiry (from the perspective of metaphysical phenomena, rather than logical linguistic analysis) by 'bracketing off' or setting aside (so far as is consciously possible) preconceived beliefs, and general epistemological presuppositions, in an effort to intuitively apprehend the essence of the thing-in-itself.

Husserl was here influenced by Brentano's notion of intentionality (or 'aboutness'). In *Psychologie vom empirischen Standpunkte* (Psychology From an Empirical Standpoint) (1874) Brentano proposed that mentality, what is in or of the mind is determined by a number of mental acts, which he characterized in relation to 'objects.' For Brentano 'acts' and 'objects' are relational. In his use of the term 'empirical' Brentano propounded a form of descriptive psychology. Defining mentality in terms of the type of object to which the mind actively tends, Brentano revived the scholastic idea of *intentio animi*, the tending of the mind towards an object. According to Brentano's view of intentionality, what is distinctive of mental phenomena is that they are directed towards an object (of thought) that may or may not now exist. Brentano's idea of *intentional inexistence* implies two main theses: an ontological metaphysical thesis (concerned with being) and a psychological thesis (concerned with the mental acts of the subject in relation to objects of thought). The musicalized-literary writing process necessarily involves the writer in a metaphysical dialogue in her own mind with imaginary objects of thought (including sound, image, concept). The notion of intentionality as developed by Brentano has renewed relevance in relation to recent and contemporary debates about the construction of the *subject* in language, and *subjectivity* in literature in the creative writing process.

Brentano postulated that a mental act that exhibits intentionality, one such as hoping, willing, desiring, wishing, or fearing, has 'included within itself' an 'inexistent object', an object of thought, which that mental act is directed toward. The object of this kind of mental act is not one that necessarily has a physical actual existence in the external world (although it can be *of* or *about* real things in the physical world); rather, it has a mental existence—or 'intentional inexistence'—in the human subject's mind. Brentano defined intentional inexistence as: 'the reference to a content' ('reference', here, referring to the mental act, 'content' to the object of thought), a direction upon an object (by which we are not to understand a physical reality as such). On Brentano's account *intentional inexistence* is a distinguishing feature of mental phenomena, that which differentiates mental, psychological acts and their content from physical phenomena.

Taking a phenomenological self-based approach to literary writing will comprise actions Brentano that calls judgements, conscious (and unconscious) selections of language elements that performatively create existential and affective propositions (including one's beliefs, desires, fears, revulsions, depending on the material). In the process of literary writing the writer's thoughts, beliefs, and desires are directed towards *objects of thought*, which (in)exist independently of the physical objects, in her conscious apprehension of them. Such objects have an internal relation to the act of their intention, or tending, and do not exist, as such, in any other way, except in that relation. Examples of this can be seen for instance in De Quincey's passionate Romantic evocations of doomed maidens in his *Dream-Fugue*. Although associated in his mind with his deceased sister who died in childhood, and, a reader now might think possibly triggered in his mind as an after-affect of what is now called post-traumatic stress disorder, De Quincey's thoughts and feelings relate, not directly to his sister who died many years before, but to recurrent images of tragically imperilled maidens which have a conceptual in-existence in his imagination and which are further transformed in displaced images arising in his text. These images of doomed maidens metamorphose in a dream sequence in *Dream-Fugue*, in descending order of age. From a strong woman commanding a sailing vessel to a girl running into quicksand to an infant girl, a baby in a 'fairy carriage'. All are described with intense passionate imagistic emotion, as the reader imagines De Quincey surrendering to the dream-like hallucinogenic power of the images of his imagination.

Comparable intensities of condensed displaced emotional rapport with the imaginatively conjured-up fictionalized images of lost loved ones are considered in the studies, in Part 11. In Proust's *À la recherche du temps perdu* (In Search of Lost Time), for instance in his narrator's images of his mother who will not come up to his bedroom to kiss him good-night; in his narrator's feelings for Gilberte and later Albertine. In Joyce's 'Sirens' episode, in Bloom's anxieties over Molly's infidelity; and Celan's wrenching references to Sulamith, based on his mother murdered in a concentration camp, in *Todesfuge* (Deathfugue), and in Plath's father-figure in *Little Fugue*. The writers relate to their characters in the conceptual world of imagination. The relation is performed with the intensity of Brentano's (and later Freud's) phenomenological 'objects of love and hate'. In the act of writing, the writer relates not to a real person in actual reality, but to the fictive object in their imagination. This is a remembered (or forgotten) conceptual object that they conjure up, embellish, and re-create in literary form. It may have only the slightest bearing, or reference, to actual reality, although it has been triggered in the experiences of the author's life and becomes for them the evocation of the affective object of love or hate.

In musicalized literary narratives, the 'directedness' of writing is intentionally directed towards translating, adapting, transforming, or converting a displaced 'object' derived from a musical text into another: a literary text. During this process the author, inwardly focused in the mental act of writing, involuntarily and unconsciously enters into the *fugal modality* of writing. This dialogue of performativity positions the author in a practice of deep transformation involving the processes of *reception* (receptiveness to the imaginary intentionally inexistent object), *judgement* (selection and revision), and *becoming*. This, according to the Freudian psychoanalytic accounts discussed below, involves the author's unconscious internalized phenomena of love and hate. It can also be seen as an active unconscious modality that involves elements of concepts of condensation, displacement and conversion that Freud developed in his dream analysis.

The process of fugal, introspective investigation of consciousness by the writing subject (self) can be seen, or heard, particularly clearly in sustained literary works of memoir and involuntary memory, such as Proust's *À la recherche du temps perdu*; heard, too, for example, in the motifs of doomed maidens which recur throughout the body of De Quincey's oeuvre. I have suggested that it is a function of this mental directedness, an inner flight in mental space (towards an inexistent object of thought), which constitutes the 'intentionality' of the un/conscious fugal writing process. This is 'un/conscious' because it fugally involves the author's simultaneous 'mental' presence and absence. By this, I mean that in the process of creating the work the author weaves together conscious and unconscious elements, immaterial (thought) and material (textual) processes and objects. The creative process of writing is thereby partly unconscious, and intermedial, in that it consists in bringing into consciousness elements that were not conscious, and weaving these into a musicalized compositional form.

The fugal modality of writing is the modality by which objects of thought are actualized in the imaginary (mental space) of the writer's mind and body, in the obscured consciousness of the writing process. The types of thoughts that come to the writer in this fugal mode of writing are of the kind known as *de re* thoughts. Thoughts of objects of (mimetic) representation in the writer's mind. The notion of *de re* thoughts (where necessity attaches to a thing's phenomenological possession of phenomena) is contrasted with *de dicto* thoughts (which are descriptive, relate to propositional attitudes and in which necessity is attributed to a whole assertion).[6]

The existence of thoughts which can legitimately be said to engender a direct relation between thought and object of thought—when that object of thought is a material thing in the physical world—could constitute a major challenge to traditional theories of methodological solipsism which hold that psychological states do not require the real existence of anything other than the subject. This would refute the premise of Cartesian dualism, that there is a fundamental division between mind and matter; and consciousness and material objects. The existence of thoughts which constitute as an essential part of their content an object which is external to the mind of the thinker could seem to be at variance with the widespread 'common-sense' view that thoughts are by nature essentially private; and in that sense the exclusive property of the thinker, and that the thinker is necessarily the best authority on what she or he is thinking, as Wittgenstein showed (Wittgenstein 1953). Ways in which *de re* thought is fundamental to the modality of writing, are important in understanding the authors in consideration, challenging traditional or common-sense conceptions concerning the mind and its relation to matter, as well as affirming the unique creative power of inventive affective poetic self-based writing that Thomas de Quincey called 'literature of power'.[7] This investigation explores what is also specifically modern about this approach to writing—the subject and subjectivity in the literature of modernity.

Broadly speaking, a *de re* thought or belief engenders a contextual, as opposed to a conceptual, relation between the relevant thought or belief and the object, or thing, which the thought is *of.* That intentional object may be an actually existing physical thing as will constitute the content of all immediate perceptual or sensory-based thought or belief; or more abstractly, it may be an object of thought such as a memory, hope, certain introspective beliefs or desires which may but need not necessarily precipitate action, such as the desire to write.

But to say a thought is contextually of an object can be seen to imply that it literally contains that object within it. So that if I say I am thinking of my brother this implies that in some sense, my brother is in my mind (the mental space of my thought). This does not mean that my brother is physically in my mind. It only makes sense to talk about *de re* beliefs if they are seen not as propositional attitudes but as another type of belief—a mode of belief, a mode or modality of the imaginary. This has relevance to the modality of literary writing and creative composition in the subjective, individually authored, 'fugue' literature of modernity.

The notion of *de re* belief has direct relevance and usefulness in understanding the *fugal modality* of writing and the particular kind of intentionality involved in the relation of the writer to their objects of thought in the obscured consciousness of the writing process. It is constitutive of the modality of writing that the writer relates to an object of thought in the writing process; by the same token, these objects of imaginative thought are constituted in the fugal modality of writing.

Such objects of thought therefore and thereby have their truth and meaning bestowed upon them in the writing process by the individual writing 'subject.' In the process of writing literary works of imagination, objects of thought are constitutively conjured up, composed, and arranged into conceptual written work. For example, there is not a real steeple, or apple blossom, contained within Proust's work, but conceptual representations of these that have been constitutively composed performatively from, and in, his objects of thought in the mental space of his writing. To elaborate, there is not a real village of Combray in his continuous novels but a conceptual mimetic representation of the village evoked by Proust in the memories that emerged constitutively in the process of his writing. Yet contextualization is necessary to this form of conceptualization. In the social, cultural reality of Proust's life, 'Combray' was a village by the name of Illiers, which to add even more layers of complexity was changed to Illiers-Combray in honour of Proust's work, an example of reality imitating fiction imitating reality. This is a good example through which to consider the significance and relation in *de re* thought to (authorial) conceptualization and contextualization (of the objects written of or about in the social and cultural contexts of their lives).

How can we understand the relation between an author's thought of a thing, and the actual existence of the thing they are thinking of, for instance Proust's thoughts of the village of Combray? I propose,

Proust does not think about Combray in a descriptive, analytical linguistic way (in the form of a linguistic proposition). Instead, he thinks intentionally of 'Combray' in his performative process of writing. The *de re* aspect of the thought is constituted in its performativity within the mental space of writing, coming into being in his literary composition, from his memories, voluntary and involuntary.

Proust's thoughts of Combray are of a specific mode of thought or belief, one comprised from his own memories and understanding of Combray, internalized experiences which have a conceptual mental component but also physically-based memories for him of his childhood, that is memories which are triggered by physical sensations such as taste and smell and sound, garnered and built up in layers from his experiences through time in/of 'Combray.' The memory traces of his experiences of Combray are within the unconscious physical memory of his cells. These experiences have an unconscious presence in his Being. They manifest in performative (*de re*) writing processes, transformed into writing in a process of becoming.

In numerous ways: renaming, condensing, transposing, distorting, Proust exemplifies how a modernist author 'fugally' replays and transforms self-based memory through the prism of narrative fiction.

In the conceptual subjective inner processes of writing, an author makes her, or his, own the objects of their thoughts grounded on their own experience of living in the social context of their lives. This can involve the fugal 'puzzle canon' of coded messages, and in-jokes (for instance, the transformation of a forbidden male into an acceptable female form, or vice versa). Writing thus becomes an individualistic, self-based process, subliminal, a form of authorial ownership. As the writer searches to understand the objects of thought arising from personal experiences in the world, she or he (may believe they) come to 'own' those objects in their writing, the writer captures these perceptual objects of thought ('objects of love and hate') in the process of writing. In this way the author (may believe she, or he) is able to control, and order their characters in the notional world of their writing like a form of play, but total control proves illusory. There is an aspect of incommensurability, beyond control, that is to do with memory and forgetting, with the unconscious of language and the individual writer. It is this complexity of (the writer's) experience of Being in time, in the contrapuntal polyphony of the text's becoming, out of time, searching for a lost sense of time, involving conscious and unconscious processes of thought, dream, memory, and imagination, aspects immaterial and material, conceptual and contextual, which Proust deeply conveys and expresses in prismatic poetic prose.

Intentionality is suggested in Brentano's theory that phenomenological 'truth' is ascertainable through intuition and 'self evidence'. In *Cartesian Meditations: An Introduction to Phenomenology*, Edmund Husserl (1931) developed phenomenological accounts of self-evidence, introspection and self-examination. He rejected empirical phenomenology for what he termed 'transcendental' phenomenology, in order to consider objects of phenomenology (including the phenomena of mental acts such as desiring, fearing, wishing, and so on) as standing in necessary relations, independently of any solely psychological consideration. Husserl argued against Descartes' empirical deductive natural science, claiming:

> the idea of an all-embracing philosophy becomes actualized...as a system of phenomenological disciplines, which treat correlative themes and are ultimately grounded, not on an axiom, ego cogito, but on an all-embracing self-investigation.[8]

Husserl continues:

> The path leading to a knowledge absolutely grounded in the highest sense, or (this being the same thing) a philosophical knowledge, is necessarily the path of universal self knowledge—first of all monadic, and then intermonadic....
>
> The Delphic motto, "Know thyself!" has gained a new significance. Positive science is a science lost in the world. I must lose the world by epoché, in order to regain it by a universal self-examination. "Noli foras ire," says Augustine, "in te redi, in interiore homine habitat veritas. [Do not wish to go out; go back into yourself. Truth dwells in the inner man].[9]

The notion of *epoché* resonates with a fugal concept of temporarily losing awareness of the world and the social self in order to apprehend the intuitively authentic 'being' of oneself and of what one is writing about, the objects of *de re* thought, in one's process of writing. Husserl urged that in order to discover the truth or essence of phenomena in the actual world we 'bracket off' all that can be known about these, all presuppositions, until we arrive at what cannot be bracketed off. Using this method, he suggested we should find that consciousness itself is the one thing that cannot be bracketed. Translated or applied to the author in the writing process, intentionally relating to objects of thought, this achieves self-reflexive resonance.

Husserl's reductionist methodology would appear to lead to a form of methodological solipsism, unless one gives consideration to the potential of *de re* thoughts as giving genuine modal access to objects in the real world. In a fugal modality of writing, in a state of obscured consciousness, the individual writing 'subject' transforms objects of thought derived from experiences of trauma in the world, into musicalized conceptual textual objects. Notwithstanding the possibility of the reconceptualization of *de re* thought revolutionising phenomenological intentionality, literary texts such as Proust's *À la recherche du temps perdu* do have solipsistic elements: involving the imaginary.

Husserl's transcendental phenomenology urges an active examination of the internal objects of the consciousness of the transcendental ego and what is left after 'bracketing' is consciousness. This consciousness may presuppose an ego, however it is a transcendental ego'.[10] All the intentional relational acts occur within this consciousness, in Husserl's account. Heidegger developed this idea, referring after Husserl to the Greek meaning of epoché of suspension of belief or 'to hold back', in relation to his philosophy of Being.

Suspending disbelief, of being in suspension, in between, holding back, bracketing to reveal the essence, a discipline of restraint and formalization, is characteristically evident in the musicalized fugue works examined in Part II. It is due to this authorial, fugal, holding back and sublimation of possibly traumatized emotion into musicalization, that the literary musicalized textual work figuratively speaking 'takes flight' and becomes itself. The conscious and unconscious authorial practice of *epoché* gives rise to the textual becoming of the intermedial, melopoetic literature of modernity.

The 'fugal' approach this investigation is taking to cultural, social and political contextual analysis of literary narratives in relation to the construction of the subject and subjectivity in literary language is positioned within, or at the edge of, a field of contemporary cultural criticism suggested, as Scher acknowledges, by Lawrence Kramer's aim to 'find a meeting ground for literary criticism and musicology as both disciplines aspire to become vehicles of a more comprehensive criticism of culture.'[11] Kramer claims: 'a serious musical hermeneutics is beginning to establish itself, an interdisciplinary enterprise that not only draws on the resources of non-musical fields of study but also has something to offer those fields in return'.[12] Kramer makes a claim about a cultural agency of music that is relevant to this inquiry when he argues:

> The major force behind this emerging hermeneutics has been a call for understanding musical compositions in their cultural contexts. I would like to carry this project a step further and claim that music can also be understood as a cultural agency; that is, as a participant in, not just a mirror of, discursive and representational practices.[13]

This can also be a methodological direction for interdisciplinary inquiry: in what ways can the music of the fugue be said to participate in 'discursive and representational practices' of literary writing? What mimetic and/or performative manifestations do these 'disciplinary and representational' practices take in literary-textual compositions, and how? What are the performed functions of the creative, and cultural, agency of musicalized fugue narratives? Overall, can fugue musicalization be said to translate into and work as a form of cultural agency in literary texts? If so, what form does such agency take? These questions inform the approach taken in the studies in Part II.

On the literal level, communication through writing and reading is a form of agency. More interpretively, the cultural agency of writing and reading can take many diverse forms, depending on context, and perception of context. For instance, the cultural agency of a literary narrative may be that of 'subversion' of a dominant paradigm. This cultural agency may manifest overtly, as in satire or parody or in more subliminal unconscious ways. The cultural agency suggested by the symbolic and rhetorical structures of the fugal modality of writing and textual literary fugue narratives can be understood as one of subversion of inauthentic, and socially oppressive, forms of writing. Cultural 'subversion' may be secondary effect and not necessarily part of the primary intention—or drive—of the author. In some cases, for instance in Joyce's and Plath's fugal writing, a conscious subversion of dominant language structures was a part of their drive. Use of fugue techniques and structures implies openness to change and chance, a reluctance to bring about closure, a perhaps coded articulation of the emotional inner life experienced by the individual. Above all, perhaps, the fugue structure or form in literary form enacts a form of 'waking dream' writing, a connection to unconscious subliminal realms of imagination and intoxication; it might be read as a form of escape and surrender yet within that surrender to *jouissance*, it denotes resistance to external totalitarian or fascistic state-imposed authority. The composer of the fugue makes their rules generated by the form of the writing itself. The melodies chosen by the writers are the subject themes from which their fugues commence and develop. The agency of this practice is profound and subliminal, communicating the message to readers of the possibility and published reality of different or other ways of writing, of thinking and feeling. The fugue is a symbolic and rhetorical figure of conversion and translation and free invention. This cultural agency of fugue writing may travel via subliminal cultural routes crossing borders and language barriers, to affect another culture in another time and place. This is seen in poet Charles Baudelaire's translation of De Quincey's *Confessions of an English Opium Eater* and *Suspiria de Profundis*.

Phenomenological hermeneutics can enable theoretically competing disciplines to collaborate, and be analyzed, in a mode of mutual influence, whilst still retaining their differences. Husserlian phenomenology is used here to analyze the textual evidence of literary fugue narratives.

Interdisciplinarity must confront the challenges of vagueness and superficiality. Roland Barthes has anticipated some of the problems of the 'violent' jolting displacement or dislocation of interdisciplinary studies:

> Interdisciplinarity is not the calm of an easy security; it begins effectively (as opposed to the mere expression of a pious wish) when the solidarity of the old disciplines breaks down—perhaps even violently, via the jolts of fashion—in the interests of a new object and a new language neither of which has a place in the field of the sciences that were to be brought peacefully together, this unease in classification being precisely the point from which it is possible to diagnose a certain mutation.[14]

This interdisciplinary *jolt*, not unlike the Surrealist 'jolt', is designed to shatter preconceptions and reveal a new object, a new way of seeing. Barthes qualifies his argument about the violent jolt of this field of studies with the acknowledgment that the 'mutation' it produces is 'more in the nature of an epistemological slide than a real break'.[15]

In other words, the jolt does not so much signify a deathblow, as the shock of the new, or the active progression of change. This can be seen as a dialectical progression, producing a new synthesis from its thesis (traditional discipline), antithesis (interdisciplinary study), to synthesis (a new object of study). Barthes' argument that 'there is now the requirement of a new object, obtained by the sliding or the overturning of former categories',[16] is pertinent to contemporary word-music intermedial studies.

Fugue literary narratives comprise relatively recent 'intermedial' works. They start with De Quincey's *Dream-Fugue*, where it is shown that fugue structures constitute a particular literature of modernity. Connections and mutual influence between music and literature originate in Ancient Greece. In *Die Geburt der Tragödie aus dem Geiste der Musik* (The Birth of Tragedy from the Spirit of Music) (1872) Nietzsche argued that tragedy grew out of music linked to the frenzied release of Dionysian rituals. Following the theory of Walter Benjamin,[17] and in addressing modern literature, this book considers ways in which 'tragedy' is transposed into traumatic shock experienced by the individual author in modernity and written into literary form.

But if in these texts there is a particular link with tragedy then it is internalized, and possibly repressed, or sublimated. It emerges in the form of musicalization that is 'unconsciously' used by the author—De Quincey for example—like the mechanism of dream displacement, as a modality of articulating or translating (traumatized) aspects of the subject, into the cultural objectified subjectivity of literary language.

PSYCHOANALYTICAL THEMES: MIMESIS, TRAUMA, AFFECT

Questions of representation and mimesis in writing are fundamentally to do with the psychology of perception. In Book Ten of *The Republic*, Plato argued against the 'false representation' of poets, and sought to banish poets from the ideal Republic. Aspects of Plato's argument are reprised in mid-twentieth century debates around authorial intentionality, originality, and authenticity in writing. Mimesis, or imitative mimesis, is the imitation of human behaviour, nature, or events. How may imitative mimesis function in relation to the use of musicalized techniques in literary narratives, and how useful and significant is this way of conceptualizing 'representation' in relation to the construction of the subject and subjectivity in literary writing? How does it relate to the notion of *de re* thoughts? Is fugal mimesis a form of *waking dream* condensation and displacement?

But what are the functions and uses of imitative mimesis in relation to the psychological use of fugue? Freud, in his work on empathetic imitation and mental contagion,[18] throws light on this key problem of the mimesis of creative writing. Freud suggested melancholic mimesis is narcissistic; a condition in which we identify with 'the other', the ego cannibalistically wishes to (literally) devour the other in order to take it into inside itself. This mimesis involves an unconscious (phenomenological) pattern of loss, love and hate of the other which is indistinguishable from the loss, hate, and love which narcissistically the subject feels for himself or herself. From a psychological rather than a purely musicalized 'fugal' perspective, mimesis in fugue narratives enacts a desire to performatively reconstitute the lost loved object in writing. This is a way, or an attempt, to make the lost object, Lacan's '*objet petit a*,' part of the author. According to Lacan,[19] when a child first enters the 'symbolic order' of language (*langue*) by making its first intelligible utterances, and writing its name, it effects a separation from its mother and thus starts the long process of individuation, which may (ideally) lead to the individual becoming an independent self as language user in modern linguistic western society. However, Lacan emphasizes that this separation from the mother is not effected without a cost. Lacan hypothesizes that from the time at which a child first becomes aware of itself as a separate being, coinciding with when it first becomes aware of itself through language use, as a speaking subject, by writing her/his name, it also at the same time, is aware of a concurrent sense of loss, of the primal unity it had previously felt.

Lacan's *objet petit a* symbolizes the lost object which the individual continually, not necessarily consciously, searches for throughout their life, displacing and projecting their desire onto all kinds of compensatory or substituting objects. The self-referentiality of this project is suggested by Freud's focus on narcissism in the mimetic cycle. Freud theorizes further themes of loss and desire in his exploration of phenomenological affect in *Jenseits des Lustprinzips* (Beyond the Pleasure Principle) (1920). Arguably, if the fugal writing process is phenomenologically capable of being interpreted as constituting one particular form of unconscious 'narcissism', Freud's theories of mimesis might help illuminate it.

In *Love, Guilt and Reparation,* Melanie Klein postulates her thesis of the relationship between guilt and the creative process, particularly in relation to articulations of phenomenological affects (evidence) of survivor guilt in narratives. Klein's theories of the sublimated drivers of creativity and culture may be adapted to account for the writer's fugue linked to post-traumatic stress disorder. She suggests that the creative process of writing and art-making is expressive of basic unconscious needs in fundamental ways: the creative process is a form of 'reparation,' a seeking to make good and thus redeem the guilt felt by the individual for unconscious desires (in her Freudian theory, the desire of a young child to harm a parent for frustrating its needs). But up to a point, guilt is a spur to creativity:

> Feelings of guilt...are a fundamental incentive towards creativeness and work in general (even of the simplest kinds) [but] may however, if they are too great, have the effect of inhibiting productive activities and interests.[20]

This suggests that people who feel most guilty, although they may address themes of guilt in their literary works are not the greatest writers or at least the most productive. To be meaningful, powerful, and ultimately productive, art has to be made with an ethical, humane sense, is the inference from this.

Another Kleinian idea is relevant:

> The baby's impulses and feelings are accompanied by a kind of mental activity which I take to be the most primitive one: that is of phantasy-building, or more colloquially, imaginative thinking. For instance, the baby who feels a craving for his mother's breast when it is not there may imagine it to be there, i.e. he may imagine the satisfaction which he derives from it. Such primitive phantasying is the earliest form of the capacity which later develops into the more elaborate workings of the imagination.[21]

The primal sense of security this imagined satisfaction gives arguably becomes particularly important for the traumatized individual, perhaps becoming a *need* rather than a desire. Growing up in an Ireland colonized by the English and politically struggling for independence, James Joyce, a radical free-thinking student who was frustrated by the English language and (sometimes) despaired of his fellow Irish, felt a need from an early age to reinvent—in writing—himself, his country and his language, to return to himself in an earlier stage and articulate his displaced memories in textual form (a story he writes of in his *Portrait of the Artist as a Young Man*). 'What makes Joyce a radical writer is his willingness to question not just the expressive powers of language but also the institution of literature itself', writes Declan Kiberd in his Introduction to Joyce's *Ulysses*.[22] The traumatic themes that surfaced into De Quincey's *Dream-Fugue* suggest that he felt a commensurate need to immerse himself in a simulated security to counter-balance painful memories in his writing. Without wishing to labour the psychoanalytical point, on a Kleinian-derived model, the compulsion he felt accounts in the lifelong volumes of his highly prolific intoxicated output, at least, if not wholly, for the recurring motif of the endangered maiden, as an expression of survivor's guilt. To further adapt a Kleinian theme, the fugal writer seeks to make reparation, to repair, 'heal', and reconstitute the lost shattered object (which in the back of their mind the writer feels guilty about), and at the same time, as a response to the traumatic images and memories that their writing stirs, they need to immerse compulsively in the very medium through which the trauma is replayed, namely writing. Thus writing from trauma may evoke a Romantic—or post-Romantic—idea of the artist in their writing perpetually re-opening a wound that never heals (cf. De Quincey).

Kristeva's theory of abjection in writing deepens the psychological theme. She suggests that the repetition and compulsion of the fugal writing process linked to music has its deepest psychological impetus as a manifestation of a *drive*. Kristeva refers to the 'archaic memory of language' in modernist literature. In *Pouvoirs de l'horreur* (Powers of Horror), she argues of the modern writing process:

> But what is it? Unless it be the untiring repetition of a drive, which propelled by an initial loss, does not cease wandering, unsated, deceived, warped, until it finds its only stable object—death. Handling that repetition, staging it, cultivating it until it releases, beyond its eternal return, its sublime destiny of being a struggle with death—is it not that which characterizes writing?[23]

The notion Kristeva suggests of the 'wandering,' 'unsated,' repetition of a drive propelled by an initial loss resonates with the idea of the uncanny, deterritorialized fugue of the writing process. Kristeva has also suggested that the modern author desires to reconstitute the lost object (as object of thought) in writing. Hypothetically, this may be a phase of life, or experience, which is associated with the trauma of loss. Involuntary memories may take the form of exact reproductions of a traumatic incident, but—like dreams—are more likely to be displaced projections, or Freudian 'condensations', which distort the experience, producing a series of motifs or visual images (objects of thought) which may not seem directly connected to the experience of shock, trauma and loss—thus heightening the writer's sense of alienation, anxiety, and the compulsion to keep writing. Writing in this instance becomes a releasing of symptoms of post-traumatic stress disorder, and (paradoxically) its subject's concurrent attempt to escape its painful hold. This condition, subsumed under the rubric of psychogenic fugue, involves recurrent involuntary memories. These may take the form of waking dreams, or actual dreams, or both. For De Quincey this also involved opium dreams. De Quincey's intoxication—through opium writing—has been likened by Alina Clej (1995) to a forerunner, or prototype, of the modern and postmodern *disaffected literary imagination*.

A double sense of loss and desire provides compulsion—or inspiration—to keep writing. The writing process then constitutes a sense of alienation and displacement and also projection of the 'impossible' desired (lost) object onto the writing self, thus, in some accounts creating a self-reflexive and narcissistic metafictional loop.[24]

In *Revolution in Poetic Language* Julia Kristeva puts forward a theory of signifying practices and what she terms the 'semiotic chora, which modifies linguistic structure'.[25] She writes that the 'genotext' is a process, 'it moves through zones that have relative and transitory borders and constitutes a path that is not bound or restricted to 'the two poles of univocal information between two full-fledged subjects' (or between an author and reader/s). If this distinction were to be translated into a metalanguage, the genotext is 'a matter of topology', whereas the phenotext is one of 'algebra'. It should be added here, that the phenotext, is made up of 'phonematic devices' for example the 'accumulations and repetition of phonemes [a basic sound unit in writing] or rhyme' and 'melodic devices', of intonation and rhythm. Kristeva holds that 'Writing represents-articulates the signifying process into specific networks or spaces.'[26] This signifying process includes both the genotext and the phenotext.'

In the theory that emerges in my examination of ways in which the authors of literary fugue narratives and poems have literally translated fugal devices of music, in forms of 'musicalization' (or musicalized writing) the modality of the signifying practice that operates between what Julia Kristeva terms the 'genotext' and the phenotext of phonemes in their literary compositions, is what I have called the fugal modality of writing, in the writer's fugue, activated by traumatic shock, and which articulates in a performative need to communicate, or annex, in writing, the impacts and event of this shock, and to also, in this way, to overcome its hold, as a post traumatic effect on the nervous system, as a restitution, and articulation of the 'subject' or self.

Kristeva bases her ideas on the different kinds of writing on modalities of discourse, in 'our society' distinguished by Lacan: 'the hysteric, the academic, the master, and the analyst'. She distinguishes four types of 'signifying practice: narrative, meta-language, contemplation, and text practice.'[27] She associates each of these modalities of 'signifying dispositions' with discourses. She links 'narrative and contemplation' to 'hysterical and obsessional', and metalanguage and text practices to the 'psychotic (paranoid and schizoid) economies'.[28] I propose, based on my examination of the literary compositions, that there is another modality of writing and another discourse in our society, which is that of the modality artist, as literary author. The artist-author was left out of consideration in the discourse of language and signifying practices in the mid-late twentieth century, although this is a crucial signifying practice, of discourse; it has been overlooked. Kristeva discusses the writings of authors, including Joyce, who reach what she refers to as the 'infinity' of the process of writing (from the *chora* of the genotext, in flight, to the phenotext) I add to this, and reply to Kristeva's theory that holds that these encompass a 'pulverization' of language; far from destroy, these texts and poetic narratives create, they embody what is termed a musicalization. They are not aesthetically detached, and they engage with social and political issues of their authors' lives and times, yet in processes that are plural, heterogeneous and contradictory.

Through the studies, I come to link these as a form of writing that is associated with mild dissociation of fugue, the ancients spoke of as the inspiration of the muses, and which persists as an account of losing awareness of oneself whilst in a mode of poetic creation.

In Kristeva's theory, 'abjection' in relation to the individual process of writing, the modernist author attempts to find or reconstitute the lost object through subliminally evoking in his, or her, writing Lacan's *objet petit a*.' This may point to, even account for, the compulsion of writing, also referred to as 'inspiration', for instance by musicologist Percy Scholes (1993). This compulsion to create takes the form of a mood, a desire to write which the individual feels they must heed. It was explained by Hugo von Hofmannsthal, in 1893, as the compulsive need for an individual writer, composer, or artist to 'dissect a mood, a sigh, a scruple.'[29] Alternatively it may manifest as a desire for artists to immerse in: 'Reflection or fantasy, mirror image or dream image'.[30] To adapt a Lacanian model, the shock of entering language and becoming aware of herself, or himself, as separate, individual and alone may be sufficient for sensitive individuals to feel compelled to write—using the very means by which they became alienated (language use) to seek restitution for their loss.

This may account for a specific tone of modern literary writing. However this exploration focuses on texts enacting discernible affects in response to the effects of traumatic shock, later in the author's life, beyond the linguistic shock of entering the symbolic language order. There is though a sense in which writers such as De Quincey, Joyce and Proust use literary writing as a form of individuation. They each —in the guise of the implied author—seem to affect a form of linguistic and psychological flight in their creation of an inventive self-based literary language text. Paradoxically this entails a temporary fugal loss of the sense of self in the author's immersion in the writing process, and the literary value of this cannot be underestimated. Baudelaire wrote of the artist in modernity, in *The Painter of Modern Life*, 'Few men have the gift of seeing; fewer still have the power to express themselves'.[31]

In the same essay Baudelaire wrote: 'Modernity is the transient, the fleeting, the contingent; it is one half of art, the other being the eternal and the immovable.'[32] Perhaps it is 'by chance' as Proust suggests that through this process of writing triggered by traumatic experience, the author's subjectivity emerges in writing, and this enacts and characterizes the subjectivity of the individual, alienated in modern capitalist society. Walter Benjamin puts forward a different view, in his essay *On Some Motifs in Baudelaire* (1940). Proust writes on the inadequacies of *mémoire volontaire* and intellect, that they do not actually contain the past within them. He contrasts this to *mémoire involontaire*, which he believes *do* contain traces of the past, and he considers the idea of metempsychosis, the transmigration of souls, an idea which Joyce also refers to in *Ulysses*. Proust's narrator, Marcel, writes:

> I feel there is much to be said for the Celtic belief that the souls of those whom we have lost are held captive in some inferior being, in an animal, in a plant, in some inanimate object, and so effectively lost to us until the day (which to many never comes) when we happen to pass by the tree or to obtain possession of the object which forms their prison. Then they start and tremble, they call us by our name, and as soon as we have recognized their voice the spell is broken. We have delivered them: they have overcome death and return to share our life. (*Swann's Way*, p. 57)

He concludes: 'It is a labor in vain to attempt to recapture it: all the efforts of our intellect must prove futile. The past is hidden somewhere outside the realm, beyond the reach of intellect, in some material object (in the sensation which that material object will give us) which we do not suspect. And as for that object, it depends on chance whether we come upon it or not before we ourselves must die.'[33] Whilst for Proust it is a matter beyond a person's control whether an 'individual forms an image of himself, whether he can take hold of his experience' Benjamin argues: 'there is nothing inevitable about the dependence on chance in this matter. A person's inner concerns are not by nature of an inescapably private character. They attain this character only after the likelihood decreases that one's external concerns will be assimilated to one's experience'.[34] In other words if an individual can assimilate the shocks and traumas, of loss in the world, for example, by writing of these, they can be shared and be communicated through language.

Benjamin, writing in 1940, uses this to make an argument against the kind of sensationalist disconnect in press writing of 'information' which he criticizes as it is designed to not be assimilated, everything mitigates against it: the layout, and writing style based on journalistic principles —newsness, brevity, clarity, lack of connection between the individual news items 'the linguistic habitus of newspapers' which 'paralyzes the imagination'. Benjamin contrasts journalistic writing with Proust's literary 'reporting on his own childhood' in his 'eight-volume novel' which 'gives some idea of the effort it took to restore the figure of the storyteller to the current generation.'[35]

Kristeva refers to the '*objet petit a*'—that is the (unconscious) object desired by the (writing) subject. In her theory of abjection, Kristeva questions the idea that the abject subject (writer) is driven by desire for an *'object a,'* she suggests that abjection is a 'negative' drive characterized by its lack of an object, writers write: 'a language of want... the want that positions sign, subject and object'.³⁶ Here I consider the psychoanalytic thesis that it is the desire to constitute the lost object in writing that drives the subject who is constituted in language, from language, into her, or his, own writing. This is not negative, neither is it amoral. According to Lacan, a primary loss is experienced by the individual in entering the symbolic language order, making their first utterance in speech and thus becoming self-aware as separate from the primal unity of the mother. In his famously gendered analysis, the mother represents nature, and the father represents culture, the symbolic realm of language represents and is governed by the *nom-du-père* (Law of the Father). In the individuation of the writing process, the wrench that Lacan describes is repeated as the writing subject repetitively, compulsively, leaves the natural unity of the real (the actual world), to enter the symbolic realm of language.³⁷

The lost *objet petit a*, relating to the primary unity of a child with its mother, can be projected, or displaced, onto any object of desire. Is it useful to consider that the artist-author seeks to reconstitute in writing their lost object? This object can be displaced as a character or place, such as Joyce's meticulous, almost carnivalesque, reconstitution of Dublin, the home city he left, permanently after his mother's death. He eloped, on a *fugue romantique*, with his future wife Nora Barnacle, to Europe, and did not return. The urge to write may indeed then have a primary source of origin, beyond the traumatic event written about. In Kristevan theory, 'abjection is eminently productive of culture. Its symptom is the rejection and reconstruction of languages'.³⁸

Moving beyond Lacan's notion of the *objet petit a*, Kristeva's concept of abjection focuses on two realms of writing (un)consciousness: *chora* which is pre-language, the realm of primary urges and desires which is yet a realm of (becoming) *semiosis* from which meaning is derived and made; and the *symbolic* language order. The author who draws on these realms of the space of intermedial writing might find that they germinate and generate in inventive musicalized literary writings, the phenomena that Kristeva calls 'pure signification', and 'the music in the letter'.³⁹ Signification can be seen and heard in Joyce's paronomasical play in the 'Sirens' episode in *Ulysses*, in which the signification of written language resembles that of non-representational music. This constitutes an effect of the fugal 'flight' of the language of the literary text, which Kristeva sees as cathartic: 'A single catharsis: the rhetoric of the pure signifier, of music in letters'.[40]

Kristeva argues that musicalized literary narratives, stream-of-consciousness novels, and she cites Joyce's *Ulysses*, have performative and musical quality not found in realist literature. This can be interpreted as the distinction between *de re* performative writing, which is *of* objects of thought in the writer's mind, and *de dicto* descriptive realist writing which is *about* things in the world, as if the world has a smooth order, Kristeva claims that High Modernist literary works, which enact musicalized techniques, are profoundly semiotic. In *La révolution du langage poétique* (Revolution in Poetic Language) (1984), she claims:

> Among the capitalist mode of production's numerous signifying practices, only certain literary texts of the avant-garde (Mallarmé, Joyce) manage to cover the infinity of this process, that is reach the semiotic chora, which modifies linguistic structure.[41]

Associations and connections between musical and literary compositions can be approached (as was the case with modernist experimentation) in terms of un/conscious psychic structures and the synchronistic, synaesthetic symbolic language of the unconscious. According to Lacan, in 'The Insistence of the Letter in the Unconscious':

> beyond what we call "the word", what the psychoanalytic experience discovers in the unconscious is the whole structure of language.[42]

This suggests a subliminal unconscious emerges into consciousness in language use. It, also, suggests thereby that the language we use, when apparently consciously awake, is to a degree unconscious. Aspects of our unconscious language uses are often linked to the emotions and their conscious repression, so too in the creative writing processes of literary narratives. The interplay between the subjective intentions of the individual and materialized objective aspects of the language used is most obvious in musicalized fugal narratives. A liminality, or in-between mental space, which may exist in all conceptual created works, is perhaps most immediately apparent in intermedial works.

Unconscious processes that evoke both psychological and musical meanings of fugue are detected in Proust's *À la recherche*. These unconscious processes include involuntary memory and recurring motifs.

His use of tropes of metaphor, metonymy, and recurring motifs, creates a polyphonic effect likened by Deleuze and Guattari to music.[43] Reading this lengthy complex musicalized text gives the impression of entering and inhabiting the multi-layered, unfolding realms of its narrator's mind. Or, rather, it is as if the text of this work has a complex, self-generating mind/machine, of fugally shifting systems. Motifs such as the *madeleine* and the *petite phrase de la sonate de Vinteuil* recur throughout the entire eight volume literary composition, reminiscent of recurring leitmotifs in opera. The emotional tone also shifts from predominant melancholia and nostalgia to glittering witty social satire at times bordering on farce, as narrator, Marcel, performatively searches, steadily with patience and fortitude, and a palpable sense of writerly solitude, through his involuntary memories of *temps perdu*.

It would be erroneous to conclude that the power of the author is diminished by the textuality of literary language that renders literature, in a profoundly obvious sense, 'authorless', a theory put forward in the 1960s, which fails to take into account the authentic self driven author as artist. The musicalized process of writing is a performative practice of individualistic subjective arrangement—in a literary composition. This is an associative process enacting a subjectivity of consciousness in the writing. The artist's intentional use of musicalized techniques involves an interpretation firstly on the part of the writer as to what are these musical techniques, and how to apply these in literary language. In intentionally adapting fugue techniques in 'Sirens' Joyce developed his unique *fuga* individual language of onomatopoeic and alliterative word music. Joyce devises compound words, for example: *Bloowhose, bluerobed, gigglegold, freefly, giggle-giggled, napecomb, bronzegold, goldbronze, shrilldeep*, all of which are to be found on a single page of *Ulysses*. However objective and aesthetic experiments in fugal musicalization may be, this is an emotive expressive writing process which involves firstly an author giving names to things and bestowing upon these their subjective associative meaning, in their writing, a process which makes this name-giving possible. This process creates an individualistic language use, a form of the 'language of power', to use De Quincey's term (and the contemporary author does this knowingly with awareness of the complexities) which then becomes subject to individual interpretations of readers of musicalized literary narratives. This, a practice of self-based writing that developed in the late eighteenth century, came to characterize the self-based individualistic modern subject articulated in the subjectivity of the literature of modernity. This articulation of subjectivity in literary writing emerged perhaps by chance as Proust suggests. But it is inextricably linked to social and political contexts as albeit 'displaced', i.e. parodic, reflection and critique. Both Foucault (1969) and Barthes contextualized the birth of the modern author within the emergence of laws of modern society and the rational modern capitalist secular state. These included property laws and, copyright laws, brought in with the Statute of Anne in 1710 in England, thereby bestowing the rights of ownership on the individual (provided he had sufficient property to be subject to these laws) whilst inscribing status and being as a subject within the social laws of language. Although women were protected by copyright law, they lost their property once they married, when their copyright passed to their husbands; whereas unmarried and widowed women owned the copyright for their writings. In England the Married Women's Property Act of 1882 enabled married women to own and control property, a provision extended to British Territories at the end of the nineteenth century.

Musicalized fugue literary narratives may be seen to have an aesthetic *conceptual* value, but the studies in Part II show that authors also use highly stylized and individualistic techniques in narratives that enact *contextual* social cultural criticism. This is particularly evident in 'Sirens' in *Ulysses*, which was written in the latter years of Ireland's struggle for Independence (and within the social context of intense debate around the place of women in Edwardian society).[44] The metaphorical and analogous meanings of musicalized literary narratives perform cultural functions beyond aesthetic entertainment, novelty, or self-indulgence—as some theorists, Lukács, for instance, Clej (1995), have referred to modernist literature.

The authors of literary narratives which use 'non-representational' kinetic-mimetic musicalized techniques to articulate and inscribe the meaning of experience from traumatic shock, enact the literary plight of the individual in modern expansionist capitalist colonialist society. Literary works are individualistic and original expressions of authors' experiences and perceptions, in fictionalized literary form, they were written within social and political contexts to which authors responded. Enacting and reflecting the individual experiences and concerns, and cultural and political contexts of their authors' lives, these musicalized texts enact political, ideological, and social comment. This is demonstrated alike, though differently, in De Quincey's *Dream-Fugue*, Joyce's *Ulysses*, Proust's *À la recherche du temps perdu*, and Celan's *Todesfuge* and Plath's *Little Fugue*. Interpretative and individualistic, they are literary enactments, creating representations, of subjectivity. Whilst an author may produce literary works which can be seen to have a solipsistic existence, in the actual process of writing the writers go beyond their 'mental' inner worlds and methodological solipsism to connect with and comment on, in the practice of writing, the social and cultural world in which, in an enigmatic relation, their textual works are embedded. This practice occurs to the extent that the textual works achieve manifest existence in social and cultural realms, and can continue to exist long after the physical death of the author.

The authentic poetic articulation of affect, as a literary expression of emotion, is the missing link (or note) in an explanation of how musicalized literary narratives are capable of originality and invention. To be authentic, and have the power to move the receptive reader, affect must derive from the articulation of an author's self-based emotional experience. But again, this raises a problem for critical interpretation, taking the reader into a significant area of disjuncture in the writing process of fugue narratives involving (complex) postmodern or poststructuralist interpretation. This may be simplified as the dichotomy between, first, an interpretation of creative processes of written narratives based on the theoretical view of the phenomena of involuntary memory recurring motifs as 'simulacra', as in Alina Clej's analysis in *A Genealogy of the Modern Self: Thomas de Quincey and the Intoxication of Writing* (1995) and second, an approach that connects the creative processes of the written literary text with the author and their inner psychological experiences as articulated by the implied author in the literary narrative text.

The existential phenomenological 'evidence' of the articulation of a post-traumatic shock in fugue literary narratives—manifest in recurring motifs—constitutes an anomaly for hermeneutic investigation. Should recurring involuntary memories be considered as individual objects each time they occur in an author's literary fugue works? Or should they be seen, as we might read in De Quincey's body of work, as evidence of post-traumatic memories that recurred throughout his life, prompting him to write, over and again, impassioned prose based on his secret witnessing of his sister's corpse, when aged six? Are these recurring motifs 'simulacra' or 'things-in-themselves'?

Phenomena in literature, of recurring motifs, involuntary memories, mood disturbance, and desire to reconstitute lost 'objects' in writing could be read, 'psychologically' as the transposition of symptoms and/or affects of a traumatic sense of loss and the attempt of the individual to recover or recreate a lost object in the process of literary fugue writing. Both Proust's *madeleine* and *la petite phrase de Vinteuil* (a musical phrase) are associated with affect. The chance taste of the madeleine teacake sets up an on-the-tip-of-the-tongue longing and need to recover and recall the significant lost memory object whose identity and real meaning has been forgotten. Vinteuil's 'phrase' is metonymically associated with complexity of emotion (particularly jealousy) in love relationships. Both, the reader assumes, are displacements of events and experiences in Proust's life. In comparison, De Quincey's images of imperilled and endangered maidens recur throughout the entire life's body of his work, perhaps signifying his nervous system's replaying of the shock of witnessing his sister's corpse, as a child; and in the process creating significant literature, that is so significant it is regarded as foundational to modern literary subjectivity. Here a relevant question is intentionality, to what degree are and can these techniques be used to create such effects and affects? As shown in the studies, particularly of Joyce, the authors are writing with the complex intention of adapting formalized musicalized techniques, and in so doing, wrote profound works of the *subjectivity* of modernity.

In exploring contradictions, and competing theoretical positions around concepts of performative writing, mimesis involving 'simulacra' and 'things-in-themselves,' in examination of the literary fugue works discussed in Part II, there emerges a context of 'fugal' writing involving a *fugal performance* in writing and reading. The 'intermedial' compositions of literary fugue narratives are arranged and composed by authors in the writing process from elements that have often been regarded as disjunctive, dichotomous, paradoxical, or contradictory, and anomalous. These binaries include: formalism and expression; self-reflexivity and unconsciousness; rationality and 'irrational' affect. Michel Foucault, in works such as *Discipline and Punish* has theorized that the construction of 'the subject' in modernity, and modern times, has occurred through the limiting delineation of disciplinary institutions (founded on categories of classical western metaphysics).[45] In contrast, Derrida suggested that binaries could be 'dissolved' in the transformative experience of transforming language into writing in a process of textual becoming.

For Derrida, binaries structure and limit the categories of classical western metaphysics. He claimed that authentic, 'pure' writing had the power of transformation, which he referred to with the emotive affective word 'violence'. He writes against the history of writing's notion of a 'linear norm', which he terms 'linearization', and relates to a Saussurean structuralist model, which emphasized: 'limits and marked the concepts of symbol and language'.[46] Derrida is against the conceptualization of models, which by virtue of being 'models' are inaccessible.

> If one allows that the linearity of language entails this vulgar and mundane concept of temporality (homogenous, dominated by the form of the now and the ideal of continuous movement, straight or circular) which Heidegger shows to be the intrinsic determining concept of all ontology from Aristotle to Hegel, the meditation upon writing and the deconstruction of the history of philosophy become inseparable.[47]

Such binaries are not so much 'dissolved' as, more precisely, brought together polyphonically to coexist, contrapuntally, in the fugal writing process. This process of signifying occurs in the intentional transposition of musical techniques into new literary language. Authors intentionally inscribe their existential 'being' into their musicalized literary narratives. Paradoxically, these narratives also contain elements of which the author is unaware and over which she or he has no direct control, once the work enters the public realm it is open to interpretation. Like recordings of musical and spoken word performances, these textual narratives also contain an element of 'nothingness,' an absence of the author from the text: the author is both present and absent.

3

FUGUE VARIATIONS: POLYPHONIC CONVERSATIONS

> Fuga is from Latin fuga, flight; because the parts setting off so successively, seem to fly and pursue each other—Jean-Jacques Rousseau, *The Complete Dictionary of Music*, 1779
>
> Fugue, a flight or pursuit; a fugue differs from a canon only in being less rigid in its laws; a canon is a perpetual fugue: the first a leading part gives the law to the rest in both; but in the course of a fugue, it is allowable to introduce episodes and new subjects—Charles Burney, *The present state of music in France and Italy: or, the journal of a tour through those countries, undertaken to collect materials for a general history of music*, 1773
>
> I would propose that music is a mirror of the process of thought itself... All the various symbolic methods we use to investigate the nature of the world and ourselves are to be found within music. The fugue (...) is the very exemplar of thought, working by proof and analogy, and the refinement of memory—Yehudi Menuhin, *The Music of Man*, 1979

In the Western world, the idea has long been acceptable that authentic emotion can be expressed in musical form. But expressing emotion in literary writing is perceived as a more complicated—and less direct—art. Of course, Romanticism drew on musical form and techniques in poetry and poetic prose to move the passions of the reader and express the passion of the writer—through using musicalization. Yet ever since Plato proposed banning poets from the ideal Republic there has been a body of thinking in philosophy that tends to regard the expression and articulation of affect in literary form as somewhat suspect. Through examining fugue narratives and poetic works in Part II, I aim to achieve an understanding of the scope of these contradictions, and the nature of experimental, fugal, musical writing processes.

STRUCTURAL FORM AND TECHNIQUES

Rousseau defines fugue in his 1779 *The Complete Dictionary of Music*. His definition begins:

> FUGUE: A piece of music, wherein we treat, according to certain rules of harmony and modulation, an air called subject, by making it pass successively and alternately from one part to another.

He identifies the structural 'rules' of fugue:

> There are the principle rules of the fugue, the one of which they are proper to it, and the other common with the imitation.
>
> I. The subject proceeds from the tonic to the dominant, or from the dominant to the tonic, in ascending or falling.
> II. Every fugue has its answer in the part, which immediately follows that which has begun.
> III. This answer ought to return the subject to the fourth or fifth, and by a similar movement, as exactly as possible proceeding from the dominant to the tonic, when the subject is announced from the tonic to the dominant, and vice versa. One part may also retake the same subject in the octave, or in the union of the precedent; but in that case it is a repetition rather than a true answer.
> IV. As the octave is divided into two unequal parts, the one of which comprehends four degrees in ascending from the tonic to the dominant, and the other only three. This obliges us to have attention to that difference in the expression of the subject, and to make some changes in the answer, not to quit the essential chords of the mode. It is another thing when we propose to change the tone; in that case the exactness of the answer itself, taken on another chord, produces alterations suitable to this change.
> V. The fugue must be designed in such a manner, as, that the answer may enter before the end of the first air, that we may hear each of them in part at a time, that by this anticipation the subject may be united, as it were, to itself; and that the art of the composer may be shewn in this collection. It is a joke to give as a fugue, an air, which only passes from one part to another, without any other difficulty than accompanying it immediately. This, at most, deserves on the art of imitation. (*Dictionary*: 146)[1]

In 1951, Alberto Ghislanzoni, in an article 'La Genesis storica della fuga' in the *Rivista Musica Italia* defined fugue, as:

> A musical work written for one or two or more parts—vocal or instrumental—which present initially a basic theme or subject melodically and rhythmically well-defined and easily recognizable (or two or

more such basic themes), restating this theme again and again at the fifth, at the fourth, or at some other diatonic or chromatic interval, and elaborating upon this theme and its various elements contrapuntally in a number of sections by use of augmentation or diminution (double, triple, quadruple note values etc. half, third, quarter note values etc.), by use of contrary motion, reversion, suitable rhythmic changes, increasing closer spacing of themes and answer (stretto or partial stretto), and by use of extended tones on the lower, upper, or middle voices (pedal points); all of this with the greatest possible freedom of melodic and rhythmic invention and without any particular limitations as to resulting harmonies, structural patterns, or tonal and modulatory progressions.[2]

The melodic subject theme or themes are therefore played by different parts (or 'voices') entering in turn. The initial articulation of the subject is followed by the 'fugal answer' played (or sung) by another part. This exposition is developed as the parts restate the theme in different variations, playing notes of the melody in different ways. This counterpoint occurs through 'contrary motion' through a free range of techniques that may include inversion, diminishment, elaboration, repetition, mirroring, distortion, and embellishment. The exposition may be followed by a counter-exposition.

In summary, the fugue is a polyphonic horizontal composition of imitative counterpoint for several voices, whose played notes harmonize melodically, in vertical counterpoint: enacting variations on the subject melodies in a potentially infinite mimetic, circular structure. The variations are inventive, and free, there may be a *codetta*, a short cadence, at the end of the exposition or counter-exposition. The fugue ends in a coda, with a cadence, where the subject lines are restated.

VARIATIONS IN INTERPRETATION: MODALITY TO TONALITY

Although it reached its apotheosis in the works of Bach (*Die Kunst der Fuge* (Art of Fugue) and *Musikalisches Opfer* (The Musical Offering), the fugue form is believed to have emerged in its complex structured form around 1500.[3] In Bach's later fugues, the form attained an intellectual canonical complexity, including complex use of puzzle canon, and an extraordinary enaction of infinite regression in mirror fugues. After Bach's death (1750) on the cusp of modernity, the fugue form declined. For a period in the early 19th century composers experimented with the symphonic possibilities of fugue, notably Beethoven's *Grosse Fuge*

(1822) and, earlier, Mozart's 'Jupiter' *Symphony, No. 41 in C Major* (1788). The fugue section in Mozart's symphony is a five-voice fugato (representing the five major themes) the end of the fourth movement; there are also fugal sections through the movement. Starting with four notes, it transforms into a fugal coda of enormous ingenuity and complexity. Beethoven's *Grosse Fuge* composed as a multi-movement form contained within a single large movement. Introspective and extremely technically demanding, the fugue takes fifteen minutes to play. It has been described as his most avant-garde music.[4] Each of these fugues is remarkable for its innovative, experimental and individualistic nature. Mozart's fugal work represents a more affective, emotional approach to composition and playing than Bach. In the later fugue of Beethoven, a further development in music language articulates the relationship between the composer and his text in the construction of an expression of subjectivity. This is a far more emotional, subjective fugue than any before.

Although very different in style, each of these composers had an inherent understanding of the musical language they did so much to develop and change.[5] The main change (making the classical style possible) is tonality. Tonality denotes having repetitions of the subject at different pitches in the same key, as in the fugue form. Musicologists debate whether tonality is a natural or a 'conventional' language (and whether this makes it 'artificial', and reflective of social relations rather than natural harmony). Charles Rosen, in *The Classical Style*, comments that whilst it is based on the physical properties of a tone, it equally evidently 'deforms' and 'denatures these properties in the interests of creating a regular language of more complex and richer expressive capacities'.[6] One effect of the development of tonality (by means of the circle of fifths— in comparison to the major and minor scales) is that it revealed the asymmetrical relation of dominant to sub-dominant, 'emphasizing that the centre of a tonal work is not a single work but a triad'.[7] This differentiated a hierarchical relationship, contrasting a 'modal' with a tonal system.

A modal system is one in which, as Rosen emphasizes, 'the centre is one note, each note is restricted to the notes of its mode, and the final cadences are conceived as melodic, rather than harmonic formulas'.[8] The modal system was used in sacred music. The emergence of tonality is highly significant in the development of the fugue— it is symbolically significant for the social systems of musical language approaching modernity, and for the new cultural forms of musical and literary language. There are analogies in the development of secular society, of an awareness of hierarchical relationships and regularization of language in modernizing society. Rosen argues that the music of both Mozart and Beethoven raised questions in musicology as to whether their symphonic music is technically Romantic or Classical. Mozart's 'Jupiter' *Symphony No. 41 in C Major*, and Beethoven's *Grosse Fuge* experimented with the emotional possibilities of the fugue form. The works of Bach were articulated in a more rational and scientific style, that was also, however, modal; this can be interpreted affectively as a form of gravely restrained passion.

The fugue as a compositional *form* in itself, in contrast to fugue as compositional *texture*, declined in popularity, and lost its public presence in the mid-late eighteenth century. In the early twentieth century, the *fugue l'école* emerged in France as a scholastic exercise for teaching the rules of compositional form and theory. Due to this scholastic usage, coupled with its virtual disappearance as a 'living' form, the fugue developed a new and misleading reputation for being strictly rule-governed, intellectual, and scholastic.[9] The *fuga per canonem* or fugue according to rule, has come to be seen as exemplifying rules and conventions of musical language—but this is very far from its origins, or indeed its development.

Contemporary research, Paul Mark Walker's *Theories of Fugue from the Age of Josquin to the Age of Bach* (2000), affirms earlier contentions in Alfred Mann's *The Study of Fugue* (1958), and Imogen Horsley's *Fugue: History and Practice* (1966), in defense of the authentic origins of the fugue. Their research undermines the belief that the fugue has always been a scholastic form and/or a strictly canonical form. In its origins it was a secular communal musical form, it was the opposite of a lifeless exercise; and originated as a melodic form exemplifying articulation of the living voice in the natural melody of musical form. Originating in the musical sound and rhythm of the singing voice, over time this 'natural' musical form was adapted in local communities secular settings, according to cultural requirements and social change. Even as canon developed into the complex polyphonic compositional shapes of the emerging fugue form of the fifteenth and sixteenth centuries, it was a new form 'alive with possibilities', which, Horsley writes, was:

'associated with projection of text and with the technique of formal construction—with practicality and not with pedantry.' She concludes: 'Then, as in many later periods, composers took pride in their technical skill and inventiveness, but that does not mean that they were not concerned with freedom and expressiveness'.[10]

HISTORY AND DEVELOPMENT OF FUGUE

> This quest for musical structure was associated in all its phases with the term fugue for originally, or eventually this term served each of the forms mentioned. In its first meaning, it identified the canon, but it was to be used in turn for the motet and its instrumental descendants, the ricercare, tiento, and fantasia. It was applied to the core, and at times to the very essence, of the canzona, of the toccata, and of the overture (even as late as Beethoven's Quarter Op. 133). It ruled the forms of the Baroque concerto and sonata and eventually bequeathed the structural achievements which it had gathered over three centuries to the classic sonata, yet retained its own life in the developmental technique, the "major element" that marked the "final decisive step" towards and beyond the Classic era...An understanding of the course that this search for musical form followed has grown only slowly —Albert Mann, *The Study of Fugue*[11]

From a brief overview of the historical development of the fugue in western music, several pertinent points can be made about its impact on and uses for literary construction and interpretation. The fugue was a form that adapted to social and cultural change until the dawn of modernity when it was overshadowed or superseded by new forms of more sophisticated music and tonality including the new Western harmony. The origins of the pre-modern fugue exemplify the expression, and development, of pre-modern melody; and this form still exists in the round that is sung by voices, in turn (such as *Three Blind Mice*). This was closer than later forms of the fugue to the melodic 'natural' music extolled by Rousseau, in his *Dictionary*. He wrote in *Essay on the Origin of Languages*: 'It is known that our harmony is a Gothic invention. Those who claim to find the system of the Greeks in ours are ridiculous'.[12] Instead, in the *Dictionary* he praised:

> the eastern languages, so sonorous, so musical... the Greek air, so delicate, so sensible, exercised with so much art.[13]

Rousseau heard it as evoking the 'natural' sense that he indicated of 'good melody' that takes and needs no 'supplement', it was not written down, but played by ear. The form of the fugue was flexible; in adhering to the principles of polyphony and imitative counterpoint, it did not 'degenerate' to a point where it became any less melodic. In the *Dictionary*, Rousseau criticized the 'invention of counter-point' as he saw it as the start of new western harmony, and:

> It is very difficult not to suspect that all our harmony is but a gothic and barbarous invention which should never have followed if we had been more sensible to the true beauties of art.[14]

Yet his criticism is ambiguous in relation to the fugue as it overlooks the melodic nature of the early counterpoint. The earliest forms of the pre-modern fugue articulated a musical language of dialogic communication between a group of voices taking turns to articulate the theme in different variations.

Mann records that the first known use of the term *fuga* in musical theoretical writings occurred around 1330. The *fuga* was amongst the main vocal forms—demonstrating the fugue's origins in the singing voice. In the late fifteenth century the Flemish theorist, Johannes Tinctoris, defined fuga as the technique common to both canon and round. Once imitative technique was identified by the term *fuga* it was recognized 'as a means of artistic expression, or art music', this is signified by Tinctoris referring to *fuga* as the means by which a composer may achieve musical variety. Mann writes: 'The emphasis upon free use of the imitative manner may seem surprising at a time which we customarily associate with contrapuntal art of amazing and mysterious strictness.' He adds: 'Yet it is doubtless this free, non-canonic use of imitation on which the most significant achievements of the time are founded'.[15]

As theory of musical fugal writing evolved, the distinctiveness of the form became clearer: 'moderne', requiring a certain choice of melodic material, thematic elements, variety and freedom of artistic expression and the 'imitation' of voices of each other—symbolizing secular interaction on the worldly plane, rather than reverence and worship through imitation of an idea of the sacred. In a growing reconciliation between the modal theory of sacred music and the tonalities of traditional western secular music, the modal music entered the realm of the secular. The transcendental 'sacred' exceeded the subject. The sacred was—figuratively speaking—brought down into the subject, so that the emission of the once sacred place sprang forth from the composer as subject in the form of his fugue writing (there is no record of female composers in this era of history). This symbolic exchange of transcendental idealism for transcendental empiricism—is enacted and played out in the changing secularizing form of musical language.

The Renaissance musicologist Vincentino's *modo moderne* signified a definitive break—or rupture—with the theoretical views and practices of the Middle Ages.[16] The specific principle that emerges from Vincentino's theoretical adapting of the fugal technique to the modal system has become known in modern musicological terminology as the *tonal answer*. That is, the answer of one voice to another through the medium of imitative counterpoint.

Figuratively speaking this is a shift away from the modal idea of the musical voice in a conversation with the sacred, to the tonal idea of the polyphonic musical voices of the fugue in conversation with each other, yet within a *cantus firmus*, a canonic modal form that keeps the voices within the limits of the melodic notes of the subject themes.

Seeking to interpret the history and development of the fugue raises social, cultural, and political questions concerning the relationship between the developments of musical language—at a certain time and place—and the cultural, social, and political contexts in which it developed. While it is beyond the scope of this inquiry to pursue these wider questions here, it is pertinent to go a little further into what is the basis of musical expression, and what is the relationship between music and language in specific cultural settings.

On a level of deep grammar, or psychoanalytic-linguistic language construction, what does the development (and subsequent decline) of the fugue as a musical form say about the societies and cultures in which it emerged, and then declined? These questions invite a further question. What is the basis of a national music style, in a given era? A famous dispute between Rousseau and Rameau, over melody versus harmony, focused on the Italian and French schools of opera. This dispute that divided Paris, in 1752, continued to resonate throughout the Jacobin period and the Romantic era into the nineteenth century. Interest in the wider function and application of musical language as a symbolic correlation, or analogy, to the changing social systems of modernity was to be later expressed subliminally as a dream-like counterpoint or double-voiced discourse in De Quincey's *The English*

Mail Coach with its third part called *Dream-Fugue*.

Here we can consider the significance of the practice of melody exemplified in pre-modern fugue. And what was it about melody, — what did it symbolize—that was to become so socially significant in aesthetic and political debate about 'melody and harmony' in the early European modernity of the mid to late eighteenth century? What also is the significance of the notion and practice of 'imitative counterpoint' in relation to (ancient and) contemporary discourse about 'representation' or the 'construction' of the subject and subjectivity in literary language? Aspects of these questions inform this fugal analysis.

CANON

The word *canon*, originating in Pythagorean philosophy, was adapted in Western usage as an ecclesiastical term for rule and law, and used in musicology for the rules or laws of composition of music (related to the church). Over time, it also came to mean a body of work, a collection or lists of works accepted as genuine, in music and literature. This signifies a classical connection between musical and literary language, which has continued into western modernity. The long-term cultural connections between musical and literary language development are indicated as already noted in the development of the Latin word *fuga* whose meanings include 'flight,' 'fleeing,' and 'to chase'. *Fuga* originally stood for what is now referred to as 'canon' by musicologists, that is, a style or piece with different parts taking up the same subject successively in strict imitation. The fugue however deviates from this strict imitative rule in its evocation of flight. Rather than adhering to 'strict imitation,' the voices in a fugue take turns, varying the subject theme in a range of inventive variations. Before the word and musical form of fugue came into being, the Latin *canon* (rule) meant, in music, a short motto or sentence. Associated with the Mot, or word, these mottos indicated, as may do a puzzle or a riddle the way in which a single musical part was meant to be performed or another part derived from it. Horsley gives the form of the rondeau (or round) as an example.[17]

Mann comments that it was connections to the church that tied medieval music to the notion of *Mot*, Latin for word, which referred to the sacred Word.[18] This usage was echoed in the musical form *motet*, a diminutive of 'mot.' Walker contends that motet represents a revolution in compositional process signified by the emergence of *pervading imitation*, precursor of vertical counterpoint; amongst the best-known composers of the motet were Nicolas Gombert, and Jacobus Clemens non Papa; in musical history, Clemens and Bach represent each 'end' of the main development of fugue, Clemens signifying its beginning, Bach its apex and end.[19]

Mann observes that the Church greatly increased the influence of vocal music, but as the Middle Ages declined an *ars nova* practice began encompassing musical forms beyond the church, drawing increasingly on secular texts, and then in a great leap towards secularism, on the drama of classical antiquity. This took the form of drama, and dramatic music in opera. After hundreds of years in subservient roles of accompanying dances and vocal forms, instrumental music was elevated to independent status. The ricercare, that describes a 'searching' for form, was an early form of fugal contrapuntal polyphony.[20]

Although Bach is the best known later fugue composer, who wrote fugues of great complexity, he was not the only one to do so. In Italy, Giambattista Martini (1706-1784), Franciscan friar, musician and composer wrote fugues of eight-parts, in *Esempare o sia saggio fondamentale prattico di contrappunto fugato* (1774-75).[21]

Joseph Maria Muller-Blateau's history of fugue *Grundzuge einer Geschichte der Fuge* (1923) also places the end of fugue with Bach, but Mann says it is wrong to consider fugue only as a fixed form in itself. He says the later fugues in Mozart's instrumentals and Bach's piano sonatas show that fugue has changed rather than declined, and ended. Mann argues that Muller-Blateau's book fails to conclude the history of three centuries of fugue writing did not lead to a 'formulaic' form and that the very attempt to 'freeze' it into 'the fugue' reduces this vital modality to a 'mere formula'.[22]

In *Music in the Baroque Era* (1947) Manfred Bukofzer declared that rather than fugue being a form or a texture 'strictly speaking the fugue was a contrapuntal procedure'.[23] Donald Tovey did describe fugue as a 'texture' in his entry in the *Encyclopedia Britannica* (eleventh edition): 'a texture the rules of which do not suffice to determine the shape of the composition as a whole'. He commented that 'the Italian fugue style is represented by hardly any strict works at all.'[24]

Initially confined to a church anthem, the mot eventually found a way into wider usage. It was not until the mid-late eighteenth century and the onset of modernity, that music became widely secular.

But fugue was an exception to the ecclesiastical music. As the fugue had never been based on text, but on canon, the communal fugue generated its own rules self-referentially and set its own terms (based on the sounds of its themes). When polyphony entered theory, and was first written, it had been in existence in popular music for hundreds of years. Due to its improvised nature, and its self-referentiality, in forms of song, early contrapuntal fugue music escaped the strictures placed on primarily text-based and sacred music. The fugue enacted its own live canon, generated from the polyphonic counterpoint of its interwoven voices. Both in its origins and in development after the sixteenth century it was a secular form, used for secular purposes.

POLYPHONY

Polyphony began with the interweaving of voices in singing. The beginnings of polyphony are heard in all the monophonic practices that involved the use of different yet simultaneous vocal part registers such as singing 'rounds' and these were based on melodies. Rousseau wrote:

> At first there was no music but melody and no other melody than the varied sounds of speech. Accents constituted singing...and one spoke as much by natural sounds and rhythms as by articulations and words.[25]

Polyphony was first imprinted and inscribed in musical notation in the early part writing of the Middle Ages. But before it was written, Horsley's research shows it existed in the informal yet carefully structured folk traditions of round singing.[26]

Horsley identifies the development of *Stimmtaush* as significant, it was the interchange of the melodic segments between voices, in the twelfth-century music of the Parisian Notre Dame School, and in thirteenth-and-fourteenth century motets. In some of these early motets counterpoint is found where two interchanged phrases are of equal length. 'This very early form of polyphony, and counterpoint, was created by inversion, or invertible counterpoint'.[27]

The early forms of the fugue originated through a mode of melodic dialogic music in which the voices or parts 'talk' to each other, through exposition, and answers. Across Europe, but particularly in Italy and Germany, this early 'conversation' grew in complexity and virtuosity, reaching an apex in the late fugues of Bach in the eighteenth century. Significantly the emergence of the polyphonic fugue form as a narrative plays out and enacts, as Mann observes, 'the gains and setbacks characteristic of the contest between the old and the new'.[28]

Mann writes that the *discantus*, or descant, regarded as the 'true spirit of polyphony', represents the achievement of a significant amount of melodic independence of part writing, when: 'contrary motion of different voices triumphed over direct and oblique motion'.[29] The fugue is based on melody. In its performance, it enacts a form of melodic difference, in which voices (instruments) articulate their themes in a contrary motion to each other. They do not blend or harmonize artificially in chords. Instead, the voices of a fugue retain their individual melodic integrity; a natural tonality of individuality and difference.

Fugue developed in time as a formalized art structure, in theory:

> A final reconciliation of the various polyphonic means was found when Western art music adopted and cultivated the techniques of imitation, which had probably existed for many centuries in the improvisations of popular musicianship.[30]

This meant that the use of polyphony now attained the linear strength of (horizontal) monophony, through counterpoint; it also achieved a new linear meaning as 'different voices performed the same melodic line',[31] in vertical contrapuntal formation, Mann writes. These voices were clearly distinguished through their spaced, or staggered, entries. A more definite balance of ascent and descent could now be achieved in the course of melodic lines following the principles of contrary motion and imitation. Contrary motion functioned in a move, which imitated through opposition, and thereby set up its own structural constraints or context, as the ascending passages called for a descending passage in response, countering the imitative entrance of the following part. This polyphonic motion thus created and enacted a form of musical flight.

As Max Weber also comments in *The Social and Rational Foundations of Music*, the quintessentially occidental form of polyphony, of several parts, or voices, in contrary motion or counterpoint, developed gradually. It may have represented a triumph of cultural achievement in musical accomplishment, yet when it first began to be written down, as it had emerged and developed as a sung vocal form, some problems became apparent.[32] This was because in writing polyphony what was essentially a form of naturally harmonizing voices, in a natural 'vertical' counterpoint became reabsorbed into a tradition of linear writing. The part-writings of polyphony in the twelfth century were applied to perfect consonances, and there was a narrow range, this thereby failed to provide early polyphonic writing with an unbroken melodic flow, Mann's research shows. Instead it produced some dissonant sounds, which Rousseau later criticized. However, polyphonic part writing was generally accepted and taken up. Although there were critics.

With contrary motion of ascent and descent, this complex structured form of polyphony evoked *images of voices chasing each other, or voices in flight.*

In tracing the development of the fugue form, Horsley comments that whilst the *rondellus* disappeared from use, the *round* or *rota*, the infinite form of canon found throughout the entire history of musical development, has continued to this day in the form of popular songs, and nursery rhymes that are sung as rounds. In the fourteenth century, a more sophisticated canonical variation of round appeared, known in France as *chace*, in Italy *caccia* and Spain *caca*. This type referred to the hunt or chase, and it is in this context that the fugal notion of voices chasing each other was formalized. It was at this time that the Latin word, *fuga*, was first applied to this form, Horsley suggests; *fuga* may have originally been a translation or mistranslation, of the French *chace*.[38] *Chace* remains to this day a prototype for simple compositional canons. There are significant differences in form between the round and the chace. And these extend analogously to concepts of narrative text.

The circular round is 'infinite canon', meaning that it has no natural stopping point, or end, it continues for as long as the singers decide to keep singing (compare to the form 'circular argument' or reflexive postmodern texts, and Romanticism's appeal to the infinite).

However, the hunting airs of *caccia* and *chace* ended the canon with a cadence, a rhythmic measured fall to close the musical phrase. The caccia and chace comprised two canons, one after another, as the text was divided into parts, as Horsley discusses. In these the leading voice was a long melody, which did not, necessarily, include any repetition, followed by a second part (or more) entering several measures later. Within this framework there was opportunity for variations, including madrigals, contrapuntal parts of highly developed melodic lines and imitation sounds of the hunt which included 'horn calls' incorporated into complex, virtuoso vocal lines.[34] This was in the form that was called 'hunting airs' that Rousseau writes of in his *Complete Dictionary of Music*.

Thus, we see that the musical canon or round was used to symbolically imitate the sounds of the hunt. This is an early form of musical (performative) imitative mimesis that recalls the narrative function of representation in written language where words are used to symbolically represent scenes in 'real life'.

Rounds and hunt music, were performed informally in social contexts for communal enjoyment. Music making as spontaneous social activity follows the tradition of communal, inventive, playful, social musical expression in folk and social secular settings. It would seem to fulfill Plato's criterion of beneficial health-giving social interaction through measured music and dancing. This contrasts—as a socialized cultured form—to the 'Dionysian' music making and dancing that Aristotle likened to tragedy for the benefit of cathartic release it provided for masses of ordinary citizens. Rousseau also confessed, in a 'Postscript' in *Letter to D'Alembert,* published in 1758, to a response to music and dancing in public space that is of relevance to this discussion; its relevance related not so much to any one particular musical form, but rather to Rousseau's response to a performance of music and dancing he participated in as a child, in a public square in Geneva, when he experienced a great joy. The regiment of Saint-Gervais had gathered in the public square, after finishing a meal, they spontaneously broke into song, dance, and music-making soon to be joined by womenfolk, maids and children, and Rousseau and his father: 'there resulted from all this a general emotion that I could not describe but which, in universal gaiety, is quite naturally felt.'[35] From this experience he concluded: 'the only joy is public joy, and the true sentiments of nature reign only over the people'.[36] The particular phenomenon Rousseau describes of joyful release is echoed in De Quincey's descriptions in his *Confessions*, of his rapturous experiences at Covent Garden, watching performances of musical interludes by Josephina Grassini. Rousseau's idea of beneficial entertainment in the form of musical gatherings in public squares is in striking contrast to his criticism of what he came to see as the immoral artifice of refined and sophisticated French theatre, at least for the people of his native Geneva, as he wrote in his *Letter to*

D'Alembert on Theatre.

The context of his Letter was that Voltaire had recently moved just outside Geneva, and was looking for a place to stage his plays. D'Alembert, editor of the Encyclopedia, had published an article in favour of this idea, which Rousseau was replying to. Rousseau had differences with D'Alembert, who had supported the French harmonic composer Jean-Philippe Rameau in the Querelle des Bouffons (discussed soon) and D'Alembert had published work by Rameau during the Querelle. Rousseau's criticism prefigured Brecht's didactic theatre, in which he aims to keep the audience members conscious that they are observers watching a performance so as not to identify too closely with the roles of the actors, and illusion, in trivial entertainments which might lead to the viewer losing awareness of him, or herself, rather than actively engaging in important social and ethical issues. An argument that has been waged since 'Book Ten' of Plato's Republic over the role of art in society—literary performative art as beneficial, edifying, and worthwhile as opposed to shallow, false, worthless entertainment. Rousseau believed republics should have natural assemblies of people:

> let the spectators become an entertainment to themselves, make them actors themselves, do it so that each sees and loves himself in the others so that all will be better united. [37]

Whereas Rousseau's criticism of the proposal to start a theatre in Geneva may seem contradictory (as he wrote plays as well as comic operas), he was criticizing the courtly and decadent artificial style of theatre, in Paris at that time.

VARIATIONS, TEXTURE AND NEW CONTEXTS

In the musical fugue's early development there were numerous forms that used fugue techniques or were variations of the fugue form, as Walker writes:

> There are many composers who wrote many fine pieces in many genres all of which are easily recognizable as fugal or in some way important to the fugue's development: ricercar, imitative fantasy, canzona, capriccio, toccata, verset, and occasionally fugue itself, not to mention the fugal writing to be found in sonatas for instrumental ensemble or in sacred and secular works.[38]

This seems to suggest there is something musically 'archetypal' about fugue 'texture', if not form, in musical compositional (and, too, in literary) language. This is not so surprising when one considers that the basic elements of fugue—polyphony and counterpoint—are fundamental to musical compositional language and form. It is for this very reason, as fugue techniques are used and applied in so many musical compositions, that musical scholars stress the importance of setting truth and meaning conditions, or limits by which to define the 'fugue' form.

Walker comments on the necessity felt by some scholars to attempt to define rules by which to judge and assess fugue works, arguing that in a sense this is an appropriate or understandable approach to take to the form: 'whose essence is its rigor born of rules and procedures that are almost purely musical.'[39] Of all musical forms, none can be more appropriately judged by the 'rules' it sets itself. Walker writes: 'A fugal composition succeeds or fails to the extent that its compositional creativity is held in check by a tightly controlled contrapuntal framework'.[40] Walker suggests that the modernist composer, Igor Stravinsky, might have been writing about the fugue when he spoke of the musical 'need for restriction'.

The questions that Walker raises in reference to seeking to establish criteria for defining musical fugue works also have relevance to analyzing literary composition; of course, in literary fugue narratives, the questions refer to literary context. Most particularly, if the modern creative process of writing is in some part unconscious, and its intentionality also in part unconscious, how can we set out to judge or assess a literary fugue work by its own standards, rules or terms? How can we assess these terms?

In investigating early development of the fugue, Walker emphasizes the enigma, perhaps paradox, of the fugue form. This is that, 'despite the word's infrequent use during the period as a genre designation, and thus its relatively infrequent appearance on musical manuscripts and prints, the idea of fugue, that is fugue as compositional technique remained very much alive'.[41]

Walker asks a number of questions as part of a strategy for identifying historical fugal works. These are interesting to consider since they have relevance to an interdisciplinary literary fugal analysis. Walker suggests the following approach:

> Is there a concept of fugal writing at any time during this period, and

if so how is its rigor defined? When is a composer attempting to write something that reflects this rigor and thus might be recognized as fugal? When is he not? What are his own biases in defining fugal rigor and how do they compare with the biases of earlier times? [42]

These questions may be usefully adapted and transposed to a literary fugal analysis of the development of fugue literary narratives. In the Part II literary fugue analyses, I have mainly focused on works that identify their influence by including 'fugue' in the title. While this accords with Werner Wolf's criterion for a musicalized literary work as one which makes a defining (preferably titular) reference to musical compositional form, many of the elements of fugue in its varied musical manifestations resonate strongly in the fugal form and texture in literary works.

Notwithstanding the quest for rigorous formal criteria, the fugue form has an intriguing tendency to vanish out of cultural social existence, to reappear, transformed, in another equally enigmatic cultural guise. This perhaps suits a modality of infinite variation, which generates and under-writes the processes of re-invention. Yet when new cultural forms materialize, this also calls for critical (as well as creative) re-assessment, re-reinterpretation and re-definition.

While the first known mention of the word *fuga* in a musical context was made around 1330, in *Speculum musicae* by Jacobus of Liege, it was before this that *fuga* appeared in the first known literary reference in Dante's *Divine Comedy*, written between 1306-21. In *Canto XIII* (from *The Second Circle: The Envious; Sapia of Siena*):

> Rotti fur quivi, e volti negli amari
> Passi di fuga, e, veggendo la caccia,
> Letizia presi; ad ogni altra dispari;[43]

> Beaten they were, and fled in bitter rout;
> And there thrilled through me when I saw the chase
> Such glee as 'til that hour I'd tasted not[44]

This indicates that the evolution of literary fugue was to some degree interwoven with, and paralleled, the evolution of the musical fugue, although the literary fugue most significantly developed as a form after the demise of the musical fugue. Dante's use parallels the linking of *fuga* with *caccia* or chase, an association that was occurring in the evolution of fuga as a musical form.

I suggest that Dante is, in part, in a play on words, referring to the musical form of fuga that is developing into the fugue. The next literary use of fugue was by Milton, which in turn prefigured and inspired De Quincey's *Dream-Fugue*. In Book XI of *Paradise Lost* Milton warns against the dangers of intemperance. The Archangel leads Adam to the top of the hill in an Eastern country, they gaze down at the plain. A settlement is below with tents.

> He look'd and saw a spacious Plaine, whereon
> Were tents of various hue; by some were herds
> Of Cattel grazing: others whence the sound
> Of Instruments that made melodious chime
> Was heard, of harp and Organ; and who moovd
> Their stops and chords was seen: his Volant touch
> Instinct through all proportions low and high
> Fled and pursu'd transverse the resonant fugue.[45]

In this, an ambiguous stanza, six lines (558-563) of which occur as an epigraph to De Quincey's *Dream-Fugue* (Chapter 7), Milton seems to be making a pun to do with the 'transverse...fugue' and physical congress between the people in the tents. In relation to the development of musical fugue it shows that Milton and therefore presumably (at least some of) his readers were viewing the musical form of fugue in relation to its potential symbolic and metaphorical aspects in relation to human behaviour and beginning to critically analyze received ideas about 'God' and humankind, an acknowledgment that God's 'volant' touch is everywhere. However, this represents a critical approach to the sacred which constituted an alternative viewpoint to orthodoxy, from the perspective of human-kind (in contrast to the disembodied objectified forms of writing in the Bible, for instance). Milton's use of the word fugue acknowledges its origins in *caccia*— chase.

The chase refers to the pursuit of love. But Milton also uses fugue in relation to its later development as a form of temperance and design—this meaning is suggested in the Archangel's warnings against intemperance. Milton thereby interwove the *caccia* and later meanings of fugue as a form of rationally tempered design into a narrative about God and humans, natural impulse, the chase and pursuit of love, and religious views of temptation and the follies of intemperance. These were themes that would have had a powerful presence in pre-modernity as Europe was heading towards a secular society. Milton's poem thereby held up a mirror to concerns of his day about the nature of faith, symbolically articulated in musical language of fugue.

In the Baroque era, in the works of one composer, the articulation of the 'subject' themes in the language of the fugue became increasingly complex, reaching an apex. In his use of puzzle canon, and mirror fugues, Bach mirrored the fascination, characteristic of Baroque art, with optical illusions, tricks of the eye (*trompe l'oeil* art works) hidden messages, double meanings, and invention, playing with the idea of infinity in infinite regression. In his puzzle canons, Bach wrote and sent messages coded into notations that only those who knew the fugal musical language could understand. The articulation of the subject symbolized in Bach's works included two main elements characteristic of his time, first was scientific reason; second was the articulation of a belief or desire for mystery, symbolized in a striving for infinity in his mirror fugues. Approaching modernity two major social, political, moral and aesthetic concerns articulated in Bach's fugues: which enact a dual construction of faith and reason.

It is significant for the purposes of this investigation that Bach is the 'name' that is associated with the art of fugue. This is due to the complex artistry of Bach's fugues. It is in their artistry that makes his fugues more than exercises of examples for his students to learn the art of fugue (which some sources say is the reason he wrote *Die Kunst der Fuge*). It is this artistry which sets him apart and which 'individualizes' his fugues. In this, he most resembles a modern artist—who in any artistic medium is known for the articulation of his/her individualistic 'subjectivity' in language as a medium of creative art. Bach then was a precursor to the modern artist who emerged in the late-seventeenth century, as a result of the legislation of property rights including copyright for intellectual property. But Bach was not 'modern'. His works articulate and interweave two major themes that characterized European society approaching modernity: faith and reason. In the pre-modern Baroque, music and science were seen to be unified—a system of belief that in a way evokes the beliefs of the Pythagoreans in the connection between music and mathematics. Music was considered to be a 'sounding mathematics' (in Leibniz's phrase), with Bach one of its foremost composers.

In the life and work of Bach we can see major social, political and aesthetic influences of the Baroque interweaving to shape the articulation of the 'subject' in his fugue works. It was in these works especially that can be seen the diverging currents of secularism, epitomized by reason, and the sacred, epitomized in Bach's own adherence to faith. Both these influences were given free play in his fugue works that were not composed, as was his church music as *Kapellmeister*, primarily for performance in church. Amongst scholars, Bach's attitude to Pietism is considered to be of some significance, as Malcolm Boyd points out in his biography of Bach. Recent research has investigated the degree to which Bach was a rationalist and the significance of this, including the extent to which his compositional mind can be illuminated by analogy with the metaphysics of the rationalist philosophers, such as Leibniz and Spinoza. Scholars have examined the significance of Bach's involvement in Mizler's Society which Bach joined three years before his death. Comprising composers and music theorists, this was a society of 'intellectually minded musicians' which Mizler founded on a neo-Pythagorean proposition that mathematical rubrics could be used to explain artistic, and philosophical and natural phenomena.[46] There is significance in relation to the musical mind in Leibniz's dictum published by Mizler: 'Music is the hidden arithmetical exercise of a mind unconscious that it is calculating'.[47] Mizler stipulated that a composer: 'must have a rational intention'; Bach's involvement was at least indicative of his interest in the doctrines of eighteenth-century style Rationalism.

In this chapter I have investigated several structural techniques of the musical fugue, which, as we shall see, have been transfigured in the writing of literary fugue narratives. These techniques include polyphony that converts into dialogism; the use of counterpoint that converts into the building up of narrative layers; the use melody lines or subject themes that convert into literary themes; the use of recurring motifs that convert into recurring literary motifs, images or verbal references, which recur throughout fugal literary works. Overall, the form of the musical fugue is itself a migrating figure, which lends itself to diverse and varied literary and cultural interpretation. Of particular interest to this thesis is that, as a musical form, the fugue is primarily pre-modern. It reached its apex in the Baroque era preceding modernity. By the time De Quincey wrote *Dream-Fugue,* the fugue as a musical form had fallen from common cultural use.

ROUSSEAU, RAMEAU, AND THE DISPUTE OVER HARMONY: QUERELLE DES BOUFFONS

One observation that arises from this discussion is the extent to which musical language and the systems of musical forms appear to represent and reflect a society's political and cultural beliefs. And how this in turn affects and perhaps determines the ways in which the subject is symbolized and constructed in musical and literary language. In the early musical language of fugue there is no construction of 'subjectivity' as we now understand this—as a perhaps illusory construction of an authorial 'I' that conjures an illusion of a solid presence or a personality in the coded meanings of words. This was a development in literary language that was exemplified in the affective, expressive, writings of Romanticism. And certainly preceded by Rousseau in his *Confessions*, and many other literary works.

Towards the end of the Baroque era what lay ahead in European consciousness was a split between reason and faith, the amplification of musical language and form into the arena of moral and political discourse, which was to see music used to analogously symbolize the very systems and structures of human society in modernity. On the cultural horizon, also, was a celebrated public dispute, between composers Jean-Jacques Rousseau and Jean-Philippe Rameau, the *Querelle des Bouffons* (Quarrel of the Comic Actors), also known as the *Guerre des Bouffons*, and *Guerre des Coins* (War of the Corners), over the relative merits of Italian melody and new French harmony, mentioned above. This dispute was so significant it has been said of it that it prolonged the reign of the Ancien Régime.[48] In a series of exchanges, the dispute consisted of a series of 'parries and thrusts', of rebuttals and further elaborations of intellectual positions, that took place in pamphleteering, and letter writing, in salons and in public cafés.[49]

This politicized aesthetic musical conflict emerged in 1752, following the arrival at the Opera of Eustacchio Bambini's touring company playing *La Serva Padrona* (The Maid as Mistress) by Giovanni Battista Pergolesi. This was a comic Italian *opera buffa*, an *intermezzo* or short opera performed during the intermission of the long French opera; it was the first time such an intermezzo had played in the Paris Opera. It divided the city into support for the Italian, and French operas. Italian based on the natural human voice, and French based on the principles of new western harmony, that is, on rules and 'artificial' chord-based language. The Italian style was seen as symbolizing freedom of artistic expression—that is expression of emotion and affect, and addressed ordinary people, with problems of poverty. In comparison, the French style of lyric tragedy of Rameau was seen to symbolize appearance, the 'dignity and ornate splendor of the ancient regime',[50] and its audience were from the aristocratic classes. Supporters of the Italian opera gathered in the 'King's corner', under the royal box, and French music supporters met under the 'Queen's corner'. This was also the year that Rousseau's opera in Italian folk style, *Le Devin du Village* (The Village Soothsayer) was performed for the first time, at court in Fountainbleau (on the 18th October 1752). It was highly popular and was performed again the following year at the Paris Opera (on the 1st of March 1753).

Rousseau, who wrote several operas and libretti in the Italian folk style, was a supporter of the Italian opera. 'Man was born free, and he is everywhere in chains' he wrote famously in *Du Contract Social* (The Social Contract) (1762). A liberationist who believed in the goodness of humankind, and therefore the benefit of artistic expression, Rousseau directed his attack (amplified in articles in the *Encyclopedia* later collected in his *Complete Dictionary of Music*) at Jean-Philippe Rameau, the leading living exponent of French operatic music, author of *Traité de l'harmonie réduite à ses principes naturels* (Treatise on Harmony), published in 1722 (and with whom he had personal differences). Rousseau believed that melody is closer to natural expression of the voice; and he publicly denounced the new system of harmony, as rule-bound and artificial. Rousseau's argument was given political resonance, by his contention that in art free expression is more important than following rules, on political grounds. Rousseau thereby privileged melody in what later came to be recognized as a definitive idea of Romanticism, which is that art as the expression of the free spirit takes precedence over the strict adherence to rules, codes and conventions of language. On the other hand, Rameau believed that harmony is bestowed directly from nature and that it is the means of imposing order onto chaos.

In his criticism of the style of Rameau's long operas, based on large scale dance-tableaux with fantastical mythical beings representing the monarchs and aristocrats, which were performed at the Paris Opera for the monarchy and aristocracy, he tapped into a public sentiment, prior to the French Revolution, which diverted attention and fanned a controversy that enabled the regime to continue a few years longer, as he wrote in his *Confessions*.

> A description of the incredible effect of this pamphlet would be worthy of the pen of Tacitus. It was at the time of the great quarrel between the courts [Le Parlement de Paris] and the clergy. The courts had just been dissolved; the excitement was at its height; there was every danger of an approaching revolt. My pamphlet appeared, and immediately all other quarrels were forgotten; no one could think of anything except the threat to French music. The only revolt now was against me, and such was the outburst that the nation never quite recovered from it. At Court they were merely deciding between the Bastille and banishment; and the warrant of arrest would certainly have been signed if M. de Voyer had not shown how ridiculous it all was.[51]

Rousseau at two points in his life that he writes of in his *Confessions*, rejected opportunities for a well-paid job, to instead pursue his chosen vocation as author and composer, the first time when he turned down the chance to be the cashier to the Receiver-General of Finance; after filling in this vacancy for a few weeks he became ill, and gave up the offer of a permanent position to become a music copyist to support his writing.[52] A few years later, he did not fulfill an invitation to be presented to King Louis XV (and likely patronage) for his opera *Le Devin du Village*.[53] When Rousseau published *Letter on French Music*, incensed musicians in the Opera orchestra plotted to assassinate him; and his author pass was revoked.[54] None of this seemed to hinder the popularity of his opera, or the sales of his books.

Rousseau justified his decisions: 'Nothing vigorous, nothing great, can flow from an entirely venal pen'...

> I have always felt that the profession of author is not and never could be an honourable and illustrious one except in so far as it is not a trade. It is too difficult to think nobly when one thinks only for a living. If one is to have the strength and the courage to speak great truths one must not depend on one's success. I threw my books to the public in the certainty that I had spoken for the common good, and without a care for anything else.[55]

Rousseau publicly opposed Rameau's view that affirmed the first principle of French Classicism, to wit conformity to rules and codes.[56] In contrast, for Rousseau, who professed to believe in the fundamental goodness of humankind, melody was the euphonious expression of the human voice, the free spirit. This was the most significant public expression in the mid-eighteenth century of the ongoing debate over the relative merits of appearance signified by artifice, sophistication and technique, and a deeper hidden meaning in creative art—a debate about representation that originated in Book Ten of *The Republic*.

The dispute between Rousseau and Rameau was of the zeitgeist, it struck not only at the nature of human creativity and artistic expression but even more widely at the very core of the way that modern society was organized and structured. Later, Max Weber would contend that harmony is one of the main organizational systems of rationalization in modern society.[57]

In this chapter I have lightly traced history and development of the changing articulation of the 'subject' in the musical form of the fugue, in two ways: the development of the articulation of the subject—as the subject *theme* (or themes) of the musical fugue; and the concurrent evolution of subject as the *composer*, articulating the subject and subjectivity in the form of musical language. This is a symbolic difference with echoes in contemporary discourse about representation in writing and the articulation (or representation) of subjectivity.

As with origins of dramatic literary art and poetry in ancient times, the origins of the fugue form have been shown to be not textual but canonic—of the musical sound of the singing voice, transposed into the musical sound of instruments in Europe in the Middle Ages. In the climate of Rationalism and Reason, there were those who continued to associate music with mathematics and scientific principles into the mid-late eighteenth century. This represented a form of dissociation between emotion and reason, which was fundamentally challenged by Rousseau, and that has resonated throughout modernity. The form and especially the texture of the musical fugue have rich associations and analogues with the fugal mode in literature.

4

IDENTITY SHIFTS, FUGAL RECURSION

'Whosoever loses his life, shall find it' (Greek proverb)

FUGAL JOURNEYS

Having mapped a number of formative ideas about the fugue and its development, the following chapters examine two main issues, both problematic, which arise in the methodology of fugal analysis. The first is the psychogenic fugue used as an analogy for the writing process, particularly as it relates to the life experiences of the authors whose works are discussed in the literary studies in Part II. The second problematic area is the degree to which the polyphony and dialogism of the fugue does or does not convert into 'proper' literary terms. This includes the relevance of polyphony and dialogism to literary texts, and motifs as fixed rhetorical devices that seem to recur throughout literary narrative works. This inquiry also moves outside the terrain of literary critical terms and makes use of musical terminology per se. As part of my exploration of wider uses of musical terminology, I will later consider how some musical terms are interpreted, and function, in the textual work of literary cultural theorists including Edward Said and Mikhail Bakhtin, in preparation for the main literary analyses.

I recognize that in some respects I move outside what appear to be conventional critical boundaries. First, I list a number of terms that are or can be used in musico-literary analysis. Then I invoke fugue as a psychogenic fugue and consider it in relation to a subjective moment of writing. Closely connected to this is the way I will treat aspects of writers' biographies and specifically their experiences of traumatic life events, reflected in ways in which they write, how they write adapting musical fugue techniques, as well as what they write of. Methodological issues arise in drawing on fugue as documented in medical and psychiatric literature. I do not intend to pathologize writers in relation to the psychogenic fugue, nor am I making reductionist claims that diminish the notion of a fugal modality of writing into a psychogenic condition of fugue. But my argument does draw on aspects that have an application of conversion in relation to the writing process. Later on, I draw on medical accounts of post-traumatic stress disorder as a limited model in relation to some elements I have noticed in biographies of the authors whose work I consider in the case studies.

This approach thus extends the affects of reading to the psychogenic fugue, and it extends the critical terminology of literary terms to make use of musical terms in relation to literary writing. A certain symbolic, as well as rhetorical, structure of writing is identified in the works of the literary case studies. Issues of affect, the quality of the experience of the writer, and the quality of affective experience performatively embodied in the writer's writing necessarily arise in considering the psychogenic fugue as it can be applied in writing.

MUSICO-LITERARY TERMS

Intermedial Synaesthetic Textual Fugue:
The textual fugue is kinetically, articulated and inscribed into language form that can be musical or literary (or visual). It uses techniques of fugal musicalization. Textual literary fugues (analyzed here) range in length from a short poem to voluminous, continuous novel. Its length and use, function and form will be determined by its composer who decides on the melody themes, and on the notes of the melodic phrases. The textual literary fugue involves constitutive multi-sensory input, and is synaesthetic, and intermedial. As with fugue music composition, a writer (composer) arranges the 'rules'.

Fugal Recursion:
A concept of reflexivity, which 'puts on hold' one voice, whilst another picks up and plays the theme.

Fugal Melody:
The fugue, which emerged strongly in Italy and German, exemplifies the polyphonic secular use of European pre-modern melody.

Literary Polyphony:
The musical art of polyphony (exemplified in fugue) translates into writing of polyphonic literary narratives in several main ways: voices

of many interwoven characters, as in Joyce's *Ulysses*; the multiple voices of a narrator engaged in a search through their own consciousness, and memory, articulating different aspects of themselves, a (remembered or lost) time, as in Proust's *À la recherche*. Rather than implying a schizophrenic kind of dissociation on the part of the author, use of multiple narrative voices by an implied author is an exercise of the flight of the fictionalizing imagination.

Dialogism- Mikhail Bakhtin:
Bakhtin's term for the interplay and intertextuality of voices in cultural production. The term dialogism refers to uses of polyphony, derived in part from analysis of Dostoevsky's novels. Bakhtin's rhetorical terms associated with these uses include: cultural hybridization, the mutual influence of diverse cultural forms and speakers on each other; heteroglossia, the mixing of diverse languages, cultures and races in overall context such as a novel or a social grouping; juxtaposition, the conceptual and material patterns of form in which this mixing occurs in textual literary works: and utterance, the articulation of expression of any communicating being or entity whose understanding and meaning is on Bakhtin's view necessarily modified and shaped by the context in which the utterance is a) made by an addresser (sender) and b) received by the addressee (receiver). This constitutes Bakhtin's concept of addressivity according to which all cultural and creative processes are a form of dialogue/communicated in a tripartite relation of addresser, addressed, addressee. Literary dialogism is characteristic of modernity. It was relatively rare until the Renaissance. Chaucer's *Canterbury Tales* with its rendition of traveller's tales was one of the first examples of a dialogic, polyphonic novel. The terms in which Bakhtin perceived the creative role and function of the dialogic novelist recall the finely tuned art of polyphonic musical fugues. A dialogic, or polyphonic style is also particularly apparent in the use of forms of pastiche, parody and satire. The tradition of polyphony, or dialogism, stretches back in Western literary history to Menippean satire—a form of satire Kristeva refers to as 'carnivalesque', that has been used since Ancient Greece to satirize and comment on ideological pretensions, worldly aspirations and to react to the use of language as the 'law'.

Counterpoint:
Interweaving of 'voices' (not necessarily verbal, a visual image of effect can be a 'voice'). Counterpoint works in literary writing on a more

conceptual level than musical counterpoint for the simple reason that polyphonic literary voices cannot be literally enacted in writing. Whereas it is not possible to literally replicate the effect of instruments playing different melody lines simultaneously, the effect of simultaneity is produced in writing through alternating voices. Awareness of the previous voices therefore informs the readers' reading of each voice or section in turn, thus developing a contrapuntal effect in the reader's mind. The narrative is therefore not linear, but multi-linear, comprising a complex interweaving of voices and points of view. Literary writers have adapted the musical concept in new forms of contrapuntal language.

Western Instrumental Rationality- Max Weber
Weber contended that modern Western societies are rational and systemic, dominated by instrumental reason based on principles applied impersonally. These systems are: the economy, law, science, architecture, and music. Weber based his views on music on the rise of the tempered scale in Western counterpoint and harmony, and the Western system of notation that emerged in modernity. An extreme application of Western music as an instrument of scientific irrationalism occurred in the World War II holocaust, where music was instrumentally used to choreograph the unspeakable routines of forced labour camps and death camps.

Contrapuntal Reading- Edward Said:
A term coined by Edward Said in the context of reading, in a postcolonial context, cultural texts written and produced by authors from colonizing cultures with an awareness of the wider contexts of the colonized, who may not even be referred to directly in these literary texts. A contrapuntal reading of *Jane Eyre*, for instance, is to have awareness of the context of the wider social, cultural, and political conditions of colonized peoples on the sugar plantations in the British colonies of the time. Derived from counterpoint, the term evokes the polyphony of a fugue where all voices take turns and have parity in the musical 'conversation'. It extends to indicate a reading where 'voices' that may be imperialistically overlooked according to dominant ideology are given parity of consideration by the reader.

Cultural Hybridity- Homi Bhabha:
A term developed by Homi Bhabha in observation of the creation of cultural artifacts such as art works by artists who change locations in

cultures. It relates to the fugal analogy in reference to different aspects and elements of cultural artifacts brought into conversation in new arrangement. Cultural hybridity infers a process of heterogeneity in contrast to homogenization.

Recurring Motifs:

In a musical fugue, a recurring motif takes the form of a melody, a sequence of notes that recurs. In a written text, a recurring motif may comprise any phenomenon—such as an image or phrase that recurs in the text and/or in the writing. In modernist literary narrative (non realist) phenomena may comprise a token of evocation of a person, in visual image, a line of words, a phrase of music, mood, expressed in different ways and forms at various times throughout the narrative. Well known recurring motifs include Proust's 'madeleine', and 'Vinteuil's little phrase'. Recurring motifs function as a mnemonic device, memory aid, in the text, in the process of writing.

Subject and Counter-subject (Answer):

A fugue has subject lines, melodic themes, which are counterpoised. As in a dialogue, a counter-subject answers a starting subject line. This begins the fugue.

Voices:

A fugue's voices enunciate, play, and develop the melodic subjects or themes. There are usually about four voices, and two themes though Bach's fugues were more complex.

Variations on the theme:

Reversal, inversion, repetition, elaboration, embellishment, mirroring are forms of variation (in Bach's most complex mirror fugues his mirroring regressed to infinity).

Exposition:

The beginning part of the fugue in which all the voices make their entry.

Staggered Entry:

Voices enter in the exposition in a staggered entry after another.

Stretto:

(In quicker time) Stretto may be used at any point in the fugue. It has been suggested that some parts of De Quincey's *Dream-Fugue* enact an impassioned form of literary stretto.

Free Episodes:

The voices play with, or freely state their themes.

Double-Counterpoint (and Discourse):
A form of counterpoint for voices in which the dominant voice switches place with the subordinate and vice versa. This fugal device has obvious uses for literary depictions of changing power balances in social relations. The musical concept, practice and term double counterpoint evokes Bakhtin's concept of a dialogic double-voiced discourse—that is discourse that contains a deliberate reference, though not overtly stated, to other words. Bakhtin identifies several specific types of double-voiced discourse. Those that have received most attention in contemporary cultural theory are parody and hidden polemic. These operate on a subtextual level, imparting messages to the reader on a subliminal level. The type of parodic writing referred to by Bakhtin as 'doubly-oriented discourse,' subliminally recalls fugal counterpoint. This is seen when, for instance, a modernity novelist (or anti-novelist) may adopt a deliberately 'inappropriate', contrasting ironically (too) 'appropriate' narrative style to write a story. For instance, Joyce uses a mock classical-heroic style in *Ulysses*, which may seem to parody the decidedly unheroic modern life of his protagonist Bloom. It may also seem to satirize the classical concept of a heroic epic Homecoming journey. Yet perhaps it also expresses a subliminal desire and will, for Home: a poignant desire in the context of colonized Ireland prior to Independence, and Joyce's self-exile and sense of *unheimlich* in his life, and the English language.

Coda and Cadence:
The last movement of a fugue. A coda of cadence can end with all or just a couple, of the subject voices.

Imbrication:
Overlaps like tiles. An adjective used in relation the fugue to describe 'overlapping' of voices in stretto. In recent years imbrication has been used in contemporary critical discourse to refer to an intense overlapping of concepts and ideas.

Word-music:
A term used by Steven Paul Scher and also by Werner Wolf to denote the musicalized use of words, where a musical effect is achieved in onomatopoeia, rhyme, and rhythm. Joyce makes word-music, when he creates new musicalized words to express the music of his text.

Verbal Music:
A term to describe the articulation of word music with which it is interchangeable.

Melopoetics:
The complex relationship of poetry and music, involving a musical quality in poetic words.

Memory Involuntary:
Memory and loss of awareness of self-identity constitute an a-semantic link in the writing processes of composition—particularly in the 'inspirational' mode of compulsion to write poetry and make art. Paradoxically this process of invention from memory also involves forgetting, a form of fugal recursion—putting on hold parts of the composition whilst working on other parts.

Arrangement:
In Music to arrange is to compose, put into order the voices, elements of the composition. Bakhtin developed a meaning of 'arrangement' as juxtaposition. Arranging elements in juxtaposition to each other can give rise to and create new meanings—in the arrangement. Analogies between elements and aspects of musical and literary composition provide a conceptual plane and field for mutual influence in which techniques, and modes of each form may be subliminally adapted, transposed and rearranged. Exact transposition between music and literary language appears literally impossible (although it is now happening visually in digital media), yet music-word intermediality is the affective mode of writing of many writers who wish to create original works in literary language.

FUGUE NARRATIVES

There are significant examples of modern literary works that include the psychogenic dissociative fugue as a symbolic structure, such as Mann's *Der Tod in Venedig* (Death in Venice) (1912). In Mann's novella, Aschenbach wanders away from his normal life on an untypically spontaneous journey, a metaphorical flight to Venice. This takes him beyond the safe boundaries of his highly disciplined life and self-identity as a successful author in Weimar Germany into areas of desire and homoerotic yearning that Aschenbach has long repressed. He follows his desire into a kind of poisoned Arcadia, losing his old identity in the city of Venice gripped by cholera. Entranced by the sight of Tadzio, a young boy staying at the same hotel with his family, Aschenbach gladly ignores the warning signs of the epidemic and instead *in a fugal haze* embraces his own death.

Der Tod in Venedig enacts a symbolic fugue structure in several ways. First, Aschenbach wanders off on an impulsive journey of which he informs no one. Second, is a loss of awareness of his previous identity. He behaves in ways out of character for the esteemed literary writer, Gustave von Aschenbach. His lack of stability, increasing self-deception and state of denial are physically demonstrated in an ill-conceived cosmetic enhancement at a hotel barber shop in Venice, where his appearance is transformed through rouge, powder, and black hair dye. This is a symbolic attempt to disguise more than his age. Hitherto unknown or suppressed aspects of his personality emerge to take control of his destiny. Whereas fugue is often a temporary condition, in *Death in Venice* it leads Aschenbach to his death that coincides with the novella's end, thus the fugue is symbolically enacted as literary structure in itself. This kind of fugue narrative enacts a journey into an underworld, in which a physical journey is accompanied by an inner journey into a protagonist's own unconscious desires. It may be accompanied by a loss of previous self-identity, the assumption of a new identity. The symbolic structure used by Mann can be read in Moore's *In the Cut* (1996). In this contemporary novella the main protagonist Frannie, like Aschenbach, is a writer who lives a solitary life, and who also falls into a self-negating obsessive love for a 'fatal' object of desire. In Frannie's case, her object of desire is a corrupt, murderous detective who leads her on a journey into an underworld of sexual risk-taking, and her fugal death—when she is murdered by her lover's male detective 'buddy', his partner in crime.

Such symbolic structures have a mythological or even archetypal ancestry. In Greek mythology: fugal symbolic structures in the story of Persephone, a myth of renewal or rebirth; the myth of Orpheus where the musician god, bereft at losing his beloved wife Eurydice, is struck by fatal guilt when due to his own actions (looking back when Hades warned him not to) he loses the chance he has almost won of her resurrection.

These symbolic structures carry associated themes of desire and loss of awareness of identity, traumatic shock, grief, mourning, melancholia and metamorphosis in the form of rebirth or metempsychosis. Whereas in the Persephone myth the goddess re-emerges each spring from the underworld, in the Orpheus myth Eurydice remains in the underworld and Orpheus too loses his life (after Eurydice's death he can love no woman—and he is torn apart and devoured by frenzied maenads, female devotees of Dionysus).

NEW LIMITS OF REPRESENTATION

Recently, the problem of representation has been reactivated and re-assessed in relation to artistic representation and academic theorizing, after the Holocaust, and following Adorno's controversial dictum: 'To write poetry after Auschwitz is barbaric'. (Nach Auschwitz ein Gedicht zu schreiben, ist barbarisch).[1] Adorno later retracted this statement, in its extreme form as a literal exhortation, and said he may have been wrong, and contextualized it within the horror of post traumatic shock and survivor-guilt following the Holocaust.[2] This is discussed in relation to *Todesfuge* by Paul Celan, in Chapter 9. The link between authorial post-traumatic stress disorder and the uses of the (archetypal) musicalized structure and techniques of fugue as a form of writing is evident in relation to Holocaust poetry. But there is another specific issue of representation confronting art from the unspeakable horror of the Holocaust, which Susan Gubar identifies in her article 'The Long and the Short of Holocaust Verse' in *New Literary History* (Vol. 35, No. 3. 2004). She draws attention to two types of poetic representation, based on and articulating extreme trauma.

> The enormity of the event [Holocaust] often propelled poets in two diametrically opposed directions: on the one hand, towards ellipses, fragmentation, in short poems that exhibit their inadequacy by shutting down with a sort of premature closure; on the other, towards verbosity in long poems that register futility by reiterating an exhausted failure to achieve closure.[3]

Gubar quotes Deleuze and Guattari's dictum, the deterritorialization of language: the traumatized de-homed nomad may creatively utilize expression when 'Language stops being representative in order to now move beyond its extremities or its limits'. Gubar makes a symbolic connection between the *form* of poetic expression and the traumatic *experience* articulated by its author. She claims: 'Severely limited and extremely elongated Holocaust poems communicate how alienated their authors are from the native idioms they deploy or how estranged their adopted idioms are from the disaster they seek to address'.[4]

This implicitly references the concept of dislocation, *unheimlich* or as *Die Unheimlichkeit* literally 'unhousedness' or 'not-at-home-ness', but which has also been translated as 'uncanny' or 'uncanniness'. Felstiner suggests this concept (that is associated with Heidegger) has relevance to Paul Celan in reference to his position as Jew, survivor of the Holocaust, poet and exile, in relation to the German language in which he continued to write poetry.[5]

The 'extremely elongated' writing Gubar identifies as performatively demonstrating: 'an exhausted failure to achieve closure' is the most extreme case of fugal writing from trauma. Its form has taken it beyond the limits of representation to a kind of exhausted psycho-linguistic self-referentiality of traumatic shock. Some of the poems Gubar refers to—in *Poetry After Auschwitz*—were written by people who were murdered in the Holocaust, their poems found posthumously, for instance in pockets of their clothes. They wrote from their experience of unspeakable horror, bearing witness to one of the crimes against humanity in European history. Their poems are testimonies to the strength, courage and beauty of the human spirit. They are memorials showing that in times of absolute horror, and unspeakable inhumanity, there were still *people* who could write poetry. The perpetrators of barbarous murder could not take away their humanity, and integrity.

For those who survived and wrote, the trauma, of course, does not end. Fugal writers unable to achieve closure of the originating experience have replays that recur in involuntary memories through their waking and sleeping dreams (in the form of nightmares). This is a sign and symptom of what is now termed post-traumatic stress disorder. A form of writing chosen to express this authentically, performatively reflects this state of mind. It may be uncomfortable to read Holocaust poetry in the same context as the other fugue narratives. The purpose is not to make comparisons, but to draw attention to the reality and authenticity of writing from emotional trauma in extreme situations. This kind of writing at times seems to unconsciously find, and express, itself in a highly condensed, archetypal fugal form.

Friedlander discusses a crucial facet of representation and limits in the context of postmodern culture. He acknowledges there are problems in theorizing, discussing and representing the Holocaust, in an academic theoretical context. He identifies problems specifically related to the epistemological, aesthetic, ideological position of postmodernism, as opposed to traditional and modernist modes of representation, the problem is one of limits and boundaries. Postmodernist thought rejects 'the possibility of identifying some stable reality or truth beyond the constant polysemy and self-referentiality of linguistic constructs'.[6] Postmodern thought postulates the multiplicity of infinite interpretation over 'grand' or master meta-narratives of totalizing views of history—and literary narratives. This was intended to counter totalitarian or hegemonic thought. Whilst, Friedlander argues, an acknowledgment of ambiguity is certainly useful, if not necessary, in relation to representing and discussing unspeakable horror, a context of limits is also necessary.

Postmodernist thinking (and he mentions Lyotard), questions the validity of: 'any totalizing view of history, of any reference to a definable metadiscourse, thus opening the way for a multiplicity of equally valid approaches'. Friedlander claims this may lead to 'any aesthetic fantasy'.[7] He argues that in relation to discussing, theorizing and representing the Holocaust (Shoah) it is important to establish a stable truth. Friedlander's discussion suggests it is important to establish a context of truth and interpretation for the reading and understanding of *all* the modern literary narratives, derived from experiences of traumatic shock, some of which—like Celan's work—involve representations of the Holocaust (Jewish Shoah). The cultural 'misreading' of Celan's *Todesfuge* shows that postmodern notions of openness and multiplicity can be and are used against those who support freedom of expression—especially by the totalitarian, or hegemonic, powers postmodernism 'ironically' purports to refute. The issues arising may indeed extend beyond the domain of traumatic shock.

In postwar Germany, *Todesfuge* was included as a text in secondary schools to help foster the reunification of Jewish and German children. This publicly showed the acceptance of Celan as a poet, however he publicly made clear that he did not intend the meaning of the motifs of 'golden haired Margarete and 'ashen haired Sulamith' to be 'reunification.' In 1953 Celan was accused of plagiarism by Claire Goll, wife of the deceased French Jewish poet, Yvan Goll, which led to Celan needing to have a spell in a psychiatric clinic. He was accused in an open letter of 'stealing' the metaphors of 'Todesfuge'. John Felstiner, Celan's biographer, writes that the ensuing debate in West Germany profoundly disrupted Celan, who detected deeper sinister reverberations in the accusation. Celan answered those who rebuked him for writing in the language of his parents' murderers, which was the language taught to him by his mother who loved the German language: 'Only in the mother tongue can one speak one's own truth. In a foreign tongue a poet lies'. In 1960, the plagiarism accusations were declared unfounded.[10]

Celan did not intend *Todesfuge* to be interpreted in 'black and white' terms as a postwar reunification text, in which the two iconic female figures, Margarete and Sulamith, representing German and Jew were interpreted in the end as metaphorically linking arms, when he meant it to say something quite different (which it certainly does). His poem also points to the 'grey' area of moral ambiguity and guilt, of survivors.

Primo Levi writes in of the moral dilemmas facing the victims, who were, for a while, spared death, for collaborating under coercion from the Jews who were coerced by their Nazi captors, to execute the orders and operate the machinery of death whereby millions of their fellows were killed. Levi termed this a 'grey zone' in relation to representing the victims who were coerced into actions that sent fellow inmates of ghettos to their deaths in concentration camps; and in death camps, the Jewish victims in the one-thousand strong 'Special Squad' who operated the machinery of mass murder, the gas chambers and ovens of Auschwitz, where hundreds of thousands of innocent people were murdered on an industrial scale. Squad members did this in return for food to keep themselves alive, and copious amounts of alcohol. Every few months, each Squad was replaced, by a new group of 'crematorium ravens' selected by the Nazis, their first task was to kill and incinerate their predecessors. This was meant to ensure that the Nazis' mass murders were kept secret, writes Levi who was a prisoner in Auschwitz for one year, before the end of the war. He wrote of this in *The Drowned and the Saved* (1986),[8] Levi argues that one should not judge the decisions and actions made by the Jewish, Roma and others captive in concentration camps and ghettos. He believes that whereas perpetrators should be judged, it is morally wrong to pass a judgement on the victims who, under coercion, compromised and collaborated, and thus lost or had, further, stolen from them their humanity and selves.

The reply to this argument is that if no one had compromised or collaborated then such an atrocity could not have happened. For the same argument is used in defense of the German citizens who did not speak out to stop this from happening: they collaborated because, it is said, because they were following orders, and the law. They adopted the evil ways of the Nazis, and oppressed and murdered their fellows, on orders, and in anticipation of orders, many relished this, yet if they had all, or enough of them, refused on moral grounds they would have been a lot happier now: they sold their humanity, integrity, and soul to the devil. Hannah Arendt, in *Eichmann in Jerusalem* (1963)[9] commented on the 'banality' evil administered by bureaucratic systems of totalitarian control, and says: 'They know that the system which succeeds in destroying its victim before he mounts the scaffold . . . is incomparably the best for keeping a whole people in slavery'. It is because of the people who have the humanity, nous, and the moral integrity to resist that humanity survives. Children are the hope for the future.

Levi recommends a kind of moral ambiguity for judging the privileged victims in the grey zone: calling for the public sparing of moral judgement of those who were under pressure, whilst at the same time he is unable to not pass some moral judgement. It was after Levi published this book, that Felstiner then published his work on the need to establish the moral limits to representation. Levi's essay shows that for those who were involved, this is very difficult and he argues no one can know how they would behave unless they were in a similar situation. A question this also raises is to do with reliability of traumatic memories, as testimony in bearing witness. It is through the collection of different perspectives, voices, and accounts, of atrocities, from those who were the victims and perpetrators, that the record of what happened is best served, enabling a juxtaposition and comparison, and it is through the writings of authors that we come to know of what happened, in their stories, and hear the ambiguities, and moral complexities, and horror in their individual accounts. The Freudian account of 'Remembering, Repeating and Working Through' is relevant for understanding traumatic memories. One symptom of post-traumatic stress and PTSD is forgetting, and it might take decades to be able to remember and think about the times, places and the events of the trauma.

This is however shifting the emphasis away from the actual perpetrators, the Nazis and German supporters, the ones who implemented genocide, of an industrial scale by the Nazis. Gathering strength is a movement to research and find out more about what happened, things which have suppressed. There has been widespread cultural amnesia.

In the creative processes of writing authors cannot always be fully consciously in control of all that they write, just as readers read within a conceptual context of which they are not always conscious, aware or in control. In writing, authors bring their works into the social cultural realm through a creative process of interplay between consciousness and the unconscious, psycho-linguistic articulation and emotive affect, a doubled form of mind/body mediation in which they work up their manuscript, their narrative (often through many drafts and rewritings) usually in intense conceptual solitude, until (if circumstances prove propitious, and they are able to assert this control) they feel it is ready for public view.

The fugue narratives in the literary studies in Part II provide a new perspective and challenges a 'postmodern' approach to interpretation and representation in several main ways. First, they provide evidence of authorial 'intention' in use of techniques of musicalization by fugue authors. They intend at the least to adapt techniques from music or specifically fugue into literary form—and they fulfill this intention.

Second, these authors adapt musicalized techniques intentionally as a mode, or modality, to authentically articulate emotional affect deriving from their experiences of traumatic shock, loss and a deep need for restitution. Although, paradoxically, they may not necessarily be aware that this need for restitution of what has been lost to them in the moment of trauma is what is driving their desire to write.

Third, these are not narratives written to an external formula, such as an Aristotelian unity of beginning-middle-end. Their unity is provided by their use of techniques of musicalization that articulate and unify the chaotic emotional experiences of their authors, and form the driving modality of musicalized fugal narratives. These narratives are thereby performative in that they self-reflexively 'perform' themselves. The possibility for a 'stable truth and reality' in relation to fugue narratives I investigate lies in the body and minds, the life, being and psyche of the authors who wrote them. Even if their lives, minds and bodies were not 'stable', they still provide the real, material (and conceptual) context for their writing. This reality is also contrapuntally interwoven if not exactly embedded in the mundane social and cultural contexts in and of which they were writing, the issues, events and experiences with which they were engaged, and to which their authors were responding and paradoxically escaping, through re-playing and symbolic reconfiguration in their writing.

FUGAL PARADOX: THE DICHOTOMY OF WRITING

There is another potential source of misunderstanding in relation to literary fugue narratives. There might appear to be a dichotomy between the use of formalized techniques to performatively express and articulate the subjectivity of personal experience. I define the dichotomy as one that symbolically locates the individual in a doubled position in relation to language. Echoes of this dichotomy can be heard in the words of those who do not feel at home in the language that they use. It can be heard in Irish novelist John Banville's heartfelt declaration: 'The language that we speak is not our own, even after a century and a half of English: listen to any Irish conversation at any class level, and you will clearly hear the suppressed melodies, as well as the hesitations and disjunctions, of the deep grammar of Gaelic'.[11] It is heard in the narrative of women's struggle to find their own voices in 'phallocentric' language in the diverse discourses of feminism and female writing, as variously articulated, for instance, by Virginia Woolf in *A Room of One's Own* (1928), Hélène Cixous in works such as *La Venue à l'écriture* ('Coming to Writing') (1986), Luce Irigaray in *Ce sexe qui n'en est pas un* (This Sex Which is Not One) (1977), and Kristeva (1974). In *La Revolution du langage poétique* (1974) Kristeva put forward her thesis that art and literature, through reliance on the notion of the subject: 'is the privileged place of transformation or change: an abstract philosophy of the signifier can only repeat the formal gestures of its literary models'.[12] A similar belief drove the movement and creative practice of *l'écriture féminine*, the 1970's intervention with which Irigaray and Cixous are linked although acknowledging the difficulties of defining such a concept Cixous has (on occasion) publicly rejected the term and instead she has talked about writing a 'feminine speech', 'white ink',[13] and in her novel *Illa* extending this to a search for a *langue maternelle*.[14]

This is a dichotomy that is acutely felt and expressed by ones who are marginalized, outside the 'dominant' language structure or what such a (hostile) structure is believed to be. And as Freud refers to in the concept of a 'special entity' or *instanz*, for example, in his essay 'On the Introduction of Narcissism' this is often a shadowy kind of conception of authority and linguistic dominance, an apprehension of surveillance experienced by the individual subject, perhaps as the voice of censorship.[15] The search for linguistic freedom is heard in the voices of the early Romantics who developed a new approach to writing as individualistic and transformative, guided by ideals of freedom and inspiration, which transcended the institutional structures of modernity and the trappings of capitalism. It is the voice of the individual who is aware of herself or himself, affectively, emotionally prior to or outside the language that she learns, in dreams, and in emotional states. This realm of affect is subjective and might feel as if it is private. But, Wittgenstein insisted, there is no such thing as a private language. Once a thought is expressed in language, it becomes by definition public, defined in language, which is public and communal.

The dichotomy of literary writing is in the struggle of the writer to articulate herself effectively and affectively in a language that she learns, which ultimately is not hers alone, as it is shared. The dichotomy begins with the phenomenological evidence that a baby does not have to learn feelings and affective emotive responses. A baby does not learn hunger, cold, fear. She does not consciously learn attachment to the mother. She does not learn deep inherent emotions of love, hate, loss, and desire. These are experienced as pure unconditioned affect; the baby just knows how she feels. But as she grows she does learn how to (try to) articulate these affects in a language that by virtue of its learning reveals to the child the first paradox of language use. In order to express her 'private' affective responses and experiences she must enter a discourse which by virtue of being public is to a degree impersonal and not hers alone. As the child grows, she realizes that the language she has at her disposal to seek to articulate her subjective feelings and affective experiences in writing is the objective language of public discourse, which might be read and interpreted by others in ways she did not intend. And this, perhaps, has never been more clearly, widely and publicly, shown than in the new social media communication,

In an individual sensitive to nuance this can compound a feeling of alienation and abjection, which in some, may lead to a self-reflexive fugal flight into language experienced as *jouissance*.[16] This could certainly be considered to constitute the appeal of *l'écriture féminine*, and certain kinds of affective poetic writing from Romanticism onwards. In the women's writing movements of the 1960s and 1970s self-consciously revolutionary radical alternatives to dominant discourses of authoritative language proliferated, and there was an efflorescence of writing—both about and of—a certain kind of self-reflexive poetical free writing (*écriture*) a pleasurable experience in itself, an experience in which writers feel themselves transformed through writing. The joy of writing may be connected with the deep desire to write; this may be a faintly guilty pleasure, as is suggested by Klein (1975). Paradoxically, again the experience of writing may suggest to the writer a connection with a force that is mysterious, unknown, and beyond the individual. This perhaps suggests a realm that the ancients referred to as the domain of muses and divine inspiration.

Yet using formalization may well be the only way an author can approach and write of traumatic emotional content, and a reader read of it, a point that Susan Gubar also makes about writing, reading and thinking about art after the unspeakable horror of the Holocaust. This may have been so with Celan's choice of techniques for *Todesfuge*, his first published poem, which he began to write before the end of the war and the end of the Holocaust, perhaps when he was still interned in a forced labor camp, as Felstiner speculates.[17]

In relation to literary works written using techniques of musicalization it seems that the authors' decisions to use the 'formalization' of musicalization is a project and approach that has received little attention. Werner Wolf's 1999 book *Musicalization of Fiction: A Study in the Theory and History of Intermediality* is pioneering, in its focus on 'musicalization' in *narrative* fiction intermediality. In his investigation, Wolf acknowledges there may be emotive links and connections between use of musicalization and an author's desire to articulate emotional affect. In my studies, in Part II, Wolf's analysis is extended to explicitly investigate the links between the use of affect in literary fugue studies based on the evidence of the authors' biographies and further writings that shed light on their life experiences.

Existing analyses of musicalized works tend to focus on techniques of musicalization, primarily if not solely from an aesthetic or technical point of view. They seek to analyze the effectiveness of transposing musical effects into literary form often objectively assessing success or failure without looking much further at why the author might have chosen to use these techniques, and what she or he might have been articulating in their writing in a biographical political sense, and evaluating the works in a broader subjective, cultural and social context.

Whilst insightful, such purely aestheticized, and technical, readings bracket the psychological aspects of musicalization expressed as affect.

They omit to read the works within the social and cultural biographical and psychological context of the author's life, and life experiences from which literary work derives. This, as the literary fugue studies show, can mean missing out on 'real', more comprehensive, meaning of the works, which, it turns out, can only be ascertained and understood in relation to searching for the author's intentions in writing even if these may not have been fully articulated, or possible to know.

Friedlander's (2001) analysis suggests that there is a new onus on the critical reader interpreter to read within appropriate, relevant, adequately researched limits. Ideally, it should not be incumbent on the author to go to endless lengths to try to make their works understood by readers (especially when they may be unsympathetic).

FUGAL RECURSION: A PERCEPTUAL FUNCTION OF MEMORY

The fugue is developed through polyphonic counterpoint, which is the constitutive basis and principle through which the musical form is developed in exposition and counter-exposition. The function of this form of musical structure and technique, which is dependent for its audial meaning on the memory of its performer and listener, has been described as a form of recursion.

The human ear makes sense of the 'shifts' that recursion represents writes Douglas Hofstadter in *Gödel, Escher, Bach*.[18] He suggests a model from computer language systems, of stacking, to explain how minds remember, in music, that we can apply to written or verbal language, the shifting elements, which go to make up a recursive system (i.e. in prose a story within a story, or a polyphonic story told through different characters' monologues; or in musical fugue, the original starting subject line/melodic phrase/theme). How do we remember the subject line/melodic phrase/theme? Hofstadter says we 'put it on hold', as we may put on hold person A, whom we are talking to on the phone, to take a call from person B, whom we talk with before switching back to person A.

A *rondellus* or round represents a simple formal infinite recursion. By the time the fugue form had been developed to the complexity of Bach's later mirror fugues, recursion was so artfully complex at points it gave way to infinite regression contained within the fluid polyphonic structure that to the listener represented a complex but apparently unified listening experience. To give an analogous literary example, in Proust's *À la recherche du temps perdu*, the recursive elements of the narrative (the stories within stories of the narrator's memory) build up and fade away in complex layers comprising an enormous range of different elements which are yet contained within the unified whole of his narrative. Herman Hesse explicitly explored the recursive aspects of fugue in the *Die Glasperlenspiel* (The Glass Bead Game) the story of Joseph Knect, who ascends from genius grammar school student into Ludi Magister Josephus III, Master of 'the Game' in the Castalia brotherhood. This intricate system of authorized thought processing, which Hesse likens to the innovative processes of a musical fugue, describes the theory of digital computing many years before it became a technological reality:

> The Game of games had developed into a kind of universal language through which the players could express values and set these in relation to one another. Throughout its history the Game was closely allied with music, and usually proceeded according to musical or mathematical rules. One theme, two themes, or three themes were stated, elaborated, varied, and underwent a development quite similar to that of the theme in a Bach fugue, or a concerto movement. A Game, for example, might start from a given astronomical configuration, or from the actual theme of a Bach fugue, or from a sentence out of Leibniz or the Upanishads, and from this theme, depending on the intentions and talents of the player, it could either further explore and elaborate the initial motif or else enrich its expressiveness by allusion to kindred concepts.[19]

This not only describes the theory of digital computing through which a masterly programmer can convert an idea, thought or number into mathematical binary chains of numbers which can be arranged (like musical notes) into all kinds of combinations; echoing Leibniz's concept of a utopian language machine. It is also an allegory for the innovation and 'freedom' of language use, the conceptual games of language invention that writers play. The difference however between a human mind and a computational Game, is that humans have emotions. And are subject to, perhaps defined by, struggling to articulate, understand or move beyond, effects of traumatic experience.

↻ 5
STATELESS.
THE DISSOCIATIVE FUGUE

> A fugue can be defined as a syndrome in which there is (1) a sudden loss of memory, which involves (2) autobiographical memory and the sense of personal identity, usually associated with (3) a period of wandering, and (4) there is a subsequent amnesiac gap upon recovery from the fugue—*Michael D. Kopelman, 'Focal Retrograde Amnesia and the Attribution on Causality: An Exceptionally Critical Review'.*

Medical researchers have mostly tended to agree that a 'dissociative fugue' is defined by an individual's sudden autobiographical amnesia: loss of memory of personal identity, accompanied by a journey from home in an obscured state of consciousness, and that it is a temporary condition. But the ambiguous subjective quality of fugue has been a topic of uncertainty since it was first diagnosed in 1887 in a medical doctoral thesis by student doctor Philippe Tissié, in Bordeaux Hospital. Psychological research shows that dissociative fugue is caused by severe stresses that affect the ability of an individual to remember herself, or himself, and which triggers a dissociative survival 'flight' response. In this era of massive displacement of persons and the most refugees since World War 2 there is a resurgence of dissociative fugue and of research into fugue. This chapter discusses fugue stories from the media and others in medical journals, and the recent story of an Australian resident Cornelia Rau, a young woman who fled the controversial Kenja Communications 'sect' or 'cult' only to be locked up in asylums, prison and then immigration detention centre in the desert. In a Kafkaesque journey to the far Northern tip of Queensland and a fateful encounter with the forces of Border Protection because she could not remember her name, she was confined in a solitary punishment in a "processing centre" of indefinite imprisonment in the desert. This chapter interweaves references from media articles and the report of the Government inquiry into this, following a description of the dissociative fugue from recent research in medical journals. She was treated as if she was 'stateless', like the children born in Australia's immigration prisons, who have no identity papers.

Medical researchers have investigated thinking, conclusions, and problems on the ontology of the dissociative fugue and the attribution of causality over the past century, to unravel this mysterious condition. In this chapter, some of the medical findings are contextualized within the cultural history of the psychogenic fugue. Elizabeth Glisky writes: 'Psychogenic fugue is a disorder of memory that occurs following emotional or psychological trauma and results in a loss of one's personal past including personal identity'.[1] According to Markowitsch: 'stress conditions and depressive states may modify the release of steroids (glucocorticoids) and transmitter agonists at the brain level with the consequence of selective memory disturbances which may manifest as a 'mnestic block syndrome'.[2] Although there may be an appearance of a semblance of convergence of research findings, researchers take somewhat different approaches. They range from Hans Markowitsch's mechanistic neurological perspective based on changes in brain function and neurological chemistry to Michael D. Kopelman's findings of psychological aspects of memory loss considered in relation to the wider social and cultural contexts of subjects lives.[3] Kopelman et al defined the fugue state in relation to psychogenic amnesia, with a focus on its relation to an 'offence':

> The term 'psychogenic amnesia' encompasses a number of phenomena. These include so-called 'fugue states', amnesia for specific situations such as committing, witnessing, or being the victim of an offence, and simulated or malingered amnesia. Of these a 'fugue state' refers to a specific syndrome, consisting of a sudden loss of the sense of personal identity and of all past autobiographical memories, usually associated with a period of wandering, which lasts a few hours of days and for which there is a virtually complete amnesiac gap upon recovery. (M. Kopelman et al. 1994, p. 675)

In 2000, Kopelman refined this:

> A fugue can be defined as a syndrome in which there is (1) a sudden loss of memory, which involves (2) autobiographical memory and the sense of personal identity, usually associated with (3) a period of wandering, and (4) there is a subsequent amnesiac gap upon recovery from the fugue. (M. Kopelman 2000, p. 587)

There are accounts in recent psychiatric medical science literature of fugue narratives, with personal stories researched, tested and documented as cases. From this evidence researchers have attempted to draw conclusions from and about this mysterious condition. Elizabeth Glisky et al (2004) document the case of a male German-English bi-lingual patient:

> Patient F.F. was a 33-year-old-male, who after walking along unfamiliar streets for an indeterminate length of time on evening, entered a motel and asked a clerk to call police, stating that he believed he had been pushed out of a van by two men. He claimed not to know who or where he was and he had no identification on him. The police took him to the University Medical Centre, where he was seen by emergency room personnel and admitted to the psychiatric ward of the hospital. The patient spoke English with an accent that was later determined to be German but he claimed to have no knowledge of German and did not respond to any German instructions.[4]

According to the records he gave staff a first name, which turned out to be his. Amytal (a 'truth drug') tests revealed only results, which Glisky et al report 'clearly were false'.[5]

When a photograph of F.F. was shown on American television, two women came forward who claimed to have dated him. They each gave information that F.F. arrived in the United States less than three months previously, with expensive luggage, clothes and a considerable amount of money. A roommate was found who was brought to the hospital. F.F. was 'clearly scared of the room-mate', he said that his roommate armed with a shotgun had attacked him, stolen his money and possessions. These were never found. His passport was found, verifying his German nationality and his recent arrival in the U.S. but F.F. claimed to have no knowledge of German.

Tests with bi-lingual and German speaker control groups produced inconclusive results as regards his amnesia. The researchers conclude: 'Although in these studies, as in the lexical decision study, it is impossible to be certain that F.F. was not feigning his amnesia, the patterns of his performance did not resemble that of simulators who were told to lie'.[6] The findings of 'difference across three paradigms, which could not have been predicted a priori, provides some confidence that this patient was experiencing a true psychogenic amnesia'.[7]

On re-discovering or remembering, his nationality, F.F. contacted the German consulate for assistance. His brother was subsequently located in Germany, and he sent him a plane ticket home. His brother offered the medical researchers information that F.F. was the owner of a computer business that was in financial difficulties. Furthermore his marriage was also in difficulties. Apparently F.F had disappeared suddenly from his home in Germany four months before. His brother indicated to the US medical researchers that his brother had 'done something wrong'.[8] When F.F. returned to Germany police met him at the airport. Although the medical researchers did not obtain information as to what exactly had happened, they found: 'he was arrested and put in jail immediately on disembarking from the plane'.[9] They wrote: 'Although we were unable to discover the exact nature of his crime, we do know that it concerned his business, and that he was given 18 months probation'.[10] The researchers added: 'F.F. contacted us a little more than a year later, asking for some help in understanding what had led him to 'denying everything' during the period of time that he was in hospital in Tucson'. Glisky et al. observe that F.F.'s comments to them in recent communication:

> are instructive and consistent with a view of psychogenic amnesia as a temporary state of disrupted consciousness...F.F. stated that "I just neglected my whole life...The break even point, where not knowing the answers and ignoring the knowledge of the answers is difficult to find...I was aware of knowing German in written and spoken form somehow after about 10 days...It was part of my life I just wanted to lock away in a dark chamber. I can't even say if it was active will or passive defense...The point where this disorientation was replaced by neglecting the truth is not easy to find and somehow undefined...In the last test, the lie detector, some of the things were common [familiar] and my mother's name went through my 'personal barrier'. (E. Glisky et al., 2004, p. 1138)

The researchers concluded that their patient's remarks are consistent with other cases of fugue amnesia 'which have often reported a mixture of fantasy and reality, some islands of memory, and awareness of some aspects of the past'.[11] They further concluded: 'All cases of psychogenic fugue are associated with emotional trauma that provides a powerful motive for psychological and often physical escape as well'.[12]

Kopelman et al.(1994) concluded from their findings from their review of the literature: 'fugues are always preceded by a severe precipitating stress (e.g. marital or financial), very commonly by depression and/or suicidal ideas, and there is often a past history of transient organic amnesia from head injury, epilepsy, hypoglycemia or some other cause'.[13] The past history of amnesia is important as it provides a model, or precedent, from which the mind learns. Kopelman et al. also summarize main problems or objects of inquiry, which are identified as setting an agenda or defining the terms of recent phenomenological medical research into the psychogenic fugue:

> The role of awareness in the impaired memory processes of patients who have an organic amnesia is an important preoccupation of the current neuropsychological literature.[14]

A main object of inquiry was:

> The differentiation of hysterical from simulated amnesia[15]

They acknowledge the medical interest in researching causes and patterns of amnesia caused organically, for instance in brain disease, dementia, and head injury. Against this, they identify the field of their research: amnesia that is defined as 'hysterical amnesia'. Kopelman et al.'s literature review raises the hypothesis that a state of psychogenic fugue may co-exist with brain disease, perhaps following a 'minor' head injury or some form of brain disease. This is a hypothesis that Kopelman et al. (1994) set out to investigate.

In the medical science/psychiatric literature on fugue causality the type of organic cause suggested is minor, such as a 'minor head injury' (one that does not cause any brain damage beyond immediate concussion) or evidence of childhood meningitis or small anomalies on CT scans—anything considered more serious is diagnosed under rubrics of organic amnesia caused by physical changes in the brain—which psychogenic amnesia of fugue states is differentiated from due to a defining characteristic loss of awareness of personal identity. Kopelman et al state: 'the loss of personal identity distinguishes them from transient "organic" amnesia'.[16] What they found was that the patient they tested who had experienced a sustained 'fugue' episode (functional retrograde amnesia) for seven days, had patterns of performance on an autobiographical and a news test, amongst other tests, that 'differentiated her from patients with organic amnesia...' Kopelman et al suggest that patients with psychogenic amnesia may also manifest different levels of awareness for differing memories.'[17]

EARLY DEFINITIONS OF PSYCHOGENIC FUGUE

The psychogenic fugue was first diagnosed as a medical condition in France in 1887, where it rapidly achieved epidemic proportions. It remained a regularly diagnosed condition until the period following World War II, after which it lapsed for a few decades as a clinical diagnosis. According to Kopelman et al writing in 1994: 'Fugue states appear to have been more common during the first half of the century, especially during wartime, but they are still reported in the literature and the loss of personal identity distinguishes them from transient 'organic' amnesias'.[18]

In the 1980s-1990s the focus of medical science on the psychogenic fugue appeared to undergo some resurgence in diagnostic practice and reporting. There was an increase in reports in the media in the UK, of conditions that could seem to come under the rubric of psychogenic fugue including psychogenic amnesia. In the US and Australia, precipitating cultural factors included, most significantly, the Vietnam War, and specifically the after-affects of stress on Vietnam veterans. Indeed, the diagnosis of Post-Traumatic Stress Disorder emerged into diagnostic, media and public discourse following the end of the Vietnam War.[19] The (re) emergence of fugue phenomena included a range of dissociative disorders constituting variations of dissociative amnesia such as 'repressed memory syndrome', and 'multiple personality disorder' as noted by Hacking.[20] Such conditions have been likened, by Kopelman, to 'Freudian' hysterical amnesia.[21] Hacking's cultural theory suggests these might include things such as increased interest in and reporting of Unidentified Flying Objects, extra-terrestrial encounters, and a range of ambiguous cultural phenomena, such as 'taken by aliens' reports; and reports of 'satanic ritual abuse', which were reported frequently in the mainstream and tabloid media in the 1980s (in the UK). (However, perhaps there are more sinister explanations for these, so they are not to be dismissed without investigation).

Research into the ambiguous condition of psychogenic dissociative fugue tends to focus on the two main inter-related problem areas, as stated, the nature of the causality of the psychogenic amnesia for autobiographical memory; and to what degree the patient is genuinely experiencing loss of memory of personal identity; to what degree loss of autobiographical memory and identity is feigned (if at all) therefore deliberate deception; and to what degree it is a genuine loss of awareness of personal identity. Can this be understood as self deception? Sartre explored this territory to some extent, in *Being and Nothingness* with his notion of 'bad faith' a form of deception of self and others and the attempt to rationalize one's life through religion or science or other operative forces, denying the necessity of relying on her or his moral insights and fallible will, attempting to escape the burden of responsibility for choices, and regarding herself, or himself, as a passive subject of external influences. By which she or he evades taking moral responsibility for her or his choices.[22] Yet this is not relevant to the dissociative fugue and the cases, which suggest instead that there are clear strong reasons and causes that precipitate dissociative fugue, that these are severe stresses and traumas; it is therefore not self deception, nor 'made up' but a genuine amnesia of self and life caused by catastrophic stresses; this is the conclusion of the medical experts who have researched it extensively.

Numerous articles have been published on the nature and causality of the psychogenic and dissociative fugue in medical science psychiatric journals and collections of papers, such as *Memory and its Disorders (Handbook of Neuropsychology Vol. 2)* (Cermak, ed. 2000) and *Memory, Consciousness and the Brain: The Tallinn Conference* (E. Tulving, ed., 1999).

Kopelman's paper 'Focal Retrograde Amnesia and the Attribution of Causality: An Exceptionally Critical Review' shows the complexities of researching psychogenic fugue, reflected in questions surrounding the qualitative experience and symptoms of a patient in dissociative fugue documented in the medical science literature as to the nature of the fugue, and the degree to which the patient lost their autobiographical memory of personal identity. Whereas some medical researchers in the past placed greatest emphasis on 'loss of personal identity', others have emphasized the 'period of wandering'. Kopelman concludes that 'Although it is very difficult to "prove" psychological causation':

> Given these problems, in uncertain or equivocal cases, it is as critical to present the relevant psychological data for the reader to evaluate as it is to provide the pertinent memory test scores: this is unpreemphasized in many of the studies reviewed. Publication of cases in the absence of such data may lead to faulty clinical, neuro-psychological, and cognitive conclusions. (M. Kopelman, 2000. p. 585)

Kopelman writes that: 'Fugue states are not the only or the most common form of psychogenic amnesia' but he believes they are 'probably the most pertinent to this discussion' (on focal retrograde amnesia). Kopelman surveys and presents a range of predisposing factors to fugue episode from the medical research literature, which he writes suggest there are three main predisposing factors to fugue episodes:

> fugue states are always preceded by a severe, precipitating stress such as marital or relationship discord (Kanzer,1939), bereavement (Schacter et al., 1982), financial problems (Kanzer, 1939), being charged with an offence (Kopelman, Green, Guinan, Lewis and Stanhope, 1994b; G. Wilson, Rupp, and Wilson, 1950), or stress during wartime (Parfitt and Gall, 1944; Sargant and Slater, 1941). Second, depressed mood and suicidal ideas are very common antecedents for a fugue episode (Abeles and Schilder, 1935; Berrington et al., 1956; Kopelman et al., 1994b; Schacter et al., 1982; Stengel, 1941). The third factor is a past history of a transient, organic amnesia, such as epilepsy or head injury. (Berrington et al., 1956; Stengel, 1941)[23]

Kopelman summarizes from this that those who are most likely to 'go into a fugue,' and wander off in a state of personal-identity amnesia are people under severe stress who have experienced a previous transient organic amnesia (perhaps caused by a 'minor' head injury), and have subsequently or later become depressed and/or suicidal.

Markowitsch et al. emphasize neurological changes in the brain. But these may be similar or indistinguishable from changes that occur in the brain of a patient whose amnesia is of an organic origin (excluding any evidence of physical injury), commenting that 'Focal retrograde amnesia may occur with and without manifest organic brain damage' and 'minor or no manifest brain damage at all may result in severe and sometimes lasting retrograde amnesia for autobiographical material'.[24] This is further evidence of the intriguingly unpredictable nature of the psychogenic fugue. Whereas a severe head injury may cause no trace of fugue, which is defined by loss of awareness of personal identity, a very minor bump to the head or no head trauma at all can lead to major states of psychogenic amnesia.

Markowitsch concludes: 'functional retrograde amnesia' or loss of autobiographical memory, personal identity, can be caused by organic and psychogenic amnesia. Markowitsch et al. cite the incidence of a patient, 'B.T.', a 30-year-old male who was 'referred to our hospital because of his complaint of having lost his memory for his whole life span'.[25] 'B.T.' said that he had left home to make a phone call. Instead, although he had no recollection of this action, he went to his bank, and withdrew a large sum of money from his account. The next thing he said he remembered was waking up next to a road with no money and no documents, 'feeling disoriented and with no memories of his personal past. He realized he was abroad and had in fact gone from Germany into Czechoslovakia'.[26] B.T. expressed his fear of contacting police or medical doctors. He returned to Germany and as he did not regain his memory, he contacted the 'Travellers Aid' of a big city train station, from where he was taken to a psychiatric clinic.

Neuropsychological tests on B.T.'s intelligence, attention, concentration, and anterograde and retrograde episodic 'showed no cognitive defects, except for retrograde memory', Markowitsch et al. write: 'The patient's only defect was in the area of old memories and here disproportionately so for autobiographical life events'.[27]

During these tests, Markowitsch et al. note differences to normative brain function. However, the conclusions to be drawn from this, or what it may mean, were rather sketchy. Markowitsch et al. conclude that there may be similarities in the mechanisms activated in both an organic and psychogenic amnesia. Markowitsch et al. describe psychogenic dissociative amnesia in mechanistic neurological terms of changed circuitry that somehow effect a mnemonic block: the failure to access retrograde autobiographical material, or fugal memory loss, may be the result of a 'highly specific process which can be caused by mutual influences of psychic alterations and organic brain changes'.[28] This descriptive account however takes us no nearer to understanding the deeper (or precipitating) causes for this psychogenic phenomenon.

Kopelman, and Markowitsch et al., each state that in many respects phenomenological symptoms of psychogenic fugue resemble those of organic amnesia (caused by a minor head injury, epilepsy or other organic damage). Kopelman et al. summarize findings from 1907, 1939 and 1982, that state in a psychogenic fugue there may be 'islets' or 'fragments' of memory preserved within an 'amnestic gap', and the person in a fugue may adopt a detached attitude towards their memory fragments describing these as 'strange and unfamiliar'.[29]

The medical evidence cited above is a recent demonstration that the psychogenic fugue is a mysterious state of absence, a vexed form of amnesia, 'dissociation of the personality', which had baffled physicians from the nineteenth century. In such a state, the subject appears dissociated and will 'wander off not knowing who or where she is.'[30] The fugue was diagnosed as a dissociation of the personality. In dissociation, Rycroft writes mental states are believed to co-exist 'without becoming connected to or influencing each other'.[31] Before Freud's theory of 'hysterical amnesia', dissociation was a term liberally used by psychologists and alienists to describe and account for a spectrum of maladies and symptoms that would later on be regarded as neurotic. Conditions subsequently viewed as neuroses were assumed to result from a functional defect in a person's constitution. After Freud, such maladies became instead subject to the complex explanations of psychoanalysis, premised on the existence of the unconscious and also, if more dubiously, the lifelong effects of repressed (infantile) memories.

Belief in the existence of the unconscious might seem to imply that the human being exists in a state of continual dissociation. Yet, in 1986, in his entry in the *Oxford Book of the Mind*, Charles Rycroft commented that since Freud, the term 'dissociation' had largely fallen into disuse in the medical profession. He acknowledged there was one exception to this trend: Freud's concept and diagnosis of 'hysterical dissociation' was still in use. This kind of altered state of mind involves a particular form of temporary amnesia. For a sustained period of time, or for a course of a particular action, the subject appears to not be his or her usual self, unaware of her or his usual store of memories, stocked with personal information. Rycroft states, the dissociative subject

> appears not to be actuated by his usual self—or, alternatively...his usual self seems not to have access to the recent memories that one would normally expect him to have.[32]

In a state of obscured consciousness, a person in a fugue literally forgets who she or he is. In the DSM-5 (2013) dissociative fugue has been reclassified as a specifier of dissociative amnesia rather than a separate diagnosis; and criteria for dissociative identity disorder have also been changed to recognize gaps in recall may be for everyday events as well as traumatic events.[33]

To summarize these diverse strands: the dissociative fugue is a rare form of dissociative disorder, involving an experience of temporary self-amnesia, in which an individual forgets her or his personal identity. This typically involves 'wandering off', or metaphorical 'flight' from his or her environment, and the assumption of another identity.

Fugue as a medical phenomenon has been extensively researched and discussed with results that indicate that the dissociative fugue is a 'flight' response of self-survival following extreme stress or stresses.

FIN DE SIÈCLE AND THE EMERGENCE OF FUGUE

Although states that can be retrospectively linked to 'fugue' have been identified in the distant past, Ancient Greece for example, the condition known as psychogenic fugue was not defined by medical diagnosis until 1887, in Bordeaux. In a series of published Page-Barbour lectures *Mad Travelers: Reflections on Transient Mental Illness*, Ian Hacking gives an historical and cultural account of the changing uses of the term 'fugue'. Hacking re-conceives and contextualizes the term historically and culturally, with a range of what he terms 'transient mental illnesses'. By this, he means mental illnesses that appear in certain times and places in history, and later fade away:

> It [the illness] may spread from place to place, and reappear from time to time. It may be selective for social class or gender, preferring poor women or rich men. I do not mean that it comes and goes in this or that patient, but that this type of madness exists only at certain times and places. The most famous candidate for a transient mental illness is hysteria, or at any rate its florid French manifestations toward the end of the nineteenth century. Cynics would offer multiple personality today as another transient mental illness and go on to compose a list of other disorders that will prove transient.[34]

Tissié, a 33-year-old doctor, published the first diagnostic account of dissociative fugue, based on the case of a man Albert Dadas, a gas fitter, in a ward of the Bordeaux hospital of Saint-Andre, whom he found in the ward, crying and distressed after Dadas came around from one of his strange journeys across Europe. He had long conversations with Tissié. He told him how it all started: he had been voluntarily enlisted in the 127th Infantry Regiment, by chance he met a childhood-friend, whom he encouraged to join up but the friend had been enlisted to the 16th Dragoons, and as they could not billet together they deserted. They walked hundreds of kilometres through Belgium and Holland and on this journey, in the bitter winter, his friend died of exhaustion, hunger and cold. Dadas continued to travel, when he heard that there was an amnesty for deserters, he made his way, by a roundabout route, home to France, hundreds of miles by foot and train. From then on he went on many strange long journeys by foot, rail, and boat. He would overhear a place name, such as 'Algeria', and set off to visit the place. Tissié wrote:

> He could not refrain when the need took him; then, seized, captive to

an authoritarian compulsion he left family, work, habits...and set off briskly walking 70 kilometres a day.[35]

After walking for hundreds of kilometres, ending up in cities such as Moscow and Constantinople, he would 'come to', sometimes after being arrested for vagrancy and imprisoned, sometimes without identity papers and no money, in distress having to make his way somehow to France. Under hypnosis he recalled fragments of scenes and details from journeys, which were otherwise an amnesiac blur. Tissié (a musician), applied the term 'fugue' in his diagnosis of Dadas' mysterious condition in *Les aliénés voyageurs* (1887); the condition was referred to as *automatisme ambulatoire* ('automatic walking') by Janet, and Charcot.

Nowadays, in French usage, to '*faire une fugue*' can mean to take an 'inconsequential getaway' from home, according to the Larousse Dictionary, the term is also applied to the *fugue romantique* of elopement, *fugue amoreuse* of love escapades; as well as to musical fugue. In contrast, the English translation in the Collins dictionary is 'to run away, to abscond'.

Ian Hacking describes the epidemic of 'mad travellers' that broke out in 1887.[36] Hacking was writing in the 1990s and published his main work on fugue, in 1998. Yet he describes fugue as an example of a 'transient mental illness' which no longer exists. But strangely, my research shows the resurgence of fugue as reported over the last twenty years, since Hacking's books were published. It is now acknowledged that it is a rare condition but is far more frequent in times of large scale wars.

Dissociative fugue has recurred during the war on Terror, and the global wars of the last twenty years, combined with the environmental catastrophes, which have displaced millions of people, and which have witnessed the new failure of globalization, and the return to nationalism, and an increasing focus on borders, and identity.

Such illnesses in the nineteenth century included hysteria, trances, and neurasthenia, nervousness, which Proust was said to suffer from.[37]

Dissociative fugue is a 'flight' response of self-survival in situations of unbearable stress, usually where there are several stressors such as relationship breakdown, financial difficulties, being diagnosed with a life-threatening illness, or being charged with an offence; connecting with aspects of the individual that are unconscious and releasing.

Might it be significant that the 'fugue' was diagnosed, and thrived, in the *fin de siècle* France, the era in which literary modernism emerged and burgeoned? A further cultural and social factor that may be linked with the diagnostic emergence of psychogenic fugue was the European advent of tourism. All three cultural phenomena, the art movement of modernism, package-tour tourism, and psychogenic fugue are juxtaposed in Hacking's *Mad Travellers*. These cultural phenomena were self-starting responses to the ideological tensions of capitalist society under modernity and colonialism, at the height of empire.

All three of these phenomena are associated, like colonialist imperialist expansion, with travel, yet each interprets the notion of, or 'does', travel in different ways, according to the individualistic propensities, backgrounds, and social and cultural opportunities of its proponents. The relatively unproblematic luxury travel was only available to, and availed by, the well-to-do bourgeois class, and the international Cooks package tours were beyond the means of many. According to Hacking, fugueurs in the 'epidemic', which swept France in the late 1880s and 1890s, were mainly 'lower class men' who lacked the means to avail of tours and holidays. Instead they disappeared from their surroundings, in states of obscured consciousness, on idiosyncratic journeys by foot and rail, which took them thousands of kilometres from their homes. Markowitsch's case of the male German subject, 'B.T.', who wanders on a journey into Czechoslovakia, recalls this fugue 'tradition'.

Modernist artists also took flight, in an escapist sense, as suggested by Hugo von Hofmannsthal.[38] This was an escapist self-based flight into the subjective realms of individual creativity. For some artists and writers this also did involve concurrent journeying and travel, often linked to the trade routes of colonialist expansion. This was the case for instance with French poet Arthur Rimbaud, who travelled to North Africa, and the French artist Gauguin who journeyed to French Polynesia. For Joyce travel was a form of escape from English colonization and the First World War. For De Quincey the association of imperialist expansion and colonialism affected his inner journeys in the form of the opium to which he was addicted and which came from enforced British trade in China.

For the modern writers whose works are discussed, their writing was in part triggered and influenced by experiences of traumatic loss. The effects of shock, alienation and displacement exemplified in their musicalized works became the subjectivity of literary modernism, as Benjamin suggests in his study on Baudelaire (1989). However, what is important to remember, is the distinction between 'fugue' as a medical condition and the fugal elements and analysis of literary creation.

There are cultural, medical definitions, diagnoses, and prescribed cures for fugue maladies, which exist therefore as specific narratives (or narrative-clusters) within the topography of medical discourse, at least in the cases in the UK and US discussed. It is their status as defined and diagnosed narratives within medical discourse, which makes their status as 'hypochondria' or 'imaginary' rather ambiguous. Ian Hacking uses the facts of historical record that these ailments are transitory (specific to a time, place and cultural context) as evidence on which to base an argument that fugue disorders rather than being social constructions, are 'ecological' emergences. He proposes: 'The most important contribution here is the metaphor of an ecological niche... Such niches require a number of vectors...'[39] Hacking argues that disorders arise from the 'ecological niche' of four 'vectors'. First, a medical definition including diagnosis and 'taxonomy of illness'; second, cultural polarity, 'the illness should be situated between two elements of contemporary culture, the first romantic and virtuous, the other vicious and tending to crime'. And he qualifies this with the statement that these values, of vice and virtue, are, also, culturally constructed and temporal in their nature, they belong to a place. Third, he suggests, the vector of 'observability...the disorder should be visible as disorder, as suffering, as something to escape'. The fourth vector he claims is provided by the release that the illness brings, even though it may cause pain, a release that is not found elsewhere in the culture in which it, nonetheless, thrives.[40]

What would happen if we were to apply this concept of vectors to the writing process in relation to the cultural context of literary movements, such as Romanticism, Modernism or *écriture féminine*. Adapting this vectored theory of social and cultural change might suggest that literary movements come into being through people, writers, in a particular time and place to fulfil a psychological, cultural and social need for expression, and group identification, and then after a while fade away. The process of a certain kind of self-based writing as art may be understood to 'work' in a cultural dimension that parallels Hacking's account of the cultural framework of the 'fugue'. Like wandering into another country, introspective self-based writing that is derived from traumatic experience in the world, involving a sense of alienation, is a form of metaphorical inner journey that provides a release, albeit painful, perhaps, which the writer cannot find anywhere else, or in any other way, in the culture in which she lives and writes. This operates in two domains of communication. First, that of the individual within herself or himself; second, that of the individual with others, as part of a literary movement. After a certain time, these movements fade away, although sometimes elements may be revived, in a new form.

The main problems associated with the phenomena of dissociative fugue identified in recent medical and psychological discourse are to do with the subjective nature of subjectivity, memory, self-consciousness and personal identity. These issues, which concern self-awareness and loss of personal identity, are areas of ambiguity in the philosophy of mind and phenomenology that have long posed questions with no conclusive answers for philosophers. So far, they have evaded the categorization of empirical medical knowledge. Kopelman takes a holistic approach that considers the wider narrative of the fugueur's life.

Kopelman et al published a study *The Great Escape: A Neuropsychological Study of Psychogenic Amnesia* (1994) which seeks to consider the wider social and personal dimensions of a fugue narrative, and which is paraphrased below.

The female subject in this case study reportedly 'came around' on a London Underground train between Liverpool Street and Bethnal Green. Her report recorded on video-tape, a month later, reveals she went to a phone box, rang the police, and was, eventually, taken to the hospital, disoriented and confused. She had a bag with her that contained nothing but clothes and a letter addressed to 'Alice Thornton.' (Researchers later found it was not her name). Two weeks later she was taken to another hospital. Orientated in time and space by now, she claimed to have no recollection of who she was, although she admitted to some 'macabre' memories including that her husband and son had been killed in a car accident the previous December. Administered Amytal (a 'truth drug' that is supposed to stimulate true recall of information) she recalled information which turned out to be false. She was discharged and was an outpatient on a regular basis for a couple of years. The researchers comment that she proved adept at survival, since she quickly established herself in London, securing emergency accommodation, a voluntary job with a charity, and a 'man friend' (a fellow outpatient who had a job as a paramedic). Meanwhile through

Scotland Yard's Missing Persons bureau her family in America located her. It turned out that she had three children and a husband in a town in the Southern U.S. 'A.T.' as she was known by Kopelman et al. continued to deny any knowledge of her previous identity and on being shown photographs of herself from her old life expressed surprise 'that certainly looks like me but it cannot be me.' On further administration of Amytal, 'A.T.' remembered more information about her past life and volunteered information that she had been in a difficult marriage; her husband drank heavily and was violent. She told the doctors, 'I think that I—I would if I were in that kind of situation, now I would, I would try and get out of it somehow.' Her last self-reported memory of being in the U.S. was dropping off her three children to school

> I remember being very sad, but I don't know why, unless maybe that's when I was planning to leave, I don't know. [41]

Kopelman et al observe at the end of their report that the travel agency where she booked her flight was called Great Escapes and its logo was a hot air balloon.[42]

CORNELIA RAU: A CASE OF MISTAKEN IDENTITY

A recent case in Australia would seem to fulfill the psychological definition of a fugue; it has also been the subject of an official Inquiry and was reported in the mainstream media. Cornelia Rau, 39, resident of Australia, and German citizen, who had worked for years as a flight attendant, went into what seems to fit the descriptions of a dissociative fugue state, following her traumatic encounters in a group described as a 'cult' or 'sect', and she temporarily forgot her identity. She ended up unlawfully held in prison (six months) in Brisbane, and an immigration detention centre (four months) in South Australia. Her wrongful imprisonment later became the subject of a government inquiry, the Inquiry into the Circumstances of the Immigration Detention of Cornelia Rau, and the *Palmer Report* (2005) which strongly criticized the culture of the Immigration Department and proposed recommendations for systemic change[43] referred to below.

Cornelia Rau was born in Germany to middle class parents, in the Baltic city of Hamburg. Her father, Edgar Rau, worked for a pharmaceutical company and he brought his family to Sydney in 1967 when she was aged one, and he was establishing an Australian branch office.

When she was aged twelve, they returned to Hamburg. They moved to Indonesia for two years and back to Australia, after her father left the pharmaceutical company. In Sydney Cornelia matriculated from high school, on Sydney's North Shore, went to art school, took a diploma in leisure and recreation, and worked for Qantas. When she was working as a flight attendant, she had an apartment in harbourside Rose Bay. In 1998 she attended Kenja Communication, to do ballroom dancing, and became involved in the sect.

In his long investigative article Robert Manne goes into some detail quoting an anonymous source, about the tactics of the group to secure vulnerable 'sexually insecure and romantically lonely' recruits by surrounding them with attention, and, the feeling of being in a romantic relationship; she was affected by the courtship of a young man in the group 'which she took to be a love affair'. Kenja members moved into her apartment with her. Kenja Communication founded by Ken Dyers a World War II veteran and partner, Jan Hamilton, who studied acting in London, promoted itself as a self development organization.

They ran ballroom dancing, singing, 'Klowning', theatrical productions, eisteddfods, sporting events, and one-to-one Energy Conversion sessions where a 'meditation consultant' would stare into the subject's eyes in prolonged sessions of 'holding a person still', whilst listening to their deep thoughts, to free inner energy blockages to spontaneity, in 'confront' sessions; members were confronted without warning with these in front of others.[44] Cornelia Rau had an unsettling experience whilst in a performance with Kenja in Melbourne, and she fled in distress. Little did she know then she was about to spiral into a years-long nightmare, that would end up with her being held still imprisoned for almost a year hidden away in an indefinite detention centre for asylum seekers, in the remote south Australian desert.[45]

After what happened to Ms Rau, and her involvement with Kenja became known, and after the parliamentary inquiry and report, (discussed below) Luke Walker and filmmakers made *Beyond Our Ken*, an award-winning documentary, which features Ken Dyers and partner Jan Hamilton (Kenja combines the first letters of their names).[46] They gave the documentary makers access to film the Kenja sessions, and spoke at length to camera on the group; the action reaches a dramatic climax when Dyers becomes incensed when asked about allegations of sexual abuse.[47] It includes footage of sessions such as a scene where

Dyers performs a ritual to, as he puts it, clear a young girl of 'negative sexual energy'. One reviewer praises the film:

> Think cultish self-help gurus are the exclusive provenance of gullible Yanks? Then this skilful Aussie doco's for you. [48]

The Age reviewer Jim Schembri described it as

> an extraordinary, powerful, unflinching look inside the workings of Kenja Communication, the proudly Australian "self empowerment" organization.[49]

The documentary vérité footage shows:

> The group's chief asset is a technique called "energy conversion" during which a Kenja member sits opposite a client in a closed room for meditation sessions that can go on for hours. The object of the exercise is to offer a form of enlightenment by purging a person's cluttered spiritual energy of unwanted emotional residue. [50]

In his feature article 'The Unknown Story of Cornelia Rau', published in *The Monthly* (2005) Robert Manne, an Emeritus Professor of Politics at La Trobe University, notes that these 'Energy Conversion' sessions called 'holding a person still' cost $130 and attendees were required to attend expensive workshops; the organization had acquired substantial assets since foundation in 1982. There are Kenja centres in several cities. (Manne's article is referred to throughout this account).[51]

The *Sydney Morning Herald* published an article on the documentary made about the group, in which a 'basic tenet' was described as 'that a human is a spirit whose potential is blocked by 'negative spirits'.'[52]

> The film culminates in a scene in which Dyers responds to a question by poring over a young girl's body, explaining he needs to clear her of negative sexual energy. He then launches into a seven-minute tirade in which he accuses his persecutors of tactics used by Hitler, Mussolini, the Spanish Inquisition and the Salem witch hunt.[53]

Jim Schembri wrote: all was not 'Nirvana' at Kenja. 'Amongst its many happy customers have been those who have accused the organization of brainwashing, cash draining and sexual abuse.' And 'Some who have been involved with Kenja have ended up disappearing—sometimes never to be seen again.' [54]

The documentary seeks to give balanced coverage of 'Kenja's operations and the scandals that brought the organization into the news.'[55] The filmmakers spent hours filming Dyers and Hamilton, who appear to be presenting themselves with transparency, giving them the chance to explain the organization's rationale and operations. *Beyond Our Ken* was voted a third most popular documentary in the 2007 Melbourne International Film Festival, and was then featured at the international film festival in Toronto. Kenja member flew from Australia to protest against the screening, which they tried to disrupt; which only added to the publicity. *Beyond Our Ken* is also available on DVD.[56]

Kenja Communications includes members of adults with children, and members who are teenagers; Ken Dyer committed suicide in 2007 whilst facing fresh allegations of sexual abuse, as reported by Fairfax Media.[57] Urban Cinefile includes this in its documentary synopsis:

> In July 2007, police requested an interview with Dyers about an allegation by Kenja attendees that he'd sexually abused their daughter. The following day Dyers shot himself- shortly before the premiere of this documentary at the Melbourne Film Festival.[58]

Manne contextualized the story of what happened to Ms Rau in relation to the history of reports and investigation into the Kenja group.

> Kenja created for its members an ersatz community. The state of mind to which all aspired was called "havingness". Nothing said in Kenja was confidential; information was centrally controlled. Those who left were thought of as failures and known as "security risks". Inside Kenja, despite the leader's occasional bursts of rage and his mania for control, Ken Dyers' wisdom, authority and goodness were the unquestionable postulates.[59]

In 1992 there had been a parliamentary inquiry into Kenja and parliamentary report by Liberal parliamentarian Stephen Mutch, after his constituents appealed to him following their daughter's 'recruitment to' the group. Many 'victims' brought their testimonies to him, in 1993. Mutch described Kenja in terms of serious concerns about 'psychologically vulnerable young people, especially from the educated middle class'.[60] Manne writes that one young man, who had 'been inside Kenja between 1988 and 1990' told Mutch that he had become 'a diagnosed schizophrenic who had been hospitalized five times'. Manne writes that he spoke 'of four others who had developed severe psychological problems following time inside', and that after writing to Mutch, the young man committed suicide.[61] Ms Rau began Kenja classes in 1998 and attended for six months. An article in the *Sydney Morning Herald*, in 2005, reported that:

> Even though her attendance at classes such as ballet, choir, and drama were infrequent, her "scattered, disoriented" behaviour was noticed. She was asked to leave after an incident at a Kenja eisteddfod in Melbourne where, according to Ms Hamilton Ms Rau "walked off."
>
> As Ms Hamilton spoke, defending the organization's role, her lawyer sat with the green ring binder that summarized six months of Cornelia Rau's life- observations and evidence of the state of mind of a young woman about to topple into a mental nightmare that would lead her to the Baxter Detention Centre. (12/2/2005)[62]

The same article, by Robert Wainwright, reports that in 1998 Ms Rau was diagnosed with bipolar disorder. Manne reported in *The Monthly* that a former member of the group sent an anonymous letter detailing what she had witnessed being done to Ms Rau, which involved 'unveiling an individual's innermost secrets and feelings in a public forum without prior warning'.[63]

Two days after this incident, Ms Rau was in Sydney. She was driving on the wrong side of the road, and stopped by police, who took her to a hospital where she was diagnosed for the first time with psychosis.[64] Over the following five years she was hospitalized several times with diagnoses of different mental illnesses. In 2003, as a voluntary patient she discharged herself from Manly Hospital during or facing psychiatric assessment with a possible community requirement of intravenous medications; she had previously withdrawn her savings from her bank account, so had means to travel.[65] The following account of her journey from the government inquiry's Palmer Report, is supplemented with further additional details from media reports.

Ms Rau travelled, thousands of kilometers, to far North Queensland, and arrived at the Hann River Roadhouse. The reports state that she told the proprietor she was planning to hitchhike to Weipa, a settlement further north on the Cape York Peninsula. The proprietor was concerned about her safety. She took a lift with painting contractors to the Exchange Hotel in Coen. The proprietor of the hotel was also concerned, it was 'the wet' (rainy season) when travellers can become stranded for weeks. At the Exchange, 'Anna' gave different names, Anna Schmidt, or Anna Brotmeyer, and gave varying accounts of how she had arrived and how long she had been in Australia. She was speaking in English and German. The publican called the Coen police constable, James Foy.[66] When he arrived and questioned her, 'Anna' did not provide any identity documents.[67] The police constable contacted the

Department of Immigration (DIMIA) compliance officer John Wisegibber in Cairns who carried out 'travel movements and identity checks' finding no record of her arrival into the country.[68] 'Anna' stayed the night at the Exchange Hotel, the local police tracker paid for her meal, and the publican did not charge her for the night's accommodation. The next day, police went to the Hotel, but she had left; been given a lift, the police found her walking on a road fifteen kilometres north of town, according to the Palmer Report, they:

> explain that the road north is flooded and invite her to accompany them to Coen Police Station to help them confirm her identity.[69]

When asked, she could not remember her name, giving the surnames Schmidt and Brotmeyer, and said she could not recall her date of birth, 'her origins in Germany' her arrival by air or boat, and her movements around Australia. The constable contacted the DIMIA compliance officer in Cairns again, and he ran further checks.[70]

> Unable to identify 'Anna' he asks the constable at Coen to detain her in immigration detention under s. 189 of the *Migration Act 1958*, under suspicion of being an 'unlawful non-citizen.'[71]

Ms Rau was driven on an eight-hour car journey to Cairns watchhouse, where she was interviewed, but she could not remember who she was.

> provides the names Anna Sue Brotmeyer, Anna Schmidt and Anna Sue Schmidt and a birth date of 21 March 1970. She again gives conflicting accounts of her origins in Germany, her arrival in and travels around Australia, and how long she had been here.[72]

DIMIA arranged for Honorary Consul for France and Germany, Mrs Iris Indorato,[1] to interview 'Anna' in Cairns, and the interview was conducted in German. ABC 4 Corners reports 'Anna' spoke German which was reported to be very childlike in terms of vocabulary. 'Anna' could not recall personal identity details and was not issued with a German passport. After three days she was locked up in Brisbane Women's Correctional Centre prison, with the general prison population. The compliance officer visited her in prison, interviewed her and took photos. The report states she gave 'fictitious details of her arrival in Australia, family life in Germany and personal information.' Five weeks later she applied for a German passport, but still could not remember her identity, so her request was refused.[73]

---

1 See ABC Four Corners, *Cornelia Rau Chronology* 04/04/2005. www.abc.net.au/4corners

According to the law, Migration Series Instruction 244, detaining an 'unlawful non-citizen' in jail is 'a last resort'. Although a DIMIA case officer was meant to make weekly contact and visit her once a month, the Palmer Report records that this did not happen. Her 'case officer' Ben Stonely visited her only three times in six months, writes Manne.[74]

'Anna' was one of twenty-five prisoners interviewed by an Ethical Standards Unit investigation team, an independent investigator, and a representative of a support group, Sisters Inside. In a taped interview she describes being punished, put into solitary confinement in the 'Detention Unit' for trying to get a newspaper to read:

> EDU Where would you like to start? What would you like to tell me?
> CR Well I just got put into the DU [Detention Unit] for just want to get the newspaper. Like, basically, I went out of my unit wanting to get a newspaper from the other unit and the officer just said 'NO' for no reason. And I said 'Why?' and he said 'NO' and then he just...
> EDU And did he breach you?
> CR He breached me for just getting a newspaper, and that's not right. I had to stay for five days in that terrible setting where you can only have one room and there's nobody else, you, normally there's someone else there, one room that you have to put up with, to not have anything in the room, there's only a Bible that's all in the room.[75]

'Anna' was kept in prison for six months. In this time, she was held in solitary confinement for five weeks, states the Palmer Report. Robert Manne reports that she had expected to be deported to Germany.

> Her deportation had proved more difficult than DIMIA had hoped. She had now to be regarded as a long-term detainee. In the Brisbane women's prison something peculiar occurred. Anna was informed that she was about to be deported to Germany. In preparation for this deportation, she was moved from the Detention Unit to the Health Centre. Anna was clearly very excited. The handwritten prison note for September 28 records her buoyant mood: "0330 hrs. Awoke and dressed and was ready to leave. Requesting door opened. Says 'My time is up. It's time to go. People are waiting outside for me.' Either sat on end of bed or @ door, repeatedly requesting above." Her escape plan, it seemed, had worked. As it turned out, the news was false. Anna was returned to the Detention Unit...[76]

Two days later, paperwork was dropped off at the prison to authorize transferring her to Baxter detention centre for illegal immigrants. Ms Rau declined to sign the papers. She was then forcibly transferred, thousands of miles by plane to the Baxter Immigration Reception and

Processing Centre, operated by private contractors Global Solutions Limited, in desert land in South Australia. As emerged in the Inquiry, to take her there against her will she had to be 'sedated' and 'placed in restraints' according to the Palmer Report.[77] Baxter was an indefinite detention centre, where writers and a journalist (see Chapter 12) were held for years, exiles from repressive countries they has fled to save their lives after revealing political corruption.[78] 'Anna' was imprisoned in Baxter for four months, and held in punitive 'behaviour management' 'Red Unit'; the Palmer Report records that, on the basis of its interviews at Baxter:

> The Inquiry became aware of a belief among many of the GSL detention officers that before her arrival at Baxter Anna had been in gaol in Queensland for drug use or that she had been living with Indigenous Australians in far north Queensland and had been sniffing petrol. These misinformed stories about Anna's background led many GSL officers to see her odd behaviour as consistent with that of someone who had been involved with drugs or had suffered brain damage as a result of sniffing petrol.[79]

She was held in 'isolation' in 'Red Unit' high security management, for almost three months, subjected to measures which the Inquiry reported 'defied commonsense'.

> for example, in 'week one' a detainee was allowed access to books; in the following week the detainee was allowed to have reading glasses. This is another demonstration of the focus on process at the expense of commonsense.[80]

Asylum seekers at Baxter were concerned about her, and talk to refugee advocate Pamela Curr, who calls the German consulate, and writes to the Immigration detention Advisory Group and Amanda Vanstone the Minister for Immigration. In December 2004, Father Arno Vermeeren and Christian ministers who visit, brief IDAG (Immigration Detention Advisory Group) on concerns about 'Anna''s treatment and her health. In late December psychiatrist Louise Newman's group visits but does not see her. In January, the Germans conduct final searches of databases and say 'Anna' is not a German citizen (ABC Timeline). On the 24 January, 'the German Consul-General in Melbourne advises DIMA that after extensive investigations and final checks by authorities in Germany, it has not been able to establish any verifiable identification that Anna is a German citizen' (Palmer Report).[81]

The Asylum Seeker Resource Centre, which visited asylum seekers at Baxter, lobbied the German consulate, DIMIA, and IDAG. Information on a 'Anna''s plight appeared on a website for asylum seekers and advocates, where journalist Andra Jackson saw it; her article 'Mystery woman at Baxter may be ill' about a young German woman 'aged about 18' appeared in the newspapers *The Age* and *Sydney Morning Herald* on 31 January 2005. It was read by family friends of Ms Rau's family (who had reported her as missing in August 2004); they showed the article to Ms Rau's family.

The Palmer Timeline records that on 3 February, Mrs Rau contacted the New South Wales Police, who emailed DIMIA officials at Baxter with details and photographs; 'Anna' was identified as Cornelia Rau.[82]

> 3 February 2005 At 22.43 South Australian time Cornelia Rau -who is not an illegal immigrant and consequently may not be kept in immigration detention- is removed from Baxter by South Australia police and ambulance officers and taken to Port Augusta Hospital.

> 4 February 2005 Cornelia Rau is transferred from Port Augusta Hospital to Glenside, where she is committed for psychiatric care.[83]

Glenside is very different now, of course, but it is named after the former Glenside Hospital, an institutional asylum for the 'city's unwanted citizens', including 'unmarried women with children', founded in 1836. The state-run institution that was termed the Public Colonial Lunatic Asylum operated from 1846 till 1852. Parkside, which was on the same site, created in 1870, had wards for 'difficult men and women, hospital wards, for the intellectually disabled, tuberculosis wards, and finally at the end of the series of wards, 'Z Ward' for the criminally and mentally insane'.[84] An illustration of what Foucault called the trajectory of enclosures, in administered society, in the nineteenth century, society abandoned the unwanted, the poor, people with intellectual disabilities, and those who did not otherwise fit in; they were all incarcerated in a State enclosure, where separation was administered by location.[85]

Parkside was created in a time believed to be one of enlightenment for mental health treatment, in an ABC report local historian, Senior Clinical Psychologist at the Flinders Medical Centre David Buob says:

> We were no longer chaining people up putting them into water baths, because the concept of being possessed by the devil and needing to be spiritually cleaned had passed.[86]

Ms Rau's sister, Christine Rau, wrote of her despair and shock:

> How could the system allow Cornelia to suffer such horror? [87]

Christine Rau writes of the sister she remembered:

> she was a vibrant, gregarious, empathetic person who loved her work as a Qantas flight attendant because it fulfilled her restless nature. People who met her commented on her talents: multilingual, artistic, tertiary-educated, beautiful. She seemed to have it all.[88]

Christine Rau commented on the double standard for 'unnamed illegal immigrants' and residents.

> While she was an unnamed illegal immigrant, the only treatment she received for mental illness was longer periods in lock-up as punishment... As soon as she became an Australian resident she was whisked away to a teaching hospital, seen by consulting psychiatrists and medicated. During which leg of her flight from Baxter to Adelaide did she suddenly gain the basic human right to medical treatment?[89]

In 2005 Cornelia Rau was awarded 2.6 million dollars in compensation, but in a final irony this was not awarded to her directly but to be managed for her by lawyers.[90] According to her Wikipedia entry she is now studying Indonesian and French at Flinders University.[91]

When Ms Rau was imprisoned, there was no centralized Missing Persons Bureau in Australia, this made it difficult for her to be traced, the Palmer Report states. According to the report, there was no communication between the separate State's Missing Persons offices (Ms Rau's journey took her into New South Wales, Queensland and South Australia). Furthermore, there was a reluctance to release photographs and details of missing people to the media in Australia at the time due to 'privacy concerns', according to the report. All these factors are cited in the Palmer Report as contributing to the long, unlawful, imprisonment. As a result, following the recommendations of the Inquiry and Palmer Report, a centralized Missing Persons Bureau was established.

MEDICAL CONCLUSIONS

After years of research and testing of fugueurs, Kopelman (2000) concluded by invoking Freud's principle of 'psychic determinism'. Freud wrote of this:

> If you think that what occurs... might be anything in the world...then

> you are making a great mistake...a deeply stated faith in undetermined psychical events...is quite unscientific and must yield to the demand of a determinism whose rule extends over mental life...[92]

Kopelman declared that even though he is 'not a Freudian' he would like to utilize Freudian principles and postulate what he terms a principle of 'applied psychic determinism' in relation to the psychogenic fugue and specifically the inconclusive results of medical research into this condition. Kopelman's principle states:

> If you have not found a cause (organic or psychological) for an amnesia, then: either you have not looked long enough (patients may take 2 to 4 years before they give critical personal information), or you have not looked hard enough, or you have not looked in the right place.[93]

Interestingly, Kopelman says that, in order to gain a better awareness of the dissociative fugue it needs to be contextualized within the social and psychological context of the individual undergoing the subjective qualitative experiences of a fugue:

> In cases where mild concussion was accompanied by disproportionate consequences, these matters need to be considered in detail. A patient's initial assertion that 'there is no (psychological) problem' cannot be accepted at face value, and it may take considerable time, patience, skill and effort to find out what really has been occurring in any patient's life. Given the difficulties in the attribution of causality, the social and psychological context needs to be presented for the reader to judge for himself or herself (with reasonable safeguards taken for patient confidentiality): this can be just as crucial as presentation of the memory test scores.[94]

Kopelman concludes: 'Psychogenic amnesia does exist, is important, deserves to be studied, and cannot simply be 'dismissed''. Perhaps the search to understand the qualitative nature of the fugue, which is a subjective condition, could yield more fruitful (albeit less 'objective') results if medical researchers turned to the realms of literature and art, as Freud did, in his representing of psychic phenomena as 'Oedipal'.

The domain of the subjective writing self is where the meaning of the polyphonic and multivalent fugue is perhaps most imaginatively expressed, articulated, and understood in the affective poetic language of literary works derived from the author's experiences of traumatic shock and loss. An enduring figurative trope of literary history is the narrative of the fugue: a protagonist's journey into the underworld (of their unconscious desires) predicated on loss of awareness of personal identity and often involving an ultimate transformation of the self, or a rebirth of the self. This forms the symbolic structure of *Death in Venice*; although the journey ends in Aschenbach's death, it is a deeply Romantic death as the protagonist is overcome and consumed by the idealized image of classical aesthetic perfection (unattainable beauty). The Freudian 'return' of Aschenbach's repressed desire overwhelms him in a fugal loss of awareness of his former identity, leading him to ignore obvious warning signs of cholera in Venice and to succumb to his delusory fantasy and longing in increasingly feverish solitude.

Thomas Mann who was awarded the Nobel Prize for Literature in 1929, was an outspoken critic of the Nazis and fled Nazi Germany. After the outbreak of war, he criticized the Third Reich, in recordings broadcast by the BBC. His diaries which were released after his death show that he had struggled with his own sublimated desires, his attractions to men, and even boys. *Death in Venice* can be read as an account of a struggle between the Apollonian ideals, represented by esteemed, and ennobled Professor von Aschenbach's scholarly works, and the Dionysian pull of his repressed desires overcoming the author-narrator in a fever of sickness, recognizing this as a 'fall', and a forgetting of himself, which the author-narrator expresses in literary form. In his fever, at the climax of the novella, this is played out in delirious hallucinations of Greece. A critique is introduced in Mann's references to Aschenbach's earlier works which led to his rise, in which Aschenbach had participated in the dubious 'nationalistic' or fascist idealization of a beautiful blonde youth.

OBJECTS OF LOVE AND HATE, COUNTERING NARCISSISM, AND SADISM, IN WRITING

When applied to the literary writing process, the two main meanings of fugue may suggest not so much a dichotomy but a contradiction in terms. The meaning in music, in its most complex forms, signifies the language of a high degree of creativity, self-discipline, judgement, and rational consciousness. But the psychological meaning might seem to signify something quite different: an unconscious surrender to impulse and amnesia, an idiosyncratic response to unknown factors that lead to a 'subject' or person breaking away from the social conventions of their known world, and, in an obscured consciousness, wandering on a solitary journey into the unknown. This signifies a radical deterritorialization in which, on some level of their being, the fugueur allows her or himself to give in (to a subliminal desire) to follow an unknown imperative. How is it that two such seemingly disjunctive concepts, with their Dionysian and Apollonian echoes, may be applied consistently to the creative process of literary writing?

Whilst, in many ways a writer's fugue is defined by paradox, contradiction and disjuncture; in relation to this particular dichotomy, it is not such an 'impossible' contradiction in terms to put aspects of these meanings together. When one considers, as Gubar suggests in *Poetry After Auschwitz*, the efficacy of formalism (techniques of musicalization) in articulating (including discussing and theorizing) emotional experience of trauma that goes beyond the limits of representation, the subliminal ('fugal') logic of the paradox emerges. Using formalized, 'objective' organizing techniques of musicalization can, I suggest, provide limits and a context of 'truth and reality', which makes possible the transformation of deterritorialized emotional experience in the writing process.

The missing link here is suggested by fugue's meaning as flight. The writing process constitutes and occurs in, the imaginative, conceptual flight of the imagination. Flight is suggested in the musical fugue by the idea of voices taking flight, fleeing from, and chasing each other. Flight is suggested in psychogenic fugue when the fugueur takes flight from their usual self and their social and cultural environment and sets out on their unknown journey, driven by forces beyond their control. Flight is suggested in the process of writing in which the writer (in conceptual and metaphorical flight) deterritorializes their chosen words and concepts from rule-governed language and transforms this language, according to her own 'rules' or specifications—into writing.

> I suggest the reconsideration of the definition of the dissociative 'fugue' as an exceptional group of phenomena which have it in common that the subject maintains for a considerable length of time some line or course of action in which he (sic) appears not to be actuated by his usual self—or, alternatively that his usual self seems not to have access to the recent memories that one would normally expect him to have.[95]

Although Rycroft, above, is writing about the fugue for a psychological entry on the mind, this description could be applied to writers during the (dissociative) imaginative literary/poetic writing process. The obscured consciousness and specific memory disturbance of the writing process is evidenced by the phenomenon of 'involuntary memory', a term coined by Proust to describe memories which arise unbidden in the writer's consciousness, and are inscribed during their writing process. Recurrent involuntary memory is a phenomenon that is also associated with post-traumatic stress disorder. In some fugue literary narratives these intersect. Literary writing occurs in a kind of obscured consciousness, a mild form of dissociation, involving the driving 'psychological' project of mimesis. In the deterritorialized, liminal obscured state of writer's fugue, hypothetically, the fugal writing subject seeks (not fully consciously) to reconstitute in words, in their 'own' writing, a lost loved object. In Freudian accounts of mimesis, in *Beyond the Pleasure Principle* and *Mourning and Melancholia* (1917) this enacts and reflects the narcissistic drive or desire to 'cannibalistically' devour and thus make part of herself the object of desire. Freud theorized mimesis, as already noted, as the means and form of emotional identification with the other. He iterated his belief that emotional identification is a mimetic process in which the subject's ego narcissistically takes the other into itself; thus internalized, the objectified other becomes an object of love and hate, and desire and loss, that is indistinguishable from the subject's narcissistic love and hate, desire and loss of herself. Freud associates what he terms 'object love' with the sadistic drive, which involves internalizing and destroying the loved object.

> But how could we possibly suppose that the sadistic drive, which aims to harm its object, derives from Eros, the preserver of life? Isn't it altogether plausible to suppose that this sadism is actually a death drive that has been ousted from the ego at the insistence of the narcissistic libido, and as a result only become apparent in conjunction with the object? ...In the oral stage of the organization of the libido, 'taking possession of the love object' and 'destroying the object' are still coterminous; later, the sadistic drive separates off, and ultimately, in the phase of genital primacy, it serves the purposes of reproduction by taking on the role of subjugating the sexual object to the extent necessary for the fulfillment of the sexual act. Indeed, one could say that, following its expulsion from the ego, the sadistic element shows the libidinal components of the sexual drive which direction to take; in due course they follow its example and strive to reach the object.[96]

Freud draws the following rather disturbing conclusion: 'Where the primal sadism element does not undergo any mitigation or dilution, the outcome is an erotic life marked by the familiar ambivalence of love and hate'.[97]

Hypothetically, if writing as an articulation of the inner voice can in some way symbolically evoke the 'oral stage' of Freud's theory, then in the practice of mimesis this means that the writer is in this sense cannibalizing or, less dramatically, consuming the loved object internalized in imaginary realms of the writing process.

This connects with a sense of guilt Klein associates with the artistic creative drive. However if the Freudian oral stage may also be associated with musicalization and polyphonic singing voices, then another meaning is suggested in a very different account of the writing process. Amongst women writers who have insisted on an open approach in writing alternatives to phallocentric authoritarian texts Hélène Cixous is a leading voice reminiscent of views on the primacy of the melodic accented voice, though from a different, contemporary, feminine perspective. Conley writes: 'she insists on the origin of writing as song, as something that comes from the body'.[98]

In her writings, Cixous has challenged the Freudian idea of consuming and becoming the other in the writing process. She has put forward accounts of the related phenomenon of the subject internalizing aspects of loved, desired and lost objects in the imaginative flight of the writing process. This involves the practice of musicalized poetic-prose emerging from and transforming personal experience. Cixous seeks to offer a positive feminist alternative to Freudian theories of 'guilt' and inadequacy that marginalize women in a hierarchical relation to patriarchal authoritative law in social language use, to the Freudian idea, in which the writer must symbolically become the internalized symbolic object which she or he writes about or of—and thus devour. Thus she recalls the homogenous union of harmony in which the melody notes (and some individual voices) become symbolically and materially overtaken. In *La jeune née* (The Newly Born Woman) co-authored with Catherine Clement, a title that has multiple layers of meaning including a psycho-linguistic paronomasiac paronym in the English language—Cixous insists on displacing the desire for sexual recognition which she claims always ends symbolically in the battle of the sexes and the subjugation of one of the partners.

Cixous replaces this symbolic scene of sexual conquest with a desire for alterity, the difference of the other, which encompasses a journey towards the desired other that goes as far as possible so that the self is affected by the other without becoming the other. This recalls a fugue in which the melody notes are affected by the others, responding to each other, but do not take over and dominate each other. They do not harmonize into one. Responsive to the other, and others, each subject retains its own selfhood.

Writing against phallocentrism, in *Jours de l'an* (First Days of the Year) (1990), Cixous personifies the drive that compels her to write, as 'the Queen'. She has to leave the known world of her family on a journey to visit the Queen in the other world. When she is 'over there at the Queen's',[99] the narrator enjoys a pleasurable license. This allusion to the metaphorical unconscious of the writer recalls Persephone, who is both Queen of the Underworld, and Goddess of Spring, sending up the shoots of new life. When Cixous's narrator crosses into that 'other' realm of foreign tongues, she is 'in the secrets... I pleasure everything'. This suggests the flight of writing takes the author into a fluid, semiotic underworld of meaning making where anything is possible and all things are given meanings.

> Light of my life. Truth of my days that from afar I perceive burning, burning at the stroke of midnight. I am Hers. I give her all I have, I kill my oxen and distribute them, I kiss my mother and my daughter and the people who are all I have, and I follow her. Leaving, leaving. Translating my whole life into this foreign tongue, where the words, the same words as here, shine with a secret. Over there at the Queen's I am in the secrets, I pleasure everything. Moreover, there I understand that we can take pleasure in everything: pain, happiness, all is joy. The darkest emotions, the nastinesses, the pigsties, all in the end is good.[100]

In this underworld of fluidity 'everything' defined as affective emotional states of pain and happiness, is capable of transformation into the 'joy' of writing. Cixous's flight of writing involves a pleasurable, joyous translation of the words from 'here' into the deeper meanings of 'the secrets'. These dual states of 'here' and the semiotic queendom of 'the secrets' are located within the experiential realm of the female writer. Cixous's understanding of writing's 'pleasure' evokes a sense that even the 'nastinesses' and pigsties of experience 'here' can be redeemed in the secrets, the foreign tongue, of writing. Even the darkest emotions are 'good' if they can be translated and transformed into the writing of 'feminine speech'.[101]

Cixous, and the various writers of *écriture féminine*, and poststructuralist feminist theorists responded to Lacan's view of the symbolic order of language. In diverse ways, feminist writers challenged the idea that, according to Lacan, there is no room for the female child to develop her own female language or voice in the symbolic order in which language is symbolically depicted as male in his concept of the *Nom–du-père*. (Lacan was clearly writing from the perspective of the 'symbolic order' of the 'traditional' family structure). According to Freudian theory, the male as possessor of a phallus is dominant. The female is thus defined by her lack of phallus. In *The Four Fundamental Concepts of Psychoanalysis* Lacan developed and enlarged upon Freud's views in relation to the *Nom–du-père* in 'patriarchal' language. In works such as *Coming to Writing*, Cixous positions women outside the patriarchal system implied by Freud and the patriarchal law. She challenges the Freudian concept of 'symptoms' as a form of pathologising the other. Women have often been pathologised as hysterical in patriarchal medical discourse. In *Writing and the Law: Blanchot, Joyce, Kafka and Lispector* Cixous writes, 'we are not hysterical, or mad, or anything at all, if we do not legitimize the system of moral laws that is in reality already a system of political laws upon which civilization, as Freud has described it, is founded'.[102] Cixous's solution is to see women as being outside the patriarchal order. She writes that one has a choice between the moral laws, the asylum, or being asocial:

> Or one can have recourse to another logic altogether. Where morals are concerned, everything has always been done in the name of reason and reason did not fall from the sky. It is the very discourse of half of humanity. But one can have another reason, another logic. One can have interest in something that again does not interest half of humanity. There is a kind of creation in the world, a cosmos having nothing to do with the classical creation that is immediately hierarchizeable.[103]

One way out of this disempowering impasse for women is to see the phallus as a symbol of active strength and capability. If the phallus is only a symbol, many things might represent it. In this way, anything that empowers a woman can be her phallic symbol, including writing.

Cixous seeks to pioneer a way in which a woman can be a writer, an author in her own right. She seeks to recover and enact feminine discourse in terms of plurality. Her concept of plurality differentiates feminine from masculine. For instance, Cixous asserts that whilst the male remains forever unified and autonomous, the female body and self is literally divided, doubled, and multiplied in the acts of giving birth and in breast-feeding. Cixous suggests that it is the female body in its nurturing of new life that comes into direct contact within itself with the other. She develops a theory of mothering, and the maternal as a 'gift economy' (rather than a sacrifice). This is an economy of the creative process in which new life is given. It has a parallel or a metaphorical immaterial corollary in the process of artistic creation in which the writer gives of herself, in creation and nurturing of a new work. The expressive experience of childbirth, and of nurturing, for Cixous, suggests a genuine encounter with the other that disrupts the self. In this utopian gift economy, everything is given whilst nothing is expected in return. Cixous attributes this generosity to women in general. In *The Laugh of the Medusa*, she writes: she gives more with no assurance that she'll get back even some unexpected profit from what she puts out, so there may be some life, thought, transformation.[104]

Cixous believes this gift economy is epitomized in women's bisexual relationships. The *jouissance* or joy of such relationships, involves an interplay of difference and the other that is distinct from male desire and pleasure, and which does not involve the hierarchical emotional/social economy of dependence, stereotypical gendered sex roles of 'traditional' western heterosexual marriage.

Cixous asserts that her notions of *jouissance* and *écriture* cannot be theorized, for that would be to subject feminine writing to the patriarchal authoritative critical gaze. Cixous has evolved a way of writing, and a theory of writing, which resists and eludes the 'traditional privileged concept' of the author. This in her view is the dominant, male, speaking position of the centralized locus of rational humanism that represents and articulates patriarchal authority. Whilst, in a subtle sleight of hand, she maintains, she gives birth and wings to her own creative power to express herself in language in her own fugal feminine way. Cixous's perception of writing may be understood as expressive and joyful, an attempt to gain freedom through writing, a very different approach to Freudian theory of the repressed sublimation of artistic creation which is disciplined by the reality principle.

Cixous's writing performatively articulates her deep understanding of women's affective experience in the process of writing. Propelled by a desire for freedom and *jouissance*, in writing she connects with her abject experience that she transforms in her own writing. Cixous writes in several 'voices' or forms, she is an essayist, a dramaturg, critic, and author of poetic-prose novels. Her poetic intertextual writing uses elements of musicalization, and melopoetics, finding additional layers of meaning on a phonemic, rather than a purely lexical, level.

THE WRITER'S FUGUE: PARADOX OF MODERN SUBJECTIVITY

There are particular paradoxes and contradictions in relation to the social and cultural significance of the writer's fugue in the articulation of modern subjectivity. Althusser drew attention to a paradox inherent in the articulation of modern literary subjectivity through his writings on the ideological work performed by the functions of address in which he emphasized 'interpellation' or 'hailing'. This concept problematizes the doubled position of the individual 'subject' in modern society; Althusser argues: 'the ideas that make up an ideology impose themselves violently, abruptly, on the 'free consciousness' of men: by interpellating subjects in such a way that they find themselves compelled 'freely' to recognize that these ideas are true—compelled to constitute themselves as 'free' 'subjects'.[105] Ideology is expressed and maintained in and through language. The contradiction which literary writers have to negotiate in their writing is crystallized in two different meanings of the word 'subject' and the relational positions to language which are entailed. In the first sense, the subject is as an active principle, an actor, or an author, writer. The second sense is that in which an individual is subject to the Law, or state, expressed and maintained through language. The individual, who may choose what they write, has no choice when it comes to the second sense of being a subject, in which she or he is subject to the state 'Law of the Father' in Lacan's terminology. Whereas the writer may believe herself (or himself) to be a free agent and desire to express her free spirit, her 'own' perceptions, the medium she has available to do this is also, at least in one way, the medium of the 'Law' of the State, the pre-existing language in which she becomes aware of herself as a state subject at the same time as becoming subjected to its externalized authority.

This is relevant to the works in the Part II case studies in different ways. After the Holocaust, Paul Celan continued to write in German—a language in which he felt, or was made to feel, un-homed. James Joyce frequently expressed his dissatisfaction with English, language of the colonizers of his native Ireland. It was when he was in exile in Zurich that he set about creating his fugal literary language. Given such constraints, perhaps the only way that authors can write is in the state of metaphorical fugue, a form of deterritorialization of the imagination. In order to escape the confines of the 'Law', the sense that the words they use are the words of rules and regulations, the writer must become a fugueur and wander off in an inner state of obscured consciousness, to create her own rules and strategies of narrative composition. This is a seemingly irrational escape with an unconscious rational purpose. Some altered state of writing and reading, an intense dream-like state, of liminality or intermediality—a waking dream in between conscious and unconscious worlds—has been written about since classical times, when poets, and poetic flight, were believed to be inspired by the nine muses of poetry.

Yet there are particular problems involved in this double nature of subjectivity, and the writing process which writers are compelled individually to address. The struggle of the author is to articulate and write herself in a way which is an authentic expression of her individuality, her perceptions and experiences within (or against) the context of the modern social and cultural world, which she inhabits and is a part of—as a modern subject. This indicates not only the conceptual difficulty of theorizing a coherent account of the 'subjective' process of writing and authorship; it also indicates the psychic struggle facing the writer as a creative artist who desires to write literary work that is original, and true. In the mid-nineteenth century, in Paris, Baudelaire was writing of 'modernity', and on the shock of modern life in the city, in his literary and art criticism, and poetry. As Benjamin commented,[106] he writes of characters as motifs. These included: the artist, the man of the world, the man of crowds, the child, the soldier, the dandy, women: honest ones and others... In his writing he takes the streets as the authentic theatre peopled with characters on the fringes as well as high society. The fugueur was another character in the streets, though not named until 1887. 'Carriages' is a motif of life on the streets (which has relevance to the narrative of De Quincey's *Dream-Fugue* in his *The*

English Mail-Coach which Baudelaire translated).

Hacking has recently written of opposing 'environmental vectors' (of virtue and vice),[107] from which diagnoses of 'transient mental illnesses' emerge, and which applies to the 'neurasthenia' of modernist authors, which Proust and Baudelaire were both said to suffer from. Another relevant environmental perspective for writers in modernity is put forward by Foucault, in the mid-late twentieth century in *Discipline and Punish*, of the enclosures which enclose the individual, starting with the family, the school, the barracks, the factory, the hospital, the mental asylum, and the prison... In his essay 'What is an Author',[108] Foucault writes of the modern author, and the 'question of the author' emerging as 'a privileged moment of individualization in the history of ideas, knowledge, and literature'. He writes of the relationship of the author to the text and writing as implying an action that is 'always testing the limits of its regularity, transgressing and reversing an order that it accepts and manipulates.'[109] He talks of the kinship between writing and death and the idea of a spoken or written narrative providing a protection against death which has passed into the idea of immortality of the author, through her, or his, work, and their name living on, after their death. The modern author's name 'characterizes a particular manner of existence of discourse', Foucault writes. 'Discourse which possesses an author's name is not to be immediately consumed and forgotten' and 'its status and its manner of reception are regulated by the culture in which it circulates'.[110] Foucault posits that the naming of the modern author is a way of holding the individual responsible for their writings, subject to censorship, punishment, and imprisonment:

> Speeches and books were assigned real authors, other than mythical or important religious figures, only when the author became subject to punishment and to the extent that his discourse was considered transgressive.[111]

It was at the time of the establishment of a system of ownership and copyright rules at the end of the eighteenth century and beginning of the nineteenth that 'transgressive properties' he sees as intrinsic to the act of literary writing became the imperative of literature.[112] Foucault sees this as an unconscious compensatory dynamic of restoring an element of danger and risk to the action of writing just as it had assumed the safer status of individually owned property. (He does not focus on the impacts of cultural and psychological trauma in the motivation to write, although these are not mutually exclusive.)

These are also enclosures which fugueurs might seek unconsciously to escape, and writing was a 'protection against death' which modernist and modern authors and artists sought to escape, in journeys in the world, and in their art.

Deleuze and Guattari write, in *Kafka: Towards A Minor Literature*, of the individual seeking to escape in a line of escape: 'right, left or in any direction as long as it is as little signifying as possible.'[113] Deleuze has also written of his concept of the 'dividual', rather than 'individual', the 'dividual' is divided into 'constituencies' from within.[114]

Another way of thinking of escape is in terms of music, as a polyphony, a fugue which the writer practices, by inhabiting other characters and selves, in their imagination in the writing of narratives. Baudelaire flies lyrically in imagination and pen portrait across the city and its inhabitants, from all social stratas. Benjamin describes the identification of Baudelaire with the characters or motifs in his writings, his aerial descriptions in terms: 'of being himself and someone else... Like a roving soul in search of a body, he enters another body whenever he wishes.'[115]

Meanwhile in the mid-to-late-eighteenth century in London. The story of the Irish statesman Edmund Burke in London, reflects aspects of the emergent modern author, and the fashioning of a self in literary subjectivity, which was to effect and show the comparable social and cultural contexts of the author and publishing in the political and literary intellectual circles of London, in comparison to the musical and moral disputes of Rousseau and *philosophes* in Paris. Burke who came from a well-to-do Irish family became a successful author in London after being accepted into the circles of literature and politics, when he published his first full length manuscript entitled *A Vindication of Natural Society:, or, A View of the Miseries and evils arising to Mankind from every species of Artificial Society* (sic) (1752). This work tapped into the zeitgeist, and the debate between the natural and the artificial, of the republic of Letters, in Ireland, and Europe and was the start of his career as a professional author, which made his reputation intellectually and provided his income. This work was followed by: *Philosophical Enquiry into the Origin of our Ideas of the Sublime and Beautiful* (1757) and in collaboration with William Burke, *An Account of European Settlement in America* (1757). Yet his career as an author was fraught by accusations of not being authentic as a writer, and of not having a legitimate, or true voice. He was involved in the political turmoil of the time, and the revolutionary spirit, which heralded the revolution in France, and he was later accused of betraying or repressing his leanings to safeguard his financial well-being. Rousseau wrote that he could not be an author if he had a 'venal pen', but Burke was accused of just this. He defended himself, saying that it was due to his minority and outsider status as an Irishman in the political establishment of London. Although he was a supporter in principle of the French Revolution he exhorted diplomacy over bloodshed, as he wrote in his highly influential *Reflections on the Revolution in France* (1790).[116] This triggered a pamphlet war. Within a few weeks, Mary Wollstonecraft had published *Vindication of the Rights of Men*; followed by Thomas Paine's *The Rights of Man* (1791). At some points, Burke acknowledged that his survival as an Irishman in parliament and the British political and literary establishment depended on repressing his feelings, his loyalty to his home country. In 1796 Burke's passionate reply to attacks by the Duke of Bedford, the radical whig aristocrat who accused him of repressing his real feelings about the revolution in France to secure the patronage from parliament that he had just been awarded for services to his country, led to his publishing *A Letter from the Right Honourable Edmund Burke to a Noble Lord, on the Attacks made upon him and his Pension in The House of Lords, by the Duke of Bedford and the Earl of Lauderdale* (London, 1796). His anger burst out in powerful rhetorical prose, of the type De Quincey termed the 'literature of power'. He replied:

> At every step of my progress in life, (for in every step was I traversed and opposed), and at every turnpike I met, I was obliged to shew my passport, and again and again to prove my sole title to the honour of being useful to my Country, by a proof that I was not wholly unacquainted with its laws, and the whole system of its interests both abroad and at home. Otherwise no rank, no toleration, even for me.[117]

This snapshot briefly illuminates the deeper historical backdrop to the subliminal story in the 'Sirens' episode in Joyce's *Ulysses*, of the plot to bring down Charles Parnell, one hundred years later, as he almost secured Home Rule in Ireland, at the end of the nineteenth century, which is the context in which another long home-coming journey was written by Joyce, also a self-imposed exile from Dublin. Parnell faced oppositions in the British political establishment in London, and in Ireland, and his downfall was his affair, then marriage to Katherine O'Shea, the separated wife of a political rival, references to which are woven into the story of the decoy in the 'Sirens' episode. Joyce relays this story in a double-voiced discourse, through songs, and references, in motifs of seduction and decoys. These are discussed in more detail in Chapter 9. One of the songs, the ballad, is represented in a painting by Charlotte Schreiber, *The Croppy Boy (The Confession of an Irish Patriot)* (1879). *The Croppy Boy* relates the story of a young Irish patriot who was tricked and killed in the 1798 Rising. The song began its life in 1798 as a ballad sung by street peddlers. Its lines and sentiments run throughout the 'Sirens' episode of *Ulysses*, it is sung by Ben Dollard in the Ormond Hotel. The context of the Rising and its rapid defeat included bad luck that would not be out of keeping in the trials that beset Odysseus and his doomed comrades in their fateful 19-year homecoming voyage by boat, in Homer's *Odyssey* (after winning the war which was started by Paris stealing Helen). It was planned that French supporters would sail to the west coast of Ireland, and meet up with the Irish fighting to regain their homeland. The plan was they would defeat the colonizers, and restore Ireland to the Irish. Bad weather at Bantry Bay prevented the French ships from landing; and, without their support, the uprising that went ahead was defeated. It is this epic story that Joyce adapts, in varying degrees of parody, in his *Ulysses*.

It was by replying, in writing, answering back, freedom of speech and expression, that these authors fashioned or articulated a persona, a self, in powerful prose and poetry, perhaps in a coded way in fictionalized narratives or poetry, or directly, in letters; this is the emergence of the modern subject in literary language and the subjectivity of the self as a modern citizen, a subject of the state, or in contrast, as an outsider, an illegal alien, and stateless; until proven to belong, or granted the right of residency, as the history of Australia, and the true story of Cornelia Rau shows.

Proust in his *Search* uses recurring motifs in the narrated memory of Marcel, to metonymically stand for the objects of memory, including the 'little phrase' of music, which individuates Marcel, and propels or unfolds the narrative. Joyce adapts recurring motifs in the 'Sirens' fugue to stand for the characters in the episode through synecdochical devices, including use of onomatopoeic sound-words. As in musical fugue the recurring melodic motifs create texture and movement in *Ulysses*, which he wrote in self-imposed exile from Ireland still under colonial rule. In *Deathfugue* (Todesfuge) Paul Celan speaks back to the murderers of his mother in a concentration camp, using the language of German, his mother-tongue as a Romanian Jew in the province of Bukovina, born after the break-up of the German and Austro-Hungarian empire and redrawing of boundaries, and before the redrawing of boundaries again after the Second World War, which saw the province he grew up in, of Chernivtsi, Romania, disappear, annexed, into the Soviet Ukraine. For decades there was a widespread cultural denial and amnesia about the holocaust in Romania, and until only very recently one of its former leaders, the pro-fascist General Ion Antonescu, who was executed for war crimes in 1946 for his part in the 1941-42 Odessa massacre and similar crimes in Transnistria, was treated like a hero.[2]

In Sylvia Plath's writings of emotional and psychological depth she explored taboo subjects in the nineteen sixties of nervous breakdown, damage by electroconvulsive therapy and being a mother, abandoned by her husband with their two infant children, in London in a freezing winter, struggling to overcome her deeply traumatic shocks.

Deleuze and Guattari asked questions of relevance to each of these authors, writing their fugue works in counter-exposition to the 'master language':

> How many people today live in a language that is not their own? or no longer, or not yet, even know their own and know poorly the master-language they are forced to serve?
>
> How to become a nomad and an immigrant and a gypsy in relation to one's own language? This is the problem of immigrants, and especially their children, the problem of minorities.[118]

How can a writer achieve individuation, symbolically effect a separation from the 'law of the father', escape the enclosures, and differentiate herself from the narratives of the society in which she lives? In what ways and to what extent can writers create their own original inventive true works? An indication of the interpellation, or influence, of social and cultural texts into the literary polyphonic narratives of individual authors is discussed in regards to the authors and their works in Part II. Amongst those discussed, in different ways, each author negotiates the contradictions through using a strategy of contrapuntal fugal writing.

---

2   The subject of the documentary *Odessa* (2010) by Romanian filmmaker Florin Iepan.

PART TWO

6
Literary Fugue Studies

> Ricercar n. (Music.) Instrumental composition of study or fugue type esp. of sixteenth and seventeenth centuries.

Ricercar, *Italian for 'to seek out,' was the term ascribed to an early form of the musical fugue. In literary terms, the ricercar may be seen to function in relation to the fugue in ways not dissimilar to the musical genre. De Quincey sought to develop a powerful expressive literary form, developing his own distinctive etymology of rhetorical terms.* The Dream-Fugue *exemplifies his intentional use of musicalization in his 'literature of power. Whereas Proust (1871-1922) did not write his works intentionally referencing fugue form, the functions of fugue as a ricercar can be seen to operate in his* À la recherche du temps perdu, *an eight-volume narrative fugal composition operating on many levels. In it, at least seven first-person voices can be detected. Each belongs to the narrator Marcel, speaking in different times, and modes. Marcel's voices interweave in a ricercar of complex, monumental proportions. Proust's novel not only provides the literary approximation of an individual author's multi-layered memory but is also an exemplar of the fugal nature of self-reflective autobiographical narrative. Joyce went further in rhetorical, political and aesthetic psycho-linguistic experimentation in his search to develop a unique, individualistic form of language. Growing up, an Irish citizen of colonized Ireland, he was driven by a belief that the English language was incapable of articulating feelings, thoughts, and cultural knowledge, that, as a self-exile in Europe he expressed in the musicalized literary form of his invention, accented with the speech rhythms and word-play of Dubliners. In this, he intentionally adapted techniques of a fuge per canonem in the 'Sirens' episode in* Ulysses. *Paul Celan's* Todesfuge *exemplifies the conversion of traumatic experience into poetic writing that characterizes the fugal modality. Sylvia Plath contrapuntally responds to Celan's fugue, in her poem of emotional and psychological depth* Little Fugue.

In their writing they each sought to reconcile experiences of trauma, which found release in the dissociated formalized musicalized rhetorical figures of fugue forms. Each of the literary composers, De Quincey, Proust, Joyce, Celan, and Plath are driven by profound imperatives, conveying the integrity of loss (of their loved object/person/place) and jouissance as they write of inner truths of being, *truth dwells in the inner man*. The desire to write, is a healing drive for restitution, to reconstitute lost objects in words, in writing, after trauma, to restore dignity, and to bear witness; and speak truth to power, in the literature of poetic power.

1. *Thomas De Quincey: The English Mail Coach*, part 3: *Dream-Fugue: on the Above Theme of Sudden Death* De Quincey was haunted throughout his life by the death of his sister, when she was eight, and he, six years old. Images of sudden death and doomed maidens, whom the narrator tries to save from 'sudden death', recur throughout his writings.

2. *Marcel Proust: À la recherche du temps perdu (In Search of Lost Time)* Following the death of his mother, and his onset of chronic ill health, Proust locked himself away from his life as a Parisian high-life dandy and socialite, and began writing—a life of isolation that ended only in his death. He wrote about the life he had lived until his seclusion.

3. *James Joyce: 'Sirens' in Ulysses* Joyce mourned and celebrated his homeland, Ireland, which was colonized by British invaders. He left Ireland in his early twenties to live in self-imposed exile in Europe. In *Ulysses*, his homeland is reconstituted in extraordinary detail.

4. *Paul Celan: Todesfuge (Deathfugue)* Paul Celan mourned his parents, and the Jewish people murdered in concentration camps. *Todesfuge* is an expression of his feelings, and an elegy for his mother.

5. *Sylvia Plath: Little Fugue* In her homage to Paul Celan's *Todesfuge* Plath mourns her father and the loss of humanity in the Holocaust. Each of the 'fugue' composers returns to lost objects that they seek to reconstitute in the solitary process of writing. Their writings are peppered with recurring motifs of what has been lost, the lost object, and the lost object of desire, which despite their often superhuman efforts in writing they nonetheless cannot recover. Like the musician-god Orpheus, despite a descent into the Underworld of the creative imagination, cannot bring back their Eurydice, alive to the surface. When they emerge from immersion in the writing process, they are still alone.

The studies are examples of literary fugues, for a variety of reasons.

They are significant literary works with high degrees of agency. They each, variously, use techniques inspired by the musical fugue in their language and structure. The works range in time from early nineteenth century narrative to mid-twentieth century poetry. Three were chosen because they intentionally reference the fugue in their titles. Proust's work was selected for its subliminal use of fugue techniques, polyphony, counterpoint, recurring motifs, involuntary memory and word-music, and because (although it is much longer) its style bears some discernible if indirect signs of influence by De Quincey's *Dream-Fugue* (translated by Charles Baudelaire) and his 'literature of power'.

De Quincey's text demonstrates the interpellation of nineteenth century ideological narratives: the glory of volition and global colonial communications (the opium trade with China), symbolized by the English mail coach. He implicitly criticizes the dangers and traumas of the individual in modern society through his individualistic writing based on his childhood experience of traumatic shock. Proust reflects aspects of the narratives of the desirability and glamour and prestige of high society, which he criticizes by focusing on its denizens' foibles, absurdities, double-lives, and deceptions in a society which prohibited homosexuality. Using tactics of hidden polemic, Joyce revolutionizes the English language with techniques of musicalization. In *Deathfugue* Celan answers back to the '*meister*'. This is echoed in Plath's *Little Fugue*.

The works fulfill the three criteria herein identified as characterizing a literary fugue. These are, *first*: intentional or even unintentional use of musicalized fugue influences. *Second*, evidence of a mood, or mind-set, generated by personal experience of traumatic shock. This is signified by a loss and desire for restitution of a 'lost loved object' in writing. Such motives are transformed in the process of writing, into the musicalized, affective writing, that De Quincey called *impassioned prose*. The *third* criterion involves the writer, reflecting on, critiquing and transforming reality through language aesthetically and politically, in an 'escape' from the mundane social cultural world, which, paradoxically, generated the experiences of which they indirectly or directly write. In this metaphorical flight, the author's experience of trauma is worked through. These literary fugue narratives also exceed these criteria to create the formalized, musicalized articulation of the individualistic subjectivity of modernity.

7

THOMAS DE QUINCEY'S
DREAM-FUGUE

Before he began publishing his literary writing, Thomas de Quincey was a self-proclaimed gentleman-scholar—and a self-confessed opium eater. He was a Greek scholar, and a contemporary and friend of the Romantic poets. In his writing he reinvented classical rhetorical categories and invented rhetorical terms and forms of writing that he called the 'language of power' and 'impassioned prose'.

The life of Thomas De Quincey (1785-1859) spanned a large part of a century of modernity. His essay *The English Mail Coach,* with its Section III, *Dream-Fugue: on the Above Theme of Sudden Death,* exemplifies a new form of writing based on the self. Not realist or naturalist writing, it is antithetical to the consciousness of Enlightenment reason and rationalism. It is derived from the fractured self of dreams, and traumatic affect, desire and longing and a deep sense of loss displaced into vivid dream images. The *Dream-Fugue's* musicalized writing is synaesthetic and sensational, articulating and evoking musical sound in its rhythm and syntax. It exemplifies the affective inventive language of power, an impassioned prose style driven by motive force, a persuasive will to move the reader, combined with a compulsion to write of traumatic memory. Written in a sequence of five parts it thereby delivers and recalls in a dream-like association the five canons of Greek rhetoric, rearranged through the prism of opium intoxication.

The powerful self-based writing of *Dream-Fugue* and similar works in his *Suspiria de Profundis,* evoke a fusion of Romanticism, rhetorical invention and intoxication. This revolutionary style of poetic writing was to prefigure and profoundly influence the subjectivity of modernity articulated in modernist poetic literature.

THE ENGLISH MAIL-COACH

Some twenty years before I matriculated at Oxford, Mr Palmer, at that time M.P. for Bath, had accomplished two things very hard to do on our little planet, the Earth, however cheap they may be held by eccentric people in comets: he had invented mail-coaches, and had married the daughter of a duke...

...The mail-coach, as the national organ for publishing these mighty events thus diffusively influential, became itself a spiritualized and glorified object to an impassioned heart; and naturally, in the Oxford of that day, all hearts were impassioned, as being all (or nearly all) in early manhood. (From *Section I- The Glory of Motion*)

But the lady----But the lady---! Oh, heavens! will that spectacle ever depart from my dreams, as she rose and sank upon her seat, sank and rose, threw up her arms wildly to heaven, clutched at some visionary object in the air, fainting, praying, raving, despairing? Figure to yourself, reader, the elements of the case; suffer me to recall before your mind the circumstance of that unparalleled situation. From the silence and the deep peace of this saintly summer night—from the pathetic blending of this sweet moonlight, dawnlight, dreamlight—from the manly tenderness of this flattering, whispering, murmuring love—suddenly as from the woods and the fields—suddenly as from the chambers of the air opening in revelation—suddenly as from the ground yawning at her feet, leaped upon her, with the flashing of cataracts, Death the crowned phantom, with all the equipage of his terrors, and the tiger roar of his voice. (From *Section II- The Vision of Sudden Death*)

Passion of Sudden Death! that once in youth I read and interpreted by the shadows of thy averted signs;—Rapture of panic taking the shape which amongst tombs in churches I have seen, of woman bursting her sepulchral bonds—of woman's Ionic form bending forward from the ruins of her grave with arching foot, with eyes upraised, with clasped adoring hands—waiting, watching, trembling, praying, for the trumpet's call to rise from dust for ever!—Ah, vision too fearful of shuddering humanity on the brink of abysses! vision that didst start back—that didst reel away—like a shrivelling scroll from before the wrath of fire racing on the wings of the wind! Epilepsy so brief of horror—wherefore is it that still thou sheddest thy sad funeral blights upon the gorgeous mosaics of dreams? Fragment of music too stern, heard once and heard no more, what aileth thee that thy deep rolling chords come up at intervals through all the worlds of sleep, and after forty years have lost no element of horror? (Opening, Section III *Dream-Fugue: on the Above Theme of Sudden Death*)

'INTO MY DREAMS FOREVER'

Dream-Fugue: On the Above Theme of Sudden Death, is the concluding section of the three-part article series *The English Mail Coach* written by De Quincey for *Blackwood's Magazine* first published in 1849. Masson who compiled *Collected Writings* (1897) writes in his Introduction that it has revisions by the author. There are several published versions. This chapter refers to the version in Masson's 14 volume *The Collected Writings of Thomas de Quincey, Vol. XIII Prose Tales and Phantasies* (1897), and its republication in *The Works of Thomas de Quincey*, in 21-volumes, published under the general editorship of Grevel Lindop (2000-2003).[1]

Dream-Fugue is the first modern narrative in English to consistently explore different levels and layers of consciousness, and unconsciousness, which the reader is led to infer may operate simultaneously, and contrapuntally in the author's mind. This judgment, however, may be an effect of contemporary psychoanalytical or post-psychoanalytical interpretation. It may not have been the author's conscious intention although De Quincey did emphasize the significance and meaningful unconscious power of dream, beyond the understanding and control of the rational mind.

De Quincey's attention to aesthetics was actively political, as well as reflectively philosophical. He was writing in the Romantic era when aesthetics and politics were imbricated, if not inextricably interwoven.

In *The English Mail-Coach* De Quincey was writing spectacular, social and political critique—which provoked some outraged critical reaction. It seems fair to say that De Quincey's *English Mail-Coach* performs the semantic function of a symbol of modern progress. Through this symbolic device, he offers a moving, dynamic and fast-paced social and political critique of early modernity from the perspective of the individual subject. This effectively constructs the 'subject', the active principle of the individual narrator with a powerful personal identity, driven by passionate feeling and trauma: subject formation constructed in the medium of affective writing.

Each of the main sections of the *English Mail-Coach* are narrated in a distinct style, effecting a transposition of topoi and style from the rhetorical digressive witty style of *The Glory of Sudden Motion*, through the reflective articulation of traumatic shock triggered by the near-accident in *The Vision of Sudden Death*, to the hallucinatory spectacular intoxicated performative writing of the *Dream-Fugue*.

Taken as a whole, *The English Mail-Coach* triptych effects a series of transpositions that can be analyzed as a 'double-voiced' articulation and reflection in a narrative form of De Quincey's critique of social and political changes of early modernity. Simultaneously, in a contrapuntal reading, these transpositions can be interpreted as a series of changes performed in his writing of the consciousness and the unconsciousness of subject formation articulated in writing as self-based art.

This pattern of change occurs in sequential order. On a subliminal level, the writing is antithetical to the supposed progress of modernity, in relation to its traumatic and dissociative effects on the 'subject'—the narrator/implied author. The rationally constructed 'subject' of the first movement of the triptych is deeply shaken through the traumatic shock of the second movement; and in the third movement is deterritorialized, disassociated into a spiritualized bodiless perspective of observation, like a fugueur in the imaginary phantasmagorical 'simulacra' of his own dream images.

The triptych positions the individual author, as author, within the wider context of the antithetical Romantic explorations into human consciousness, 'hidden' truth and meaning. De Quincey's writing was antithetical to the 'artificial' rule-governed harmonies of sophisticated industrialized society that Rousseau identified in his criticism of Western harmony. There is perhaps a political edge to the symbolic choice of the musical fugue, exemplifying pre-modern melody, in the subliminal social critique in *The English Mail-Coach*. Is there a hidden polemic, and/or a double-voiced discourse in his impassioned articulation of affect and expression of the free artistic spirit?

Read in *The English Mail-Coach*, the *Dream-Fugue* contrasts to, and counterpoises, the earlier sections, performing a state of altered consciousness, spectacular, symbolic 'waking dream' of fantastical images, and rhythm producing strong emotive affects. The first sections of the triptych set the scene for the dream fugue, an intense excitation, concentration, and overflowing of impassioned emotion. The three parts of *The English Mail-Coach* triptych constitute a narrative providing an insight into multi-layers of consciousness in the imagined mind of the implied author/narrator and perhaps also the reader.

The English Mail-Coach begins in humorous, witty, informative style on the theme of the English invention, the mail-coach, in *The Glory of Sudden Motion*. Its content is autobiographically based, drawn from De

Quincey's experiences as a student at Oxford, using the royal mail-coach as his, and his peers, preferred form of transport, the only mode they deemed worthy for themselves, to and from home, London, and Oxford.

Through anecdote and reflection, De Quincey relates a rhetorical account of experiences riding as an 'aristocratic young gentleman' on the box of the mail-coach, which after careful consideration, the students deemed the most desirable seating arrangement, preferable to riding closed inside. He discusses the social hierarchy of this:

> the illustrious quaternion, [who] constituted a porcelain variety of the human race, whose dignity would have been compromised by exchanging one word of civility with the three miserable delf-ware outsides. Even to have kicked an outsider might have been held to attaint the foot concerned in that operation, so that perhaps it would have required an act of Parliament to restore its purity of blood. (*Collected Writings Vol. XIII*: 273)

Thus they rearrange the order of the social hierarchy of the mail coach seating arrangements. As the narrator puts it: 'Great wits jump', and it was not long before this debate over the merits of inside or outside the mail coach had, somewhat improbably, travelled to China where:

> The question was soon asked in China when a state-coach was sent as a gift by George III to the Emperor of China in Pekin. The grand state question, 'Where was the Emperor to sit?' (296)

Thus, the narrator relates

> A revolution of this same Chinese character did young Oxford of that era effect in the constitution of mail-coach society. It was a perfect French Revolution; and we had good reason to say *ca ira*. (296)

De Quincey's narrator draws out the most spectacular elements of the experience: the volition, horses, the power and style of the royal mail-coach, including the superior size and tasteful design of the coach and the livery of the 'royal' coachman with his whips and hard-won decorations. Yet, this is a foil, for the mail-coach has a more ominous culturally symbolic, and personally significant, function as a vehicle for the narrator, which is about to become clear.

The Glory of Motion concludes with the ominous—albeit thrilling—acknowledgment that in bearing news of victory in the great battles of the times, the news was not always gladly received by everyone:

> The mail coach it was that distributed over the face of the land, like the opening of apocalyptic vials, the heart-shaking news of Trafalgar, of Salamanca, of Vittoria, of Waterloo. (271-2)

The narrator describes the female relatives whose menfolk have been slaughtered, with examples of grieving mothers and mothers yet to discover their bereavement. The glorious motion of the mail-coach—symbolizing volition, the speed of communications and the power of modern life—now suddenly appears shadowed by, if not causally connected to violent and sudden Death.

The Glory of Sudden Motion introduces a panoramic topos of England in early modernity, connected to the moving figure of the mail coach. It is written in a rhetorical style of persuasive appeal. It functions on a level of factual, rational narrative consciousness. The essay's tone is high-spirited, social, confident, recounting the recollected perceptions of the implied author's Oxford youth, discussing a dazzling array of affairs of the day related to the theme of the mail-coach, the social hierarchy of seating arrangements, politics, Empire, battle, communications, romance. Towards its end, the eloquent, empirically grounded style gives way to an increasingly 'impassioned,' ominous tone with the introduction of the theme of sudden death.

The second part, *The Vision of Sudden Death*, focuses on an incident of near-fatality involving an imperilled maiden, one of a romantic couple, in a traumatic near-collision at night, between a 'reedy gig' and the mail-coach. Evoking a figure of dissociation, the narrator/implied author is both spectator and participant. Whilst the incident happened 'almost forty years ago,' the narrator relives every detail in traumatically shocking, vivid imagery and sensation. The incident is recounted as if the narrator is split, observed and observer, frozen and caught in the 'infinite' moment of traumatic shock. Matching this, the writing style is anchored ('forever') in the facts of traumatic memory, recalled in an increasingly impassioned tone.

The Vision of Sudden Death is prefaced with a discussion of the cultural relativism of the concept of 'sudden death'. For instance, the narrator comments, sudden death was considered 'glorious' to the Romans, yet 'tragic' in Christendom. Yet this discussion has an emotive, increasingly impassioned tone, suggested by the subject matter and a certain, increasing, velocity of language that implies and evokes a sensational, impending, sense of alarm.

It was during the Assizes (19th century periodic criminal court sessions held in 'assizes towns' which 'justices of assize' judges travelled to)—the reader is informed—and roads were unusually still at night, as so many horses and carriages had been out during the day, by night the horses and people were generally too exhausted to travel as usual. The narrator, in the guise of De Quincey the implied author, tells the reader that, when travelling through the country at night in a mail-coach, he was almost involved in a fatal collision with a small 'reedy gig' coming from the opposite direction, down a narrow avenue of 'umbrageous trees' which met high overhead, giving it 'the character of a cathedral aisle' (p. 314). The coach driver had fallen fast asleep. The six horses were galloping uncontrollably fast—down the wrong side of the road. Riding in the reedy gig was a young couple, who escaped death by only a few seconds. The narrator was the only one who was in a position to act and he struggled to avert the accident:

> What could be done—who was it that could do it—to check the storm-flight of these maniacal horse? Could I not seize the reins from the grasp of the slumbering coachman? You, reader, think that it would have been in *your* power to do so. And I quarrel not with your estimate of yourself. But, from the way in which the coachman's hand was viced between his upper and lower thigh, this was impossible. (*Collected Writings Vol. X111*: 313)

In desperation, the narrator remembers Homer's *Iliad*.

> Strange it is, and to a mere auditor of the tale, might seem laughable, that I should need a suggestion from the *Iliad* to prompt the sole recourse that remained. But so it was. Suddenly I remembered the shout of Achilles, and its effect. But could I pretend to shout like the son of Peleus, aided by Pallas? (314)

Fortified by this symbolic appeal to classical culture, the narrator/implied author, shouts twice and succeeds in alerting the oncoming reedy gig to swerve just in time.

Over 'in the twinkling of an eye', the incident was never to leave the narrator's mind: 'the turn of the road carried the scene out of my eyes in an instant, and swept it into my dreams forever' (318).

The third part of the triptych, *Dream-Fugue: on the Above Theme of Sudden Death*, relates to the previous realistic essays, as a dream relates to the incidents, events and thoughts of a dreamer's waking life. All the elements from the preceding essays are rearranged in a dream-narrative of five parts. Spectacular visual images of endangered maidens, battles, volition, warships, childhood, Christendom, and death and redemption, jostle and metamorphose, in rapid succession, in the dream narrator's hallucinogenic fantasies of horror and redemption. The mode of writing is poetic musicalized prose, surreal, dream-like, and impassioned.

Through its use of musicalization, and visualization, the writing of *Dream-Fugue* performs a paradoxical semantic function of conveying a 'deep' semiotic meaning beyond words. This evokes the displaced symbolic meanings of dreams, performed in the realm of the spectacular imaginary. In this way, the *Dream-Fugue* links the narrator's dreams to the incident that caused his trauma. Another 'truth' is alluded to in relation to the divine, to De Quincey's narrator's appeal to the Christian God of his childhood. Two incidents are alluded to in this sequence. Most obvious is the near-accident observed in the mail-coach. But the more formative is an experience of childhood trauma, when the young De Quincey's sister, Elizabeth, died suddenly, at the age of eight, and he, aged six, secretly visited her corpse.

Dream-Fugue is the first literary fugue narrative ever written. Poems written before this had allusions to fugue, such as Dante's *The Divine Comedy (Purgatory)*, and most significantly Milton's *Paradise Lost* whose reference to 'the resonant fugue' De Quincey quotes in the intertextual epigraph to *Dream-Fugue*. But De Quincey's poetic fugue narrative appears to be the first sustained narrative intentionally to adapt musicalized fugue techniques and visualization, performatively enacting a polyphonic, multi-layered, fugue. Whilst this is achieved through use of polyphony, recurring motifs and counterpoint in *Dream-Fugue*, the highly impassioned and affective form of the fugue achieves greatest semantic meaning in the overall context of *The English Mail-Coach*.

DE QUINCEY'S 'LITERATURE OF POWER'

De Quincey, in *Style; Rhetoric; and Letters to a Young Man Whose Education Has Been Neglected* (CW Vol. X, 1897), conducted a 'philosophical investigation' into the language of literary writing. In a move that is reminiscent perhaps of a fugue composer, he enumerated his 'rules' (or method) for his original style of musicalized poetic prose. His purpose was to devise a practical, aesthetic system of concepts and criteria by which to recognize, define— and write—what he termed the literature of 'power'. In a discussion which uses Milton as an example, he set forth theoretical terms for the literature of power:

> I presume that I may justly express the tendency of the *Paradise Lost* by saying that it communicates power; a pretension far above all communication of knowledge. Henceforth, therefore, I shall use the antithesis power and knowledge as the most philosophical expression for literature (that is Literae Humaniores) and anti-literature (that is Literae didacticae Tiaideca). (49)

De Quincey argues this latter may include:

> ...Parliamentary report, a system of farriery, a treatise on billiards, the Court Calendar...and generally all books in which the matter to be communicated is paramount to the manner or form of its communication. All that is literature seeks to communicate power; all that is not literature, to communicate knowledge. (48)

His criterion for authenticity in literary language is the power to move the reader, and writer; a power that he insists must come authentically from the deeply felt experiences of the author. This implies an aesthetic value judgment attached to the sensibility of the author and the reader— reliant on an ability to differentiate what is worthwhile, and profound feeling and affect. De Quincey contrasts authentic, moving poetic prose, which he terms 'eloquence', and 'impassioned prose', to artificial sophistry which he terms 'rhetoric'. He refers to false representation, or 'rhetoric', variously as 'ostentatious ornament' (82), 'artificial structures' (130), 'an art of sophistry' (82) and fraud' (130) (*Collected Writings Vol. X*). In his impassioned prose, De Quincey determined to create prose in which the words, images and concepts 'reverberated' with each other, and with the concepts they evoked in the mind of author and reader. The overall effect of this reverberation set up between words, images and ideas, he likened to music, which has the power to move the listener's emotions.

From his emotionally-based imaginations— most likely originating in his psychological state of post-traumatic stress disorder, originating in his furtively visiting Elizabeth's corpse as a child—throughout his life De Quincey created a form of writing which enacted emotional affects of post-traumatic disorder, an enactment closely connected to the notion of fugue as flight.

However it appears that De Quincey may have been unaware of

the extent to which his own writing, and theories of writing were connected to his experience of childhood trauma. We read De Quincey through the lens of psychoanalytic or post-psychoanalytic theories.

The term 'reverberation' which De Quincey applied to his poetic prose recalls his impassioned experience of shock and trauma:

> I sate, and wept in secret the tears that men have ever given to the memory of those that died before the dawn, and by the treachery of the earth, our mother. (D-F: 446)

The narrator/implied author's anxiety is mimetically evoked in the 'trembling' of reverberations and in the pathos of associations set up between words and concepts. A self-reflexive vital power of shock paradoxically reverberates between words, images, concepts in *Dream-Fugue*, paradoxical because the impassioned language of the narrative itself is self-referential yet it originates in emotions, and unconscious memories, of the writer:

> Tidings had arrived, within an hour, of a grandeur that measured itself against centuries; too full of pathos they were, too full of joy that acknowledged no fountain but God, to utter themselves by other languages than by tears, by restless anthems, by reverberations rising from every choir. (D-F: 446)

De Quincey believed passionately in the power of music to genuinely express emotion and move the listener. The music he loved and publicly supported (through writing reviews and articles and his attendance of the opera in Covent Garden) was Italian.

THE YOUNG ROMANTIC AND ROMANTIC WITHDRAWAL

A rebellious and romantic youth, in 1802, aged 17, De Quincey ran away from Manchester Grammar School, where he was a boarder. His discontent was fuelled by the physical environment and dehumanization of the industrial town. At this early age De Quincey had already written to Wordsworth whom he deeply admired. He had expressed a wish to visit him in the Lake District, rather than return to school. As he wrote of this: ' It had been my intention originally to proceed to Westmoreland, both from the love I bore to that country and on other personal accounts. Accident, however, gave a different direction to my wanderings, and I bent my step towards North Wales' (*Confessions*). He walked around North Wales, staying in lodgings, then set off to walk and live on the streets of London for a few months, in extreme poverty, homelessness, and starvation, before moving back to his mother's home in 1803, followed by a studies at Oxford supported by a small allowance and borrowed moneys before he came into his inheritance (Works Vol. 1; Confessions).

In his twenties, De Quincey forged a deep connection with Wordsworth. An active participant in London's literary life, where he had met Charles Lamb, and closely involved with the Lake poets Wordsworth and Coleridge and others—from 1807 he stayed at Dove Cottage in Grasmere with William and his wife Mary, their young growing family and William's sister Dorothy; when the Wordsworths moved in 1808 to the larger Allan Bank in Grasmere, De Quincey remained until 1820.

In 1818 his marriage to local farmer's daughter Margaret (they had twelve children) compelled him to find a bigger house, Fox Ghyll, near Rydal. In 1825 the De Quinceys moved permanently to Edinburgh, the centre of magazine publishing. In 1813, after eight years as a 'dilettante eater of opium', as De Quincey wrote in *Confessions of an English Opium Eater* (1821) his post-traumatic reaction, of grief and depression, to the death of Wordsworth's young daughter, drove him to eat more opium, in the form of laudanum, in increasing quantities and as 'an article of daily diet'.[2] The cost of this addiction was to dramatically change his life, and it resulted in him becoming a publishing author. He moved between Edinburgh, London, and the Lake District, settling in Edinburgh in 1825, where his essays and serialized works were published in the new journals *Blackwood's Magazine*, *Tait's Edinburgh Magazine*, *North British Review*, *MacPhail's Edinburgh Ecclesiastical Journal*, *The Glasgow Athenaeum Album*, and others.

De Quincey did not begin publishing his writing until he was almost forty years old—hence there has been some confusion surrounding the somewhat misleading dates of his works. He started from necessity, when due to the opium addiction, the money from his inheritance ran out and he had to support himself and his wife and daughters. He described the effect of solitude in his development as a writer in *Letters to A Young Man Whose Education Has Been Neglected*:

> If there has ever lived a man who might claim the privilege of speaking with emphasis and authority on this great question, By what means shall a man best support the activity of his own mind in solitude? I am probably that man; and upon this ground, that I have

> passed more of my life in absolute and unmitigated solitude, voluntarily and for intellectual purposes, than any person of my age whom I have ever either met with, heard of, or read of. (CW Vol. X, 1897: 14)

In his withdrawal to write, De Quincey set a modern precedent for the literary retreat from the social world into an obsessive all-consuming intoxicated realm of subjectively-generated writing, a pattern based on his memories of the life he had left, that was later echoed in the art and life of Proust.

RE/CONNECTING LIFE, WORK AND ART: INVOLUTES

> At six years of age, or thereabouts (I write without any memorial notes) the glory of this earth for me was extinguished...the love which had existed between myself and my departed sister, *that* as even a child could feel, was not a light that could be rekindled...I sate I stood, I lay, moping like an idiot, craving for what was impossible, and seeking, groping, snatching at that which was irretrievable for ever.[3]

For understanding the deeper psychological and cultural significance of the themes and motifs in *Dream-Fugue*, an obvious starting point is De Quincey's own extensive writings about his life. He was conscious of the enduring impact of his early traumatic experience on the rest of his life.

De Quincey came from a large family. His father was a prominent linen merchant in Manchester. The young Thomas's mother has been described by Lindop as emotionally distant, rather stern and strict.[4] Yet De Quincey describes his mother warmly in *Confessions*, as an 'Intellectual Woman'. He describes his father too as a literary man. The sibling Thomas was closest to was Elizabeth who was two years older than he. When she was eight years old, she became ill and died a few days later.

The death of his sister, upon whom he was emotionally dependent, was a shock from which his writings show he did not ever fully recover. The theme and motifs of 'sudden death' and mortally endangered girls and women recur throughout the copious body of his work; interrogated repeatedly in the triptych beginning with *The English Mail-Coach*, ending with *Dream-Fugue: On The Above Theme of Sudden Death*.

De Quincey wrote about his sister dying, and his secret visit to her dead body in the room that was her death chamber. Traumatized and reeling beneath the shock, Thomas forged his own secret plan:

> On the day after my sister's death, whilst the sweet temple of her brain was yet unviolated by human scrutiny, I formed my own scheme for seeing her once more. (CW Vol. 1: 38)

It was high summer, and De Quincey confides that ever since then the enormity and awfulness of death has been heightened in his mind by its (cruel) contrast with summer. On entering the death chamber:

> From the gorgeous sunlight I turned round to the corpse. There lay the sweet childish figure; there the angel face; and, as people usually fancy, it was said in the house that no features had suffered any change, had they not? (38)

He considers each feature in turn and concludes that although 'the serene, noble forehead' might be the same that is all:

> the frozen eyelids, the darkness that seemed to steal from beneath them, the marble lips, the stiffening hands, laid palm to palm, as if repeating the supplications of closing anguish—could these be mistaken for life? (38)

They cannot (of course), for if they had, he adds, that he would immediately have sprung to kiss his sister on the lips. And as he stands and gazes at the corpse, 'awe, not fear, fell upon me'.

Now a vision begins to take him over. Whilst he stood:

> a solemn wind began to blow—the saddest that ear has ever heard. It was a wind that might have swept the fields of mortality for a thousand centuries. (41)

And he recollects the many times he has heard this wind again in his traumatized recollections:

> Many times, upon summer days, when the sun is about the hottest, I have remembered the same wind arising and uttering the same hollow, solemn, Memnonian, but saintly swell, it is in this world the one great audible symbol of eternity. (41)

This wind has achieved a significance and force in his thoughts that echoes unrelentingly. In *Dream-Fugue*, he associates this, perhaps unconsciously with another divine wind, the wind of the Aeolian harp representing the 'volant touch' that blows through Milton's 'resonant fugue'; (Memnonian wind alludes to the Collosus of Memnon in ancient Egypt, a statue near Thebes that was said to produce a musical sound, when touched by the first rays of the dawn sun). In the death chamber, once the wind blows, he writes:

> instantly a trance fell upon me. A vault seemed to open up in the zenith of the far blue sky, a shaft which ran up for ever. I, in spirit, rose as if on a billows that also ran up the shaft for ever; and the billows seemed to pursue the throne of God. But that also ran before us and fled away continually. (42)

It is as if, in his words of writing, the narrator, De Quincey, is trying to follow his sister in his imagination to heaven and God, but the heavenly vision keeps running away from him, he cannot reach her. De Quincey refers to the inner mechanism within the psyche that processes and deciphers sensory information, as the 'deciphering oracle' (42). This, in a sense, is the function of the self's inner subjectivity, the subjective deciphering machine which determines and defines the self through experience. It is also this unreachable part of the mind that is responsible for generating the uncontrollable rush, repetition and recurring series of images and motifs associated with post-traumatic stress disorder. De Quincey is aware of this, although helpless to control it. As a child in the death chamber, he went into a trance and:

> I slept—for how long I cannot say—slowly I recovered my self possession; and when I awoke found myself standing as before close to my sister's bed. (42)

It is this loss of consciousness, when the shock is so great that he cannot comprehend what he is seeing and loses awareness— whether at the time or in his recollection of the event which he cannot fully remember because it was too awful, that the phenomenon of traumatic shock is most clearly evident. It is what he cannot remember, what he repressed at the time of shock in the death chamber, that comes back to him in an endless series of involuntary memories for the rest of his life. De Quincey writes of the impressions that made their way into his mind, unconsciously in those moments, and from this experience, as an adult, he drew a theory of the mind and perception that accounted for unconscious perception through 'involutes'. He introduced this conceptual term into his *Autobiography* in recollection of his entry into his sister's death chamber:

> And, recollecting it, I am struck with the truth, that far more of our deepest thoughts and feelings pass to us through perplexed combinations of <u>concrete</u> objects, pass to us as <u>involutes</u> (if I may coin that word) in compound experiences incapable of being disentangled, than ever reach us <u>directly</u> and in their own abstract shapes. (38)

De Quincey's use of 'involute,' which he coined, is interesting as it relates to a labyrinthine spiral of associations which has resonance—to both the musical and psychological meanings of fugue. His adaptation of the term involute is complex in its relation to the writing process. Recently, John Barrell comments that conchologists used the word for a tightly whorled shell of gastropods.[5] Baudelaire, in *Les paradis artificiels* (1860) commented on De Quincey's use of involute, which he regarded as a fitting metaphor for his particular approach to writing. De Quincey's thought was 'naturally spiral.'[6]

EMOTIONAL AVOIDANCE, TRAUMA AND FUGUE :

> Blank anarchy and confusion of mind fell upon me. Deaf and blind I was, as I reeled under the revelation. I wish not to recall the circumstances of that time, when my agony was at its height, and hers in another sense was approaching. (CW 1: 37)

In cases of trauma, nowadays, it is considered expedient to talk about, and be counselled on, the emotional effects of traumatic occurrences such as the sudden death of loved ones. But it seems that (as he was not supposed to have gone into the death chamber) the young Thomas bore his grief in silence, not wishing to say what he had done, unconsciously using the automatic psychological defense mechanism of denial or avoidance. The significance and potential long term effects of De Quincey's reluctance to recall the circumstances of that time can be seen in terms of the Freudian view on the effects of trauma on memory. Thomas's six-year-old inability to consciously acknowledge and attempt to resolve his agony at that time, when his sense impressions and emotions swam in a 'blank anarchy' of 'confusion of mind', rendered the traumatic experience into one which was not consciously remembered, and which therefore had the power to recur in involuntary memories. As Lindop puts it, young Thomas's trauma and avoidance, his dissociation, 'provided the motive force which drove Elizabeth's image into his dreams'.[7] In psychoanalytic terms, this becomes 'flight' response symbolizing the traumatized subject's attempt to escape from stress or shock.[8]

De Quincey's kind of intensely subjective writing—drawn from the inner dislocations of trauma and loss—is characterized by or enabled through intense solitude. He says in *The Solitude of Childhood* (1891) that

Elizabeth's death increased his predilection for solitude. This solitude was one that harbored the seeds of his future impassioned prose, his morbid obsession with death and his writer's fugue:

> As nothing which is impassioned escapes the eye of poetry, neither has this escaped it—that there is, or may be, through solitude 'sublime attractions of the grave'. But even poetry has not perceived that these attractions may arise for a child. Not, indeed, a passion for the grave *as* the grave—from *that* a child revolts; but a passion for the grave as the portal through which it may recover some heavenly countenance, mother or sister, that has vanished. (CW 1: 13)

In De Quincey's work, the fugue of mourning, loss and melancholic solitude are crucially connected in, and to, his development of impassioned poetic prose. His seedling writing first stirs in his impassioned solitude as a child. His creative process of future writing originates in this moment. His solitary grief over the lost loved 'object' involves a reverberating desire for the unattainable that has strongly romanticized overtones verging on manic hysteria:

> Through solitude this passion may be exalted into a frenzy like nympholepsy. At first, when in childhood we find ourselves torn away from the lips we could hang on for ever, we throw out our arms in vain struggles to snatch at them, and pull them back again. But when we have felt for a time how hopeless is that effort, and that they cannot come to us, we desist from that struggle, and next we whisper to our hearts, might not we go to them? (13)

This passage strikingly foreshadows a passage in Proust's *Du coté du chez Swann* (Swann's Way).The motif of the lonely boy longing for his mother's goodnight kiss as he lies awake in bed. Young Marcel's formative subjectivity, his propensity for jealousy and loneliness, is shaped by his longing for his mother who does not appear to kiss him goodnight, instead partaking with his father in the 'unknown pleasures' of their distant social world—without him.

Grevel Lindop suggests in his *The Opium Eater, A Life of Thomas his de Quincey* (1981) that the young Thomas sought to barricade himself from pain and grief by losing consciousness and memory as he gazed at his dead sister. I suggest the traumatic shock caused him instead to have a spiritualized, dissociative experience (perhaps of a kind known as an out-of-the-body experience). Lindop proposes that this was the child's way of protecting himself from the terror of shocking experience. But the terror, which he repressed—or transcended in the moment at the deathbed—very soon returns in what I interpret to be a post-traumatic pattern of delayed affect. The child's recurrent bouts of terror began after Elizabeth's death in the form of visions, experienced when he was gazing at the stained glass windows in church, and at home listening to Bible stories. Seeing the glass turn red, as if with blood, the vision of a female image appear in it, were later re-enacted in *Dream-Fugue*, amongst other works.

Clearly his visions were significantly connected with his six year old ideas of heaven and God, and Death; and connected to his belief that Elizabeth was in heaven with God. De Quincey writes of the impact of the Bible on himself and his siblings, 'It ruled us and swayed us as mysteriously as music' (CW 1: 38). And it is this influence—the association of the Bible and religious stories with the trauma of death and God's will—which later emerges and runs throughout his 'literature of power'.

'AUTHOR'S POSTSCRIPT' TO THE DREAM-FUGUE

Critics in De Quincey's time did not understand the fugal writing style or content of *Dream-Fugue*, according to De Quincey's 'original intentions' ('Author's Postscript', *Collected Writings Vol. XIII*: 329). The critical reception was so unsympathetic that De Quincey felt compelled to write an 'Author's Postscript', explaining what he was doing in the *Dream-Fugue* to unimaginative critics. In sketching a brief abstract of its 'original design', De Quincey explains that '37 years ago, or rather more', he witnessed the accident that he describes in *The Vision of Sudden Death*. He writes of the fugal affect this memory had on him: 'a movement of horror, and of spontaneous recoil from this dreadful scene, naturally carried the whole of that scene, raised and idealized, into my dreams, and very soon into a rolling succession of dreams'.

He likens the sequential, kinetic, movement of this process, from experience to waking dream, to that of a musical fugue:

> the actual scene, as looked down upon from the box [on top of the mail coach where he rode], was transformed into a dream, as tumultuous and changing as a musical fugue. (CW XIII: 329)

He describes this dream as 'troubled' befitting a traumatic memory replayed in dreams. It is highly significant, and perhaps unconsciously prescient, that De Quincey likens the progressive, sequential movement of a perceptual experience of traumatic shock to the movement of a musical fugue.

But De Quincey is not trying to force his dream sequence into an unnatural 'musical' or 'fugue' structure. Instead he captures, in words, the vivid images, and sounds, of his dream sequence that have natural music and poetry as well as a tragic logic, harmonizing with the music of the poetic unconscious. This is a 'music' beyond conscious control of the writer, and dreamer:

> the Dream knows best; and the Dream, I say again, is the responsible party. (CW XIII: 330)

De Quincey takes flight into the intoxicated dream of writing in which he gives himself to the power of his unconscious mind, and develops the symbolic meaning and images of his dreams; dreams that have their own inner law, logic, archetypal patterns, and power to communicate.

POST-TRAUMATIC STRESS DISORDER

In the elevated, traumatic consciousness of crisis and disaster, the individual functions automatically, and, with no time to prepare, is powered by adrenalin, instinct and a pre-conscious animalistic will to survive. Being alone in traumatic experience means there is no one else to talk to about, and perhaps contextualize, the experience afterwards. According to Freud's theory, fright has greater significance in the 'absence of any preparedness for anxiety'.[8] In *Charles Baudelaire: A Lyric Poet in the Era of High Capitalism*, Benjamin writes of Freud's thesis that the memory has two functions, remembrance which works to protect and conserve consciousness and the 'protection of impressions', and memory which 'aims at their disintegration'.[9]

It is when trauma occurs unexpectedly and is unprepared-for, that its affects on the brain, body and mind of the subject are most profound, lasting and perhaps damaging. Over and over, in compulsive, arresting vivid images the scenario replays through dreams in endless fugal variations. Over and over again, through the years, they are compelled to write it once again, in a futile attempt to lay the ghost to rest. It is as if the fugal subject is paradoxically attempting to subliminally anchor, find, or cure himself, or herself, in writing.

The *Dream-Fugue* symbolizes an experience of alienation and dislocation, through which, paradoxically a renewed growth of (dislocated) subjectivity emerges and is reconstructed. A new sense of the self—as traumatized—is born as the individual struggles to resolve the tension of the trauma. The most traumatic shock of all enacts an experience which is not remembered which disappears into the memory of the person, to appear and reappear in apparently random recurrences such as recurring dreams and involuntary memories—perhaps over a lifetime—over which the 'subject' or person has no control. This is particularly pronounced, perhaps, if, like the narrator of De Quincey's tale, the subject, or survivor, of traumatic shock is thrown into a position where they alone are in the position to act. In his mind, *a voice says to him audibly:*

> One way lies hope; take the other and mourn forever! (CW XIII: 315)

MUSICALIZATION IN DREAM-FUGUE

Dream-Fugue has a five-part structure, five dream-sections, and an introductory paragraph. Written in De Quincey's style of impassioned prose each part reads like a prose poem. Here I will refer to the Robert Morrison edition (2003). This differs, in some parts quite markedly, from the version of the article published in Masson. The article in Masson's edited works is based on a version that may have been changed by Japp, perhaps an unhelpful if well-intentioned practice of supposed 'improvement'.

The *Dream-Fugue* has an epigraph. This is a quotation from Milton's *Paradise Lost*, which refers to the fugue, and indicates musicalization, in the use of the musical term 'Tumultuosissimamente':

> Whence the sound
> Of instruments, that made melodious chime
> Was heard, of harp and organ; and who mov'd
> Their stops and chords, was seen; his volant touch
> Instinct through all proportions, low and high
> Fled and pursued transverse the resonant fugue (D-F: 442)

Milton's reference to an ambivalent God is echoed in De Quincey's *Dream-Fugue*. The term 'Volant' refers to flying, evoking images of the intangible flying hands of God playing the resonant fugue, perhaps on an Aeolian harp, a concept that also suggests the Pythagorean idea of the harmony of the spheres. There is another significant allusion here to De Quincey's autobiographical description of the 'wind' he hears blowing as he gazes at his dead sister. This is a resonant fugue whose subject themes of life and death are contrapuntally interwoven.

One subject theme of *Dream-Fugue* is 'sudden death'. The other is suffering life, signifying the consciousness of the one who is left traumatized and suffering after the loss of a loved one. The trauma and suffering sets up reverberations of the fugal movements and variations, like 'sighs from the depths'. Whilst this fugue of associations is triggered by the incident in the mail-coach, it develops in a counterpoint of association to cover numerous aspects—and variations—related to sudden death through processes of association (in a recursion to an originary or earlier trauma).

The introduction refers with veiled references, or 'averted signs', to the shock and trauma of 'sudden death' of his sister Elizabeth.

> Passion of Sudden Death! that once in youth I read and interpreted
> by the shadows of thy averted signs (443)

The narrator laments the traumatic recurrence of the image that continues to return to haunt his dreams so many years after the event. The narrator likens this fragment of memory to a scrap or fragment of melody that forms the basis of a fugue developing and continuing (potentially to infinity in Bach's mirror fugues) through repetition that enacts variations on the theme of that melody-memory fragment. De Quincey's narrator asks of this fugal melody line:

> Fragment of music too stern, heard once and heard no more, what aileth thee that thy deep rolling chords come up at intervals through all the worlds of sleep, and after thirty years have lost no element of horror. (443)

De Quincey's association of recurring fragments of memory with a fragment of music has several significant functions.

The first dream-part, in itself a fragment, begins in summer, with an expansive opening gesture: 'Lo it is summer, almighty summer!' in which 'The everlasting gates of life and summer and thrown open wide' (443) as if inviting or drawing the writer and reader into the vast vaults of eternity. This evokes the season in which Elizabeth died. On the ocean, the narrator is floating with 'the unknown lady from the dreadful vision... She upon a fairy pinnace, and I upon an English three-decker' (443). She is on a fantasy boat, he upon an English war ship. This image immediately displaces and refigures the coaches of the memory in *The Vision of Sudden Death*. The modes of transport and the element upon which those modes are borne have transformed into forms, as in a dream, which this is. There is mention of place, England, 'the domain of their common country' in which 'a wilderness of floral beauty was hidden' (443)—this may refer to England under industrialization—a process that was an anathema to De Quincey. Beautiful young people, women and men dance together on the pinnace, it is a vision of beauty, life, laughter, summer flowers moving

> amidst music and incense, amidst blossoms from forests and gorgeous corymbi from vintages, amidst natural carolling and the echoes of sweet girlish laughter (443)

Echoing, perhaps, the laughter of a sister. The pinnace moves beneath the bows of the three-decker. This symbolically provokes guilt. Suddenly all the music, laughter, gaiety, all sounds from the magical fairy pinnace 'all are hushed' (443). The dreamer-narrator is bemused, what has happened he asks himself, he blames himself, in the sturdy three decker with its 'dreadful shadow' and he asks himself helplessly, "Was our shadow the shadow of death?" (443). He looks over the bows to see what has become of the magical vision of the fairy pinnace but there is nothing there, all is gone. And suddenly the man at the masthead cries out that the weather has come upon them, 'in seventy seconds she will founder!' (444).

This ends the first paragraph-fragment.

In the second paragraph, the bad weather rolls in and takes hold. In the ensuing storm, a frigate runs across their bows, recalling the near collision in the English mail-coach. Yet just as with that, as the frigate bears upon them, just in time, it swerves away. As the frigate passes, the narrator sees: 'As she ran past us, high aloft amongst the shrouds stood the lady of the pinnace' (445). Images follow, of the ship shrouded in mist (echoing the previous images in his writings of his dead sister in her death shroud; and the young woman in the carriage facing a vision of sudden death).

The third paragraph opens 'Sweet funeral bells' (445), leading to possibly one of the most expressive and saddest images ever written about the sudden death of a child, swallowed by quicksand.

> Already her person was buried; only the fair young head and the diadem of white roses around it were still visible to the pitying heavens; and, last of all, was visible one marble arm. I saw by the early twilight this fair young head, as it was sinking down to darkness—saw this marble arm, as it rose above her head and her treacherous grave, tossing faltering, rising, clutching as at some false deceiving hand stretched out from the clouds—saw this marble arm uttering her dying hope, and then her dying despair. The head, the diadem, the arm, —these all had sunk; at last over these also the cruel quicksand had closed; and no memorial of the fair young girl remained on earth, except my own solitary tears, and the funeral bells from the desert seas, that, rising again more softly, sang a requiem over the grave of the buried child, and over her blighted dawn. (D-F: 445-446)

In this way the image of the young woman, seen only from the rear in the reedy gig, as she rises and falls upon her seat, clutching at the air is transformed into the image of the young girl rising and falling as she sinks into the symbolic clutches of the quicksand.

In the fourth movement, the narrator 'immediately, in a trance' (446) is 'carried over land and sea to some distant kingdom' (446). This is the movement that De Quincey's critics did not understand for its mention of the battle of Waterloo, but which De Quincey later felt compelled to explain in his Postscript was a logical development of dream thought working on the mail-coach's associations with Empire and victory. Night falls now on the narrator in a carriage surrounded by crowds. The mail-coach has transformed into a dream-carriage, the bearer of good news, a victory that

> we that sate upon the laurelled car had it for our privilege to publish amongst all nations...At midnight the secret word arrived; which word was–Waterloo and Recovered Christendom! (446)

By introducing and associating the victory of Waterloo and Christendom, and the carriage in which the narrator ascends towards a 'mighty Minster', De Quincey introduces the theme of the glory of God, Empire and victory in battle—all themes which relate by association to depictions and representations of Christianity and Empire in nineteenth-century England, which relate back to his upbringing. This dream association moves to the carriage entering through 'golden light' (446) at a 'flying gallop...the grand aisle of the cathedral' (448). The organ and the choir are sounding.

Continuing the association of Empire, battles and cathedrals he:

> became aware of a vast necropolis rising upon the far-off horizon—a city of sepulchres, built within the saintly cathedral for the warrior dead that rested from their feuds on earth. (447)

De Quincey's stream of associations has swung to death again in the way in which it is associated for him with Elizabeth's death, with religious visions and imagery.

Looking up, and in the stained glass window of the cathedral a rosy glow appears:

> within that crimson radiance, suddenly appeared a female head, and then a female figure. It was the child—now grown up to woman's height. Clinging to the horns of the altar, there she stood—sinking, rising, trembling, fainting—raving, despairing; and behind the volume of incense that, night and day, streamed upward from the altar, was seen the fiery font, and dimly was descried the outline of the dreadful being that should baptize her with the baptism of death. (447)

Now, in the last of five movements, the battle for deliverance is played out and enacted in associations. As in the beginning, the implied author links this movement with the music of a fugue, giving the narrative a circular structure:

> Then rose the agitation, spreading through the infinite cathedral, to its agony; then was completed the passion of the mighty fugue. (447)

De Quincey is said to have misunderstood the fugue in music—a form that is usually thought of as more cerebral than passionate, observes Werner Wolf.[10] Yet contrast can appear to exaggerate, enlarge an object, throwing it into sharp relief. Through associations with cathedral music, fugue is adapted a vehicle for the passions which for the narrator are repressed behind, or suppressed in, the controlled, grave beauty of the fugue, performed in a cathedral setting—by celestial voices, with a choir and an organ, which threw up 'columns of heart-shattering music' (447). Just as the cold pain of Elizabeth's death seemed to De Quincey to be horribly magnified by the cruel contrast of summer, a time associated with holiday and the fullness of life, so the restrained beauty of cathedral music kindles and creates a heightened passion in the dreams of the narrator. His fugue grows more frantic.

> We that spread flight before us, heard the tumult, as of flight, mustering behind us. (447)

The narrator asks if it is death, or resurrection that 'had wrapped me in the reflux of panic?' (447). He confides his affliction that never could hear the 'sounds of joy without sullen whispers of treachery in ambush'. He cannot enjoy or trust anything without suspicion, for 'from six years old' he:

> didst never hear the promise of perfect love, without seeing aloft amongst the stars fingers as of a man's hand, writing the secret legend— "Ashes to ashes—dust to dust". (447)

He asks himself why he should always find fear when other men found cause for rejoicing. His 'reflux of panic' alludes to and represents the panic of post-traumatic stress disorder, which cannot let him rest. He cannot love without fear of death to what or whom he loves.

And then, in a dreamer's wish–fulfillment, he hears a voice from the heavens say:

> Let there be no reflux of panic—let there be no more fear, and no more sudden death! Cover them with the joy as the tides cover the shore! (447)

And now all the 'children of the grave' hear this, and, as one, the narrator and the armies of dead children rise up and ascend together 'to the skies we rose' (447).

Resurrection leads to deliverance, a form of reunion and oneness as the dead return to life. And the throngs ascend 'from Waterloo—in the visions of peace' (447). And all are rendering thanks to the young girl, his sister:

> —suddenly did God relent; suffered thy angel to turn aside his arm; and even in thee, sister unknown! shown to me for a moment only to be hidden forever, found an occasion to glorify his goodness. (447)

In this way, Elizabeth's death is given a meaning, or a justification, a reason that may make it worthwhile. For if Elizabeth's death could lead to a deliverance of all people from sudden death this would not only reunite the dreaming narrator with his 'sister unknown', but also perform a glorious service to all humanity—which the dream hordes of the resurrected acknowledge and applaud.

Now the narrator acknowledges that all the images of the girl and young woman, are representations of the 'sister unknown,' whom he could not know because she was taken from life by sudden death. He confides that

> A thousand times, amongst the phantoms of sleep, has he shown

thee to me, standing before the golden dawn, and ready to enter its gates—with the dreadful word going before thee—with the armies of the grave behind thee; shown thee to me, sinking, rising, fluttering, fainting, but then suddenly reconciled, adoring...(447)

The narrator recognizes that God has shown him images of his sister in all the guises that we have seen her in *Dream-Fugue*.

The upstretched arm in mortal danger echoed by the gesture of hope of divine resurrection. And the fugue ends on a note of symbolic optimism after plunging through dark realms of terror and despair, the dreadful resurrections that haunt the dreams of post-traumatic stress disorder—or fugues.

WRITING ACCIDENTS

There is a coded semiotic meaning, one could call it a form of subliminal double-voiced discourse, that emerges from the etymology of two concepts that structure this piece of textual writing.

The first is to do with the concept of *an accident*, which De Quincey uses as a symbol to structure the entire sequence of the triptych.

The noun, *accidence*, is a part of grammar dealing with the variable form of words. Its etymology stretches back to medieval Latin, as in *accidentia*, and before that it has its origins in the Greek, *parepomena*; it is the plural of *accidens* as folly.

Accident: means an event that is without apparent cause or unexpected. It is used for irregularity of structure, a property of quantity not essential to the conception of a substance; or accessory, or ornament in music of flats or sharps (this evokes the word 'Baroque' deriving from French 'misshapen pearl'). Symbolically this might refer to a modern awareness that the world is not designed according to plan, that there is an irregularity, incommensurability—a forerunner of the modern secular world; humans are not here by 'design', but by 'accident'.

Accidental: In Music, it means a sign attached to a single note, not in a key signature and it can be in sharp, flat or natural key.

This etymological sketch reveals some interesting associations and connections between musical language, literary language, and incommensurability of events—accidents—that cause trauma. Connections made in tragedy between incommensurable events, the unknown, and unconscious, and accidents causing trauma—such as the 'accident' of Oedipus marrying his mother and killing his father. In Greek tragedy, musical language and literary or dramatic language were also inseparably linked.

From this perspective, the *Dream-Fugue* can be read as commenting on the changes that were occurring in society as it became increasingly secular, with the progress of modernization. *Dream-Fugue* makes the powerful symbolic point that this progress can lead to accidents. It is telling that it not an actual accident that occurs but that the accident is conceptualized in terms of its psychological impact on the narrator/implied author—and that it is psychological affect of trauma that then defines the event as an 'accident'.

There is a more symbolic semiotic meaning in the use of accidental in relation to the use and meaning of the musical term accidental. This has significance in relation to the development of the fugue form and to the use of the form of fugue.

CRACKING THE PUZZLE-CANON OF THE DREAM-FUGUE

As De Quincey was a music lover who wrote about music, *Dream-Fugue* signifies a paronomasiac play on musical and dramatic/performative literary language. The text is making a pun that ironically comments on the flexible handling of accidents—drawing a contrapuntal comparison between the divine modality (of God) and fugal modality (of humanity). According to a divine modality perhaps there are no accidents, or at least they can be handled flexibly. According to a human fugal modality, the individual cannot exactly handle the accident flexibly being deeply affected and traumatized by accidents. The way that the subject seeks to handle the accident flexibly is through his or her writing in a musicalized style. Prior to modernity the main 'musicalized' style of writing was enshrined in sacred texts; symbolizing an unbroken conceptual connection with faith in the multivalent notion of canon/the Word signifying divinity. The fact that authors and poets such as De Quincey were now using this musicalized style to write of secular experiences is highly significant and modern. On a symbolic level, of double counterpoint, *Dream-Fugue* performatively writes a complex and nuanced comparison between the notion of God as the divine modality writing the world of events and the destiny of all of its inhabitants, representing the Word; and humankind, mortal, writing his or her own destiny in his or her own hand.

De Quincey's text is thereby on a semiotic level of 'deep' grammar commenting on the counterpoint of the modal system representing the sacred system—represented by canon—in musical language and dramatic church language; and the fugue which stands for the accidental, incommensurable, creative innovative invention of the individual artist/composer, which in music reached its apex in the Baroque; and which foreshadowed and gave rise to the society of modernity, industrialized capitalism, and individual subjects.

By using Milton's quotation from *Paradise Lost* to precede his fugue, De Quincey acknowledges the loss of paradise on two levels. First, this symbolically applies to the industrialization of England; second, it applies to the loss of his sister in childhood, thus closing the door on the 'paradise' he had experienced as a young child when she was alive, and which he never felt again. In this way, by chance or accident, the traumatized sense of loss experienced by one individual accorded and came to symbolically signify the zeitgeist of early modernity.

There are further coded messages, to be found in the *Dream-Fugue*. Another puzzle canon is provided by the structure of the fugue in five paragraphs parts. This suggests two possible interpretations. One, that De Quincey had in mind Mozart's fugue section in the *Jupiter* symphony, which has five parts. And as Mozart was one his favorite composers, as writes Sackville-West (1930), this seems plausible. Another interpretation is that he was subliminally playing with the concept of the five canons of Greek rhetoric (beheld through De Quincey's opium-dream prism). This may seem far-fetched but if one analyses the fugue, paragraph by paragraph one can see correspondences by association to the five canons. And De Quincey was an exceptional Greek scholar.

For instance, the first canon is Invention. In the first paragraph the scene of the dream is 'invented' or rather re-invented. It is summer, 'almighty summer' (the season of his sister's death). The second canon is Arrangement, and senses are 'rearranged' by the experience of losing sight of the young woman in the fairy pinnace. The third canon is Style. In De Quincey's paragraph the girl's death is evoked in wrenching impassioned prose. He displays the 'style' of Romantic writing in its most profoundly persuasive mode. The fourth canon is Memory. De Quincey remembers his childhood experiences in the family pew at church gazing at the stained glass window in which he saw blood red visions of a young girl. The fifth canon is Delivery. De Quincey's fifth paragraph turns this into a narrative of 'Deliverance'. This subliminal hidden polemic continues in a subtextual comparison between Greek canon and the fugue that occurs in the structuring of the text into five paragraphs. Opposed to the use of empty rhetoric in oratory and literature, here De Quincey subverts empty rhetoric and replaces it with performative writing of his own deep authentic affective experience.

The *Dream-Fugue* articulates and plays with themes of dissociation, dialogism and polyphony in affective performative writing. In its subliminal poetic subversion of the conventions of classical rhetoric and its detachment from Sacred canon, it articulates the dissociated perception of a traumatized individual subject alienated in modernity.

INTERPRETATIONS OF DREAM-FUGUE

Recent critical interpretations of De Quincey deploy a range of contemporary critical angles including intermediality (Wolf 1999); gender (Clej 1995; Burwick 2001); addiction (Clej 1995); the Other in relation to British expansionist imperialism (Barrell 1991); and capitalism (Clej 1995); as well as investigating more humanist psychological concerns in relation to De Quincey's impassioned narratives of trauma and his life experiences (Lindop 1981).

In one of his pieces of writing in *Suspiria de Profundis*, De Quincey likens the mind and processes of thought, dream and association to a palimpsest. This piece, and others, were translated by Baudelaire (*Collected Writings Vol. X111* 1897; Baudelaire undated).

A self-reflexive significance resides in De Quincey's reference to the palimpsest. Like music, and the visual images of dreams, De Quincey's dreamlike associative poetic-prose has a vivid impressionistic quality that renders it particularly open to individual interpretation. Numerous critics have found different meanings in his evocative words. Some earlier readers, such as Japp (1891) and even, to a lesser extent, Masson (1896; 1897) went so far as to make their own meanings by selectively rearranging his work according to their views. Baudelaire's translation of De Quincey's work in *Les Paradis Artificiels* was to a significant extent a selective representation, and was profoundly influential not only on Baudelaire's poetry but on the *fin de siècle* 'decadent' imagination (Pierrot, 1981).

Julian North has surveyed the critical responses to De Quincey's *oeuvre*. He suggests that even the most renowned critics have read De Quincey according to their own agendas.

He comments somewhat wryly:

> For David Masson, the scholar and polyhistor, De Quincey is first and foremost a scholar and polyhistor; for Virginia Woolf, De Quincey is an embryonic Virginia Woolf; for J. Hillis Miller, suffering from the disappearance of the author, De Quincey is a writer suffering from the disappearance of God...for the deconstructionists of the late 1970s, De Quincey anticipates the insights of Derrida. De Quincey's autobiography is no longer a coherent expression of the authorial voice, but it is now an allegory of deconstruction.[11]

De Quincey's writing enacting the sublime heightened sensibility and symbolic affects of post traumatic shock, has had a profound, if subtle and subterranean influence, not only on modernist literature but on the enduring modernist, and postmodernist imagination of contemporary writers and critics.

MUSICALIZED READINGS

Dream-Fugue is cited by Wolf (1999) as the first literary work to intentionally have used the musical structure and techniques of a fugue as a structuring form for a literary narrative.

Few literary critics have sought to analyze the musical aspects of *Dream-Fugue*. Others include Hopkins (1967), Porter (1980), Aronson (1980), and Jordan (1985). The first intermedial analysis of the *Dream-Fugue* was published in 1938, by Calvin S. Brown. He attempted to read *Dream-Fugue* as analogous to a musical fugue in a technical sense, and was disappointed: 'there is no working out of the complete musical pattern'.[12]

Werner Wolf suggests that the *Dream-Fugue* may be read in three key ways. First, as a 'psycho-narration' of the traumatic events concerning Elizabeth's death. Second, as a political allegory of 'England's history between the French Revolution and the victory over Napoleon at Waterloo'. Third, as a religious allegory of the resurrection.

However—and as De Quincey pointed out—a dream has its own dream logic; in the *Dream-Fugue* all these elements are combined and intermingled, each plays its part through association, in analysis of the whole.

Wolf says *Dream-Fugue* is a worthy candidate for consideration as a musicalized, intermedial narrative on the grounds that it:

> contains the basic constitutive elements generally requested of this microgenre: a) the existence of a narrator (in our case a first-person narrator, who plays a central role in what happens), and b) the existence of a 'story' (or, in our case, of several stories or versions of one story).[13]

He points out that the narrative status of the text is further indicated in the framing section, the introductory paragraph, and the *Author's Postscript*. The writing practice of musicalization and intermediality can be seen to depend upon the exercise of a certain mandatory intentionality on the part of the author—deliberately composing a literary text, using musicalized intermedial techniques. Wolf comments on the 'massive signalling' used by De Quincey in alerting the reader to his use of what are now called techniques of musicalization:

> Thus the intratextual as well as the paratextual contain concrete and specific indications of music and even a particular musical form, so that there is persuasive evidence that *Dream-Fugue* is in fact conceived of as a musicalized fiction.[14]

Wolf uses the criteria of what I refer to as *performativity*; to 'showing', in contrast to telling, as a measure of the musicalization of a text. He comments that the *Dream-Fugue* contains little word music 'apart from a certain tendency of De Quincey's prose towards rhythmic order'.[15] Therefore he seeks to find 'symptoms' of musicalization in the two further categories he uses to define effects of the techniques of musicalization, namely 'structural and imaginary content analogies to music: in unusual or recurrent patterns and images, and in a tendency towards auto-referentiality and dereferentialization;[16] Wolf expects to find such effects to be related to the imitation of the musical form of the fugue, as indicated or signalled in the title of the composition.

Seeking to identify a semantic 'fugal subject', Wolf argues against Brown who suggested 'speed, urgency and a girl in danger of sudden death'. Wolf accepts speed as 'quite near the mark' but argues that the image of the girl in mortal danger appears only once in parts I to III, analogously representing the entry of the subject (in a three part fugue). This would constitute a very odd kind of fugue where the exposition lasts a disproportionately long time (from parts I-III). In his reading, the subject is instead the general idea of a 'horizontal movement'. Wolf therefore offers an alternative to a figurative reading in which images constitute fugal subjects, and suggests instead a non-figurative kinetic reading of the subject—a use that he detects in the works of several authors of musicalized narratives. The kinetic subject is comprised of allusion and references to movement, such as 'drifting towards us'; 'fled', 'Down she comes', 'with the fiery pace ran', 'running along the strand' and so on.

Wolf is the author of the *Musicalization of Fiction*. This is a theory of mimesis, of the imitation of music in fictional narrative texts, which he qualifies under the more general rubric of 'musicalization', a term adapted from Aldous Huxley's *Point Counter Point*: Huxley wrote: 'The musicalization of fiction. Not in the symbolist way, by subordinating sense to sound....but on a large scale, in the construction'.[17] Of primary significance is Wolf's concept of intermediality, the participation of more than one medium of expression in the signification of a human artefact. Wolf suggests that what links the terms intermediality and intertextuality is a distrust of 'closure', which he identifies with the anti-essentialist wider cultural context of the times.

This distrust of closure has generated interest in widening horizons, expansion and opening up to new possibilities and hybrid combinations of cultural ideas and concepts and artefacts, which reflects the expanding (yet also contracting) realm of global communication. Wolf identifies a cultural zeitgeist, which involves:

> a stress on signifying processes which involve a plurality of discourses, an emphasis on discursive exchanges and contacts rather than on essential qualities and logocentric differences, as well as a concern with various kinds of 'Others', with regard to what traditionally had been in focus...
>
> As far as literature and its traditional links to the print media are concerned, a further motive for intermediality research may be to (re) affirm the flexibility, openness and adaptability of a verbal medium which some fear may be a loser in the present competition in the non-print media.[18]

The fugue is a symbolic, rhetorical and signifying form of language creation which exemplifies 'plurality of discourses', 'exchanges and contacts' rather than essential qualities, as well as a concern or accommodation of various kinds of 'Others'.

Wolf analyses *Dream-Fugue* musicalization focusing on the mimetic imitation of musical structure in literary textual form— amongst the interesting observations of his analysis, is a focus on De Quincey's use of counterpoint.

The problem of portraying counterpoint in literary form is solved by De Quincey, writes Wolf, who argues that 'the different, (partially) simultaneous and independent parts in which the subject must unfold is a fugal one, they could be identified not as consecutive scenes, as Brown does, but as three characters of groups of characters who are all repeatedly described as being engaged simultaneously or individually in various kinds of (rapid) horizontal movement.' Of these figurative groups, 'at least one is always imagined as present in the fictional situation evoked in the text: a) the female figure, b) the narrator-1 and c) as a third part'.[19]

Wolf suggests this third part is played by several 'instruments' at a time. It is as part of his analysis of literary counterpoint that Wolf invents the concept of 'imaginary content analogy' to account for the transposition of the effect of this kind of musical technique into literary form.

The transposition of effects of musical techniques of polyphony, which operates in its most complex form as literary counterpoint, are dependent on the capacity of the reader's imagination to hold in their mind the voices they have read, and 'sound' the new voices they are reading against this backdrop, thus creating in their reading a contrapuntal polyphony, sounding through what they have already read, and now know. In the writer's and reader's imagination characters and events which the text can 'only unfold consecutively...can be... simultaneously present' in the reader's mind, Wolf argues. 'They can "sound" together and enter in 'contrapuntal relationships of similarity or imitation and opposition, according to the reader's mental reconstruction of textual contents.'[20]

This form of *kinetic* articulation navigates the problem of polyphony and counterpoint as existing as an imaginative detour in the reader's imagination. This is a way of attempting to describe in technical or scientific terms how elements such as characters and their experiences can 'sound' together in the imagination, and set up 'reverberations', to use De Quincey's term, so that whilst writers can only write one voice consecutively the reader reads these whilst holding in their imagination the voices of the polyphonic counterpoint of the literary text.

REVERBERATION AND 'IMPASSIONED PROSE'

De Quincey's musicalized concept of reverberation in impassioned prose is most useful in the contemporary context of intermedial studies, in relation to the questions involving the function and uses and analogous transposition of musical concepts of counterpoint and polyphony, in literary narratives. The concept of reverberation set up between, and in the arrangement between ideas, concepts and images in writing is a clear and persuasive way of describing, or accounting for, the kinetic energies of the writing process, which are most evident in musicalized narratives.

Can we directly compare the structure of the *Dream-Fugue* with the structure of a musical fugue? Due to its highly imaginative nature, a direct comparison is not feasible, and in any case would not be the most productive approach. If one searches to find a direct scientific analogy of musical and literary structure one may be disappointed, even accepting that this work is arranged into five dream-like pieces, animated by a form of intense kinetic dynamism—and this does evoke the intense *stretto* of a fugue by Bach. A more promising approach is through texture or tone, not form. Using an array of musical techniques, De Quincey succeeds in evoking a passionate dream state that evokes, and/or mimics the emotional feeling of the fugue of a traumatized individual. De Quincey interprets the fugue in his own style. The fugue is a flexible form which has traditionally stretched to meet requirements, so Brown's (1938) argument that *Dream-Fugue* does not correspond with the structure of a Baroque fugue, due to its emotional nature, which results in different tones or emotions being played out in each of the five sections is not convincing.

'DREADFUL RESURRECTIONS THAT ARE IN DREAMS'

Throughout *Dream-Fugue*, in each part, the memory-image of the lost girl, the dead girl, victim of sudden death, is transformed, appearing in five different variations. This is a transformation that begins with the image of the young woman in the carriage. The symbolic dream-image, a visual motif, undergoes a series of dream changes until in the last part the female figure is acknowledged and openly recognized—even in the dream—as the implied author's dead sister.

This sequence enacts a process in which the narrator attempts to come to terms with his loss, to explain this loss in a way that will end on a positive note. This is provided by his faith that his sister will, with the narrator himself, be resurrected. They will join each other in resurrection, and will thus meet again. The fugue thus enacts a series of transformations from 'the dreadful resurrections that are in dreams' to the 'endless resurrections of his love' (referring, of course, to God).

The image of a lost girl and her catastrophically shocking, untimely, sudden death recurs in a series of fugal variations in which she is transformed, and rearticulated, like the melody of a fugue. The recurring motif of the girl/woman is like a fragment of a melody that the narrator cannot, and does not want to, clear from his mind and his involuntary memory. The image will return fugally and play forever in the ocean, cathedrals, savannahs and beaches, the quicksand, battlefields and heavenly realms of his dislocated, displacing dreams.

In the interpretations of writers, fugue structures also have a dream logic, the logic of dreams in which motifs, images and scenes recur in an endless fluid series which repeats endless variations on a theme, in a sequence the dreamer struggles to interpret.

RAPTURE AND RAVISHMENT

De Quincey was a self-professed music lover (who chastised his fellow Englishmen for not sufficiently appreciating music) who attended musical performances in London. These may have had fugal themes, or texture; we can imagine that they would have included motets by Clemens, and Mozart's *Jupiter* Symphony, but would not have included public works by Bach as he was forgotten about for one hundred years following his death. Sackville-West writes about De Quincey's musical tastes in his biography of *A Flame in Sunlight* (1936):

> As he grew older, music became more important to him. Though the expeditions tired him, he never missed hearing a good concert in Edinburgh; and at home, [daughters] Florence and Emily would sing to him, from the operas of Bellini. Listening, his mind would recur to those days in London, thirty or forty years ago, when he had sat in the gallery at the opera house, on Saturday nights his intellect lulled by Grassini and the music of Cimarosa, Cherubini and Mozart—his favorites to the end. (291)

Of later music, De Quincey liked only Beethoven and Mendelssohn—particularly in performances of Sophocles *Antigone*. For De Quincey, the 'supreme instrument was the violin. There is an *infinity about the violin*, he said' (291).

De Quincey invokes figures from music including the operatic performer Josephina Grassini in his recollections on 'being-on-opium' in *Confessions*. Grassini's physical presence is as significant as her voice in De Quincey's accounts of the effects of opium; this casts light on the romanticized or 'eroticized' affiliation or 'conflation' in De Quincey's writing. Daniel O'Quinn perceives interwoven threads of erotic and nationalistic imperatives, a conflation of romantic and patriotic desire symbolized in De Quincey's attraction to and admiration of Josephine Grassini (Napoleon's mistress) when she is singing Italian at the opera. De Quincey's opiated 'ravishment' as a spectator at live musical events, in his account in his *Confessions* reveals his recurring predicament: the experience of 'the suddenly undecidable moment when one is both inside and outside oneself.'[21] This is suggestive of the fugues he heard when he went to the opera.

De Quincey's descriptions of his response to Grassini, his transports of rapture at the Covent Garden Opera House recall, also, Rousseau's ideas about loss of awareness of identity in the experience of music performances and dancing in public places, and the public good.

In Rousseau's idealized public celebration of life, each participant performs the whole and temporarily loses awareness of her or his individual identity. This is an idea that is concordant with—and more on the lines of—the musical form of the fugue, as each subject line (individual voice) plays the theme, it picks up and becomes the shared subject theme that all the voices play in their diverse ways to make the musical composition as a whole. Through the performative process of imitative counterpoint, each individual voice 'becomes' the Other.

De Quincey immersed himself in performances of Italian Opera in the public space of the Covent Garden Opera House. It is congruent with this that he should focus on the 'transporting' effects of this experience, which took him into transports of raptures and carried him out of himself. Again, this evokes the loss of awareness of identity of the fugue, as much as it evokes the transportation and intoxication of opium dreams.

Nationalism, violence, and romanticism, all collide in *Dream-Fugue* in an invocation of sublime ravishment of the senses—in which the narrator loses himself in a swirling series of impassioned, violently affective impressions, Freud suggests that eroticism is a restoration of the pleasure principle, an unconscious attempt for the traumatized individual to achieve an inner balance. However De Quincey's musicalized impassioned literary writing, may have been a more relevant attempt to restore balance, counterbalancing his opium habit.

In his selection of themes for *Dream-Fugue*, De Quincey reveals a sound understanding and reasons for his choice of this musical form. Although it has been argued, by Wolf (1999), that his understanding of fugue was idiosyncratic, De Quincey's use of the fugue form was in many ways a logical choice, as Wolf concedes. Musical strategies have been used since classical times by writers to attempt to unify works, solving problems of harmony in overall structure or form, through musicalized techniques. This echoes a very early belief of the Pythagoreans in the 'harmony of the spheres' or the ability and function of music as enacting and enabling cosmic order.

Given De Quincey's traumatized thematic content, the fugue may also have been, intuitively, the most fitting choice of musical form to choose to use to narrate his impassioned prose work. This was De Quincey's strategy for resisting the 'potential chaos' of the dream/s on the formal level of discourse, and it also relates to the thematic level of the work, indicating common dynamic qualities considered typical of music and the musicalization of narrative. The function of music to establish harmony and restore order to chaos may also be seen in the narrative progression through darkness and negativity in the first four dream-parts, to the ending of the resurrection on a positive note.

Dream-Fugue has been criticized by Brown (1938) for not containing the appropriate set of elements to exactly represent a musical fugue transposed into a literary narrative. But this is not necessarily the aim of a literary author who chooses to use musicalized fugue techniques in their writings. In De Quincey's case, he was striving to authentically articulate visions and—effectively—attempting to find a way, or a technique, of writing to contain the chaos of his dreams. He achieved this paradoxically through use of 'ordering' yet wrenching, fragmented form of fugue. *Dream-Fugue* is the first literary work that suggests a modern contradictory way that we can look at deep structural elements of the text that involves the musicalized fugue, and the psychogenic fugue, coming together and taking flight in literary composition.

POSTMODERN READINGS OF *DREAM-FUGUE*

Charles Baudelaire was one of the earliest modernist writers to detect the symbolic and rhetorical significance of the extreme romantic tension, the inventions and seduction of words wrested from language in his translation of De Quincey's works into French.

Baudelaire' *Les Paradis Artificiels* (1860), a treatise on the uses, functions and effects of hashish and opium, comprised as its second part, Baudelaire's translation of De Quincey's *Confessions of an English Opium Eater*, following Baudelaire's *Le Poème du Haschisch*. Baudelaire writes:

> La pensée de De Quincey n'est pas seulement sinueuse; le mot n'est pas assez fort: elle est naturellement spirale. D'ailleurs, ces commentaires et ces réflexions seraient forts longs à analyser, et je dois me souvenir que le but de ce travail était de montrer, par un exemple, les effets de l'opium sur un esprit méditative et enclin à la rêverie. Je crois ce but rempli. (1860, no page numbers)

It is here Baudelaire identifies De Quincey's prose as naturally spiral, a reference to his involuted poetic prose that spirals in dream-like association (as Baudelaire might have intended to infer smoke spirals from a hashish pipe).

The supposed degeneracy of De Quincey's opium induced writing, commented on (somewhat ironically) by Baudelaire, a critique picked up and developed by Alina Clej, in *A Genealogy of the Modern Self*; and Virginia Woolf's comments on the two levels of his writing which are 'beautifully if unequally combined', calls for a fugal answer.[22]

It may be closer to the actual experience of writing that there are diverse sources or origins, of what authors write. Particularly when the possible origins of the shock that causes the displacement into writing are traumatic, as Freud argues, the unconscious mind throws up all kinds of disguises and deceptions, displaced images and projections of which the individual is often largely or wholly unaware. Whether this was so in De Quincey's 'dream sequence' is of less interest than the richness of writing, which a fugue analysis discloses. Moreover, such an analysis brings forth his significance for and influence on contemporary literary cultural theory. Clej positions De Quincey in historical perspective as foreshadowing modernism. Clej also proposes a notion of historical emergence, which I suggest is also a form of individual becoming, in De Quincey's writing:

the birth of the modern self...is paradigmatically embodied in De Quincey's work...[which] ...could ...be described in terms of Michel Foucault's notion of emergence of, in which a number of discursive practices and historical factors come together: the acceleration of publishing means of production, the commodification of Romanticism, and the elocutionary and rhetorical movements of the eighteenth century, which gave a mass extension to such privileged concepts as passion, voice, and the sublime.[23]

De Quincey's concepts of 'impassioned prose' and the 'language of power' certainly exemplify these notions.

His writing has been seen in a variety of post modernist contexts, for example, as evidence of guilt over the death of his sister, a guilt that has been linked to fear of the oriental Other symbolized by his opium addiction. Barrell locates within De Quincey's writings evidence of 'a fear which is repeated throughout his writings, and which runs back and forth between the most private space of his own childhood and the most public terrain of the British Empire in the East'. He finds evidence for this in De Quincey's metaphorical reference to death as a tiger, in *The English Mail-Coach*: 'the animal which...represented more fully than any other the fierceness and the violence of the demonized Orient, of India and China imagined as places of unutterable terror'.[24]

Barrell sees the Orient symbolized by De Quincey in 'the stiffening hands' of the dead Elizabeth, 'laid palm to palm' and in images of 'oriental' palm trees, repeatedly invoked in his writings. And he suggests that De Quincey's recurring dreams and obsessive visions of sudden death are due to his feeling of guilt, not only that 'De Quincey imagines he has committed a sexual crime' (33) of incest by observing the dead Elizabeth and kissing her on her death bed (51)—but also, and perhaps more pertinently—survivor guilt, caused by the fact that he 'failed to stand between Elizabeth and the wild beast that [metaphorically] killed her'(48). Alina Clej extrapolates further ramifications from the contextual connection and influence of colonialism on De Quincey's work practices (as an opium addict):

> De Quincey's addiction mirrors the imperialist fantasy of combining reckless expansion with control and containment. His emphasis on 'the most exquisite order, legislation and harmony' brought by the opium rapture, is an attempt to pre-empt any danger of dissemination and dissipation of the self through the contagious influence of the (feminine, proletarian, or oriental) Other.[25]

It is above all useful to acknowledge, now, the significance of the context of De Quincey's life experiences on his writing. As well as providing a relevant context for understanding, more nuanced significances emerge from contextual observation and understanding.

Taking this wider view of De Quincey's writing in relation to his psychological experiences and history, it follows that the texts which have struck a chord with the mind of modernism and postmodernism, were those generated by an individual writing from an inner state of dislocation and trauma. This inner state of post-traumatic stress disorder, and its lingering, 'waning', after affects, has come to be seen as characterizing the enterprise, the mind and consciousness of modernism and the increasing disaffection of postmodernism.

De Quincey wrote in *Suspiria de Profundis*:

> Ah, reader, you will think this which I am going to say too near, too holy, for recital. But not so. The deeper a woe touches me in my heart, so much the more am I urged to recite it. The world disappears: I see only the grand reliques of a work—memories of a love that has departed, has been—the record of a sorrow that is, and has its greyness converted into verdure—monuments of a wrath that has been reconciled, or a wrong that has been atoned for—convulsions of a storm that has gone by. (CW Vol. XIII: 19)

De Quincey's 'urge to recite', communicate and express the feelings and images of trauma in a continuous, driven flow constitutes the writer's fugue. In this way—through a transformation of affect enacted in the writing process—the psychogenic fugue becomes a writer's fugue.

A sense of survivor guilt is clearly articulated in relation to Elizabeth's sudden death. And in his descriptions of his 'warship' running over her 'fairy pinnace', which has a symbolism of survivor guilt. And in his castigation of himself, as the sister as infant proceeds down the aisle of the cathedral in a 'fairy' carriage. I would hypothesize although it cannot be conclusively proven that without this childhood trauma of losing his sister, his writing career might have had a different humour, or he might not even have become a writer. Yet there are also significant social-cultural 'vectors', to use Hacking's (1998) phrase, which gave rise to the particular themes of his writing's topoi, which have been indicated in this fugal analysis. De Quincey's writing, which came to prefigure the mood of modernism, was created as an 'inner' individual response to 'outer' social and cultural factors of his environment. The forces of modernity are beyond an individual's control. But within the environment in which he lived, to a significant extent, De Quincey's life and writing was determined and shaped by the intentional choices that he made. He initiated significant communication with the leading authors of the age, who were to profoundly shape his life, he was one of them; and he responded to the currents of political, social and cultural life. In so doing he became one of the leading authors of his time.

So whilst 'chance' dictated the traumatic events that would affect his work; in adulthood, it was his own intentional, contextual choices which enabled this to happen. It was De Quincey's combination of idiosyncratic, scholarly, self-willed authorial responses to the subliminal zeitgeist that enabled his significant, subliminal, influence on the *dream fugue* of literary modernism.

8

MARCEL PROUST'S FUGUE OF *LOST TIME*

> For a long time I used to go to bed early. Sometimes, when I had put out my candle, my eyes would close so quickly that I had not even time to say 'I'm going to sleep.' And half an hour later the thought that it was time to go to sleep would awaken me; I would try to put away the book which, I imagined, was still in my hands, and to blow out the light; I had been thinking all the time, while I was asleep, of what I had just been reading, but my thoughts had run into a channel of their own, until I myself seemed to have actually become the subject of my book: a church, a quartet, the rivalry between Francois 1 and Charles V. This impression would persist for some moments after I was awake; it did not disturb my mind, but it lay like scales upon my eyes and prevented them from registering the fact the candle was no longer burning. Then it would begin to seem unintelligible, as the thoughts of a former existence must be to a reincarnate spirit; the subject of my book would separate itself from me, leaving me free to choose whether I would return and I would be astonished to find myself in a state of darkness, pleasant and restful enough for the eyes, and even more, perhaps, for my mind, to which it had appeared incomprehensible, without a cause, a matter dark indeed.
> (Opening paragraph, *Swann's Way*)

THROUGH THE 'I'S' OF LOST TIME

The unique aesthetic resonance of *À la recherche du temps perdu* is caused by the interplay between the various temporal modalities which operate concurrently at any given time, and spatial point, in the narrative. The narrator's creation of 'infinite' chains of coded associations evoke for the reader—including the narrator, who is also a reader—the languid, poetic timeless motion of remembered and half-remembered, the waking dream of 'lost time'—which is, ostensibly, both the object and the subject of the text. Proust's modernist narrative métier was to attempt to capture in his writing the flow of consciousness, or the dual language-act of memory, which involves a continual inter-play between what is known—present—to the individuating consciousness of the writing subject; and what is 'lost' to it, in the past, recalled from unconsciousness—that which is not now here—through an act of memory. In Proust's writing, memory has two main functions and effects voluntary—or unproblematic—and involuntary.

Proust, significantly, coined a phrase for this last type of memory. He termed it *mémoire involontaire*, involuntary memory. This was in response to, and as a development of Bergson's *mémoire pure*. Proust's conception of *mémoire involontaire* reflects conditions of his writing. As Benjamin observes: 'This concept bears the marks of the situation which gave rise to it; it is part of the inventory of the individual who is isolated in many ways'.[1] Proust explored and investigated the unconscious aspects of involuntary memory but did not problematize it in the antithetical way of Freud. Despite the unconscious, subliminal, nature of involuntary memory, Proustian memory was not unreliable, either in the Freudian sense, as unconsciously deceptive and therefore unreliable as a gauge of any external truth, or in the literary usage of unreliable narration. Marcel is not an unreliable narrator, who might reveal unconsciously more about himself through being dishonest—narrative voices are meant to be believed as the narrator reflects on his emotions and thoughts. For Proust, memory functions in good faith, and due to this his work is tinged with a melancholic pathos, a sense of authentic nostalgia, intensely affective and emotively realized. These emotive affects are realized through uses of fugal techniques of musicalization, including development of subject themes, recurring motifs, variations on his themes of memory and the creative process and the subtle polyphony of his multiple 'Marcel' narrative voices.

The work is memorably driven from the outset by narrator Marcel, unable to recollect the significance of the remembered taste of the *madeleine* and striving to recall its significance. A critically celebrated instance of a sensory impression which triggers involuntary memory, this begins a narration through the narrator's memory, a highly complex many layered 'search', through recollection of a seemingly never-ending stream of involuntary memories of the narrator's life, his relationships, social world, reflections on art, life and relationships.

The recurring motif of the madeleine in *Du côté du chez Swann* (Swann's Way) introduces the narrator into the text, and the reader into the vast and complex realm of Marcel's mind/world which begins to open up in these pages, to use an analogy from *Du côté du chez Swann*, like Japanese 'paper crumbs' that unfold into character and form when floated in a porcelain water bowl (SW, p.62). But the musical motif, the refrain of Vinteuil's little sonata—first introduced in Combray in *Du côté du chez Swann*—is the main recurring device. Proust was a music lover, an amateur pianist who kept a grand piano in his apartment, and Proust's biographers note that in his later years he actively sought the late quartets of Beethoven to play on his piano. Ronald Hayman notes in his biography: 'At the beginning of 1913, getting up, on average only once a week, and only for an hour or two, he felt hungry to hear Beethoven's late quartets'.[2]

Amongst the influences for Vinteuil's 'little sonata' was Beethoven's *Grosse Fuge*. In April 1913, he went 'with George de Lauris to the Salle Pleyel for a performance by the Capet quartet of two late quartets and the *Grosse Fuge*'.[3] Proust 'had been trying to imagine the music of his fictional composer, Vinteuil, and the chamber music recital laid the foundations for listening to César Franck's violin sonata, 'which I love so much', played ...at a hall in the rue de Rocher', Proust wrote admiringly of the music. 'Now I found it *admirable*, the doleful chirping of his violin, and the moaning appeals in response at the piano, as if from a tree, from mysterious foliage.'[4]

In Proust's continuous novel the motif of Vinteuil's sonata works by linking *affec*t, in the narrator's emotional reflections; and *character*, in the vast cast of characters associated by Marcel with the Guermantes 'way' and the Méséglise 'way', the two 'walks' of his childhood holidays at his aunt's house in Combray that represent two ways or walks of life which run throughout the narrator's life. These 'ways' may be seen by a contemporary reader to involve all kinds of symbolic binary distinctions: bourgeois and aristocratic; ancient regime and nouveau riche; heterosexual and homosexual; conscious and dreaming; action and reflection; Art and Life, through the duration of Time and the prism of the narrator's memory. These function contrapuntally as the work as a whole brings these 'ways' together in a complex fugal composition. Like a recurring motif in a sonata, Vinteuil's 'little phrase' provides the synaesthetic structural unity of the whole vastly complex edifice.

In variations and nominal forms, Vinteuil's 'little phrase' reappears throughout Proust's composition: 'Vinteuil's septet', his 'little sonata', 'Vinteuil's theme' denote the diminutive musical passage. *La Prisonnière* (The Captive) includes a scene of the full playing of the whole of Vinteuil's sonata, to a high society audience (high society hears the full production, the bourgeoisie an excerpt). Vinteuil's 'little phrase' develops and transforms from an entrancing enigmatic piece of music by an unknown composer played in a bourgeois salon, to the fullness of a social sensation in Parisian high society, applauded by musicologists and critics.

The little phrase is first heard in diminutive form as the andante movement of Vinteuil's sonata for the piano and violin, which has been discovered by the Verdurins. They arrange to have the andante movement played to 'the clan' at their 'Wednesday evening' (*Du côté du chez Swann*). Swann does not hear it as it were afresh but as a delightful resounding of a piece of music he had heard the year before and not been able to forget; it is emotionally associated with his growing love for Odette. 'La petite phrase de la sonate de Vinteuil' proceeds and recurs as a metaphor, and motif, for the hidden, difficult, tumultuous emotions of love experienced affectively by the narrator including 'variations' of hate, jealousy, revenge, despair, anxiety (sexual jealousy is a main theme in the narrator's emotional range).

This musicalized device functions as an alternative to the structuring device of a three-act structure of beginning middle and end, providing an overall structurally thematic unity. Like the novel itself, the little phrase is a musicalized metaphor for itself. Hints are given throughout the work that the main—if not only—source of enduringly meaningful experience in the narrator's difficult and complex social life, following the death of his parents and grandmother, is the transmutation of life-experience into Art (as symbolized by 'the little sonata' and expressed in ruminations which surround and accompany its playing in the narrative). This is seen in a passage from *La Prisonnière* (The Captive). One afternoon as the narrator is alone in his apartment, awaiting the return of Albertine, ruminating on the 'anxiety' his feelings for her cause him, 'I sat down at the piano, opened at random Vinteuil's sonata which happened to be lying there, and began to play...' (173). Concurrently, and by association, this is how the device works, the narrator begins:

> approaching the sonata from another point of view, regarding it in itself as the work of a great artist, I was carried back on the tide of sound to the days at Combray—I do not mean Montjouvain and the Méséglise way, but to my walks along the Guermantes way— when I myself had longed to be an artist. In abandoning that ambition de facto, had I forfeited something real? (TC, pp. 173-4)

In its ending, the novel reveals that the transmutation of life into art has after all and unknown to the narrator (perhaps even to the author) been the performative 'purpose' and scope of a vast narrative work. Built from first-person narrative memory and rumination, Proust's work exemplifies the individuality of 'great art'. How do the musicalized transmutations 'work,' and what makes it 'fugal'?

In his associated, highly associative, recollections, the accuracy of the narrator's recall is taken as verbatim. Rather than embodying such devices as 'Freudian slips' that reveal unconscious motivations at work in consciousness, Proust's narrator reads, and interrogates, the events of his past life as 'signs,' deciphering their significance. What Proust as author and narrator, via Marcel, reveals about the mind of Marcel, in the telling of his life story, is the enormously tricky and sustained feat of revealing the *chora* or immaterial conceptual substance of the mind of the narrator (and by extension the implied author): his thoughts, feelings, emotions, his forgetting and his labyrinthine many-layered memory.

The self-referentiality of Proust's narrative pertains to consciousness, the *roman-a-clef* nature of the work, and also to the games Marcel as author/narrator plays with the reader. It does not pertain to the structure of the work in terms of memory, although this memory is involuntary. This labyrinthine work is constructed from involuntary memory, the involuntary memories triggered by the material objects in which they are contained, for instance the madeleine, the steeple, the cobblestones, the three trees, and most of all Vinteuil's little sonata. Yet it appears that authorial belief in the veracity of these involuntary memories underpins everything. It is the supposed veracity of the narrator's involuntary memory that creates the seeming solidity of the edifice of shadows, layers and suggestions, and 'literally' holds it together.

By interrogating his memory in the repeated reprisal of memory fragments, the narrator is engaged in an act of reading and re-reading his own past, his own life, with the aim of interpretation and understanding. His driving intention is to discover, 'remember', or work out the meaning that is the significance of his recurrent memory images and sensations, epitomized in the early part of *Du côté du chez Swann* by the *petite madeleine*, and taken up symbolically and rhetorically, in the recurring refrain of Vinteuil's little sonata. The re-appearance of the septet is always a narrative occasion for affect-based self-interrogation of emotions and situations of love relationships. Whereas this is initiated in a reflection from the point of view of Swann (in *Du côté du chez Swann* when Marcel is a child) this point-of-view shifts in the next volume, *A l'ombre des jeunes filles en fleur*, to the perspective of the narrator symbolically indicating Marcel is old enough to have adult feelings. The 'little phrase' in its many variations of setting and playing, is connected and associated in its replaying, its resounding, with the unresolved longing and sense of loss, the feelings of anguished emotions which literally resound throughout the narrative. His sense of desire and loss, anguish which becomes intertwined with his sickness, neurasthenia, does not go away or 'get better', he does not find satisfaction in love, no matter how many passing relationships and friendships he has. Like neurasthenia, agonizingly painful emotions of loss and longing keep recurring. In this regard, Proust's writing recalls that of De Quincey's *Dream-Fugue*, where the signified lost object (his long dead sister) is re-envisioned, throughout the body of his life's work, in a seemingly endless series of displaced visual motifs.

It has been suggested by critics Vladimir Nabokov, and Geraldine Brée,[5] that some may focus on the surface of the text, its 'superficial' depiction of Parisian social life in la Belle Èpoque; reading the work simply as story. Yet (as the narrator repeatedly hints in dwelling on his youthful ambitions to be an artist, a writer) the underlying conceptual content of the narrative, and its structure, is of and about the philosophical nature of his mind, human reality, consciousness, memory, and the creation of art from life.

The subject themes of the subliminal fugue of *À la recherche* are first, the narrator's search in memory for what he cannot remember, the involuntary memory triggered by his sensory responses to material objects such as the taste of the *petite madeleine*, the sight of the steeple, the sound of Vinteuil's sonata, the sound of the bells. These have profound hidden significance to him. Second, is the narrator's lifelong desire to become a writer and write a complete work of literary art. By the time he had begun to write *À la recherche*, after the death of his mother, Proust had published a volume of short stories, *Les Plaisirs et les jours* (1896), translations of Ruskin's *Bible of Amiens* (La Bible d'Amiens, 1904), and *Sésame et les lys* (Sesame and Lilies 1906). He had written numerous critical essays and literary pastiches including those published for the first time in 1954 in *Contre Sainte-Beuve*. But he had abandoned his first novel *Jean Santeuil*.

Both these themes are played with in countless fugal variations which develop through exposition and contrapuntal development, constituting the metaphorical narrative music until at the end of the work, the themes coalesce in the self-reflective realization of the narrator, and reader, that their interplay has all along been the subject and object of *À la recherche*.

SHIFTING PERSPECTIVES

Operating in many temporally differentiated registers, the *Search* constitutes a structural discourse between a disembodied, deterritorialized narrator, or narrative voice, and the projected object of the *Recherche*, which comprises the narrated memory content of *temps perdu*. The constantly shifting emotional registers of the Search reflect and comprise an elaborate, labyrinthine, sensation-based interrogation as the narrator, Marcel, seeks to articulate the meaning and significance of memories from his childhood and young adulthood, a time in which he longed to be a writer and write a work of art. It is only at the very end that the subliminal unconscious significance of the narrator, Marcel's, recurring recollections of lost time, his life gone by, is paradoxically revealed to be no more and no less than the purpose of the writing process itself, that is the process of producing a work of art in the form of a novel of writing consciousness (and unconsciousness). The object of the *Recherche*, therefore, becomes its subject and its subject becomes its object. *À la recherche du temps perdu* is an account and an embodiment of its own genesis, of its material and conceptual being. De Quincey's dream image by contrast is not in this way self-reflexive or dialogic, but is a recurrence and an elaboration of memory fragments from the author's past, infused with unresolved emotion.

Proust's novel series is written as an extended narrative speech-act of memory. The labyrinthine, baroque, nonlinear narrative of search unfolds in the guise and form of a first person dialogue. This is a paradoxical, 'impossible' conceptual discourse between the first person narrator, his former selves evoked in recollection and lost time itself, the past, which, we are told, was once lived and which is now brought back, re-lived, or represented, in fictional form in the author's narrative. It would be more accurate to say *lost time*, in the sense in which it functions for author, and narrator, is a conceptual space, a zone in which time is suspended and accelerates with the speed, and fragmentary, arbitrary volition of memory itself, memory of, and about, itself. Gilles Deleuze describes Proust's notion of 'lost time' as 'not simply 'time past'; it is also time wasted, lost track of'.[6] Deleuze sees this loss or lost-ness, the nature of this lostness, or loss, in terms of a forgetting, and therefore as the impetus for the narrative project: namely to regain or to remember, to search for what is, or was, lost: 'Consequently memory intervenes as a means of search,' he maintains, 'of investigation, but not the most profound means; and time past intervenes as a structure of time, but not the most profound structure'.[7]

It might be more accurate to see 'lost time' as in no structural or imaginative sense 'wasted' but 'timeless' or out-of-time zone of writing which Proust, the author, enters when he is writing, the arena of the literary narrative which is created in his writing. *Temps perdu/lost time* is the space of Proust's writing, of memory and creation, contained and inscribed within the narrative work which is accessed, or capable of being accessed and set into motion by, and through, the writer's and reader's attention.

PROUST IN TIME: LA BELLE ÈPOQUE

As the researcher engages with, and attempt to metaphorically deconstruct the narrative structure it is impossible, as reader, not to contextualize Proust's work within the well-documented philosophical beliefs that informed his approach and methodology. Proust's personal background, and the society and era in which he grew and lived, are captured by his writing. In a lecture, Nabokov sounded a cautionary note in this regard:

> One thing should be firmly impressed upon your minds: the work is not an autobiography; the narrator is not Proust the person, and the

characters never existed except in the author's mind.⁸

Nabokov clarifies his point further: 'Proust is a prism. His, or its, sole object is to refract, and by refracting to recreate a world in retrospect'. Because of this Nabokov cautions:

> The [Proustian] world itself, the inhabitants of that world, are of no social or historical importance whatever...Proust's prismatic people have no jobs: their job is to amuse the author.⁹

Despite, or perhaps because of, Nabokov's cautionary note, and the fact that the researcher is pursuing a deep structural reading, it is impossible to simply read Proust without recognizing that the novel is written in time, with innumerable references to 'its times'. And Proust's elegantly written poetic prose sparkles numinously in the light of the Proustian 'myth'. What is more, 'the author's mind' is not a deracinated entity, but a lived experience in and of its own time.

Marcel Proust's background has been examined in detail alongside his novel. Proust scholars know his history almost as well as they know his prose. Born in 1871, the son of a prominent, wealthy, and very highly regarded doctor, young Marcel was, it is said, very close to his mother, Jeanne Proust, so close that Roland Hayman (oddly) imagines a 'semi-incestuous relationship'.¹⁰ Whereas Jean-Yves Tadié's biography *Marcel Proust* (1996) denies this 'posthumous psychoanalysis' of his primary relations Tadié also points out the powerful primal feelings of Marcel to his mother.¹¹ Proust's father, Adrien Proust, who was associated with the Salpêtrière hospital, specialized in the fields of sexuality, and 'neurasthenia', the recently identified 'nervous' disease of modernity, from the earlier research into nerves by George Miller Beard that developed a neurological approach to the affects of 'nerves'.¹² He coauthored with Gilbert Ballet *L'hygiène du neurasthénique* (The Treatment of Neurasthenia),¹³ and this environment affected Marcel's health and writing. Tadié writes of the subtle influence of Marcel on his father's research:

> In fact his view on neurasthenia had been influenced by watching his son's behavior, but the influence was reciprocal: reading his father's articles and books about neurasthenia, Proust could hardly fail to recognize himself in them, and they had an effect on both his self-image and his early fiction.¹⁴

The young Marcel grew up in the fashionable society of Paris during *la*

Belle Époque. This nostalgically labeled period (itself seen as something of a glorious 'lost time') ended with the outbreak of the First World War in 1914. It was an era romanticized for its relative prosperity and social ease, for the bourgeoisie and aristocracy. During this time well-to-do Parisians enjoyed the conveniences, and few of the problems, of inventions such as automobiles and household appliances (although Proust was to suffer terribly from the consequences of an aeronautical accident). In the era when Proust was growing up, the middle and upper classes sported in the country, as did narrator Marcel's family, annually staying with Marcel's Aunt Leonie in her house in Combray, a village once named Illiers, but due to the fame accorded by its later Proustian association, the town is now Illiers-Combray. Those from the upper and aspirational classes comported themselves *en masse* in fashionable seaside resorts such as Balbec where narrator Marcel vacationed with his grandmother at the Hotel Balbec. Here he was to, fatefully, meet his aristocratic friend, Robert Saint-Loup, and Albertine.

Proust, a highly sensitive aesthete, was also a sharp social observer, with a dry sardonic wit, a clear eye for the foibles, excesses, hypocrisies, double standards, *faux pas* and absurdities of his social world, the upper bourgeoisie, aristocracy and their servants. A moral philosopher, he engaged as a novelist with the philosophical ideas of his time. These are integral to his narrative's content and structure. Reflected, often satirically, in the narrative descriptions of events are theories of art and aesthetics as discussed and debated in the *salons* of 'the best society' which (much to his parent's disapproval) the youthful Marcel frequented, and reduced to farce in others, such as the more philistine Verdurin's 'Wednesday evening' in Combray.

This social world comprised only a superficial gloss to the real substance and depth of the work as a whole, as befits an author who retreated from a life of fashionable salons and high society, following the death of his mother in 1905, two years after his father.

Jewish on his mother's side of the family, it has been observed that, in a climate of increasing antisemitism in Europe, Proust felt outside mainstream society. Like Joyce's Bloom, Swann is Jewish, as too is Bloch, a friend of Marcel's with whom Proust introduces the theme of racial intolerance. In his life Proust, was one of the first to add his name to a petition in 1898 opposing the charges which had been laid against Zola who faced a year's prison sentence and a fine for 'defaming' the army and supporting Dreyfus, in what became known as 'the Dreyfus Affair', the political and social antisemitic scandal that divided France, over support or condemnation of military captain Alfred Dreyfus who was wrongly convicted of treason and selling French military secrets to the Germans. The Dreyfus Affair, and the attitudes of those against Dreyfusards, are in his *The Guermantes Way*, *The Captive*, and *Sodom and Gomorrah*; in his earlier work *Jean Santeuil*, he writes about Zola's trial.

This indeed contradicts any views that Proust was not politically involved. He critiques and upbraids society throughout his work: for antisemitic racial intolerance, class-based snobbishness, pretensions and hypocrisies. For example, the novel's sustained awareness of the bourgeois denigration of 'lower class' or demimonde women into the fixed categories of lower class courtesan or mistress. Women at that time could not pursue independent education and careers. Swann's eventual wife, the obviously very charming upwardly-mobile Odette, started her adult life as such a woman, a cocotte of the demimonde, and ended up as the well-to-do mistress of Monsieur de Guermantes.

Chronically asthmatic, disillusioned and sick, in 1910, Proust shut himself up the family apartment at 102 Boulevard Haussmann, where he devoted himself to his work, sleeping by day and writing through the night.[15] To further muffle the sounds of the outside world, he had the walls of his room lined with cork.

Marcel, the narrator, had longed to write, with little success. Now Proust, the author, submerged himself totally in the waking dream of writing. It is recorded that he began the work in the autumn of 1906 in Paris, completing the first draft in 1912. He then continued to work and rework his novel for years, immersed in his solitary literary intoxication, a state of addictive, dependent, all-consuming proportions, which did not end until his death in 1922, at the age of fifty-one and before the publication of the final three volumes.[16] When he was well enough Proust did still manage to venture out into society, favouring the Ritz. Then Proust began to frequently complain to friends that he was dying, immersing himself in his writing, which he pursued to the hours of death.[17]

Given these conditions, it is perhaps not surprising that the work Proust created, should have as its main encompassing theme the creative process. *À la recherche* is a creative work whose major theme is the creation of itself. Integral to this theme is thus the transformation of

Self into written text; it is this flight that constitutes the fugal process of writing. Proust's work is fugal in the sense that it is deeply *of* the Self, narcissistically and symbolically embodying a flight from the self into writing of the Self; and it is tinged with the melancholia of impossible desire and regret. And yet in this fugal process, this flight in writing, all is not lost—value, credit to the endeavour may, if circumstances are propitious, emerge in the written form of the text, this (post Romantic) process of subjectivity has been alluded to by Maurice Blanchot:

> The writer plunged into dread is himself painfully aware that art is not a ruinous operation; he is trying to lose himself (and to lose himself as a writer), and yet sees that by writing he increases the credit to humanity, and thus his own, since he is still a man; he gives art new hopes and riches that return to weigh him down; he transforms into forces of consolation the hopeless orders he receives; he saves with nothingness.[18]

Proust's narrator offers up in a discontinuous flow of fragmented observation and reflection, complex, elaborate, detached commentary on the manners and mores of inhabitants of his salon-hopping social world: indifferent young ladies; capricious mistresses; good looking bachelor aristocrats, servants, sharp tongued cooks. Numerous commentators have remarked that hidden yet displayed in Proust's elaborately detailed descriptions of women as objects of desire was a masking of the reality that he was, in truth, oblivious to their charms, whilst his descriptions of men tried to hide his eye for the attractions of the male form, as many critics have observed, for example: Nabokov 1980; Tadié 2000; Hayman 1990; Carter 2006. Nabokov espies this tendency in Proust's descriptions of art works:

> in describing young men he disguised his keen appreciation for male beauty under the masks of recognizable paintings; and in describing young females he disguised under the same masks of paintings his sexual indifference to women and his inability to describe their charm.[19]

Certainly homosexuality and lesbianism and the amplified social disguises, intrigues and masks of 'the love which cannot speak its name', is theme. Proust confided in writer Andre Gide, a confession that Gide summarized in a notebook in 1921:

> He said he never loved women except in a spiritual sense and that he had only known love with men'.[20]

Ample biographical and purely literary evidence leads to the conclusion that in relation to gender, sexuality, love, and self-identity, we may well ponder the extent to which in Proust's work 'disguise' and 'flight' identify each other to converge in the fugal flight of his writing. The identity shifts of the characters can be compared analogously to the musical function and use of the double fugue. In a double fugue, characteristically the dominant and subordinate subjects change places with each other. In the world of Proust's novel, the characters are frequently revealed in new identities. This shift in values may involve a shift of gender or more often gender identity, into homosexuality, as in the narrator's discovery of Albertine's lesbianism, his discovery of the Baron Charlus's homosexuality, and the revelation of Robert Saint-Loup's homosexuality towards the end of the novel. The shift of a double fugue also occurs in relation to perception of social standing:

> [Marcel's] great-aunt and grandparents never suspected that [Swann] had entirely ceased to live in the kind of society which his family had frequented, or that under the sort of incognito which the name Swann gave him among us, they were harbouring—with the complete innocence of a family of honest innkeepers who have in their midst some distinguished highwayman and never know it—one of the smartest members of the Jockey Club, a particular friend of the Comte de Paris and of the Prince of Wales, and one of the men most sought after in the aristocratic world of the Faubourg Saint-Germain. (SW: 18)

Changing places in social class and position, a most unbourgeois social mobility for those times as the narrator points out—includes such transpositions as the elevation by marriage of the courtesan Odette to the aristocracy, and the move of Gilberte from the narrator's childhood sweetheart to the role of wife of Robert Saint-Loup, later discovered by the narrator to be homosexual. In this multi-layered world of double entendres and double-identities, reversal (of fortune or expectation), inversion (gender identity), and displacement (from previous social position) are amongst the heterogeneous variations that constitute the Proustian social counterpoint.

The identity shift is often signalled or associated with 'Vinteul's little phrase', a comparison which Nabokov notes 'Vinteuil not only brings in the theme of a recurrent musical note, the 'little theme', but also the theme of homosexual relationship which is developed throughout the novel, shedding new light on this or that character.'[21]

MEMORY/MODERNIST MÉTIER

At the end of *Le Temps retrouvè* (Time Regained), the final volume, Marcel hears the bell at the Prince of Guermantes masked ball. This is a moment of epiphany when he realizes that 'in order to get nearer to the sound of the bell and to hear it better it was into my own depths that I had to re-descend' (449).

This Orphic connection continues:

> And this could only be because its peal had always been there, inside me, and not this sound only but also, between that distant moment and the present one, unrolled in all its vast length, the whole of that past which I was not aware that I carried about within me. When the bell on the garden gate had pealed, I already existed and from that moment onwards, for me to still be able to hear that peal, there must have been no break in continuity, no single second at which I had ceased or rested from existing, from thinking, from being conscious of myself, since that moment from long ago still adhered to me and I could still find it again, could retrace my steps to it, merely by descending to a greater depth within myself. (TR: 449-450)

Thus does the search for *temps perdu*, lost self, or former selves, in lost time, become in a mythic intuitive maneuver, equated with the process of creation, of art—in Proust's sense in the form of written language. Orpheus, the musician-god, descends into the underworld (the depths of self, time, memory, consciously descending into what was or is unconscious) in order to retrieve his wife Eurydice. As Blanchot memorably put its: 'When Orpheus descends to Eurydice, art is the power that causes the night to open'.[22] In 're-descending,' polyphonic narrator(s) Marcel, the literary artist, found himself in constant movement between spatial and temporal spheres, the continuous flow to which Proust's contemporary, Henri Bergson, was directing his philosophical inquiries.

PROUST AND BERGSON

The controversial possibly mutual literary/philosophical influence between Proust and the philosopher Henri Bergson has been little remarked in critical studies over the past twenty-five years or so. But there is reason to revive the philosophical themes that Bergson and Proust each explored in different ways in their works, and to consider an analogous comparison to aspects of Bergsonian thought in relation to fugal *chora* and subjectivity, which characterize the fugal quality of Proust's writing.

Proust's writing was influenced by the ideas found in the works of the highly regarded philosopher Bergson (1859-1941) with whom he was very familiar. This was a not an unproblematic influence. Although Proust was often compared to Bergson, their (possibly mutual) influence was not publicly acknowledged by either of them.[23] They were related through marriage, meeting when Marcel was a page-boy at the wedding of his cousin to the philosopher.[24] The previous year, when Proust had enrolled at the Sorbonne to study law and political science, Bergson was one of his lecturers. This did not have much overt influence on Proust whose academic career was joined at the behest of his father, coinciding with Proust's own two preferred vocations, which he was already successfully pursuing: an inchoate social career as a dandy and habitué of the salons of Parisian society, and fledgling career as a writer. Hayman notes Proust's determination not to become a lawyer: 'In my days of greatest desperation I have never conceived of anything worse than a lawyer's office'. And he told his father, 'anything I do apart from literature and philosophy is for me so much time wasted'.[25] After he graduated with his law diploma, he settled for an unpaid job at the Bibliothèque Mazarine in the Institut de France, procured through one of his father's friends. Required to work only five hours a week this left ample time for his social and literary careers. Tadié records that surprisingly there is little recorded mutual contact between Proust and Bergson; only one conversation is documented between the two, when they were both on the jury committee of the Prix Blumenthal, after the First World War. Proust attended to make sure it was awarded to Rivière. They had a conversation on 'narcotics and insomnia' which they both suffered from. Tadié quotes Edmond Jaloux's recollection of this conversation in which he said they talked about narcotics: the way narcotics stimulated attention, the quality of mental work such stimulation engendered, and its psychological use. This also was in the time that Proust disagreed in remarks he made in his notebooks with what Bergson had written about 'the dream', these appeared in his works.[26]

Given the two cousins mutual interests in 'memory, time, instinct, laughter, sleep, dreams, morality, religion and the laws of psychology' their general lack of communication is commented on by Tadié, who hypothesizes that:

> Bergson did not like to be preceded by anyone or questioned, and he preferred to be left alone by friends and colleagues...Proust read *Matière et Mémoire*, took note of their different approaches, and in an interview, refused to allow *Swann* to be labelled a 'Bergsonian novel'.[27]

A political division had been created by their different stances on the Dreyfus affair, whilst, as previously mentioned, Proust actively petitioned for Dreyfusard, in contrast, Bergson was publicly indifferent.

Bergson was not oblivious to his younger cousin's writings, and on publication he publicly praised Proust's long, carefully executed translation of Ruskin's *Sesame and Lilies*. When Proust began to write *À la recherche*, as he immersed himself in his literary writing, he engaged with themes of psychology and philosophy of mind that by Bergson were given theoretical form.

The almost interchangeable perspective on space-time suggested by Bergson can be seen in the contrapuntal mechanisms—or literary counterpoint—of Proust's *Search*. Two fundamental beliefs central to Bergsonian thought can be seen to inform and resonate throughout Proust's literary work. In *Essai sur les donnés immédiates de la conscience* (Time and Free Will: an essay on the immediate data of the conscience) (1889) Bergson outlined these notions of time, as *le temps* and *la durée*, his related notion of *élan vital*, was as a life force, or creative animating energy that inhabits all matter. Bergson perceived of, and apprehended, consciousness as a flow. At the same time the theory of consciousness as a 'stream of thought', was published in William James' *Principles of Psychology* (1890). David Hamlyn claims that although James was influenced by Bergson they arrived at these conclusions independently.[28] Consciousness as a flow, or stream, is an idea that is explored in modernist experiments in stream-of-consciousness writing. Proust adapts similar ideas in his writings, in his method as well as content. James likened consciousness to a bird's life of an 'alternation of flights and perches', which is an idea that resounds in writings of modernity (and echoes in social media, of Twitter 'tweets').[29]

Proust, in part, incorporates the notion of *élan vital* into his literary work by structuring his narrative on memories continuously triggered by sensory perceptions. Frequent reference is made to the sensations of all five senses. Often an evocation of an incident, event, or scene will make recourse to all five senses in chains of associated metaphors and similes. Marcel refers to objects in nature, to plants, trees, sunsets, the sea, as if they are alive, in an animistic sense. This narrative sense of, and focus on, animation, the animated nature of nature, has the effect of animating the narrative, bringing writing to life, by bringing 'life force' to his writing. Benjamin proposes that Proust's creation of subjectivity is the result of putting Bergson's theory of the nature of experience in *durée* in to the test in poetic narrative.

> Proust's work *À la recherche du temps perdu* may be regarded as an attempt to produce experience, as Bergson imagines it, in a synthetic way under today's social conditions, for there is less and less hope that it will come into being in a natural way.[30]

Benjamin comments: 'only a poet can be the adequate subject of such an experience.'[31] This same comment could well apply also to the conception of time in Bergson's *Essai*. In his *Search*, Proust contrapuntally weaves together elements of time, memory, consciousness, and matter, in a continuous multi-volumed novel which develops and expands upon philosophical themes found in Bergson's theories. Despite their reticent relationship, Bergson wrote to Proust on the publication of *Du côté du chez Swann*: 'Rarely has introspection been taken so far. It is a direct and continuous vision of the inner reality.'[32]

In his theory of time, Bergson defines two kinds of time (functioning as two temporal modalities): *temps*, that is time as it exists in space, and is the time of measurement, and which can be 'lost'; and *la durée*, the time of consciousness which involves duration. In his first book, *Les Données immédiates de la conscience*, published in 1889, translated as *Time and Free Will* (1910), on time consciousness Bergson argued against the spatialization of time in physics, instead favoring a theory of the continuous flow of time as it appears to consciousness.[33] Inscribed in and prefigured by its title, *À la recherche du temps perdu*, Proust's life time's work invokes a linguistic play on these dual concepts. It is his use, in writing, of two main temporal modalities—the past of *temps perdu*, and the time of duration in which the narrator is situated in the process of actively remembering (always an unknown deterritorialized position), that results in the unique labyrinthine, baroque folds of the novel's architectonic structure: the many-voiced echoes, repetitions, distortions and embellishments of its fugal music.

Proust's inspiration, and revelation, is that these two types of time exist concurrently, it is in the creation of works of art that one form of time, *time lost*, can be accessed and preserved—out of time—in time, the time of duration. Both kinds of time are accessed in the creative act of writing together, in memory, intellect, imagination, consciousness, unconsciousness and intuition. A process in which the author loses herself or himself to find herself or himself—as in a musical fugue the subject is transformed. The author loses self-awareness in writing, to find himself in written form, a distorted reflection preserved perhaps potentially for eternity outside the flow of time, in the form of a book, a work that exists between covers in time.

Nabokov comments on what he calls Proust's: 'colored editions of the Bergsonian thought'. He regards this synaesthetic narrative technique as evidence of Proust's excavation of modern consciousness.

> Proust's fundamental ideas regarding the flow of time concern the constant evolution of personality in terms of duration, the unsuspected riches of our subliminal minds...[34]

ÉLAN VITAL AND MEMORY BINDING

The narrator in dreamy, semi-conscious, sick or almost sleeping states of mind, projects an animate nature on inanimate objects. As a child, he drifts in and out of sleep in rooms full of pieces of furniture that he perceives as having their own separate lives, their own stories. He falls in love with apple blossom. As a youth, he believes trees have secrets to tell him, literally correlating with Bergson's idea that what I refer to, here, as the *chora* of life, all that exists, is imbued with an *élan vital*, an animating life force. In *A l'ombre des jeunes filles en fleur* (Within a Budding Grove) Marcel narrates:

> I looked at the three trees; I could see them plainly, but my mind felt that they were concealing something which it could not grasp, as when an object is placed out of our reach, so that our fingers, stretched out at arms-length, can only touch for a moment its outer surface, without managing to take hold of anything...I felt...behind them the same object, known to me and yet vague, which I could not bring nearer...I watched the trees gradually recede, waving their despairing arms, seeming to say to me: 'What you fail to learn from us today, you will never know. If you allow us to drop back into the hollow of this road from which we sought to raise ourselves up to you, a whole part of yourself which we were bringing to you will vanish for ever into thin air.' (345)

'The trees' pertains to the narrator's own memory, both symbol and material representation of what he has forgotten, lost in time: where has he seen the trees before? Has he indeed seen them before?

The narrator's sense of the life force in nature, and in objects, is in striking contrast to his almost existential depiction of other people. These are portrayed as essentially and irretrievably impenetrable, and unknowable, enclosed within their notional worlds, self-contained like Leibnizian 'monads'. This view of individual self-enclosed consciousness, positions the narrator as artist removed and detached from the world he creates. Nabokov suggests that the characters portrayed exist for the author's solipsistic amusement but there are deeper forces than self-amusement in the urge to recreate such a complete self-enclosed world, that so closely mirrors, yet distorts, echoes and embellishes the author's own.

Proust's multiple first-person exploration of memory, *À la recherche du temps perdu*, is an artistic counter-point to Bergson's position that 'the humblest function of spirit is to bind together the successive moments of the duration of things'.[35] In his descriptive writing style, based on sensory-perception, Proust binds together successive moments of the duration of things, using association and metaphor, often cutting up and rearranging the successive moments through the non-linear filter of consciousness and memory. Perceptual descriptions, sentiments and intellect filtered through narrative consciousness.

> When a man is asleep, he has in a circle round him the chain of the hours, the sequence of the years, the order of the heavenly host. Instinctively, when he awakes, he looks to these, and in an instant reads off his own position on the earth's surface and the amount of time that has elapsed during his slumbers; but this ordered progression is apt to grow confused and to break its ranks. (SW:4)

This passage directly reflects in narrative form Bergson's philosophical ideas regarding movement and space, which he sees as perceptual constructs, and as such attributed with a symbolic function that in reality they do not possess. Just as Bergson's concern in *Matière et mémoire* is the gap between consciousness (or mind) and matter, the mind/body spirit/matter divide, so too does this becomes the overriding narrative device in Proust's novel. Proust in his narrative structure is negotiating in written language, tracking in words, the conscious and unconscious relation between inner and outer, between the worlds of the spirit and matter, of mind and body. He brings these together in descriptions that slide and glide, into and out of, the locus of narrative consciousness. Proust that is to say, constructs rather than represents consciousness in language.

METAPHOR, MOTIF AND METONYMY IN PROUST

Proust's narrative style conjures an illusion of the past from vividly depicted recollections, a sustained narrative of fragments. Extended non-linear evocations of Marcel's emotions, sensory impressions, social and physical observations, and moral and aesthetic digressions, constitute an infinite score of lost moments, linked by associations, which Cocteau called 'a giant miniature full of mirages, of superimposed gardens, of games conducted between space and time'.[36] The narrator's memories comprise a musicalized edifice of narrative consciousness, operating in many temporal and spatial registers.

Bergson's intention was to show, or try to understand, how a connection between the material world and the conceptual articulation of the language culture occurs and is possible. He posits that there is a kind of psychic, unconscious, animistic, vitalistic extra-sensory and sensory communication which most of us are too habit-strung, 'busy' or conditioned to recognize in ourselves. He considers recognition (and therefore object-differentiation) to be a perceptual memory-act of repetition and recollection that together form the basis of remembering. It is these that drive and structure the narrative of *À la recherche du temps perdu*. It is 'attentive recognition...a kind of circuit in which the external object yields to us deeper and deeper parts of itself, as our memory adopts a correspondingly higher degree of tension in order to project recollections towards it', writes Bergson in *Matière et mémoire*. 'The object is an interlocutor whose ideas develop within his consciousness into auditory representations which are then materialized into uttered words'.[37]

Bergson believed that time is contained in the forms of memory within objects and it is through acts of sensory perception, smelling, tasting, touching those objects that 'their' memories, their secret life, their meaning to us is released within us. The motivating force driving Proust's novel is the author-narrator's deeply felt desire to recreate what is lost, by creating art through the reprisal of sense-based memory images. The narrative, seen particularly clearly in its opening volume, is structured around a reprisal of sensory memory motifs, such as the episode of Aunt Leonie's *madeleine* teacake and her limeflower tea. The dipping of the former in the latter, imbibed by the child Marcel, and the subsequent adult recollection of this event constitutes the 'open sesame' memory that triggers, as if by magic, the novel.

The narrative has its linguistic and psychoanalytic origins in the author's symbolic ordering of his universe. It is a work representing, reflecting and embodying a subjective circular dream-like ordering, the process of exploratory creative meaning-making, in its structure. It is a life-time's work which uses memory/consciousness as its subject and its object: Time as its medium, its origin, and its end. Nabokov concluded: 'The whole is a treasure hunt where the treasure is time and the hiding place the past: this is the inner meaning of the title'.[38]

Proust articulates a refined, cultivated form of language, reflecting social origins and individual sensibility. This might at first sight appear to place him outside the criteria of the fugal in literature. He doesn't play deconstruction-games with the language that he uses. He does not attempt to represent 'raw subjectivity,' of his characters thoughts as did Joyce. Instead he enacts an exquisite, fluid, refined subjectivity, distilled from sense-memories of experience. Nabokov noted this difference arguing that whereas Joyce portrayed character omnisciently as if an objective whole 'God-known, Joyce-known', fragmented and scattered like clues throughout the space-time of his narrative for the reader to piece together bit by bit, Proust's view of other people is—as complete concepts unto themselves (to apply Leibniz's notion of monadology). 'When Proust portrayed Swann, he made Swann an individual, with individual, unique characteristics'.[39]

Proust's view of other people is almost analogous to the (inherently self-contained and isolated) monads in Leibniz's monadology: 'The monads have no windows through which anything could come in or go out' (Leibniz, 1898, par 7), and a 'monad cannot have any physical influence upon the inner being of another' (par 51).[40] Bearing out Leibniz's philosophical idea of the monad as a self enclosed entity, Proust's characters are essentially not only unknown to each other (as indicated by their multiple social masks and disguises) they are essentially unknowable to each other (and most often themselves, hence Marcel's prolonged search to remember something within his own memory). This enduring theme is the source of emotional anguish, turmoil and pain for the narrator, as well as ironic humour in terms of the 'wrong ideas' that characters have about each other's 'true' selves, or identities. Proust's secondary characters, necessarily, are never known, as characters for themselves, but comparatively, through first-person narrative consciousness, as objects of thought in Marcel's mind.

Secondary characters are mediated entirely through the prism of the narrator's consciousness and indirectly through the perceptions of the characters. Even the narrator is in a sense comparative, a shadowy, polyphonic, voice-concept, construed within and of the shifting space-time co-ordinates of a double mirror act in which the past and present reflect and eclipse each other.

I-SPY: HOW MANY I'S AM 'I'?

In the opening pages of *À la recherche* we find references to various personae who could be seen as metaphorical reference-clues to (that is reflections of aspects of) the hypersensitive author-narrator's persona (e.g. an imagined traveller; a bed-ridden invalid). Ultimately, however, the narrative constitutes a conversation between the narrator and himself. A conversation, on different levels, constructed from multiple narrative 'I' voices, each with a tense—and sense—function in relation to representing, and speaking from, different times, and places (or not, in the case of the disembodied, deterritorialized 'I' voices).

The succession of scenes from narrator Marcel's childhood, youth, and early adulthood, involves the usage of multiple narrative 'I' voices, not only in descriptions of events, but also in the narrator's equally detailed and elaborated observations of moral philosophy regarding people, society, manners and life, and the philosophical ideas which constitute the narrative. Two major temporal modalities are 'voiced'. The disembodied, detached, speaking-voice narrative 'I', in the position of Search-er, stands in relation to the described, embodied 'I' (s), the active participatory 'I'(s) in scenes of lost time. The disembodied 'I', reflecting in these scenes on the events described, is like a dreamer watching himself in a dream, from an unknown disembodied vantage point, a deterritorialized non-position of non-Being. The drama and emotions of the vivid action are felt—and observed—in the voice(s) of another deterritorialized speaking-voice 'I' (distinct to the speaking-voice of the narrative Search-er); as many as seven narrative 'I' voices have been identified in *À la recherche du temps perdu*.

Central to the shimmering layered effects of the prose is a play on reading, on readers, and on the impossibility of ever being able to truly read other people—one of Proust's enduring existential themes. On the pleasures of solitary summer reading in the garden in Combray, the narrator relates:

> Next to this central belief, which, while I was reading, would be constantly in motion from my inner self to the outer world, towards the discovery of Truth, came the emotions aroused in me by the action in which I would be taking part, for these afternoons were crammed with more dramatic and sensational events than occur, often, in a whole lifetime. These were the events which took place in the book I was reading. It is true that the people concerned in them were not what Françoise would have called 'real people'. But none of the feelings which the joys or misfortunes of a 'real' person awaken in us can be awakened except through a mental picture of those joys and misfortunes; and the ingenuity of the first novelist lay in his understanding that, as the picture was the one essential element in the complicated structure of our emotions, so that simplification of it which consisted in the suppression, pure and simple, of 'real' people would be a decided improvement. A 'real' person, profoundly as we may sympathize with him, is to a great measure perceptible only through our senses, that is to say, he remains opaque, offers a dead weight which our sensibilities have not the strength to lift. (SW: 112-3)

Thus we can know fictional characters far better than real ones, we can take inside ourselves fictional characters in a way not possible with Real People in the Real World. Similarly, we can live through reading in a way that may not be possible in our own lives. Reading and, by implication, the virtual, conceptual, fugal world of writing is therefore, this passage suggests, more satisfying than the real world of real people. What one has 'read' in, and of, the world is transformed into (one's own literal) writing capable of being read in the world. From consciousness and desire; to truth, the Book: a material object in the material world of Being. This is the Search, what is lost and found, in the self, in the fugal process of writing. What Proust searched for, and embodied, in his writing is the 'form of Time' (a spatial category) in consciousness (time-duration). It is as Milan Kundera has asserted, an exposition of how 'a man's interior universe comprises a miracle, an infinity that never ceases to amaze us.'[41]

Whereas many of the narrator's reflections on his social relations concern 'games' of inverted desires, 'playing hard to get', for example in *La Fugitive* (The Fugitive) and social deceptions of the intellect, it is traumatic shock and pain of loss of a loved one that puts the narrrator in touch with his true feelings. This begins with Albertine's flight from Marcel's apartment in Paris. Marcel then proceeds to attempt to lure her back to him by indirect mendacious means; when she is killed in a freak riding accident (which recalls the death of Alfred, Proust's secretary who lived in his apartment and whom it seems, according to William Carter's *Proust in Love*, Albertine may be based on, although Carter says he had started to write her character before he met Agostinelli)[42] the pain of traumatic loss eclipses deceptions of the intellect. In 'Grieving and Forgetting', chapter one of *The Fugitive*, in grief at her initial departure, Marcel reflects:

> I had believed that I no longer loved Albertine, I had believed that I was leaving nothing out of account, like a rigorous analyst; I had believed that I knew the state of my own heart. But our intelligence, no matter how lucid, cannot perceive the elements that compose it and remain unsuspected so long as, from the volatile state in which they generally exist, a phenomenon capable of isolating them has not subjected them to the first stages of solidification. I had been mistaken in thinking that I could see clearly into my own heart. But this knowledge, which the shrewdest perceptions of the mind would not have given me, had now been brought to me, hard, glittering, strange, like a crystallized salt, by the abrupt reaction of pain. (TF: 478)

Proust suggests self-knowledge is reached through the reflection of the individual following loss of a loved one, and the pain of the grief he felt. It is emotional pain, that puts us in touch with our true feelings. However narrator Marcel does not follow his true feelings after Albertine leaves him, even after he suggested it, and works out ingenious plans to win her back without losing face, by deceiving Saint-Loup, Albertine, her aunt whom she is staying with, and himself. When she is killed, he then feels the grief and loss he does not need to try to deceive himself about.

'INVISIBLE MUSIC' OF 'UNKNOWN PLEASURES'

> Those inaccessible and torturing hours into which she had gone to taste unknown pleasures—behold, a breach in the wall, and we are through it. (*Swann's Way*: 39)

How does Proust apply techniques of musicalization in *A la recherché du temps perdu* and what are the uses and functions of musicalization in the narrative as a whole?

In the previous chapter I have discussed how De Quincey developed techniques of fugue musicalization, in concepts of 'reverberation' and 'impassioned prose' in what he terms 'language of power', as a modality of writing through which he expresses and communicates the experiences of emotion, and recreates affect. In his recounting of trauma, in impassioned prose, De Quincey's writings focus on processes of consciousness and the unconscious, with these two main aspects of the mind brought together in use in his writing of involuntary memory.

Proust also musically explored the 'inner', emotive processes of the psyche. There is a subtle reference to the links between music and memory and his narrative processes in the title, *À la recherche du temps perdu*. The time of memory is the time of writing, which he associates with musical time. The power of music to affect emotion is a recurrent, linking theme throughout the text. A motif he uses as a vehicle to guide himself through the layers of memory and *temps perdu* is *la petite phrase de Vinteuil*, a phrase of music by the composer who came from Combray. Proust repeatedly returns to Vinteuil's septet and it becomes a motif for the creative process of writing (and composing music) which, as in a musical fugue, develops his themes in the composition of his massive fugal novel. The phrase emerges and re-emerges at different times, providing a unifying theme, used self-referentially and performatively to explore and reflect on the processes of writing.

In *A l'ombre des jeunes filles en fleur*, on the occasion of the young Marcel visiting the Swanns at home in Paris, Mme Swann plays Vinteuil's sonata for him on the piano. As he recollects her playing, it is the musical phrase, and its associations, which develop the themes of his narrative interrogation of *temps perdu*. He is drawn into inner discussion with himself (or with several 'Marcels', recollected from different times) on the association between music and memory. He begins with a clear recollection of the impression made on him by Mme Swann:

> Sometimes, before going to dress, Mme Swann would sit down at the piano. Her lovely hands emerging from the pink, or white, or, often, vividly coloured crêpe de chine housecoat, drooped over the keys with that same melancholy that was in her eyes but was not in her heart. (WBG: 118)

It is almost as if there an element of reproach in his description: should there be melancholy in her heart, should she be more serious? Or perhaps Marcel (in youthful past, or present narrating guise) sees her melancholy ironically, as akin to an abstract, aesthetic virtue, an artificial social inflection, like a cosmetic, designed to heighten her beauty and poise. He does not focus on her appearance, but on the music she is playing, for him, and its tantalizing, serious, melancholically aesthetic significance:

> It was on one of those days that she happened to play for me the passage in Vinteuil's sonata that contained the little phrase of which Swann had been so fond. But often one hears nothing when one listens to the first time to a piece of music that is at all complicated. And yet when, later on, this sonata had been played to me two or three times I found I knew it perfectly well (118).

Ruminating on 'hearing something for the first time' he continues,

> Probably what is wanting, the first time, is not comprehension but memory. For our memory, relatively to the complexity of the impressions which it has to face while we are listening, is infinitesimal, as brief as the memory of a man which in his sleep thinks of a thousand things and at once forgets them, or as that of a man in his second childhood who cannot recall a minute afterwards what one has just said to him. (118)

The narrator concludes:

> Of these multiple impressions our memory is not capable of furnishing us with an immediate picture. But that picture gradually takes shape in the memory, and, with regard to works we have heard more than once, we are like the schoolboy who has read several times over before going to sleep a lesson which he supposed himself not to know, and finds he can repeat it by heart next morning.(118)

The key phrase, in relation to memory, is 'he supposed himself not to know'. The knowledge comes back by itself. Marcel thus explores an aspect of memory: automatic recall. But he now continues in an *involution*, to use the phrase proposed by Thomas De Quincey. As his involution continues it becomes more elaborate and complex, and a tone of melancholia colors and complicates what had started as a simple observation on the sensory impression of listening to music. Marcel berates himself for not initially being able to perceive the full meaning, beauty and significance of Vinteuil's 'little sonata', in its entirety. Mournfully, he castigates himself for failing to fully comprehend then, what (it is implied) the narrator now knows about the significance of the music:

> Since I was able to enjoy everything that this sonata had to give me only in a succession of hearings, I never possessed it in its entirety: it was like life itself... (119)

In music, motifs may be elaborated and developed and exaggerated. Marcel moves from the membered sensory impression of listening to Mme Swann playing the phrase from the sonata, to ruminating on the reception of works of genius, and the time it takes for these works to be 'possessed'.

Thus, with the little sonata, he teases out a complex rumination developing and playing with the subject themes of the creative process and memory, and their shared mediums of consciousness and time. As Marcel realizes at the conclusion of the work, it is ruminations on these themes in his reflective, melancholic, obsessive interrogation of the inflections and nuances of meaning, extracted from these memory-motifs, which, ironically, constitute the writing processes and the 'work' of his writing. In this sense the *Recherche* writes itself, as the fugue constitutes itself.

Using techniques of musicalization is a way of achieving a unity in a narrative which goes beyond conventional realist representation, a unity able to account for and accommodate the fragmented states of dreams and involuntary memories—alike in De Quincey's *Dream-Fugue*, and Proust's *À la recherche du temps perdu*. It is a modality which might bring together an infinite array of associations, experiments in language involving the coining of new words phrases, and concepts, which may pass into wider currency, such as *involuntary memory*. It can therefore be suggested, following Benjamin's definition of modernist subjectivity, that literary narratives that use musicalized fugue techniques are linked to the emergent subjectivity of the modern literary mind.

Proust's use of musicalization has been discussed by critics including Deleuze and Guattari (1987) and Wolf (1999) particularly relating to 'Vinteuil's little phrase'. Deleuze and Guattari argue that Proust:

> was among the first to underscore this life of the Wagnerian motif.

> Instead of the motif being tied to a character who appears, the appearance of the motif itself constitutes a rhythmic character in 'the plenitude of a music that is indeed filled with so many strains, each of which is a being.' It is not by chance that the apprenticeship of the *Recherche* pursues an analogous discovery in relation to Vinteuil's little phrases: they do not refer to a landscape; they carry and develop within themselves landscapes that do not exist on the outside (the white sonata and red septet...).[43]

Each mention of 'Vinteuil's little phrase' acts as a trigger for an emotionally inflected involution of memories and reflections. In this way, the 'sonata' functions as an intuitive musicalized technique, unifying the narrative. That Proust's musical-literary motifs do not refer to a 'landscape' but carry and develop internal landscapes suggests the independent discursive processes of language, an understanding of literary narrative as being a thing-it-itself which exists independently of an external 'reality'.

Thus the narrative develops: through contrapuntal interweaving of the narrator's layers of memory, from Mme Swann's playing, to the complex functions of memory itself, the subliminal mental processes through which we come to develop our individual 'inner' subjective meanings and understanding from sensory impressions we receive through social and cultural experiences in our lives. Vinteuil's phrase is a signature melody, a subject theme-line of Proust's fugue of writing in the *Recherche*, which paradoxically anchors, defines and releases the novel's form. Recurrence is a symbolic rhetorical device from which develop, fugally, the contrapuntal themes and complex polyphonic variations of consciousness that performatively constitute the affective, musicalized, literary composition of *À la recherche du temps perdu*.

THE IMPORTANCE OF BEING AFFECTIVE

Wimmers (2003) argues that affect is rendered as a response by the narrator, in relation to two types of creative text. These are first, the literary texts the narrator reads, and second, the musical texts, or compositions which he listens to, and here Wimmers also emphasizes the role, function and uses Proust makes of 'Vinteuil's little phrase'.

In relation to the narrator's reading of literary texts, this can be seen as Marcel's reversal of the reader-author role which allows the reader to empathize with the narrator—as he too is a reader. Wimmers comments: 'The narrator's analyses of reading novels call attention to the central role of fictional characters in the interaction, a process rooted in the structures of exchange based on affect, primarily empathy'.[44] She notes the significance of this, in the reader's emotional identification with the narrator. 'As we watch him thus passionately engaged in reading, we get to know him more intimately and become aware of certain recurring patterns in his emotional life, patterns that leave their imprint on us'.[45] She thus draws attention to the significance of affect in the reading process of Proust's work, for the reader invited to join in this empathetic *mise en intrique*—a game in which readers play their own part in the novel's reception, an involvement which, Wimmers suggests, is aided by the insight offered by affect, that is the emotional responses invited by the narrative. Reading Proust therefore, Wimmers suggests, involves and invites an emotional exchange, and identification by the reader with Marcel the narrator (and implied author). Affect, or emotional response, is appealed to and triggered in the narrative use of Vinteuil's little phrase. This musical phrase triggers an affective reaction in the narrator as he recalls its music in his memory. Music is the privileged genre of art by which the narrator measures his emotional responses. Clearly the musical phrase carries a weight of meaning and affect—it is no musical interlude.

The musical phrase comes to be deeply associated with his personal life, for the narrator. I have mentioned the melancholic affect triggered in the narrator's memory by his memory of Mme Swann's playing. Wimmers emphasizes the role of the septet in the narrator's emotional narrative of Albertine: the neurasthenic emotions which are to torment him, stir as he is playing the septet on the piano, having just experienced the first agonizing pangs of jealously provoked by Albertine. Playing, he assimilates the music to his anguished and melancholic emotions. It is interesting here to note the associations and connections that Marcel makes between listening to Vinteuil's little phrase, the experience of listening to music, and needing to listen to music, and neurasthenia. In *La Prisonnière* (The Captive) waiting for Albertine to return, but safe in the knowledge of her whereabouts, Marcel has been playing Vinteuil's sonata on the piano.

He switches to playing Wagner and his rumination changes direction:

> I was struck by how much reality there is in the work of Wagner as I contemplated once more those insistent, fleeting themes which visit an act, recede only to return again and again, and sometimes distant, dormant, almost detached are at other moments, while remaining vague, so pressing and so close, so internal, so organic, so visceral, that they seem like the reprise not so much of a musical motif, but an attack of neuralgia. (TC: 175)

The music functions as a precipitating trigger of 'neuralgia' that can be compared to post-traumatic stress disorder, as an involuntary reprisal of traumatized memory and emotional response in a sensitive individual. Or is it caused by Wagner's music itself?

Proust also links this process with the mimetic construction of the 'individuality' of a 'person' in art: This begins with the subjective 'self' of the narrator:

> Music, very different in this respect from Albertine's society, helped me to descend into myself, to discover new things: the variety that I had sought in vain in life, in travel... (TC 175)

Marcel acknowledges that his process of constructing or constituting subjective impressions of a subject in art is built on diversity:

> As the spectrum makes visible to us the composition of light, so the harmony of a Wagner, the colour of an Elstir, enable us to know that essential quality of another person's sensations into which love for another person does not allow us to penetrate. Then a diversity inside the work itself, by the sole means that exist of being effectively diverse: to wit combining diverse individualities. (175)

The implied author hereby develops a theme of individuality, the articulation of subjectivity in art as the reflection or embodiment of an individual 'person'. Whereas this might allow us to know the creator of a work of art better than we know a lover, the ability to communicate differentiated affect is linked to the prowess, and power, of the artist. The narrator continues:

> Where a minor composer would claim to be portraying a squire, or a knight, while making them both sing the same music, Wagner on the contrary allots to each separate appellation a different reality. (175)

Is the author-narrator being ironic here? Is there a hidden polemic to be detected in his praising of the individualism, and 'joy' of Wagner?

> Whence the plenitude of a music that is indeed filled with so many different strains, each of which is a person. A person or impression that is given to us by a momentary aspect of nature. Even that which, in this music is most independent of the emotion that it arouses in us preserves its outward and absolutely precise reality.... Wagner, retrieving some exquisite fragment from a drawer of his writing-table, to introduce it, as a retrospectively necessary theme, into a work he had not even thought of at the time he composed it, then having composed a first mythological opera, and a second, and afterwards others still, and perceiving all of a sudden that he had written a tetralogy, must have felt something of the same exhilaration as Balzac... (TC: 176)

In a self-reflective turn, the implied author thereby elucidates a theory of imitative mimesis in musicalized terms in relation to literature, as the gesture indicates itself. The implied author also remarks:

> Wagner himself was filled with joy when he discovered in his memory the shepherd's tune, incorporated it in his work, gave it full wealth of meaning. This joy moreover never forsakes him. In him, however great the melancholy of the poet, it is consoled, transcended – that is to say, alas, to some extent destroyed – by the exhilaration of the fabricator. (177)

The narrator hereby alludes to musical pastoralist idealism and Wagner's use of the *leitmotif*. Whereas the musicalization of Proust's narrative text is afforded by techniques such as the recurrence of Vinteuil's septet, and it is this musicalization that gives the work its performative 'unity', what emerges as the narrative proceeds is the significant emotional tone and affective function of this modal process. The musicalized mode is created by the hyper-sensitive narrator/implied author as a means of containing and understanding his emotional affective responses, to experiences which he finds at first perhaps incomprehensible. Thus he bewails the fact that he does not 'hear' the significance of the septet until he has listened to it many times.

Proust also uses musical metaphors and analogies to signpost the feelings of either Marcel, or characters with whom he is interacting, such as the Baron Charlus, of whose homosexual desire for him the young Marcel remains for a time unaware. Using music in this way,

FUGUE OF LOST TIME 273

interspersing the characters' speeches and ruminations with musical allusions, it is as if he is articulating the music of the scene. In *Le Côté de Guermantes* (The Guermantes Way) when Marcel has been called to the Baron Charlus's house at night, from a social engagement, the Baron becomes furious, because the young man has failed to return, or succumb to the nature of his feelings for him. Charlus's outbursts are punctuated by musical passages, which effect a form of phrasing. Marcel says: 'I don't think I can have annoyed you by saying to Mme de Guermantes that I was a friend of yours'. And the symphonic music begins:

> He gave a disdainful smile, raised his voice to the supreme pitch of its highest register, and there, softly attacking the shrillest and most contumelious note, 'Oh! Sir,' he said, returning by the most gradual stages to a natural intonation, and seeming to revel as he went in the oddities of this descending scale, 'I think you do yourself an injustice when you accuse yourself of having said that we were friends. (643)

> ...like the deafening onrush of a storm. (The force with which he habitually spoke, which made strangers turn round in the street, was multiplied a hundredfold, as is a musical forte if, instead of being played on the piano, it is played by an orchestra, and changed into a fortissimo as well.) M. de Charlus roared. 'Do you suppose it is within you power to offend me?' (645)

Three pages on:

> Then in a gentle, affectionate, melancholy voice, as in those symphonies which are played without a break between the different movements, in which a graceful scherzo, amiable and idyllic, follows the thunder-peals of the opening part. 'It is quite possible,' he said. 'Generally speaking a remark repeated at second-hand is rarely true.' (648)

Two pages later, the Baron de Charlus is walking with the young Marcel to the front door. Passing through his hall, they hear music playing from somewhere in the house. Charlus points out his works of art, and his collection of 'all the hats' worn by Marie Antoinette. He indicates the Rembrandts, the Turner, and then: 'You hear: Beethoven has come to join him'.

> And indeed one could hear the first chords of the last movement of the Pastoral Symphony, 'Joy after the Storm,' performed somewhere not far away, on the first floor no doubt, by a band of musicians. I innocently inquired how they happened to be playing that, and who

the musicians were. 'Ah, well one doesn't know. One never does know. It's invisible music.' (650)

'Invisible music' refers to hidden emotions of intended seduction, to feelings, stirred by love. 'Invisible music' is the love that cannot speak its name. In *Swann's Way*, the narrator, as very young and worldly-wise Marcel, alludes to 'the woman whom we love' (39). He refers to her in terms of emotional jealousy and insecurity, as separate from himself. This begins in connection with Swann and the indifferent Odette, but primarily with Mamma, whose unforthcoming bedtime kiss, and presence, as a lonely child, grown-up Marcel imagines:

> the inconceivable, infernal scene of gaiety in the thick of which we had been imagining swarms of enemies, perverse and seductive, beguiling away from us, even making laugh at us, the woman we love. (SW: 39)

Invisible music, alluding to hidden passions and 'unknown pleasures', a source of perpetual intrigue, anxiety, and jealousy, originating in the early years; plays in unconscious desire, and loss throughout Marcel's life's-work. And in the metaphorical meaning of invisible music is the love which dare not speak its name, homosexuality, which is a central theme of the work, written and published in an era when this was socially prohibited.

MUSICALIZED SIGN LANGUAGE

In the writing of a fugue narrative, an author's unique individuality is expressed in signs, which are the literary equivalent of a visual artists' marks, or composers' self-designated motifs. Narrative signs, an author's signs, comprise motifs, images, concepts or phrases that have a coded textual meaning for both the author and reader, in the context of the narrative text. These signs may be denoted consciously or unconsciously, spontaneously, or 'automatically' through subliminal association by the author, who in the writing of the text, as narrator, and/or author, begins to realize their 'true' meaning or significance in that text. This signifies the writing of narrative as compositional, performative, formative text, created as an active Search (through, and within, a conceptual memory-based zone of 'lost time').

One salient aspect of Proust's signs (as with such texts constructed around memory loss) is that in an attempt to recall, find out, recover, make sense, find the meaning of certain supposedly significant recurring images, the narrator is placed in the same position as a reader, compelled to keep reading the signs in the narrative (which he is narrating) and puzzle out their meaning (in such narratives a reader may guess before the narrator)—a process echoing Baroque fugue puzzle canons. Marcel is compelled to read the signs, compulsively, obsessively returning repeatedly to certain motifs, for instance the *madeleine* which causes memory, Deleuze's 'resurrection of the past'.[46] Proust's signs comprise a language of motif, metaphor and metonymy, which both the reader and the narrator learn on progressing through the narrative.

The act, and processes, of memory with its multiple, selective, resurrections of the Past, is always to be seen as slippery and unreliable, Deleuze proposes. This is why he perceives the strongest narrative structure in Proust's work to be that of the objective straightforward 'signs', or motifs, such as Vinteuil's little phrase and steeples of Martinville—straightforward because they do not 'resurrect the past'—for the narrator. This means that, in the canon of Proust's narrative sign language, they do not trigger spontaneous flights of scenic memory that develop into full-fledged scenarios constructed from and within narrative recollection. The motifs or signs that *do* do this, as Deleuze points out, are the *madeleine* and the cobblestones. The narrator's obsessive return at times to these signs, which constitutes a form of self-interrogation, as he searches for the meaning of these motifs for him, creates a recursive polyphonic slipping structure, the fugal movement of the content of the narrative. Each time the narrator recalls the sign-motif of the *madeleine*, he recounts a mini-narrative; a scene or scenario that is associated, for him, with the *little teacake*, a different aspect of the story. This embodies the fugal structure of repetition of a subject line in many different ways, through different narrative voices.

But, in the wider scheme of the fugal narrative of the many-volumes one type of sign cannot be differentiated against another. The assemblage of signs, Proust's individual unique narrative language, constitutes its nature, its overall structure. Deleuze saw it as being the narrative of 'an apprenticeship of a man of letters'. How and why the narrative constitutes an 'apprenticeship' of this man of letters is what makes it fugal.

THE ART OF THE INFINITELY EXPANDING (SELF GENERATIVE, ASSOCIATIVE) METAPHOR

Proust uses metaphor, like a conjurer pulling out, seemingly from nowhere, an inter-linked memory-chain of astonishing, improbable and colourful images, one after another, linked by association and often including sub-sets of similes. Proust's metaphors are invariably triggered by an individual sense memory, which can trigger another and another, in streams of associations. His chains of metaphors can run for pages emerging out of each other like a puzzle of Chinese boxes.

Metaphor operates possibly to its most dazzling effect in *Du côté du chez Swann*, in which can be found—in the Overture, leading into the Combray section—most of the stylistic elements that run throughout the work.

From the beginning of the narrative, a series of sense memories opens one from the other, in an increasingly imaginative and dexterous display, which culminates in Proust's most famous metaphor of the *madeleine*, the taste of which triggers a memory, which opens the narrative. He is unaware of its significance until the end of the final volume, when he hears the ringing of a bell, and he realizes that the past, and all that has happened to him still exists within him, in the depths of memory. Yet, at the start of *Recherche,* Marcel has a Bergsonian presentiment:

> And so it is with our own past. It is a labour in vain to attempt to recapture it: all the efforts of our intellect must prove futile. The past is hidden somewhere outside the realm, beyond the reach of intellect, in some material object (in the sensation which that material object will give us) which we do not suspect. And as for that object, it depends on chance whether we come upon it or not before we ourselves must die. (SW: 58)

It is as the narrator *is* dying, that he realizes, finally, the significance of his memories, which is artistic significance. The written rumination on the numinous, almost 'magical,' objects of his recall, and the telling in detail of the memories they have triggered constitutes the work of art, which throughout the narrative, the narrator has continually confided he has longed to write.

Limeflower tea infusion and *madeleine teacake.* That these are going to function as sense-based aids for the active practice of writing, in solitude from the world, disconnected from social life and one's friends, is indicated, in the allusions carried by the limeflower tea to Samuel Taylor Coleridge's poem *This Lime-Tree Bower My Prison*.

It was whilst Coleridge was alone, in a lime-tree bower, unable to accompany his friends William and Dorothy Wordsworth and Charles Lamb, and his wife Sara, on their walk over the Quantock hills (as he described it to friend Robert Southey: 'Sara had accidentally emptied a skillet of boiling milk on my foot')[47] he composed a poem dedicated to Lamb (*For thee, my gentle-hearted Charles to whom/No sound is dissonant that tells of life*) which reaches the conclusion that from solitude, painful though it may be, comes the joy of meaningful creation in the writing of his poem. This is a subtle reference, which has a structural significance in Proust's work. Marcel, the narrator, is, like Proust, as it were, alone in his lime-tree bower his prison, the fourth dimension, occupied in recollection in poetic writing, and in transforming images of sensation-based memories of his experiences, in the 'lost time' of his memories of nature (and past life and loves) which, in their reflections, prove to be adequate to his needs of writing his books: for Coleridge, poetic imagination triumphs over loss and pain, as he transforms this pain and loss into his poetry, which is what happens in Proust's novels. The overall subject themes are, then, the author-narrator, and the act of writing, these motifs are reprised in Marcel's memory (and therefore narrative, constituting as it does the narrator's memory-contents) each time from a different angle adding new detail, as sound or taste or image—and their significance—is conjured up from what is forgotten. Reflecting on the dried lime (linden) blossoms purchased from a pharmacy in Combray from which his aunt's tisane was prepared and into which a *madeleine* was dipped, he narrates a sense-memory based stream of associations, redolent with branching similes:

> Presently my aunt was able to dip in the boiling infusion, in which she would relish the savour of dead or faded blossom, a little madeleine, of which she would hold out a piece to me when it was sufficiently soft. (SW: 57-58)

Once, on returning home he was served tea and cake by his mother:

> I stopped, intent upon the extraordinary changes that were taking place in me. An exquisite pleasure had invaded my senses, but individual, detached, with no suggestion of its origin. And at once the vicissitudes of life had become indifferent to me, its disasters innocuous, its brevity an illusion—this new sensation having had on me the

> effect which love has of filling me with a precious essence; or rather this essence was not in me, it was myself. I had ceased now to feel mediocre, accidental, mortal. Whence could it have come to me, this mighty joy? I was conscious that it was connected with the taste of tea and cake, but that it infinitely transcended those savours, could not, indeed be of the same nature as theirs. Whence did it come from? What did it signify? How could I seize upon it and define it? (SW: 58)

He struggles to remember what it is that the taste recalls. He sips and tastes some more. The memory is on the tip of his tongue, and then it fills his consciousness:

> And suddenly the memory returns. The taste was that of the little bit of madeleine which on Sunday mornings at Combray (because on those mornings I did not go out before church-time), when I went to say good day to her in her bedroom, my aunt Leonie used to give me, dipping it first in her own cup of tea or of lime-flower infusion... (61)

This conjures up an image so enchanting, it has appealed to many who have not read Proust, by-passing language barriers, so that in English, literate people may be familiar with 'Proust's *madeleine*', which both in the novel (and in life) becomes a metaphor for the type of startling sudden recall of long forgotten memory, triggered by a certain taste or smell.

Such is the metaphoric and metonymic force of *'the madeleine'*, it has come to stand for the 'Proustian' effect or sensibility, again a mysterious knowledge concept—held by many who have not read Proust, but yet who have 'an idea' about his work, and what it 'means'. So that, with the mere mention of Proust's *madeleine* a whole series of associations is triggered in the mind of the receiver. Such is the performative power of the metonym. In keeping with monadic, inter-connectedness of Proust's narrative structure, not only does the *madeleine* memory fragment contain a metaphor and constitute a metonym, it also functions as a powerful recurring motif and motive in Proust's work.

METONYMY: DISCREET LANGUAGE OF THE TEXT

Each text, each narrative, in a sense speaks its own language, which its readers learn in the process of reading. This is a metonymic language of association in which certain significant objects (word signs) come to represent (stand for), for the reader, that cluster of significance (significations) summonsed up by the narrator.

Proust's use of metonym, as a form of invocation, has the effect of rendering the narrative into a performative text. By using metonymic words and phrases, the *madeleine*, Aunt Leonie's lime-flower tea, Vinteuil's little musical phrase, the walks of *Du côté du chez Swann* (Swann's Way) and *Le côté de Guermantes* (the Guermantes Way), and the names of characters and places the reader comes to 'know': Albertine, Swann, Odette, Saint-Loup, Combray...he summons up 'the past', *temps perdu*, commands it to open up within, his gaze. And, one by one, memory fragments emerge, blossoming in intricate, elaborate, extraordinary metaphors and similes. One word triggers untold images and associations.

The performative trick of Proust's work, its great feat, is that what is found in the Search, in the process of writing, recollecting, reflecting is what was most wanted, most desired by the author-narrator in his youth. Desired and doubted. How could he ever be capable of fulfilling this promise? How could it be, would it be possible, the transmutation of his world into words, a narrative, a book? The transmutation or the embodiment of consciousness, his perceptions, everything in the world he has seen around him, in his family, his upbringing, his social milieu, the natural world—that flow of life transformed, embodied in words, the creation of his own work of art.

It could be seen, in a poststructuralist interpretation, that Proust achieved this transformation through the performative practice of *écriture*. Through writing one creates and makes one's language, the notes that will have an inherent set of melodic possibilities. The author writes language in his or her own image or cast.

MOTIF/MOTIVE: OBJECTIFYING OTHERS, THE WRITER'S BLISS

The motivating force, the 'leading emotional purpose', which instigates and propels Proust's narrative through its intricacies and movements, is the narrator/author's '*Recherche*' of *temps perdu*. But what does this mean? The search, through memory, in an attempt to find *le temps* in the time of duration, lived time, his writing, posits a paradoxical language-game of mirrors and tricks. What he desires is impossible, essentially nostalgic, and possibly even morbid. It is, perhaps, the desire to remain in bed alone, in the hazy hypnotic delirium of fever, in which lost memories, people, images, events swirl in hallucinogenic colours before the eye, complete with bouquets of intoxicating fragrances, impressions of touches, tastes, lingering and unforgettable; an inner world of seclusion, introspection, in which he can be alone; the world of the writer's ardours of discipline, that perhaps would not be considered 'healthy' by the rational physician, the psychoanalyst. And Marcel, the narrator, as sickly asthmatic adolescent on holiday in the Hotel Balbec, doted on by his grandmother and his aristocratic new friend, Robert Saint-Loup, admits a certain fastidious attitude to 'the outside world' when, in *Within a Budding Grove,* he confides:

> It was promptly settled between us that he and I were to be great friends forever, and he would say 'our friendship' as though he were speaking of some important and delightful thing which had an existence independent of ourselves, and which he soon called— apart from the love of his mistress—the great joy of his life. These words filled me with a sort of melancholy and I was at a loss for an answer, for I felt when I was with him, when I was talking to him — and no doubt it would have been the same with anyone else—none of that happiness which it is possible for me to experience when I was by myself. Alone, at times, I felt surging from the depths of my being one or other of those impressions which gave me a delicious sense of well-being. But as soon as I was with someone else, as soon as I was talking to a friend, my mind as it were faced about, it was towards this interlocutor and not towards myself that it directed its thoughts, and when they followed this outward course they brought me no pleasure. (364)

Proust eloquently expresses the melancholic métier of the writer, who would rather be engaged in writing about the world (of others), than having to engage directly with it. Even his justification of time spent with his friend compounds this impression:

> But I told myself that one is not intelligent for oneself alone, that the greatest of men have wanted to be appreciated, that hours in which I had built up a lofty idea of myself in my friend's mind could not be considered wasted. (SW: 365)

In writing of, and about, consciousness, deeply embedded in the melancholic pleasures and pain of writing through personal memory, the fugal narrator is engaged in a perpetual inner conversation. Mildly dissociated, psychically split in the act of writing, the author narrator becomes his or her interlocutor. He or she is talking to himself, or herself, in and to a reflection or echo of herself or himself, in the act of writing. Thus the phrasing 'I told myself' (I reassured myself, I persuaded myself etc.) is a common feature of this, a particular type of first-person fugal novel. Marcel objects to having to leave the solitary state of writing-bliss, which can afford pleasures of 'delicious well-being...surging from the depths of my being' (WBG, 364).

Having to turn thoughts and attention to communicating with a real person in the material world is painful, at least it brings no pleasure, causing the mind to have to turn away from itself, its comfortable writerly sense of anguish leading to delicious writing-bliss, Barthes' *jouissance*. He does not want to face outwards and engage directly with real objects, real things and people, events in the raw material world.

> He was no more an object the properties of which, in my musings, I sought to explore. (365).

Marcel in detached aesthetic appreciation of his friend as 'a landscape' and 'work of art', elucidates the ideas both that we can know others better than they know themselves and see things in other people of which they are unaware. (Such are the ways in which we represent other people to ourselves, attempting to make sense of them, we make metaphors of them). In so doing, perhaps unawares, he further reveals his own desired aesthetic detachment from the world of other people.

The author-narrator does this by creating a heightened and distorted mirror-world in which people, as objects of thought and memory, swirl in many-coloured images and impressions, shapes and shades in the kaleidoscopic flow of narrative consciousness. In this sense, *À la recherche du temps perdu*, through its volume, through the scale, scope and complexity of its architectural structure, constitutes a heightened example of: 'the flow of narrative consciousness', that is, the state, processes and content in which all successful complex narratives are constructed, representing, as it does, the creation of a believable virtual world in written language, which is, further, embodied and materialized in the form of the Book.

To create a believable fictional world, an author must necessarily represent people, in the form of objects of thought. There are not any 'real' people in the content of the book. The virtual language-creations, which are read from the page, 'exist' as the result and embodiment of the transposing of inexistent objects of thought in the author's mind, objects of thought which originate from an author's experienced sense perceptions of the material world. Due to the deeply introspective and sensitive nature of Marcel, this awareness (of the nature of the objects of thought, and the 'logical' —or rather illogical implications of narrative objectifying) is transferred, and is transparent in, his descriptions of his social world.

This literary phenomenon is intensified in a fugal narrator, as this form of displacement, objectifying, and transference takes place in relation to the polyphonic narrative selves. Objects of thought from consciousness, or unconsciously derived from hidden memory originate in sensory perceptions of the real world, the author's 'real life'.

In objectifying his friend, seeing him as an object of thought, and knowingly describing him as such, Marcel has taken a further logical step of the writer who writes of the world and other people, of seeing these as objects of thought, objects described, objects in his/her mind, objects of language and therefore essentially unknowable. This is a logical result of the act of writing in which the world, other people as held in ones mind/memory as objects of thought, are then transferred as objects of thought, in words, in the narrative of one's creation.

MOTION AND MOTIVE ENERGY: A MUSICAL ANALOGY TO TEMPS DURÉE AND TEMPS ESPACE

Carl Dahlhaus problematizes the nature of tonal space as symbolized by the 'vertical and horizontal dimensions of notation,' and its relation to time:

> Are the differences between tones 'distances', spatially imaginable? Does it make sense to characterize as two 'dimensions' the pitch-interval and the duration of tones and to put these 'dimensions' into perpendicular relation to each other?[48]

Acknowledging the 'difficulties hindering any attempt to describe and analyze tonal space and musical motion' as labyrinthine, Dahlhaus isolates rhythm as the 'motive energy' that 'forms the basic component of the impression of musical motion'. Thus, he writes 'Time—temps durée made into a firm temps espace—is the primary dimension of tonal space; verticality is secondary'.[49] Questioning whether the differences between tones are 'distances' (spatialized), Dahlhaus reasons that 'with chords the manifestation of any characteristic of distance or space is less than with the successions of tone' and he suggests, the hypothesis that 'the idea of tonal space represents an abstraction from the phenomenon of musical motion, and that the basic aspect of this motion, from which others are dependent, is the rhythmic aspect'.[50]

Thus we see, applied to musical composition, an elaboration of the Bergsonian, conceptual notions of Time, as *le temps* the spatialized sense of physics, and as *durée*, which underpin, and play out the narrative of *À la recherche du temps perdu*. Of course, these temporal modalities operate in the production that is writing process, of any literary narrative. What makes Proust's work a prime example, though, is that it uses this interplay as its subject and its object, and is itself a metaphor for the process.

Could it be that, as a result of the writing process, the *temps durée* of the process of writing, and of the first-person narrative, is made into a 'firm *temps espace*', in the form of the finished Book, a material object which exists in time, yet, *of course*, once opened and entered, in the act of reading, expands into its own conceptual time zone, so that in a sense it has a dual existence, in time and out-of-time, accessed in reading time, in the modality of *temps durée*?

Dahlhaus's hypothesis of musical time could be applied analogously to the notions of Time, and time, embodied in Proust's narrative. The basic aspect of the narrative motion (written and read in *temps durée*) is rhythm, the rhythm of the writing, which is indeed notably rhythmic. Drawing an analogy between musical time and narrative time, from the point of view, or perspective, of musical composition, Dahlhaus defines three functional 'levels', which are in effect operative modalities in the narratives of literary works. These are "text' (*Wortlaut*, which must be distinguished from phonetic material that realizes the text in speaking), meaning and represented object'.[51]

In order to analyze these in terms of music, Dahlhaus (1982) refers to the theories of the musicologist, Ingarden, who 'rightly no doubt, distinguishes between performances of a musical work, individual and always differing, and the work itself that remains 'the same' in all the modifications to which it submits'.[52] Thus the work is a 'purely intentional' object, drawn from time, while a single performance is real and tied to the here-and-now. This can clearly be seen to be analogous to literary textual narratives. The individual *performance*, open to interpretation and different each time, is the act of reading the work.

Not only will each reader read the same text differently according to individual background, sensibility, character, experience; but each time the reader reads the same literary work he or she will perceive it, that is, read it, differently, finding different things in it. Often it may take attempts over a period of time before a reader fully engages with a book. Many readers have had the experience of picking up and trying to read a book several times over a period of time, and not being able to become fully involved with it. Then, suddenly, unexpectedly, one day, on picking up the same book again they find that now the text engages them, they become absorbed, transported into the world of the book, finding pleasure and meaning in its narrative. Often we have to read a book 'at the right time' for it to have meaning, before we are capable of understanding it, learning, deriving enjoyment or pleasure. The context has to be right, both in minds, as regards experience and perceptions; and in physical environment. It is necessary to have sufficient time and space to read. But, ideally, it is best to be supremely comfortable, and secluded, like Proust in summer gardens of his country holidays at Combray.

> for two consecutive summers I used to sit in the heat of our Combray garden, sick with a longing I would go on with it (my book) in the garden, under the chestnut tree, in a little sentry-box of canvas and matting, in the farthest recesses of which I used to sit and feel that I was hidden from the eyes of anyone who might be coming to call on the family...Upon the sort of screen, patterned with different states and impressions, which my consciousness would quietly unfold while I was reading, and which ranged from the most deeply hidden aspirations of my heart to the wholly external view of the horizon spread out before my eyes at the foot of the garden, what was from the first the most permanent and the most intimate part of me, the lever whose incessant movements controlled all the rest, was my belief in the philosophic richness and beauty of the book I was reading, and my desire to appropriate these to myself, whatever the book might be. (SW: 111-112)

Just as the author entered and inhabited his narrative in its creation, the Proustian reader is seduced, enchanted, by the music of the text. The reader enters the imaginative world of the narrative, a performative realm of possibility, the creative imagination. Now. Time functions differently here.

CHORA

In terms of its scope, depth, and methodology, *À la recherche du temps perdu* can be perceived and defined in terms of the notion of *chora*. Postulated (without using the term 'chora') by Plato in the *Timaeus*, this notion was reprised during the mid-twentieth century. Plato's *'chora'* was reconceptualized and recontextualized in Deconstructive theory by Derrida, adapted by theorists including Julia Kristeva.[53] In *Révolution du langage poétique* (1974) Kristeva adapted another notion of *chora* to psychoanalytic linguistic theory; in her metaphorical usage *chora* denotes a deep, mobile and provisional form of articulation on the (pre) semiotic level of an individual subject's constitution in language.

The *Timaeus* postulates that the stuff theorists term *chora* (though again, Plato does not use the word) was capable of 'continually assuming new forms,' like a mass of heated gold that is, and can be, moulded and remoulded in many ways. The *chora* from which all bodies take their forms is malleable as gold. Plato's idea was considered an appropriately workable concept for Derrida and Eisenman for their collaborative project of designing a public park.[54] Developing a three-tier, tri-concentric, system to explain the connection and mediation between the intelligible and sensible, worlds of Being and Becoming, Plato speculated that the first, ultimate, principle was God, the Good, the One. (Plurality appears first at the stage of Mind). His three 'hypostases' or realms of incorporeal reality are Soul, Mind, and the One. To account for the nature of matter he speculates that for each object which exists in the material world, there must be an ideal 'Form', which exists intelligibly only in the mind of the One. This, the famous theory of forms, was elaborated in *The Republic* where it underpins the ideal state, from which the fanciful 'lying' poets were excluded.

More than twenty centuries later, echoing this view, Bach articulated the belief that the music of mirror fugues existed in 'ideal form' in the *mind of God*. To be perfectly understood a complex mirror fugue needed to be apprehended by reading the score rather than by listening to it being played on instruments in the material world. Plato, in addition to his ideal forms, posited the material physical copies, comprising all things that have a physical material existence. All of which take their place, spatially, within the *chora*. To perform this function, then, *chora* must be, according to Plato's account:

> space, which is indestructible, and is perceived by a kind of spurious reason without the help of sense. This is presented to us in a dreamy manner, and yet is said to be necessary, for we say that all things must be somewhere in space. For they are the images of other things and must therefore have a separate existence and exist in something (i.e. in space). But the true reason assures us that while two things (i.e. the idea and the image) are different they cannot inhere in one another, so as to be one and two at the same time (Timaeus: 18-19).

Chora performs the function of both 'container' and 'contained'. The Presocratic philosophers had attempted to define the nature of matter in terms of a first principle, *apeiron*, of, and in which, all material things consisted. For example, to Thales it was water. Anaximander speculated that it was indeterminate. This prefigured Plato's theory, which is an extension and development of speculation about the nature of matter. How consciousness functions, the boundaries and definition of reason, rationality, consciousness and unconsciousness, time-space, natural philosophy, quantum mechanics, higher mathematics, infinite regression in mathematics, fractal geometry and so on, all relate to, and question, the nature of *chora*, together representing the 'problematization' of all existence, of matter, and abstract entities, falling into the philosophical realm of 'questions without answers'.

Chora can be seen metaphorically and applied to writing, functioning as *receptacle*, as the narrative structure of written language, and *contained*, the narrative content. Applied to Proust, *chora* refers (at Kristeva's pre/semiotic level of an individual's constitution in language) to the immaterial nature of consciousness, immaterial conceptual flow of thought from which Marcel as narrator (and possibly Proust as author) constructs his work in the process of narrating (writing). *Chora* refers to the narrative flow of words as arranged in the narrative structure; and the contents of the thoughts themselves therein. This is not to suggest that written narratives conform to, or embody, logocentric rationalism, the rationalism of Plato's developed theory of forms. Plato's view represents the type of 'harmony' objected to by Rousseau, as Derrida documents in *Of Grammatology*. In this view 'harmony' unity comprises of different melodic parts in which the individuality of each part is sacrificed to and lost in the whole. The principle of fugal music by contrast is that the whole is comprised from the dialogic interweaving of different parts (voices), therefore each retains its individuality, and in the arrangement new variations are created.

Similarly the kind of unifying practiced by the fugal author is to bring together disparate elements without these becoming formulated and losing their individuality in the process.

In terms of defining material reality, Proust's philosophical view as embodied in the narrative (content) which draws on Bergson's notion of *élan vital*, is, as previously noted, far closer to Leibniz's monadology, according to which there is not one material substance but infinity of substances, each animated by its own spirit. Far from representing and defining an ideal, unified *Reason*, as Platonic theory outlines, this is a universe of infinitely plural entities that contain within themselves mirrors of a world in which others are essentially unknowable; motives obscured, and cross purposes and misunderstandings between people/others predominate. Marcel's refined aesthetic appreciation of beauty is more tenderly deployed in application to natural phenomena such as trees, apple blossom, a sunset, a view, than to the people he relates to, who are, true to the structural constraints of the first person narrative, necessarily essentially unknowable to the narrator.

And whereas he projects a beauty and majesty onto nature, he does not project his emotions with a similar willing empathy onto other people who are the source of feelings of desire, loss, pain, anguish and jealousy to the narrator. It is this deeply experienced rendition of first person consciousness, with its fugal tricks and plays of light and shades of darkness, which makes *À la recherche du temps perdu* such a compelling and monumental modernist narrative, reflecting and embodying the intensified, heightened, often fragile states of mind of its author-narrator, Marcel, who could not stop writing.

The *chora* in *À la recherche* comprises an immaterial mental zone, the zone of the conceptual immaterial structure and content/s of the narrative, in which a plethora of fragmented images, thoughts, ideas and narrated events are arranged (or arrange themselves?) like a choreography of Chinese-box metaphors, recurring motifs, migrating avatars and the discreet coded language of sense-based associations which comprise its metonymic structure. The application of (Plato's) *chora* is thus not meant to imply that this reflects the world as a Platonic whole. On Leibniz's model the—almost—solipsistic world of the author, which is seen to be embodied in the extended polyphonic first person narrative, represents or articulates an expression of that particular individual's 'reason to be', not a *raison d'être* for Reason as a whole, on a Platonic scale. Writers speak for and of themselves, and Proust epitomizes this.

To write from the inner world to create art from words, the writer must necessarily loses oneself in that process of transformation, in the transcendent interchange between material and immaterial, the conscious and the automatic; in which in bliss and dread, one lets go and achieves the Impossible, that fugal eclipse of self with non-self, and re/creates oneself, and past selves, in written language.

THE PROUSTIAN WRITING MACHINE: WHAT MAKES *À LA RECHERCHE DU TEMPS PERDU* A PERFORMATIVE FUGAL TEXT

In *Proust and Signs* Deleuze hails Proust's text as a representation and embodiment of the 'Antilogos' in writing.[55] Proust's life-work is, in Deleuze's view, a leading example of a narrative which has emerged authentically during, and as a result of, a process of writing. The Antilogos can be interpreted as standing in opposition to the Logos (Greek for 'word') put forward by Heraclitus, and mentioned by Plato who associated knowledge with a logos, with understanding the reason why.[56]

Logocentrism has come to mean a notion of a preconceived rationality—an uber-ordering which the existence of fugal writing—that is writing as a fugue psychic modality—disrupts and counters as it is of contingency and of the a posteriori. The fundamental dualistic opposition between an ideal Platonic (or 'God') ordered utilitarian universe of ideal (unreal) forms and the deterritorialized, wild, disruptive, contradictory, and for all these, paradoxical nature of art is expressed by Bataille who terms what I am calling the paradoxical nature of art and poetry 'the impossible'. Bataille writes of a matrix of poetry, as a zone of dream logic, brilliance, and terror. It is the zone in which one metaphorically wanders out of oneself, in which one forgets the truth of the rights of the real:

> All the mediocre qualities that railroad tracks and signals bestow on what, in spite of everything, is located in their domain... my uncontrollable, out-of-the-way laughter is lost in a world of stations, mechanics, workers up at dawn.[57]

To enter this zone, according to Bataille, implies an act of symbolic transgression against the 'serious character' of 'the real,' an act of transgression against the symbolic order which Kristeva identifies as an irruption of the semiotic, of the 'drives in the universal signifying order'.[58] This is the modern, post-Romantic, romantic, zone of beauty, eroticism, rapture, displacement, abjection ('horror' to Kristeva, 'dread' for Blanchot), and ultimately death (Thomas Mann). It is the zone of art, creation, 'the impossible' (Bataille) into which the artist falls, immerses, losing oneself. To return, if indeed one does return, doubled, out-of-order, yet assimilated into a new world order, by the rapprochement of history. Of course not all authors or artists return from this zone of immersion, this personal breakage with the prevailing symbolic order, and many commentators parallel (without exactly equating) it to pathological states such as: schizophrenia (Deleuze and Guattari) borderline psychosis (Kristeva) and madness (Artaud, whose own sanity was precarious). In a way, Proust, who did not finish his work, and died as he was still rewriting and reworking *À la recherche*, after labouring on it for twenty-seven years, never returned from a fugal zone of writing. Instead, on Kristeva's model falling more deeply, from being abject— making himself abject or 'ab-jecting himself' in his writing state, his body of work—into that most abject object: a corpse. The sense in which he did not return is that in which he existed as a person in the social world. However, as an author, doubled, distilled and transferred into a form of language essence, a trace of inscribed narrative text, a material object which can be read and held, he shall remain and return until his books go out of print and disintegrate forever. (Or remain forever in a virtual realm).

Deleuze and Guattari, in their collaborative narrative, *A Thousand Plateaux*, write of the liberational aspects of writing as a 'deterritorealization' or a breaking away of the line in the act of creation, which is anti-fascist and of the Antilogos: 'There is no act of creation that is not transhistorical and does not come up from behind, or proceed by way of a liberated line'.[59] Arguing also that:

> Creations are like mutant abstract lines that have detached themselves from the task of representing a world, precisely because they assemble a new type of reality that history can only recontain or relocate in punctual systems.[60]

This echoes Kristeva's definition of abjection, 'when that subject, weary of fruitless attempts to identify with something on the outside, finds the impossible within.' There is nothing like abjection of self:

> to show that all abjection is in fact recognition of the want on which

any being, meaning, language or desire is founded....if one imagines (and imagine one must, for it is the working of the imagination whose foundations are being laid here) the experience of want itself as logically preliminary to being and object—to the being of the object—then one understands that abjection, and even more so abjection of self, is its only signified. Its signifier, then, is none but literature.[61]

In *Proust and Signs* (1964) Deleuze's views juxtapose those of Kristeva. In accord with his theories of what he terms intentional machines (the desiring-machine; war-machine) he sees Proust's writing processes in inhuman automatic terms, as mechanic, a writing-machine, and the immaterial, intentional mechanics of Proust's writing, the interplay of imagination, memory and thought (which takes place in the consciousness and the unconscious mind, and which results in the production of text in the material world) as comprising two 'machines', which are in effect the 'dual' temporal modalities alluded to. Namely, *le temps*, Time remembered, the 'lost time' of the Narrator's lived memory and *temps durée*, the time in which Marcel, present-tense narrator, or Proust in the guise of the present tense narrator, is writing and relating the narrative. Is it more accurate to say that Marcel relates the narrative, or Proust, in the guise of the present-tense narrator, Marcel? How self consciously aware is Proust's use of this device—of oscillating between present and past tenses?

Narrative self-consciousness, authorial awareness, of writing is seen to be the hallmark of postmodernism. But in this regard, Proust can be clearly seen to epitomize modernism in fiction writing. He seemingly unselfconsciously oscillates between tenses. It's not a ruse; his narrative is not just 'seemingly' intentionally self-referential.

As noted, he does not play tricks with memory, as such; it is portrayed essentially unproblematically as a thing in itself. Of course, his use of tense is in itself not entirely straightforward. It is both idiosyncratic and unique. Many temporal modalities come into play as Marcel narrates his story's stories. No less than seven Marcel voices (all spoken through the same first-person narrator) operate in *Recherche*. In this sense the narrative constitutes a kind of first-person polyphony, incorporating a narrative dissociation. However, the dissociation that is engendered is not pathological as in supposed 'multiple-personality syndrome'. Instead, it is that of the thinker to his thoughts, the reflector to the memory contents of reflection—which we the readers are expected to take to be true, at least to the narrator's memory. Many Marcels are reflected upon, dislocating and relocating Marcel in different times and places in his 'past'; many aspects of his self in 'the past,' and past selves, are evoked and recalled as the narrator loses, and ultimately finds himself, and the meaning of his writing, in his fugal Search.

THE ANTILOGOS AND THE FUGAL MODALITY OF WRITING

Proust's writing is not Logocentric. But what does this mean? How is Proust's writing fugal? To gain a clearer grasp of Proust's methodology, that method which is cited by Deleuze as an example of the Antilogos, to understand what a thing is, it is instructive, sometimes, to look at what it is not.

If Proust's writing were 'logocentric' one might say, with accuracy, *one Proustian sentence contains references to different temporal recollections.* This would imply that the time structure, the narrative edifice of the text, pre-existed to be (capable of being) referred to by Proust. Instead, one can only accurately say of his writing that he evokes, he conjures, he summons up images, and concurrent reflections on those images, in a process that comprises the construction of his intricately sustained and complex work of art and of time, and the art of rime.

What makes Proust's narrative is its sense of summoning up what was not there, in order to reflect upon it. A process of creating images which trigger associations, which trigger associations. These all, then, are expressed in further images; as recurring motifs, that repeat in altered forms in narrative time, in metaphors that expand outwards and onwards (garlanded in similes) in a use of metonymy in which associations are coded into a language of signs, the individual idiosyncratic interlanguage, or interlingua, of the book. The book, in the process of being written, finds and creates its own language in *praxis*. The book in the process of being written searches for its own form, in words; in the process of being written, the book finds and creates its own time.

Deleuze compares Proust to Henry James (William James brother) for his 'aesthetic of the point of view' a subjective aesthetic. Proust depicts essence, according to Deleuze, not as 'something seen but a kind of superior viewpoint, an irreducible viewpoint which signifies

at once the birth of the world and the original character of a world'.⁶²
Deleuze furthermore asserts that this process is not 'individual, but
on the contrary [is] a principle of individuation'. Thus he locates the
inhuman, automatic, the machinic in the process of individuation
which constitutes a work of art realizing itself in its creation. Many
commentators have remarked on the analogous nature of Proust's
Search, that the whole vast work, is an extended comparison (of associations) revolving on the words 'as if'. *In Search of Lost Time* is a metaphor
for itself. For Nabokov:

> The key to the problem of re-establishing the past turns out to be
> the key of art. The treasure hunt comes to a happy end in a cave full
> of music, in a temple rich with stained glass. The gods of standard
> religions are absent, or perhaps more correctly, they are dissolved
> in art.⁶³

As Proust's work is composed of multitudinous fragments and signs,
associative chains of metaphors and motifs, which do not necessarily
fit together, in a linear sense, Deleuze detects a quantum theory of
Time at work, arguing that:

> Perhaps this is what time is: the ultimate existence of parts, of different sizes and shapes, which cannot be adapted, which do not develop
> at the same rhythm, and which the stream of style does not sweep
> along at the same speed.⁶⁴

In this sense, Proust's Search has a high level of musicalization, in its
rhythms and melodies, its counterpoint between consciousness and
the unconscious, between time lost and time regained, between Marcel, the implied author and the 'Marcels' of his narrator. Proust's genius is to create a work that is allowed to create itself, a self-generating
language structure, in which, as an effect of the process, the past fugally comes back by itself. It is a vast text of signs, a *chora* of consciousness
and unconsciousness, the Antilogos replete with hidden meanings,
which it realizes, embodies, and reveals within and through itself. The
Book thereby becomes an artistic fugal force or power, producing its
own world of meaning.

ɞ 9

JAMES JOYCE
SIRENS' FUGUE

> Time makes the tune. Question of mood you're in. Still always nice to hear—*Ulysses*

Critics have agreed that 'Sirens' was musical but disputed whether there was a fugue form or fuga per canonem in the text and debated for over eighty years over what Joyce meant by the term 'fuga per canonem'. Joyce's handwritten notes for his fugue, found on a long lost manuscript, show what he meant and reveal new depths of social, political and aesthetic meaning in this exemplary poetically revolutionary episode.

The relatively recently found evidence of a set of notes on a long lost manuscript of 'Sirens', gives the opportunity for a close reading of 'Sirens' using Joyce's notes, and the unique terms he invented in Italian, as well as more traditional terms, for his fugue 'parts'. This reveals his 'Sirens' fugue to be more politically and socially grounded, and musically acute, than assumed. The analysis reveals that Joyce's fugue offers a poetic critique of life under imperial colonial rule, with subject themes of love and war. By considering the formal structure of the fugue, and musico-literary techniques in the aspects of use of counterpoint, metonymy, synecdoche, and onomatopoeia, the reading uncovers a context in the play of tension between subject and countersubject, in exposition and counterexposition, interwoven with songs of seduction and rebellion. The profound contextual background of 'Sirens' fugue is that of the individual alone in a modern secular world (as epitomized by Bloom) in a land, Ireland, under colonial rule, in the struggle for independence.

This might be the first long published examination of the fugue of the 'Sirens' episode in Joyce's *Ulysses* after Joyce's notes for the *fuga per canonem* were found on the cover page of a lost manuscript of 'Sirens', in an apartment in Paris at the turn of this century, shining light on a question in the study of *Ulysses* for almost a century: What did Joyce mean by *fuga per canonem* and its 'eight regular parts', what methodology did he use to intentionally translate the musical form of fugue to his poetic writing in 'Sirens'?

This will also reveal how Joyce was inspired by Wagner's opera *Die Meistersinger* in his depiction of **maestrale stretto** or '*master stretto*' (one of the eight parts or terms for his *fuga per canonem* in his notes discovered in Paris) in the characters of the 'quintet' and themes. He had mentioned Wagner's opera and said that 'Sirens', too, had a 'quintet' in an oft-cited conversation with Georges Borach, as recalled by Borach, a businessman whom he taught language to and took walks and dined with.[1] Scholars have puzzled over this without being able to figure out how he translated a quintet into his fugue.[2] In my reading, I apply the found notes by Joyce, which show that he did do this. This will show the difference in interpretation of the text, specifically an experimental interarts narrative, with knowledge of the author's intentions, in this case.This reading also reveals and proposes, in conclusion, that Joyce was also experimenting with a dodecaphonic or twelve-tone composition method, perhaps by chance, that Albert Schoenberg developed in music, after *Ulysses* was published.

Joyce uses carnivalesque invented language to create 'intermedial' musicalized effects that are in keeping with the characters' language, humour, wit, songs and storytelling, albeit through narrator Bloom's disenchanted detached interior observations, as the men banter, and sing, and, like Ulysses bound to the mast of his ship, Bloom hears and sails past the 'Sirens' songs, in the Ormond bar.

HOMECOMING: *ULYSSES*, A STRATEGY OF INVENTION

In the early twentieth century, James Joyce sought to invent a new language in poetic writing to express what was impossible in the English language. The most inventive linguistically experimental section in *Ulysses* is the 'Sirens' episode which he wrote adapting the techniques of a '*fuga per canonem*', in his conceptual term, a fugue according to rule. In returning to the classical origins of the canon of Greek rhetoric to invent the musicalized language of the 'Sirens' episode, the text subliminally acknowledges origins of rhetorical figures in musical sound.

This connection was freely made and acknowledged in ancient Greece where music was inextricably linked to: invention, the arrangement, the style, the memory, and delivery of oratory and tragedy. Originating in the oral tradition of story telling through singing, Greek poetry developed and presented poems and plays in performances that included a chorus that relayed the narrative through singing. The delivery of the works of the poets and playwrights was, as we now say, 'multimodal' (a synaesthesia transposed onto the film and computer screen, in performance involving singing, music, and the visual spectacle of costumed performers). In Greek dramatic performance, poems—such as Homer's *Odyssey*, were delivered through oratory, the power of which depended on the delivery via the dramatic actions and musical tones and timbres of the oratory voices, backed by a chorus. In 'Sirens', Joyce invents new words, tones, phrases, rhythms using paronomasia and onomatopoeia to evoke and articulate the musical quality of the voices of the Dubliners in the musical pub, the bar at the Ormond Hotel. Of the psyche, Joyce's musicalized words evoke the dangers, and treachery, of the musical seductions, symbolized by the Sirens on the Rocks in *The Odyssey*. Considering that it is a 'fugue according to rule', we may view Joyce's use of the *fuga per canonem* to invent his new rules of literary language in writing as ironic, or as homage, or both. Or we may view his use of this re-working and re-invention of Greek canon as a deeply creative strategy of invention, returning to the psycho-linguistic origins of drama, poetry and oratory, as a musico-literary strategy in a political context, for what emerges as of most cultural significance in this episode is Ireland's struggle for Independence, and the war that was being fought in Ireland whilst he was writing *Ulysses*. He uses a classical poetic strategy in order to re-invent language in writing of ancient—and semiotic—form that consciously articulates musical sound.

In this chapter I will show and discuss how Joyce created, in words, a unique literary narrative system of synecdochical, metonymic and metaphoric signs, by reinterpreting the techniques of a musical fugue in written language. The musicalized, intermedial, acoustic language of 'Sirens', written as a literary fugue, and its socio-political-cultural context, Joyce's flight to Paris from Dublin, are discussed in the context of the modernist definition of 'escape', together with the effects of this flight on Joyce's creative practice and textual approach. Several more specific questions arise from the relationship of Joyce's stylistic literary narrative to the objective social concerns that it critiques.

The idea that a modernist narrative written in a mode of stylistic innovation and escapist flight may also be capable of constituting acerbic social critique contradicts the assertion by Georg Lukács that modernist works are incapable of delivering effective political social critique: 'The obsession with psychopathology in modernist literature expresses a desire to escape from the reality of capitalism'. He argues that modernist literature can only provide an impotent critique that falsely asserts 'the inalterability of outward reality'.[3] I contend that Joyce's 'Sirens', in which he altered the very 'outward reality' of objective language, demonstrates otherwise.

Joyce's work is considered to be an example of experimentation representing a modernist flight—but from what, into what? Is it useful, or relevant, here to attempt to make generalizations on how experiences of extended journeying from home, wandering, dislocation, and exile may affect individual artistic creation? Above all, if the specific ontological tensions inherent in literary works most intensely enacting a *writer's fugue* can be seen to cohere in the structural and thematic narrative embodiment of existential tensions concerning what it means to be human, in modernity, how are these tensions revealed and/or resolved in the quintessential modernist work, *Ulysses*, and in the musico-literary writing of 'Sirens'?

In 1897, modernist Viennese poet, dramatist, and librettist, Hugo von Hofmannsthal, proposed that 'psychic self-dissection' and artistic 'escape' were signs of the modern.[4] His identification of the new tendency to analyze inner life, reflection and dreams, and the desire for escapist flight, reflected the perceived duality of the psyche of the late nineteenth and early twentieth century evident from the psychology and art of the day.

> Today, two things seem to be modern: the analysis of life and the flight from life...One practices anatomy of the inner life in one's mind, or on dreams. Reflection or fantasy, mirror image or dream image...Modern is the dissection of a mood, a sigh, a scruple; and modern is the instinctive, almost somnambulistic surrender to every revelation of beauty, to a harmony of colours, to a glittering metaphor, to a wondrous allegory. (71)

This definition demarcates and differentiates the era of the interarts movement of Modernism—which lasted from approximately 1890-1930—within the Modern era, which began, with industrialized modernity in the late eighteenth century. Joyce's writing is a performative analysis of psychic life, through a poetic, musicalized articulation of perceptions of inner life combined with a sharp politically aware social critique. He took flight from Ireland his country of birth, physically, yet he continually returned to it in his writing. His artistic escape was predicated on his self-imposed exile.

Joyce wrote *Ulysses* in Trieste, Zurich and Paris, in the years between 1914 and 1921. At the age of twenty he fled to Paris from Ireland 'the mother sow that eats its young', as his fictional alter ego Stephen Dedalus declares in *Portrait of the Artist as a Young Man*. He returned to Dublin for a couple of years, as his mother was fatally ill, where he met his future wife, Nora Barnacle, and four months after meeting, in 1904, they left Ireland permanently, eloping to Trieste. As war shattered the Western world Joyce, a pacifist, wrote his anti-heroic epic, *Ulysses*. Then there were the events of 1916 in Ireland. As Joyce wrote *Ulysses*, in Europe, he several times took flight again, moving to safety with Nora and their two children in the encroaching approach of war.[5]

Joyce's artistic 'escape' is embodied in works which enact a powerful flight of the imagination to the outermost edges of language to create meaning. Writing, in streams of consciousness to enact the truth of the inner world of thought and impression using word-associations was a characteristic endeavour of modernist authorship. Such an engagement with the subconscious in writing has metaphorical parallels with somnambulism, as well as with the different states of awareness and variation of the 'subject' in psychological fugue. Authors in this time were using modernist approaches to writing in stream-of-consciousness to access and write subjectivity. Hofmannsthal's 'somnambulistic surrender' of modernist writing characterizes Joyce's stream-of-consciousness writing that, consciously, enacted this not only in style but content; but whilst it might seem to be somnambulistic, this is intentional: Joyce's writing has a powerful political underpinning: 'History, Stephen said, is a nightmare from which I am trying to awake'.[6]

Joyce exemplified the experimental practices typical of modernist authors when he sought to accurately write the condition of modern consciousness as lived and felt by the individual person positioned in their social and cultural life context. Whereas realist writers sought to resolve the tensions of modernity through creating an illusory unified whole in linear prose, experimental modernists exemplified by Joyce, sought instead to capture the fragmentation of modern life in writing.

Recently postcolonial theorists, and anticolonial nationalists, have identified and critiqued the phenomenon of 'derivative discourses',[7] and peoples of decolonizing countries adopting the hegemonic language structures created by former colonial rule and administration and by implication the hierarchical social structures. Laura Chrisman has critiqued this arguing that the blanket criticism of the 'Enlightenment' is a generalization, and she cites Ireland's rising of 1916 and the Irish Republic's Provisional Government's declaration as an example of a 'nationalist self-articulation' that is based on the radical discourse of freedom rather than derivative discourses of 'liberty'.[8] As Irish had been replaced by English as the dominant language this is relevant to literary authorship and to writers from Ireland. Joyce's response to hegemony was enacted in the individualistic ingenuity of his Modernist literary innovation and originality. He did not support militarist nationalism, the Cucholainoid-inspired Irish revivalist dogma, which involved a militarist mythologizing of the epic fighter of Irish legend, and belief in the redemptive nature of violence. Leaving Ireland in self-imposed exile, Joyce, who described himself as 'a socialistic artist' epitomizes the critical freedom of the individual modernist writer to take flight from the material conditions of life, detach himself, imaginatively, from language traditions and structures, and reinvent these in reconstructed musico-literary narrative structures and systems of signs; his achievement of this aim is seen, and heard, in 'Sirens'.

Joyce re-invented, performatively, in writing, his own metaphorical and metonymic literary language of signs, in what Adorno called a *negative dialectics*, or critique to comment freely, originally and critically on the social and political conditions of the (home) environment he had been brought up in and which he has escaped. In musico-literary use of language in 'Sirens', he metaphorically, and literally, takes flight from, and in, the English language, which he criticizes in *Portrait* from the perspective of the loss of the Irish language, as an inadequate vehicle for authentic literary self expression. Stephen, his alter-ego in *Portrait,* muses on a conversation with the Englishman who is university dean of studies:

> The language in which we are speaking is his before it is mine. How

different are the words *home, Christ, ale, master,* on his lips and on mine! I cannot speak or write those words without unrest of spirit. His language so familiar and so foreign, will always be for me an acquired speech. I have not made or accepted its words. My voice holds them at bay. My soul frets in the shadow of his language.

Yet, by necessity and imaginative logical design, his flight is enacted in the English language and takes him into an intermedial appropriation, or revolutionary re-reading and musicalized re-writing, of one of the classical texts of European culture. Joyce's authorial intentionality has an intermedial in-between unconscious, manifest in the objective structures of his musicalized narrative and the subjective flight of his 'escape.' The way, in which he develops his themes in language, enacts a 'fugal' modality of writing. This modality of writing constitutes a writer's fugue, metaphorically inflected with both the musical and psychological meaning of fugue. As discussed below, Joyce structures the episode of 'Sirens' inspired by the technic of *fuga per canonem*, or 'fugue according to rule', a term he used, which has caused great controversy amongst scholars.

PROTAGONISTS ON A MOCK EPIC JOURNEY

Joyce based his mock epic narrative, *Ulysses*, on *The Odyssey*. Homer's epic poem is a hero-myth, of the type that enacts archetypal themes in the analysis of the cultural unconscious. One of the modern uses for the appropriated hero myth can be to invoke deeper individual and social, archetypal meanings about the struggle and crisis of the modern individual, caught in modernity's capitalist society between (archaic/primal) emotional feelings and (modern) material obligations. Joyce's appropriation of the classical archetypal structure of the hero's journey can be interpreted as superficially ironic and parodic in terms of style, yet profound and political in terms of its underlying social comment. Homer's hero, Odysseus (Ulysses), is a god, returning from battle after sacking the citadel of Troy. His homecoming sea journey, undertaken in a boat rowed by doomed comrades lasts nineteen years, and involves his comrades all dying from 'their own sin', for despite being warned not to, they 'devoured the oxen of Hyperion the Sun, and the god saw to it that they should never return'.[9] *The Odyssey* narrates the Hero's journey, the impossible tests and trials involving confrontations with gods, goddesses, mythical beings and monsters that he encounters and is challenged by on the way home.

In contrast, the action of *Ulysses* takes place in one day and night, and involves Leopold Bloom, walking around Dublin, a mild-mannered pacifist, very aware of his body functions, and who might be more accurately described as resolutely non-heroic, rather than anti-heroic. Bloom, a sole-trader businessman, an advertisement canvasser, is of Hungarian-Jewish origins. Kiberd comments that Joyce chose Bloom, an Irishman, to be Jewish as part of his explosion of 'the myth of the fighting Irish', instead portraying the Irish as 'a quiescent, long-suffering but astute people, very similar in mentality to the Jews'.[10] Nabokov saw Joyce's choice as indicative of his rational decision to 'place among endemic Irishmen in his native Dublin someone who was as Irish as he, Joyce, was, but who also was an exile, a black sheep in the fold, as he, Joyce, was'.[11] This can be seen in a parodic pub conversation in the 'Cyclops' episode, which takes place as the narrative satirically relates,

> in the ancient hall of Brian O'Ciarnain's in Sraid ne Bretaine Bheag, under the auspices of Sluagh na h-Eireann, on the revival of ancient Gaelic sports and the importance of physical culture, as understood in ancient Greece and ancient Rome and ancient Ireland, for the development of the race. (410)

Bloom dissents from the popular support for the ideology and mythology of the Gaelic Revival movement:

> After an instructive discourse by the chairman, a magnificent oration eloquently and forcibly expressed, a most interesting and instructive discussion of the usual high standard of excellence ensued as to the desirability of the revivability of the ancient games and sports of our ancient panceltic forefathers. The wellknown and highly respected worker in the cause of our old tongue, Mr Joseph McCarthy Hynes, made an eloquent appeal for the resuscitation of the ancient Gaelic sports and pastimes, practised morning and evening by Finn MacCool [the mythical Celtic giant-hero], as calculated to revive the best traditions of manly strength and power handed down to us from ancient ages. L. Bloom, who met with a mixed reception of applause and hisses, having espoused the negative the vocalist chairman brought the discussion to a close. (411)

Nabokov comments on a tendency of critics to 'regard Bloom as a very ordinary nature', and remarks 'apparently Joyce himself intended to portray an ordinary person'.[12] However, Nabokov argues, in spite of Joyce's supposed intentions, Joyce has, perhaps unconsciously, created a 'curious character': 'in the sexual department Bloom is, if not on the verge of insanity, at least a good clinical example of extreme sexual preoccupation and perversity with all kinds of curious complications'.[13] In contrast, Kiberd postulates that Joyce's narration through the body is a carnivalesque repudiation of hypocritical bourgeois convention. He describes his character's bodily functions:

> in order to show that here was a man thoroughly free of abstract pretension or bodily self-hatred. Joyce saw, earlier than most, that the modern cult of the body had been made possible only by a century of coy evasion; and his close analysis of Bloom's daily actions expose the laughable inadequacy of both attitudes.[14]

Kiberd proposes: 'Joyce wanted to afford the body recognition equal to that given the mind'.[15] According to this argument, *Ulysses* is a highly erudite, complex modernist example of what Bakhtin and Kristeva called a dialogic and carnivalesque novel, in the tradition of Menippean satire.[16] The main characters in the work—the middle-aged Leopold Bloom; his unfaithful wife Molly, a soprano concert performer; and the young, penniless, yet highly articulate poet and teacher, Stephen Dedalus—represent three categories of ontological experience, or ways of experiencing and articulating the world. According to the schema suggested by Nabokov, Stephen Dedalus could be seen as a highbrow:

> You behold in me, Stephen said with grim displeasure, a horrible example of free thought. (23)

Leopold Bloom could be seen as a middlebrow, and possibly reminiscent of a doomed, mythical oxen eater:

> Mr Leopold Bloom ate with relish the inner organs of beasts and fowls. He liked thick giblet soup, nutty gizzards, a stuffed roast heart, liver slices fried with crustcrumbs, fried hencod's roes. Most of all he liked grilled mutton kidneys which gave to his palate a fine tang of faintly scented urine. (65)

And Molly Bloom, lowbrow, or 'vulgar':

> I'll let that out full when I get in front of the spotlights again Kathleen Kearney and her lot of squealers Miss This Miss That Miss Theother lot of sparrowfarts skitting around talking about politics they know as much as my backside anything in the world to make themselves someway interesting Irish homemade beauties. (905)

Nabokov points out 'all three characters have their artistic sides.'[17] And Bloom and Stephen discover, on comparison in conversation, towards the end of their night's wandering, they are not dissimilar in their 'parallel courses' although they too have 'views on some points divergent':

> Both were sensitive to artistic impressions musical in preference to plastic or pictorial. Both preferred a continental to an insular manner of life, a cisatlantic to a transatlantic place of residence. Both indurated by early domestic training and an inherited tenacity of heterodox resistance professed their disbelief in many orthodox religious, national, social and ethical doctrines. Both admitted the alternately stimulating and obtunding influence of heterosexual magnetism.

A romantic connection is established through Molly Bloom, soprano, and Blazes Boylan, impresario, her concert agent and lover. The artistry of the characters' artistic sides is—in contrast to, for instance, a realist description of 'artistic' pursuits—displayed and constituted dialogically by Joyce in their carnivalesque musical speech rhythms and language-inventions which the characters either express in conversation, or which are narrated through them in Joyce's third person stream-of-consciousness narration. 'Means something, language of flow', Bloom thinks to himself, in the Ormond restaurant as he writes to his mysterious correspondent Martha Clifford.

THE MYSTERY OF JOYCE'S 'FUGA PER CANONEM' REVISITED

Ulysses is of particular interest to a study of fugal literary narrative as Joyce wrote, or intended to write, the 'Sirens' section using the 'technic' of a *fuga per canonem*, as shown in his schema known as the 'Linati Schema'[18] (more on this soon). He confided his writing technique for 'Sirens' in a letter to his benefactor, Harriet Weaver, in which he wrote:

> Perhaps I ought not to say any more on the subject of the Sirens but the passages you allude to [...] are all the eight regular parts of a *fuga per canonem*: and I did not know in what other way to describe the seductions of music beyond which Ulysses travels.[19]

Two months before, Joyce had reportedly said in a conversation with George Borach:

> 'I finished the Sirens chapter during the last few days...I wrote this chapter with the technical resources of music. It is a fugue with all musical notations: piano, forte, rallentando and so on. A quintett [sic]

occurs in it, too, as in the Meistersinger, my favourite Wagner opera.'[20]

Little else had been recorded in the literature on Joyce's intentions for the fugue structure he wove into 'Sirens'. That was, until the discovery of lost 'Sirens' drafts at the turn of this century in an apartment in Paris with a list of idiosyncratic terms written in Joyce's handwriting, which has cast light on his intentions for the structure of fugue in 'Sirens'. This discovery has reignited a long-running debate and calls for rethinking the fugue in 'Sirens'.[21] For over eighty decades, scholars puzzled over Joyce's intentions for 'Sirens': *fuga per canonem*' or fugue. He was criticized for his 'confusing' use of both the terms in his letter to Weaver and conversation with Borach; several scholarly critics have forwarded theories as to how the terms affected their reading, and what his use of both the terms said about Joyce's musical (rather than literary) prowess. Much of this was to do with confusion caused by Joyce's reference to the 'eight regular parts' of a '*fuga per canonem*'. Many critics asserted that a fugue does not have 'eight parts'. As 'part' is a musical term for voice, as well as for a section, this added to the confusion. Amongst the interpretations critics have suggested are, Wolf has identified: 'constitutive element; voices or voice-clusters; horizontal segmentation, and the sequence of exposition'.[22] Although Joyce's source notes have (almost certainly) been found now, disagreement over Joyce's *fuga per canonem* remains as shown in recent articles by Susan Brown and Michelle Witen.[23]

In 1965, Lawrence Levin wrote in the *James Joyce Quarterly* on the difficulties involved in attempting to analyze the musical structure of the 'Sirens' episode: 'All the commentators concur that the musical form is fugal' but that there is 'a general disagreement as to what particular form within fugal evolution Joyce utilized'.[24] That still remains to an extent true.

The current confusion is over Joyce's term *fuga per canonem* and its relation to 'canon'. Joyce has been accused of knowing 'nothing' about music by Susan Brown,[25] and his fugue reference has been described by Knowles as a 'hoax'.[26] But my reading, using the notesheet published in *Genetic Joyce Studies* reveals that Joyce did not apply the terms of his fugue incorrectly. Given all the confusion, I shall precede this discussion with the basic comment that Joyce was not writing an academic essay on how 'Sirens' adapts the technic of fugue, in his remarks.

He was addressing an interlocutor, in letter and in conversation and as such would have been aware of the knowledge of the listener to the extent that it is very likely he used terms they were familiar with, and in referring to the *fuga per canonem* and its 'parts', in his letter to Weaver, he was very likely using a form of which she would have been aware, as it was in all the common piano teaching books of that time, and she was of a social class for whom piano lessons for girls and young women were usual. Aside from this, Joyce's usage of both these terms does not imply a contradiction in terms, as a reading using his notes, and with a basic knowledge of musical fugue form plainly shows.

Above all, as Susan Brown acknowledges, 'If we are to discover what Joyce thought he was doing when he altered his game plan for 'Sirens' and changed literature forever, the solution, as those who work with Joyce's genetic materials [texts, notes, and sources] know, is not to seek meaning from the notes themselves.' She acknowledges: 'We need to investigate the correspondence between the notes and their source'.[27] Susan Brown is one of the researchers who found the trove of missing Joyce manuscripts, in Paris. However, I shall show here soon that the source text that Brown used for her analysis was not quite accurate.

The source of Joyce's notes is the musical fugue, which has been discussed in relation to its evolution in form, and definition, earlier in this book. What light can the evolution of fugue in music, literature and culture cast on this critical disagreement?

As discussed in Chapter 2, the form of fugue evolved from 'canon' a horizontal form of melodic voices played or sung, in the round. Canon was distinct from 'fugue' as the fugue developed in the sixteenth and seventeenth centuries. 'Canon' is the derivation of polyphony from a single melodic line by imitation of itself at a fixed interval of pitch and duration.[28] Brown's genetic research in *Joycean Unions* (2013) which is a republication of her article published in *Genetic Joyce Studies* (2007) claims that *fuga per canonem* refers directly to 'canon', and the musical round; whilst 'fugue' was the form of more complex invention; on the basis of a misunderstanding of these musical terms that Joyce used in letters to friends, she claims: 'Joyce's mastery of complex fugal theory' was 'bogus to none'.[29]

In reply, historically *fuga per canonem* is not the same as 'canon'. The source of the word 'fugue'—which was a living musical form—'fuga', originally stood for canon (in ancient Greece) but it evolved through use of contrapuntal polyphony. The rules of a *fuga per canonem* are only the inventive reflexive 'rules' of notation itself. Research tracing the history of fugue has shown that it was a secular form; and not the preserve of 'monks in the 16th century' as the English composer Ralph Vaughn Williams, wrote in *Grove's* in 1906; to the contrary, fugue developed as a form of singing and instrumental music, in households, in hunt music, and art music (discussed in Chapter 2). Fugue ceased to be an extant form at the end of the eighteenth century, and he was not able to find accurate information. More is known about it now.

The published records of Joyce's letter to Weaver, and his oft-quoted conversation with Borach indicate that Joyce referred to the 'Sirens' literary adaptation as both *fuga per canonem* and fugue, which suggests that to him there was not a significant difference. Joyce's reference to '*fuga per canonem*' and 'fugue' suggest he adapted the form for literary use; in a fugue the composition is self-reflexively determined by the notations of the subject, but this does not preclude freedom of invention.

The Joyce notesheet suggests that *fuga per canonem* rather than being used prescriptively as a musical term, was Joyce's term that he used to describe the fugue he intended to adapt into literary writing in the draft of 'Sirens' which he had started, before weaving in the 'technic', or techniques, of what he referred to as a *fuga per canonem*. He wrote a list of terms in his own idiosyncratic Italian, on the inside cover of the 'Sirens' manuscript discovered in Paris, catalogued as II.ii.3 in Joyce's manuscripts in the National Library of Ireland Buffalo MS V.A.5.[30]

Susan Brown argues that Joyce referred to the *Grove's* 'fugue' entry by Vaughn Williams, as this is where the term *fuga per canonem* appears in the literature. Yet as I have just mentioned Vaughn Williams use of this term, which Gudren Budde suggested he coined, is highly vexed. Vaughn Williams wrote: "In the 16th century the word [fugue] meant a movement in canonic form; indeed the name 'canon' is merely short for *fuga per canonem*: a fugue according to rule,' (quoted from the fifth edition).

Vaughn Williams' description is incorrect as it conflates two meanings of 'canon' which can denote a compositional technique as well as rule, commented Gudren Budde (in 1995) and Werner Wolf (in 1999).

In 'The Mystery of the Fuga per Canonem Solved' in *Genetic Joyce Studies* (2007), republished in *Joycean Unions* Brown makes her claims on the basis of the entry in *Grove's*. I argue that, based on my reading of the evidence of the fugue in 'Sirens', which is revealed when read with his notes, that to the contrary, Joyce has a sophisticated and sound understanding of fugue in music, and that furthermore this shows that 'Sirens' is a deeply profound example of a musicalized literary fugue. I will discuss the criticisms below; and will outline my detailed reading of his fugue soon. Two of the general critical claims I disagree with are in this passage:

> The identification of the source also clears up the primary obstacles which have prevented Joyce critics from arriving at a standard reading: the confusion between the *fuga per canonem* and the fugue (Joyce's error while skimming); Joyce's claim of "eight" parts (his own musically inaccurate but impressionistic invention abstracted from the source); and Joyce's mastery of complex fugal theory (bogus to none).[31]

The list of Joyce's eight parts for his *fuga per canonem* as documented by Brown (2013); Ferrer (2001) and Groden (2001)[32] is copied below. Joyce translated the musical fugue terms into (idiosyncratic) Italian, in his interpretation of fugue. As Stuart Gilbert wrote: 'To the Dubliners, music was essentially an Italian art, and they always liked to allude to songs by their Italian names even though the opera whence they came was by a non-Italian composer and usually sung in English'.[33] This recalls Rousseau's and De Quincy's preference for Italian music (see Chapter 3 and Chapter 7). It is a cultural recognition of the evolution of fugue in Italy, and Germany, and also the evolution of musical terminology in Italian.

Joyce's terms with researchers' parenthetical notes.

Fuga per canonem

1. soggetto
2. contrasoggetto

(reale in altro tono: in raccorciamento)

3. soggetto + contrasoggetto in contrapunto
4. esposizione

(proposto – codetta)

5. contraesposizione

(nuovi rapporti fra detti: parecchio)
(divertimenti)

6. tela contrappuntistica

(episodi)
7. stretto maestrale
(blocchi d'armonia)
(mystery word)
8. Pedale [34]

Joyce's notes without his parentheses are published in abbreviated form in essays by the other two scholars who found the missing Joyce manuscript, Daniel Ferrer's 'What Song the Sirens Sang...is no Longer Beyond Conjecture' and Michael Groden's 'The National Library of Ireland's New Joyce Manuscripts' in the *James Joyce Quarterly*, 2001.

Ferrer, as quoted by Brown, suggested an alternative transcription and offers an Italian term, although no translation, the 'mystery word':

5) contra esposizione
(nuovi rapporti fra i detti: parecchi) (divertimenti)
7) stretto maestrale
(blocchi d'armonia)
(rovescii antesi)[35]
(Ferrer quoted in Brown 2013: 176)

Brown suggests: 'several terms and phrases could not be comfortably and logically translated; nor do they represent known musical concepts'.[36] Particularly problematic—given the melody-based form of fugue (as discussed in Chapter 2)—is the phrase 'blocchi d'armonia', which Brown claims Joyce allegedly 'cribbed' from *Grove's*: 'texture of harmonic blocks of chords is quite alien to the fugue' writes Brown.[37] She concludes Joyce was 'skimming' and got it all wrong. However in analysis of Joyce's 'Sirens' literary fugue, I found 'blocks of voices in harmony' is used quite soundly in a fugal device at the climax of the fugue, with a critically astute awareness and deeply ironic critique of the meaning of 'harmony' in its cultural ramifications. Brown's translation, with my change of (Brown's suggestion of) 'coda' back to Joyce's original 'codetta' is:

1) subject
2) countersubject
(real [answer] in other key: in diminution)
3) subject and countersubject in counterpoint
4) exposition

(proposed or leading part—codetta—ends an exposition, rather than 'coda' which ends the whole fugue)

5) counter-exposition

(new relations among several designated musical digressions)

6) (mystery word) contrapuntal web

7) masterly stretto— in my interpretation as will be discussed soon a *stretto maestrale* is one in which the whole theme is played by all the overlapping voices, as Donald Tovey puts it: a 'stretto maestrale' is one in which the subject survives the overlapping.'[38] Joyce uses this appropriately (and metaphorically) at the end of 'Sirens', and in relation to:

(blocks of harmony)
(mystery word)
8) pedal[39]

I have a different view on the translation of 'codetta' as 'coda'. A codetta is a musical device that was often used at the end of a fugue exposition, before the beginning of the countersubject and is different to a coda, which signifies the end of a fugue (though it is not essential). In his *Fugue* (1891) on how to write a fugue, Ebenezer Prout wrote:

> He should write his counter subject as the continuation of the subject. He may always introduce a short *codetta*, if necessary, between the end of the subject and the beginning of the counter subject... (Point 177)[40]

Joyce's clear use of codetta at the end of his exposition in 'Sirens' fugue is seen in my analysis that we will come to soon.

Ferrer conjectures the 'mystery word' is *rovescii antesi*. The translation I suggest is: *Retrograde-reversal*. A retrograde 'copy' is self-reflexive, a theme played backwards is known as a crab-canon.

'Rovescii', in the common dictionary definitions, offers the following variety of meanings:

> 'wrong side', 'other side', 'reverse', 'reversal of fortune', 'setback', 'back the front', 'upside down', 'inside out', 'gets things the wrong way round/the wrong end of the stick'; 'backhand'; (knitting) 'purl stitch'.

I have found that such meanings do work in 'Sirens' by re-reading the episode using Joyce's discovered notes.

A reply to Susan Brown by Michelle Witen appeared in *Genetic Joyce Studies* in 2010: 'The Mystery of the Fuga per Canonem Reopened?' She challenges the claims that: Joyce's knowledge of fugue was 'bogus to none'; that he derived the extent of his knowledge through 'skimming'; and the assertion that *Grove's* was the main or only source of Joyce's research and knowledge of fugue.

Gudren Budde, in her 1995 article, suggested that Joyce could have been referring to 'eight-part' sequence of the 'fugue d'école' or 'school fugue' using a widely available school textbook André Gédalge's *Traité de la fugue* with its list of 'eight parts' of the 'fugue d'école':

These are:

1° le sujet;

2° la réponse;

3° un ou plusieurs contre-sujets;

4° l'exposition

5° la contre-exposition;

6° les développements or divertissements servant de transition aux différentes tonalités dans lesquelles on fait entrendre le sujet et la réponse;

7° le stretto

8° la pédale [41]

This was the type of 'school fugue' that was referred to by Imogene Horsley, as discussed in relation to the cultural history of the fugue (in Chapter 3) shaped by the Italian tradition but which solidified into an academic form for teaching and learning compositional techniques in France, in the nineteenth and twentieth century, long after fugue had ceased to be a living compositional form. Two texts that Horsley identified as for teaching were published in Paris in 1901: Théodore *Dubois' Traité de contrepoint et de fugue* and André Gédalge's *Traité de la fugue*.[42] It is likely these would have been available in bookshops and libraries when Joyce was corresponding with Harriet Weaver in Paris. This was the standard form in teaching books, where Joyce was writing *Ulysses*, in Paris. His knowledge of fugue, shown in 'Sirens', was bolstered by his musical background as a tenor singer who had performed in concerts in Dublin, and he played piano; Joyce had a broad and detailed knowledge of music, recalled composer George Antheil:

> Conversation with Joyce was always deeply interesting. He had an encyclopedic knowledge of music, this of all times and climes. Occasional conversations on music often extended far into the night and developed many new ideas. He would have special knowledge, for instance, about many a rare music manuscript secreted away in some

almost unknown museum of Paris, and I often took advantage of his knowledge.[43]

Otto Luening wrote, in his *The Odyssey of an American Composer*:

At the end of this evening with Joyce I had learned more about the relationship of language to music than ever before or since.[44]

In 1918-19 when Joyce and his family were living in Zurich, and Joyce was writing the 'Sirens' episode of Ulysses he often talked with Leuning and the contrapuntist, Pierre Jarnach, about counterpoint, and about musical modes. Luening said in an interview at the 1989 James Joyce Conference that Joyce admired Gregorian chant, and (early) Schoenberg. This was a decade before 'tone rows' and twelve tone technique.[45] Twelve-tone technique has resemblances to fugue as it consists in creating compositions using only twelve-tones, the twelve pitches of the octave, without any note or tonality given a dominant emphasis. In it, Schoenberg's composition was restricted to the twelve tones, similarly to a fugue which is kept to the notes of its melodic themes, yet within that 'restriction', there are no rules, and the free invention is up to the composer. By the way, there are rare eight-part fugues recorded in the literature, such as Giambattista Martin's Eight-Part Fugue in *Esemplare o sia saggio fondamentale prattico di contrappunto fugato,* from Italy in the eighteenth century.[46] In making his *fuga per canonem* 'notesheet', it is likely that Joyce was outlining, for himself, the approach he would take in working the form into the final manuscript of 'Sirens'. Witen writes: 'More specifically, it is the indication to himself of his fugue's structure as such'.[47] As with the approach of fugue music composers, it does not mean that there is no possibility for invention in fugue, which is suggested by Browns' claim of the strictness of 'canon'. As stated, fugue is not the same form or texture as canon, evolving from secular folk and art music it is a highly complex reflexive creative composition of artistic invention.

Brown remarks that the discovery of Joyce's list makes it clear that Joyce 'intended a "subject," an "answer," and a "countersubject" as parts in the fugal structure of "Sirens."'[48] This is the usual kind of structure for a fugue beginning, or of a fugato. The strictest canons are extant in the form of nursery rhymes.

FUGUE DEVICES AND THE FUGA PER CANONEM

There is some current confusion in the literature on Joyce's fugue in 'Sirens' about the terms canon and fugue and how they relate to each other. I propose that Joyce's use of the terms *fuga per canonem* in his letter to Weaver and fugue in his recorded conversation with Borach, now clarified by his notes on fugue structure on the manuscript of 'Sirens', indicate that he was aware of the intricacies and complexities of fugue and canon and that reading 'Sirens' as a literary adaptation reveals how he used these in a complex fugal narrative with uses of canonical fugal devices, translated into metonymic and synecdochical literary devices, throughout the narrative, creating effects of fugal variation that evoke a sense of anxiety generated by the subject Love and countersubject War, in the social and political context of Ireland in the years of the struggle for Home Rule, and ultimately independence. To precede this discussion, is an exegesis on canon and fugue, so that readers will be able to gain a clearer idea of the kind of fugal musical devices Joyce adapted in his writing.

To clarify the differences. Fugue evolved from canon and it uses the devices of variation in canon, but in a freer and more emotional and artistic way, as adapted in literary devices used by Joyce.

In a canon, one subject theme is played against itself. This occurs through 'copies' in variations of the theme played by the various participating voices. There are many ways this is done. The most simple and 'strict' form of canon is a round such as *Three Blind Mice*, or *Row, Row, Row Your Boat* where a single voice sings the subject theme then after a time-delay and in the same key a second voice enters singing the theme (in the individual singer's voice) then after the same time-delay a third voice enters singing the theme, and so on. (It may seem ironic that the strictest canons are extant in the form of nursery rhymes). It is only some themes that will be able to harmonize with themselves in this way. Melodies are chosen due to their melodic qualities that allow them to harmonize when sung like this and not create dissonance. For a theme to work as a canon theme, each of its notes must be able to serve in a dual, or triple or even quadruple role. First it must be part of a melody and second it must be part of a harmonization (with the voices/parts at the same time) of this melody. When for example there are three canonical voices, each note of the subject-theme must act melodically and in two harmonic ways, and if there are four canonical voices, each note must act in three harmonic ways, as well as melodically, and so on.

There are far more complicated forms of canon. In the round, the 'copies' of the voice are staggered in time, only. In escalation of complexity:

1)   The next level up occurs when the voices are staggered not only in time (through time-delays) but also in pitch: the first voice might sing the theme starting on C and the second voice, overlapping with the first voice, might sing the copy of the theme starting five notes higher on G. A third voice might then start five notes higher than that on D, overlapping with the first two, and so on, with each voice starting five notes higher.

2)   The next stage in complexity occurs when the speeds of the different voices are altered. The second voice might sing three times as quickly as the first, and the third voice might sing twice as slowly as the first. The device of speeding up the voice is called diminution, as the theme seems to shrink in length; and the device of slowing down the theme is known as augmentation as the theme seems to expand.

3)   A further escalation is inversion of the theme, which means to create a melody that jumps down, wherever the original theme jumps up, doing this by the same number of semitones. This might sound very complicated but is used in familiar tunes such as *Good Kind Wenceslas* and *Frère Jacques*, as well as Bach's complex canons and fugues in *The Musical Offering*. Consonance or a pleasant sounding canon results when the original and its inversion are sung an octave apart, and staggered with a time-delay of two beats.

4)   The most esoteric escalation of 'copies' is where the theme is reversed or played retrograde in time. This is known as the retrograde, or crab canon, alluding to the way the crab walks. (It makes sense that this is what Joyce was alluding to in his note of **rovescii antesi**).

Hofstadter describes 'endlessly rising canon', which hypothetically goes on forever in a round, an example being Bach's rising canon in his *Musical Offering*, a canon entitled *Canon per Tonos* for three voices, which 'jumps keys', it is constructed so that after six modulation, rising upwards, it is 'magically' returned back to the starting key, and continues this ad infinitum, Hofstadter terms this phenomenon a 'strange loop', and 'tangled hierarchy'.[49] It can be conjectured that Joyce may have had this in mind with his three main characters, Stephen Dedalus,

Leopold Bloom and Molly Bloom.

6) In these devices of canon, used in fugue, the variations of the melody theme contain all the information as the original theme, in inventive variations. The theme is 'fully recoverable' from each of the 'copies'; an 'information preserving transformation', comments Hofstadter, which is also known as 'isomorphism'.[50]

A fugue is similar to canon in that it is usually based on a theme, or two themes, or three themes, and in Bach's work, on four themes, which get played in difference voices (or by different instruments) in different keys, and in variation of different speeds.

Yet the idea and practice of fugue is more flexible and open than canon, it developed as art music, and is more expressive, and beyond the standard kinds of things germane to its notes, the reflexive possibilities of the notes of the melody line/s from which the variations derive there are no rules, and it is a form of free invention. Instead of strict copies, there are free inventive variations, using the same notes. A fugue begins with a single part (or voice) singing (or playing) its theme (or subject'), for example Joyce's melodic theme, of Love, in 'Sirens', in his literary fugue. This can be sung or played in three standard ways: 'Stretto' (short theme with a short interval), 'Andamento' (a much longer theme), or 'Attacco' (a very short theme usually in staccato). When the first voice has played the 'subject' theme, the second voice enters, either five scale-notes up, or four down. Meanwhile, the first voice continues singing or playing the 'countersubject', which is a secondary theme chosen to provide melodic, harmonic, and rhythmic contrasts with the subject theme. For example, in my reading, 'War' is the countersubject in Joyce's 'Sirens' literary fugue.

After the countersubject has been played each of the voices in the fugue enters in turn, singing the 'subject' theme, often to the accompaniment of another voice singing the 'countersubject', and with all the voices playing the theme in all manner of ways, as the composer invents, in a sequence of developments and episodes. The overlapping voices of subject and answer are known as Stretto. A **stretto maestrale**, is as mentioned, one in which the subject survives the overlapping, and in 'Sirens' this is used as very relevantly, to suggest that Bloom survives the singing session, with profound carnivalesque paronomastical allusions, and double meanings in relation to Wagner's *Meistersinger*.

DOUBLE MEANINGS OF JOYCE'S DOUBLE COUNTERPOINT

There have been many suggestions about the fugue subject of 'Sirens'. Wolf has suggested desire and its inverse or negative, lack of desire, which seems close though I suggest War. He suggests it has a three-part fugal composition with three 'parts' corresponding to three groups of characters, first the barmaids/sirens as treble; second Bloom as tenor, and third, Blazes Boylan and the rest of the male characters as bass. One thing is apparent when reading Sirens in terms of its subject and counter subject is that these are not strictly limited but are manifest in variations of 'love' (desire) and 'war' (negative of desire, dislike, betrayal). This sets up an effect of vibration, or variation, and wandering of the subject, in the text, which evokes movement, and also anxiety.

I propose that 'Sirens' subject '**soggetto**' is love and its variations of desire, and countersubject "**contrasogetto**" is loss of love, in forms of betrayal, and war. These are the themes that run through the episode in many variations, of motifs, and *Love and War*, a duet for tenor and soprano from the early twentieth century, also known as *When Love Absorbs my Ardent Soul*, is one of the songs referred to and flagged in the opening sixty-three lines, which serve as an idiosyncratic prelude to the 'Sirens' fugue. As mentioned, 'soggetto' is one of the ways that fugue subjects are played. Short subjects, or themes, characteristically with an interval, which are voiced in variations by 'voices' of parts. The voices enter, playing the 'soggetto' and 'contrasogetto' and answers to the subject and countersubject. The episode is based on music, and articulates a fugal word-music by continually interweaving references to songs, a ballad, and songs of love and war from operas and popular songs.[51] The fugue proceeds through a tension of counterpoint of the elevated and the profane, in ruminations on love, and loss, and war, interwoven by the love songs, and the historical resistance ballad *The Croppy Boy*.

Parts/Voices (character parts)

The characters introduced synecdochically in the opening lines are: 'Bronze-and-Gold', 'Chips', Bloom and Boylan.

Each of these is 'doubled' through the fugue with a counterpart: Bronze (mythical Siren) with Miss Lydia Douce (Barmaid/real Young Woman); Gold (mythical Siren) with Miss Mina Kennedy (Barmaid / Young Woman); 'Chips', Simon Dedalus, father of Stephen Dedalus (who does not enter this chapter physically) identified by his 'horrid' characteristic of 'picking chips off rocky thumbnail' (a punning reversal of the 'chip off the old block' slang reference, as Simon is Stephen's father); Bloom, Leopold Bloom, whose counterpart is his rival Blazes Boylan; identified by 'Blew. Blue bloom is on the...' 'A husky fifenote blew'. There is a 'chorus' of male singers in the piano bar, and it is these men, I suggest, that Joyce likens to a 'quintet' in Wagner's *Meistersinger*. In a fugue the subject is responded to by a fugal answer, followed by the countersubject played by a voice, answered by another voice/part.

When all the voices have played subject and countersubject, and answers, fugue moves into the exposition. This initial introduction of subject and counter-subject and answers occurs in the first sixty-three lines of 'Sirens' (ending with 'Begin!'). All the characters in 'Sirens' are introduced in plays on their names or characteristics: 'Bronze'; 'Gold'; 'Blew. Blue bloom'; 'Chips' (Si Dedalus); 'Jingle' (Boylan); "Deaf bald Pat"; 'True men: Lid Ker Cow De and Doll' (the five singers).

The fugue subject call of 'Love' (seduction and desire) is answered by 'War' (betrayal or loss of what is desired) answered by Bloom's wry reflections on love and war. As in the lyrics of the song *Love and War* which is referred to throughout the episode and in the opening lines, the subject love and countersubject war, are mixed up on many ways, in the song in a mock contest of a duet between a Lover (Soprano or Tenor) and Soldier (Bass), portrayed as the attraction between Venus and Mars, which is only resolved when they sing together.

The song 'contest' in the Ormond is informal and a parody but with profound political overtones.

1) **Soggetto**/ *Subject*
Love (Amorous Love and Desire)
Signified by the words/phrases and associations:
a) 'Bronze by gold' (The barmaids' hair identified by colour). Miss Kennedy-Bronze 'rose of castille' a rose on her dress; Miss Douce-Gold. Signifying amorous desire, seduction.
b) '...a call, pure, long and throbbing. Longindyingcall.' This has references to both love and war.
Played by voices/parts: Bronze; Gold (the 'Sirens')
Answers played by: Simon Dedalus 'Chips'; Bloom
2) **Contrasoggetto**/ *Countersubject*
War (Betrayal and Loss)

Signified by words/phrases and associations:
a) 'Decoy. Soft word.'
'Avowal. Sonnez. I could. Rebound of garter. Not leave thee. Smack. La cloche! Thigh smack. Avowal. Warm. Sweetheart, goodbye!' Signifying betrayal. 'Lost. Throstle fluted. All is lost now.'

'Decoy'. 'Soft word' meaning someone who entices as into a trap or danger (parodies how the barmaids were seen as sirens in the Edwardian crusade.[52] It also refers to *The Croppy Boy* ballad on the entrapment of a Wexford rebel boy in 1798, by a British yeoman disguised as a priest; and the Irish struggle for Independence. There is another contextual allusion in the 'decoy'. The underlying reference to 'decoy' (which is mentioned previously in *Ulysses* e.g. in the 'Aeolus' episode) is to the 1882 Phoenix Park murders. British ruling administrators, Lord Frederick Cavendish, British chief secretary in Ireland and Thomas Henry Burke, were walking to the viceregal house in the park, and were assassinated by stabbing by an underground militia group The Irish National Invincibles, who had conscripted two cabs: a decoy cab, which drove a direct route out of the park, and an escape cab which went on a long meandering drive around Dublin.[53] The assassins were caught. But the ramifications were said to have slowed the leader of the Irish National League, Charles Stewart Parnell's, proposed Home Rule Bill by 24 years (to 1912, when it was not effected; it was in 1921 that Independence was finally won); this is the social and political context of the long 'homecoming' voyage of Ulysses parodied and lamented in Joyce's *Ulysses*. This incident had grave ramifications for Parnell, in its aftermath, and the 'decoy' motif (mentioned in the 'Aeolus' episode) has allusions to Parnell's relationship with Katherine O'Shea (termed Kitty O'Shea by enemies, 'kitty' was slang for prostitute) who was separated from Parnell's political rival, her first husband Catholic Nationalist MP William O'Shea; after they divorced and Parnell married Katherine, came his political downfall, and only months afterwards he died in her arms. It should be added that the implied author, Joyce (in the interior monologue of Bloom) was against violent mythologizing nationalism.

Played by character voices/parts:
'Jingle jingle jaunted jingling' (Blazes Boylan), and his sidekick Lenehan, who gives a decoy whistle.

'Sonnez' (Lenehan).

Answers played by:
'Bloo' (Bloom) writing to 'Martha' ('I feel so sad "P.S"')

3) Soggetto and contrasoggetto in contrapunto
[Subject and countersubject in counterpoint]

The counterpoint between 'Love' and 'War' (played out through the parts) continues simultaneously throughout 'Sirens'. In the first 63 lines it is summarized, in fragmented phrases from the entire chapter:

Played by voices/parts:
Lydia; Mina (barmaids); Bloom; Boylan, 'Lid Ker Cow De and Doll' the chorus of drinkers and singers at the bar.

Answered by: the seven last words of Robert Emmett: 'Then, not till then. My eppripfftaph. Be pfrwitt. Done.' Parodied by the parody-punctuation of Bloom's breaking wind.

Interpreting a musical form in a literary narrative is never going to render an exact correspondence: yet that is not its aim. Literary counterpoint is an analogous art of association rather than rule-bound science; Joyce's fugue enacts a complex double counterpoint. 'Sirens' fugue schema suggests, and creates, an interpretation of fugue within itself. This constitutes the voices of characters that enter in turn. In this doubled schema, the subject of love and the countersubject of war are articulated in thoughts of Bloom, interwoven with the fragmented conversations of the chorus of male characters drinking, bantering, and later singing. Subject and countersubject answers are voiced in the banter between the men, talking and singing the songs throughout the scene in the musical bar, mainly in the second half or the counter-exposition, and the objectified barmaids.

Another contrapuntal aspect is to do with Time. 'Bronze' and 'Gold', the barmaids, Mina Kennedy and Lydia Douce, function in different realms of time, mythical time and the time of actual performance, duration, or 'real life' as it is lived. This is also the time of association in the author's and readers' minds in the writing and reading, of the narrative. This mirrors the doubled time of reading writing. Reading a text is enacted in the duration of its performance; the act of writing and reading takes place in a time of duration yet the written text also exists in another time, within space (as discussed in Bergson's distinction between the concepts of *temps espace* and *durée*).

Musical process functions as narrator but Joyce's text has an author who created this work of artful 'illusion'. To write this musico-literary text entails elements of psychological dislocation and artistic 'escape', inflected with the double meaning of fugue. This modernist modality of writing acts out a fundamental contradiction; articulating itself in fragmented non-realist form, it enacts the absence of an integrated society and the crisis of the individual within modernity. The effect of fragmentation is created in 'Sirens' through metonymic and synecdochical device, as shown below.

'SIRENS' SETTING AND 'TECHNIC'

There are two extant schemata which Joyce created as an aid to writing *Ulysses*. One he sent to Linati in 1920; the other he provided to Benoist-Méchin in 1921, which was published by Stuart Gilbert in 1931. On this schema, the structure of *Ulysses* is broken into eighteen acts, which correspond to episodes in *The Odyssey*. Although Joyce had indicated these episodes in pseudo-Homeric titles when Ulysses was first published as a serial in the American magazine, *The Little Review*, when *Ulysses* was published in its entirety, after some hesitation, Joyce had removed the titles to avoid his work being interpreted too programmatically. When he found readers were missing the analogies, he then allowed Gilbert to publish his schema, in his *James Joyce's Ulysses*.[54]

Nevertheless, the episodes in *Ulysses* still do tend to be referred to by critics in the mock-Heroic terms of Joyce's schema. On this, not only are the eighteen episodes given classical titles, each episode is also allotted a corresponding sense, hour, organ, art, colour, symbol, technic.[55] As Joyce wrote the episode, he drew these aspects in. This might have some points of comparison with the concept of a musical 'tone row' in twelve-tone technique which emerged from the experiments of Alfred Schoenberg, in Vienna, in his decentred atonal pieces, after Joyce published *Ulysses*; Werner Wolf comments on the surprising aspect of Joyce not following this new modernist atonality, in literary experimentation, and instead in 'Sirens' looking back to the melody-based pre-modern form of fugue (Wolf 1999). But Joyce was writing *Ulysses* before Schoenberg began to use twelve-tone technique in the 1920s. It might well be possible that Schoenberg was influenced by Joyce in his development of twelve-tone technique and 'tone row', as this is what Joyce does do in some parts of 'Sirens', at least, as I shall show soon. Aside from this, it is not surprising given that the twelve-tone technique uses principles of restricted variation (on notes of the octave), as does the fugue (restricted to the notes) not to mention what might have been significant to Joyce, the significance of the rise of harmony in the eighteenth and nineteenth century. Fugue was the last complex form of polyphonic counterpoint before the full development of tonal harmony in (hierarchically structured) classical music. Joyce looked back, too, in his choice of text to ancient Greece.

In 'Sirens', excerpts introducing the main characters and themes, stated in the first sixty-three lines, in fragments, recur, develop, and expand, into the fuller narrative through the episode.

The main setting of the episode is 'The Concert Room' and the bar and dining room of the Ormond Hotel. In Joyce's time, Gifford writes, 'the Ormond bar was a favorite haunt of Dublin's amateur musicians, and the saloon was frequently the setting for the small concerts that were popular in turn-of-the-century Dublin and in which the distinction between amateur and professional musician was not considered to be of much importance'.[56] This was a logical setting, then, for Joyce to choose for 'Sirens'. According to the Gilbert scheme: The hour is 4 p.m. The organ is Ear. The art is Music. The symbol is Barmaids. The technic is *Fuga per canonem*.

To run briefly through the narrative action: 'Sirens' contains several interwoven, juxtaposed strands of action based on separate characters introduced successively as they arrive at the Ormond Hotel, where the barmaid/Sirens preside. After the first sixty-three-line 'prelude', is the esposizione/exposition following the word 'Begin'. As in a musical fugue, the entry of 'voices' is staggered. The sirens/barmaids are introduced first, as they watch, through the blinds of the bar, the viceregal coach pass, they are looking at the society personages and an attractive gentleman catches their eyes; Boots the odd-job boy brings them their teas as they are talking about Miss Bronze's sunburn from a holiday at the seaside; joking and laughing and talking of men. Simon Dedalus enters the bar, 'picking chips off one of his rocky thumbnails' (a comic allusion to the rocks in the Ulysses/Odyseus myth). He flirts with Miss Douce, 'siren', who refers to her sunburn caused by 'lying on the strand all day' He indulgently tells her how 'naughty' she is: 'Tempting poor simple males'. As they continue bantering she pours him a drink, the next to arrive in the bar is Lenehan, asking: 'Was Mr Lidwell in today' and: 'Was Mr Boylan looking for me?' As Dedalus talks to Lenehan who had earlier run into Dedalus's son, Stephen, Miss Douce pours drinks; Miss Kennedy reads a book. Dedalus comments to Miss Douce that the piano moved and she replies that the tuner, a blind young man, has been in that morning, to tune it in preparation for the forthcoming smoking concert. Lenehan tests the piano. Meanwhile, Bloom's approach has been 'heard' and mentioned, weaving through the narrative. Boylan's approach is signalled by sound-words: 'Jingle jaunty jingle'. Bloom buy sheets of writing paper to write to his secret female correspondent and looks at an image of a smoking mermaid on a cigarette poster on the door of the shop. He then spies Boylan's top hat in the jaunting car, for the third time. As 'gold' is bent over her page reading in the bar: 'From the saloon a call came, long in dying'. This is the sound of the tuning fork left behind by the piano tuner. In this passage Pat the bald deaf waiter converses with Miss Douce, Lenehan tests the piano keys and sings a few lines, and lets out 'a low whistle of decoy' as he distracts attention. Boylan, and Bloom, are approaching. Boylan enters the bar.

Bloom approaches, runs into Richie Goulding lawyer and asks if he will join him for something to eat in the Ormond. Bloom ignores Father Cowley one of the men (who will later sing in the Ormond) who is outside the sheriff's office. At the bar, Boylan flirts and banters with the barmaids and has a drink, as Bloom follows Goulding past the bar, avoiding Boylan. Although the paths of Bloom and Boylan converge, they occupy different spaces in the hotel. And this relates to the subject and countersubject of the fugue, the different registers of love and war, played out by different characters. A vignette that illustrates this, in a different way, involves barmaid/siren Lydia Douce. At Boylan's request, and Lenehan's entreaty, for her to 'sonnez le cloche', she pulls up her skirt and snaps her garter against her leg:

> Smack. She let free sudden in rebound her nipped elastic garter smackwarm against her smackable woman's warm hosed thigh...
> —... Sweetheart, goodbye! [goes the song].
> —I'm off, said Boylan with impatience. (343)

A page later, she watches him go through the bar window:

> Miss Deuce's brave eyes, unregarded, turned from the cross blind, smitten by sunlight. Gone. Pensive (who knows?), smitten (the smiting light), she lowered the drop blind with a sliding cord. She drew down pensive (why did he go so quick when I?) about her bronze over

> the bar where bald stood by sister gold, inexquisite contrast, contrast inexquisite nonexquisite, slow cool dim sea green sliding depth of shadow, eau de Nil. (345)

Her 'brave eyes' are 'smitten', 'why did he go so quick when I?' she asks herself. It's a telling motif of the human feelings within the symbolic role of Siren. The distance between the characters, the oceans of longing which consume them, or in which the Sirens wait, are indicated by allusions to water, evoking the Homeric myth in which the Sirens sing, on their rocky island, luring sailors in ships onto the rocks. In *The Odyssey*, Odysseus is bound to the mast of his ship to keep him safe, whilst his men's ears are blocked with wax so they cannot hear the Siren's songs as they sail past. In another reference to the hidden depths of the 'sirens' situation:

> They pined in depth of ocean shadow, gold by the beer pull, bronze by maraschino, thoughtful all two, Miss Kennedy, 4 Lismore terrace, Drumacondra with Idolores, a queen, Dolores, silent. (347)

Another motif was provided in the 'exposition' by the picture of the 'swaying mermaid smoking mid nice waves', in the poster on the door of the shop where, on his way to the Ormond, Bloom buys his notepaper to write to Martha Clifford. He glances at the image of the mermaid: 'Hair streaming: lovelorn. For some man' (339).

The reader senses Bloom, about to be betrayed, feels an affinity with her. Joyce might have been parodying and satirizing the furore about young women working in public bars, yet these motifs demonstrate a sensitivity to the feelings of the young women in that environment, who despite their bravado and high spirits may have suffered feelings of social inferiority; indeed heartache, romantic anguish, is an emotional theme of the episode. And as Nora Barnacle whom Joyce eloped with to Trieste four months after they met, in 1904, had worked in Finn's Hotel in Dublin as a chambermaid, he was clearly aware of the prejudices young women working in hotels faced.

The Sirens of Homeric legend sing out for company that never reaches them; the sailors they call out to are either smashed on the rocks of their island and drowned or sail by, like Odysseus, protectively bound to the mast.

Symbolically bound to Molly, Bloom does not participate in the flirtation with the barmaids, intermittently winding around his fingers an elastic band from the packet of writing paper (suggesting Ulysses bound to the mast of his ship) Bloom sits writing a letter to a mysterious female correspondent he met through a newspaper advertisement, Martha Clifford, with further undertones of a mildly masochistic relationship with her; as his dining companion solicitor Ritchie Goulding whistles *All is Lost Now*, a theme from *The Sleepwalker* whilst in the adjacent bar in the Ormond, Blazes Boylan flirts with the barmaids, specifically 'bronze'— 'sister bronze outsmiled her, preening for him her richer hair, a bosom and a rose'. Boylan has a drink before proceeding to his peccadillo with Molly. Meanwhile, 'bronze and gold', Miss Lydia Douce and Miss Mina Kennedy, the 'sirens' who symbolize musical seduction in a modern world, and all its emotional torments and dangers—in Joyce's parody of how young women were being represented in the Edwardian controversy over working in bars— preside over the bar.

As Boylan and Lenehan leave, Ben Dollard and Father Cowley enter the bar, they talk about Bloom's wife, the 'buxom lassy' soprano, Mrs Marion (nee Tweedy), Daughter of the Regiment, Bloom (Molly) whom Boylan has left to rendezvous with and whom it is implied, is the real Siren, not the young barmaids. Recounting an anecdote of the dress suit with tight trousers Ben borrowed for a concert performance, from Molly: Si Dedalus quips: 'Mrs Marion Bloom has left-off clothes of all descriptions' (a punning reference to Molly and Bloom's business of collecting and hiring out 'left-off clothes' and costumes to performers of opera and theatre productions), as well as to her affair. As the men banter, Dollard breaks into a 'bassooned attack, booming over bombarding chords' singing the lyrics: 'When love absorbs my ardent soul', and Father Cowley cries 'War! War!' 'You're the warrior!' (347). This banter soon leads into the singing session in the saloon with all the men there, except Bloom and Goulding. Bloom continues writing, musing, and listening, with Richie Goulding, firstly to Simon Dedalus singing *M'appari* from Flowtow's opera *Martha* in the exposition; and then weaving through and drawing together the threads, literally and symbolically, they all listen to Big Ben Dollard's moving rendition of the 'counter-exposition' history of the colonized, in the ballad of *The Croppy Boy*.

This ballad began, anonymously, after the 1798 rising and was sung first by street pedlars. There are several versions and broadsheet songs printed. It is still sung, sometimes to an old Irish air *Cailín Óg a Stór*.

FUGAL TEXTURE

Joyce conjures a 'non-representational' effect of musicalization that creates an overall effect of vibration, between the fugal motifs by diminution, and augmentation, which give the effect of speeding up and slowing down phrases. Dissociation, dislocation, and fragmentation are suggested and evoked through metonym (where the names of an attribute of a thing is substituted for it), and synecdoche (where body parts stand for and substitute the whole person). Synecdochical fragmentation of body parts, starts in the first words 'Bronze' and 'Gold' ('Bronze by Gold') and continues throughout the entire episode, in related words referring to the barmaid/sirens hair-colour. Scholars (e.g. Attridge 2004) have discussed the ways that Joyce focuses on synecdoche and certain body parts throughout 'Sirens' in terms of sexualization and suggestive references. Joyce uses a method of synecdochical reference that is, as Attridge suggests, almost fetishistic in its objectification of body parts, and references to persons, for instance the barmaids/Sirens in terms of hair colour 'Bronze by Gold'. As well as hair, Joyce focuses on body parts that relate to hearing, which corresponds to the 'organ' of the episode: the ear. He does this also by focusing on the voices of the characters, and lips, of the mouth. 'Miss Kennedy lipped her cup again'. There is a focus on the bodily media of aural and oral communication, listening, speaking, and singing; on sounds, and music made by the body. This functions to full effect in the evocations of the barmaids laughter, as they drink tea, whilst the bar is empty, before any of the men come in, and they are talking about 'that old fogey in Boyd's', with the playful double meanings of innuendo, laughing so hard Miss Kennedy is choking and spluttering out her tea.

Again Kennygiggles, stooping her fair pinnacles of hair, stooping, her tortoise napecomb showed, spluttered out her mouth her tea, choking in tea and laughter, coughing with choking, crying:

> —O greasy eyes! Imagine being married to a man like that, she cried. With his bit of beard!
> —Douce gave full vent to a splendid yell, a full yell of full woman, delight, joy, indignation.
> —Married to the greasy nose! She yelled.

Miss Douce makes a pun on 'greasy' which in Dublin is pronounced 'grace-y' that sends them into further paroxysms of laughter. The play of words is on the meanings of grace in musical terminology, as well

as in religion. *Gracing* is a term Burney associated, by comparison with 'the adding, diminishing, or changing a melody, or passage, with judgment and propriety...' according to *taste,* Charles Burney writes in his *The Present State of Music in France and Italy* (1753).[57] Although Joyce preferred 'a melodic statement' not 'overhung by ornamental foliage'[58] in musical notation a 'grace note' means an ornament, embellishment or flourish, an *appoggiatura,* written in smaller script above the note and is not part of the rhythm of the measure, nor essential to the melody or harmony. The term *con grazia,* means play 'with grace'. All of which Joyce would have been very familiar with as a tenor singer and musician, and are meanings that play in the association of 'greasy'
as well as a more bawdy vernacular tone, with which he often contrasts more high minded references, in his multi-toned, polyphonic style:

> Shrill with deep laughter, after bronze in gold, they urged each to peal after peal, ringing in changes, bronzegold goldbronze, shrilldeep to laugher after laughter. And then laughed more. Greasy I knows.

Their voice peal like bells, 'ringing in changes'. And then the paroxysms die down naturally, in another real and natural bodily analogy.

> Exhausted, breathless their shaken heads they laid, braided and pinnacled by glossycombed, against the counterledge. All flushed (O!), panting, sweating (o!), all breathless.

The references to love, war, women, water, the sea, lips, and the ear, are brought together and recombined in recurring motifs and vignettes, such as that of the seashell which Miss Douce had brought back from Rostrevor, held to the ear to hear the sound of the sea.

> He smiled at bronze's teabathed lips, at listening lips and eyes (338)

Lenehan is talking with Dedalus and looking at Miss Douce.

> Lenehan still drank and grinned at his tilted ale and at Miss Douce's lips that all but hummed, not shut, the oceansong her lips had trilled. Idolores. The eastern seas.

There is an allusive paronomastical reference made the membrane of tympanum, which is prefigured in the opening lines, in the fragment: 'Boomed crashing chords. When love absorbs. War! War! The tympanum' (329). After Ben Dollard sings a line meant for a higher tenor or soprano voice: 'When love absorbs my ardent soul' in a booming bass he is met with a dry response:

> —Sure, you'd burst the tympanum of her ear, man, Mr Dedalus said through smoke aroma, with an organ like yours....
> Not to mention another membrane, Father Cowley added.

This is an allusion, to the medieval religious belief that Jesus was conceived through the unbroken membrane, of tympanum, or eardrum, an explanation for how Jesus could have been conceived by the Virgin Mary. Fugal texture is also provided by the recurring motifs related to the themes of music and the sea.

The layered Joycean narrative comprises recurring motifs and repetitions building up 'Sirens' through semantic association. Metonymic and metaphorical motifs that recur earlier, in the episode include the seashell Miss Douce has brought back from her holidays in Rostrevor; the Siren-barmaids and the play on their names; the meat Bloom eats in the restaurant and the inner organs that he loves, recurring from earlier in *Ulysses*; certain watery phrases and oriental objects. Mythical, or parodic, signs that recur allude chromatically to the ocean: waves, oceandepths, the likening of women to the sea. (Bloom muses mournfully, 'Woman. As easy stop the sea. Yes: all is lost' (351)). An associated chain of motifs, like a tone row, links the ears of young women to seashells, women to the sea, wild waves, mur-murs, mer-murs, sea songs, 'Bloom-mur' (361) Echoed by: 'Murmured'(361). The barmaids-mermaids ears are recurring, linked motifs:

> Her ear too is a shell, the peeping lobe there (363).

In likening women to the sea, the tidal rush of blood sounds like waves in curve of a seashell, in their ears, as if the sea were their natural element:

> What are the wild waves saying? He asked her, smiled.
> Charming, seasmiling and unanswering, Lydia on Lidwell smiled

Musical references in onomatopoeic musical sounds abound: 'Tap tap tap' the blind stripling piano-tuner's stick, has a double meaning, the word 'Tap' is slang for copulation; it begins to appear, with repeated regularity towards the middle of the counterexposition, suggesting—in Bloom's imagination—Boylan's seduction of Molly, is occurring. 'Bloom-booms'. Songs with significant titles and lines of songs with double-meanings, double-entendres, for Bloom, are sung in the bar, interwoven through Bloom's inner musings:

> Numbers it is. All music when you come to think. Two multiplied by

> two divided by half is twice one. Vibrations: chords those are. (359)

This approach to metaphysical aspects of associations between music and mathematics, and science, that shows that the sound of chords is caused by the overtone, vibration, is followed by the 'musical' motif in fresh variations:

> Sea, wind, leaves, thunder, waters, cows lowing, the cattle market, cocks, hens don't crow, snakes hisssss. There's music everywhere. (864)

FUGAL VARIATION ON A THEME

The fugal device of repetition, variation, is used throughout Sirens in many ways, through playing with the synecdochical reference terms such as 'gold' and 'bronze'; and names and characteristics of the characters: Bloom, Bloo, Pold, Poldy, for example. Joyce also uses repetition variation in a fugal way of repeating a passage three times, in the reiterations, rearranging the words, after Simon Dedalus has sung *All is Lost Now;* Richie recalls another performance of a song he has never forgotten sung by Dedalus:

> Richie, admiring, descanted on that man's glorious voice. He remembered one night long ago. Never forgot that night. Si sang 'Twas rank and fame: in Ned Lambert's 'twas. Good God, he never heard in all his life a note like that he never did then false one we had better part so clear so God he ever heard since love lives not a clinking voice he can tell you too.
> Goulding, a flush struggling in his pale, told Mr Bloom, face of the night, Si in Ned Lambert's, Dedalus' house, sang 'Twas rank and fame. He, Mr Bloom, listened while he, Richie Goulding, told him, Mr Bloom, of the night he, Richie, heard him, Si Dedalus, sing, 'Twas rank and fame in his, Ned Lambert's house. (856-357)

This is an effective adaptation of the musical fugue technique of variation on a theme, and it also reflexively, comments on memory, and the process of thinking, and articulation, and how it works, as indeed does the whole episode, in its form of narration, through music and song, story-telling and listening.

Before Joyce's notes were found, critics speculated that the opening sixty-three lines of 'Sirens' could be read as the 'prelude' to his fugue. A series of rhythmical fragmented sense-based motifs that introduce the subject, counter-subject, characters, and prefigure exposition and counter-exposition development of the fugue. It has been suggested, by Gifford, that the first sixty motifs comprise a figurative 'keyboard on which the fugue is to be performed'.[59] It is still relevant to consider these in terms of how fugal devices work. Each of the fragmented metonymic motifs is later expanded, developed and played using musical devices of variation: distortion, embellishment, mirroring, augmentation, of metonymic and synecdochical phrases through the exposition and counter exposition, through variations on the subject and counter-subject. The variation of the terms in a phrase, diminished in some, augmented in others sets up a reverberation. The opening introduces the Sirens-barmaids synecdochically and visually by their hair colour, 'bronze' and 'gold', the principal metals in the Homeric world, and the sound of horsedrawn carriage on the cobbles of the street: 'Bronze by gold heard the hoof irons, steelyringing' (328) This short motif is eleven syllables in length. But in the exposition in which the subject of love (or desire) is developed, this one line expands into 42 lines of narrative:

> Bronze by gold, Miss Douce's head by Miss Kennedy's head, over the crossblind of the Ormond bar heard the viceregal hoofs go by, ringing steel. (331)

The sirens/barmaids are watching luminaries in the Vice-Regal procession passing down Ormond Quay—outside the bar's window:

> —Is that her? asked Miss Kennedy.
> Miss Douce said yes, sitting with his ex, pearl grey and eau de Nil.'
> —Exquisite contrast, Miss Kennedy said.
> When all agog Miss Douce said eagerly:
> —Look at the fellow in the tall silk.
> —Who? Where? gold asked more eagerly.
> —In the second carriage, Miss Douce's wet lips said, laughing in the sun. He's looking. Mind till I see.
> She darted, bronze, to the backmost corner, flattening her face against the pane in a halo of hurried breath.
> Her wet lips tittered:
> —He's killed looking back.
> She laughed:
> —O wept! Aren't men frightful idiots?
> With sadness.
> Miss Kennedy sauntered sadly from bright light, twining a loose hair behind an ear. Sauntering sadly, gold no more, she twisted twined a hair. Sadly she twined in sauntering gold hair behind a curving ear.
> —It's them has the fine times, sadly then she said. (331)

On this note, Joyce then introduces into this expanded fragment of the fugue the voice-part of Bloom—an example of 'A man', referred to as 'Bloowho', who is walking the streets.

> Bloowho went by Moulang's pipes, bearing in his breast the sweets of sin, by Wine's antiques in memory bearing sweet sinful words, by Carroll's dusky battered plate for Raoul.

Bloom is walking, past Moulang's pipe shop. The 'sweets of sin' is no indicator of his own dalliances but, in a touch of—possibly passive, possibly masochistic—wry irony, the pornographic popular novel he has selected to give to his unfaithful wife, opera singer Molly, who is having an affair with Blazes Boylan, her concert booking manager, a gift which Bloom has secreted in the breast pocket of his jacket.

As Bloom walks on, Joyce cuts back to the Ormond Bar where the barmaids have been brought tea by 'boots', who is the general 'busboy' or odd-jobber. Throughout all this narrative detail, Joyce is still taking flight in a fugal expansion of the first motif-line:

> The boots to them, them in the bar, them barmaids came. For them unheeding him he banged on the counter his tray of chattering china.
> —There's your teas, he said... (331)

The busboy, ignored by the barmaids, bangs down his tray on the bar impatiently. She places it below the bar level:

> Miss Kennedy with manners transposed the teatray down to an upturned Lithia crate, safe from eyes, low... (332)

Boots questions her for looking out the window at her 'beau'. In the doubled narrative, a parodic play between mythic and ordinary levels of narrative, once the barmaid asserts herself she ascends to the symbolic mythic archaic level of the Siren.

> —I'll complain to Mrs de Massey on you if I hear any more of your impertinent insolence.

The prelude now moves to its second motif fragment:

> Imperthnthn thnthnthn

In the expanded exposition, this is taken up and repeated by 'boots' or 'bootsnout' as Joyce fugally distorts his metonymic moniker.

> —Imperthnthn thnthnthn, bootsnout sniffed rudely, as he retreated as she had threatened as he had come

Bloom, sounding like 'boom', for the second time, Joyce intercuts the spatial-time sequence, jumping to another place, with reference to the whereabouts of Bloom. Like an approaching melody, we hear Bloom coming, iambic pentametre of his footsteps walking, interwoven with the narrative action of the bar, and its iconic, symbolic, figureheads, the barmaid/Sirens.

The foregoing illustrates the way Joyce treats the fugue in terms of its opening. From a contracted 17-syllable motif, he expands a detailed narrative, which unfolds in a way that recalls Proust's Japanese 'paper crumbs' opening into flowers. He then goes back to Gold and Bronze and back further to the mythical references to move forward in the narrative. Association of this kind was an original project in the context of a phenomenological modernist approach to narrative, which depended on associations (melded in the unfolding narrative structure). This entire narrative expands fugally and recursively by linguistic-psychological association, from the subject Love-Desire, and answers, and countersubject of War-Betrayal and answers articulated in the 'voice/parts' of characters, Bronze and Gold, Bloom and Boylan, and the 'chorus' in the Ormond, referred to in metonymic and synecdochical motifs (e.g. hair colour). The fragmented motifs of the opening are impressionistic and musical in their elaborated metonymic and synecdochical effects, also suggesting leitmotifs in Wagnerian opera, where motifs recur, building up a circular, multi-layered narrative of semantic associations. Using onomatopoeia and composite word-effect Joyce creates new portmanteau words. He slips, too, into a mythical use of language when describing the Sirens, in terms of the ancient precious metals, bronze and gold. Hence: 'gold by bronze'; 'bronze from anear, gold from afar'; 'gold from anear by bronze'; 'sisterbronze'; 'peepofgold'; 'deep bronze laughter'; 'goldbronze'; 'gigglegold'; 'Bronze by a weary gold'. (328-376)

The iconic barmaids/Sirens feature prominently as symbolic figureheads at the start of the episode, prefiguring the theme of the call of ancient instincts. This theme is symbolized, in the words of songs sung in the bar, and lines of poetry running through Bloom's meandering stream of consciousness reverie. Poetical and political, Joyce's catchy cadences of associations catch 'Will Shakespeare' —'Music hath charms Shakespeare said. Quotations every day of the year' (363), 'To be or not to be. Wisdom while you wait' (363), 'God's curse on bitch's bastard' (338)—Homer, lines from the song The Croppy Boy, amongst others, interwoven with sense impressions (338). Joyce plays not only with the signifier of mythical dimensions, but also with the Sirens' names as ordinary girls: 'Miss Kenn', 'Miss Dou', 'Lidlydiawell', 'Kennygiggles' (328-376).

Sometimes mixing symbolic-linguistic levels of 'reality': 'Bronzedouce', 'girlgold'. Joyce plays with the names in fugal development, describing (or enacting) Miss Kennedy being asked a question as she is reading, paying minimal attention, continuing to read:

> Miss voice of Kennedy answered... Miss gaze of Kennedy, heard not seen, read on...No glance of Kennedy rewarding him he yet made overtures...Girlgold she read and did not glance... (337)

In fugal diminution and augmentation, motifs are repeated in different variations, played by and through different voices. Appropriately to the technic, Bloom is aware of wind, his flatulence. It is with this carnivalesque cadence that the fugue ends. His uncomfortable awareness is repeated, developed and elaborated through the latter part of the **tela contrappuntistica** 'contrapuntal web' of counterexposition, after he leaves the Ormond, and ends on the irreverent note of Bloom's flatulence, and the word, 'Done,' the last word of the court speech that consigned to death patriotic Irish hero, Robert Emmett. 'When my nation takes her place among the nations of the earth then and not till then, let my epitaph be written. I have done.' Kiberd discusses how the 1903 centenary of Emmett's execution had been marked by articles in the Irish press conjecturing the whereabouts of his grave, which was never located, and this was a current and controversial issue in the lead up to Irish Independence.

SONGS OF SEDUCTION AND REBELLION

Interrelated musical fugal techniques, or devices, that iterate, reiterate and deepen the counterpoint of the subject of *love* and countersubject of *war* are the songs which run through the 'Sirens' episode; and the motif of the 'decoy'. The episode is divided into two main horizontal parts, exposition and counter exposition, signified by the songs, one of love; and the other of war *The Croppy Boy* a ballad of the 1798 Rising about the entrapment and execution of a young 'croppy' 'rebel'. The codetta occurs at the end of *M'Appari* as a climax. The main songs are sung by the men. Si Dedulus sings *M'Appari* from the opera *Martha* by Flowtow. Ben Dollard sings the *The Croppy Boy*. There are several other songs sung in snatches or as background. And barmaid/siren Miss Lydia Douce ('bronze') sings lines from the light opera *Flora-dora* (1899), a colonial opera set on a South Sea island. The songs comprise one of the 'voices'/strands of the counterpoint interwoven in the counterexposition, comprising a) Bloom's interior monologue on love and loss (in general); b) the songs sung by the men and 'trilled' by Miss Douce; c) the journey of Boylan across Dublin to Molly, mused on by Bloom.

About half way through the exposition the music and song begins with a tuning up, and a call, the call of a tuning fork:

> From the saloon a call came, long in dying.

This is laden with profound meanings, to do with the call of both ancient instincts and the call to rise up, and regain the colonized land:

> 'You hear? It throbbed, pure. purer, softly and softlier, its buzzing prongs. Longer in dying call.' (339-340)

The first song line is as if an interior one.

> —*The bright stars fade*

A voiceless song, sang from within, singing:

> —*...the morn is breaking* (340)

Si Dedulus is testing the newly tuned piano, and singing the love song, *Goodbye, Sweetheart, Goodbye.*

> A duodene of birdnotes chirruped bright treble answer under sensitive hands. Brightly the keys all twinkling, linked, all harpsichording, called to a voice to sing the strain of dewey morn, of youth, of love's leavetaking, life's, love's morn. (340)

There is a subtle play on the meanings of morn, as in daybreak, and mourn, to grieve, and the Mountains of Mourne (mountains in County Down), 'faraway mourning mountain eye', throughout the episode.

> —*The dewdrops pearl...*
> Lenehan's lips over the counter lisped a low whistle of decoy.
> —But look this way, he said, rose of Castille (340)

The first lines of song in the 'Sirens' episode are sung by Si Dedulus in the exposition—as Boylan is about to, and does, enter the Ormond, followed shortly by Bloom with Richie Goulding who both go into the dining room together.

The word 'Decoy' first enters in the 'prelude' at the start of line 15. 'Soft word' belying its uses in betrayal. It is used in various subliminally paronomasiac ways, as meaning someone, who entices or allures as into a trap or danger (which alludes to the way the barmaids were represented in the Edwardian crusade against barmaids, which Katharyn Mullin has discussed (2004)). It also refers to *The Croppy Boy* ballad. As well as the two main songs, also adding colour are quotations from opera songs and music hall songs, amongst those that recur are as I have mentioned lines from *Goodbye, Sweetheart, Goodbye* (lyrics by Jane Williams, music by John L. Hatton) which Si Dedulus sings as he is test playing the piano alone; and *Tutto è sciolto* (*All is Lost Now*), a tenor air from Bellini's opera *La Sonnambula* (*The Sleepwalker*).[60]

This is another way in which Joyce engages with social and political themes in the songs of the Irish people, to whom music and song was an integral part of culture. Songs about actual historical events passed on the stories, preserved the culture, and kept up morale, in a country that was struggling for independence.

The use of songs has resonances that were also personal, as Joyce was a tenor singer, who had himself sung in concerts in Dublin (including with two leading singers of the time who are referred to by their actual names, J.C. Doyle, baritone, and John McCormack, tenor).[61]

Earlier, that day, in *Ulysses*, before Bloom left the house, Molly had received a letter that he noticed under her pillow, he asked her who it was from and she replied Boylan, and that he was bringing the programme for their performance, when he asks what she will be singing, '*La ci darem* with J.C. Doyle, she said, and *Love's Old Sweet Song*'. (*La ci darem* is a seduction aria from Mozart's *Don Giovanni*).

The lyrics wend through Bloom's meandering thoughts in 'Sirens.

Joyce's use of the songs in Sirens highlights social and cultural significance of songs and singing in Irish culture as stories were passed on, and events commemorated, through songs, such as in *The Croppy Boy*. At the time in which the episode is situated, which reflects the first years of the twentieth century when Joyce had lived in Dublin, music concerts were highly popular forms of entertainment. As Bloom, using the name of 'Henry' is writing to 'Martha Clifford' in the dining room, Simon Dedalus appositely sings Lionel's aria *M'appari* from Flowtow's opera *Martha* (he sings a translated version).[62]

The codetta, signifying the end of the exposition occurs at the end of the singing of *Martha* by Si Dedulus in the saloon, in Bloom's inner associations, as he muses on:

> Words? Music? No: it's what behind (354)

Here in this codetta Joyce brings together ideas of physical orgasm and the transcendental divine. Bloom is musing on orgasm, and music as the 'Language of love':

> Bloom. Flood of warm jimjam lickitup secretness flowed to flow in music out, in desire, dark to lick flow, invading. Tipping her tepping her tapping her topping her....(354)

Thinking not of his own experiences but of Boylan with his wife.

As the song continues, and comes to a climax:

> —*Co-me, thou lost one!*
> *Co-me thou dear one!* (355)

He thinks of Martha, trying to find comfort.

> —*Come!*

Then, in contrast, segues into the climax of the codetta in a eulogy to the notes of the tenor's voice that rises and soars and flies.

> It soared, a bird, it held its flight, a swift pure cry, soar silver orb it leaped serene speeding, sustained to come, don't spin it out too long long breath he breath long life, soaring high, high resplendent, aflame, crowned, high in the effulgence symbolistic, high, of the ethereal bosom, high, of the high vast irradiation everywhere all soaring, all around about the all, the endlessnessnessness...

> —*To me!* (355-356)

In this codetta, Joyce links physical love, orgasm, with divine flight of the spirit in the voice, and music which suggests by association that it is through the body, the voice, and singing, and hearing songs sung by a beautiful voice, that the spirit soars, and that this is the comfort and counter-balance, and outlet of expressive healing, for the pains of love, and betrayals, in life.

The Croppy Boy is a ballad of the Rising of 1798, against the British colonizers; it was rewritten by William B. McBurney, nom-de-plume of Caroll Malone released in the nineteenth century, and was a well-known ballad when Joyce was growing up in Ireland and writing. It tells the story of a young 'croppy' the 'rebel' boys and men from Wexford who were known by their cropped hair in the uprising of 1798, which was defeated. In the ballad the young *bouchal* [Gaelic: boy] was tricked by a 'yeoman captain' a decoy in disguise as the priest, Father Green, who has been captured and already executed. In the ballad, which is not quoted in full in the episode, the boy goes to see Father Green for his blessing before he goes to the Wexford uprising and the yeoman is waiting for him wearing the priest's robes, in the priest's chair. In making his confession of minor things, that he has done, of cursing, going to play instead of going to mass, and passing the churchyard in a hurry and forgetting 'to pray for my mother's rest' the croppy boy makes another confession:

> *At the siege of Ross did my father fall,/and at Gorey my loving brothers all,/ I alone am left of my name and race,/I will go to Wexford and take their place*
> *I bear no grudge against living thing;/But I love my country above the king./Now, Father! bless me, and let me go/To die, if God has ordained it so.*[63]

That is when he hears a 'rustling noise' looks up, the priest's robes are off and there sits in his place the 'a yeoman captain with a fiery glare'. For background, although not quoted in full in the episode,the verses to *The Croppy Boy* include the lyrics:

> With fiery glare and with fury hoarse,
> Instead of blessing, he breathed a
>   curse:-
> Twas a good thought boy to come
>   here and shrive,
> For one short hour is you time to live.

The boy is taken and hung as a traitor.

> At Geneva barrack that young man
>   died.
> And at Passage they have his body laid.

The ballad ends:

> Good people who live in peace and joy,
> Breath a prayer and a tear for the
>   Croppy Boy.[64]

The men call for Ben Dollard to sing *The Croppy Boy*.

> —No, Ben, Tom Kernan interfered, The Croppy Boy. Our native Doric.

— Ay, do, Ben, Mr Dedulus said. Good men and true.
—Do, do, they begged in one.

Ben Dollard sings in the **contraesposizione**, which has another layer of meaning, as the counter movement. He gives a resounding rendition of the ballad in his bass voice and all are profoundly affected. The lyrics are woven through the narrative. As Bloom and Goulding listen in the dining room, Richie Goulding lawyer says to Bloom,

> Ireland comes now. My country above the king. She listens. Who fears to speak of nineteen four? (368)

1904 is the year in which *Ulysses* is set, on the 16 June, that day (the day that as mentioned Joyce and Nora Barnacle had first 'walked out' in Dublin, in the year in which a few months later they eloped, permanently, to Europe).

> -Bless me, father, Dollard the croppy cried. Bless me and let me go.
> Bloom looked, unblessed to go. (368)

Bloom is daydreaming of the letter he has been writing to 'Martha' being read out in court, 'for breach of promise', to laughter.

> The false priest rustling soldier from his cassock. A yeoman captain. They know it all by heart. the thrill they itch for. Yeoman cap. (368)

Bloom is captivated by the sight of 'Bronze' listening, and the effect the music and song is having on her. 'Thrilled, she listened, bending in sympathy to hear' (368)..Bloom is still thinking about sex and women, and ruminating on 'Bronze' whom he is looking at as she is listening, and speculating on whether she is a virgin, as he thinks of Molly.

> With hoarse rude fury the yeoman cursed. Swelling in apoplectic bitch's bastard. A good thought boy, to come. One hour's your time to live, your last.
> Tap. Tap. (369)

Bloom reflects on the affect of the song on Bronze, and how women are moved by martyrs. 'For all things dying...For all things born' (369).
And as Miss Douce pulls the beerpull, whilst Bloom makes an inner innuendo on the appearance of the beerpull sliding through her hand, 'All lost in pity for croppy'. Bloom ruminates, as the song continues:

> At Geneva barrack that young man died. At Passage was his body laid. Dolor! O, he dolores! The voice of the mournful chanter called to dolorous prayer (370)

Here Joyce interweaves an echo of the lyrics of another song *The Shade of the Palm*: '*I, dolores, queen of the eastern seas*' that earlier barmaid Lydia Douce has been 'trilling'. And Bloom gets up and leaves.

> Pray for him, prayed the bass of Dollard. You who hear in peace. Breath a prayer, drop a tear, good men, good people. He was the croppy boy. (370)

The theme songs in 'Sirens' allude to the voyage of homecoming of *The Odyssey*, which Joyce appropriates, parodies and develops. *Ulysses* can be read as symbolizing a long 'mythical' voyage of national homecoming for Ireland, fraught with frustrations and setbacks, as well as the homecoming after a long day and night's wandering for Bloom. Ireland was fighting for independence from the British and fierce turbulence surrounded proposed Home Rule. The Irish were compelled to take matters into their own hands; Pearse declared the formation of the Provisional Government of the Irish Republic, on the steps of the Dublin Post Office on Easter Monday in 1916. The British subsequently executed all the founders of this new government. During the rising, Joyce's former university classmate and 'fellow pamphleteer', Francis Sheehy Skeffington, was murdered by a British officer as he tried to stop looting of shops which was bringing discredit to the nationalist movement.[65]

This was deeply shocking to Joyce, whose murdered friend's qualities of 'civic-mindedness' were reproduced in the character of Bloom comments Kiberd, who adds that readers might interpret it as signifying a 'rebellious' spirit to fight for one's homeland. 'I bear no grudge against living thing/But I love my country above the king' is one of the original lyrics. Kiberd argues otherwise, he points out that Joyce's attitude to his countrymen was that they were not warlike, which is a theme of Joyce's anti-heroic *Ulysses*. 'Leopold and Molly Bloom may disagree, like all spouses, on many things, but they share a principled aversion to war, violence and licensed coercion'.[66]

However, it is the context of the songs that were sung to pass on stories and to keep the spirits high, and part of this was revolutionary, the Irish did win Independence in 1921 and regained their homeland that had been invaded and taken over.

In keeping with his linguistic dexterity the 'Sirens' fugue constitutes a double-counterpoint, entailing a contrapuntal reading. Transposition and analogues do not achieve a perfect symmetry, but that is not required in a balanced fugal structure. His musico-literary contrapuntal strategy symbolically takes apart and rearranges the symbolic hierarchical language of the falsely unifying bourgeois world—whose concerns and interests, Lukács has asserted in *The Ideology of Modernism*, were represented and reflected in the form of the realist novel.[67] Realist prose may have supported the unifying conventions of capitalism's hegemonic language order, but literary modernism ran contra, unmasking the artificially smooth surfaces of realism. Joyce's modernist aim was social, ideological and political as well as aesthetic. Using intermedial techniques of fugue, he aimed to articulate modern consciousness in its contradictions and fragmentation, as experienced in the inner life and through the body of the modern 'ordinary' individual.

In addition to the subliminal story of Parnell and Kitty O'Shea that is hinted at in this episode, there is second story of love and political or public downfall that Joyce alludes to in 'Sirens', that of the Revolutionary Robert Emmett and his fiancée Sarah Curran. After the Rising of 1803 he was leading failed it is conjectured that he could have escaped, and fled Ireland for France. But he did not want to leave Sarah Curran without saying goodbye, in hiding near to where she was living, he was caught, and subsequently executed. The seven last words of Emmett's last speech before he was executed wind through Bloom's thoughts in the 'Sirens' episode.

Within the context of critical theory discourse on narrative using a musical strategy, 'Sirens' constitutes an analogue for non-representational musical fugue 'structure' enacted through a fluid and musical use of poetic language. *Ulysses* is also read as an inverted variation, in the form of a High Modernist parodic, carnivalesque appropriation, of a heroic mythical epic structure. Joyce's revolutionary poetic language not only deconstructs and rearranges the classical, Aristotelian unity of narrative form, it also plays with the performative, paronomasiac, punning potential of metaphoric, metonymic and synecdochical poetic language, in textual innovation of 'musical' effects. Joyce's fugal, narrative double-strategy also raises questions about the liminality—or in-between space—between the arts of music and literature.

COMPARATIVE MUSICO-LITERARY INTERPRETATIONS

It is useful to analyze the musicalized language of 'Sirens' fugal devices such as counterpoint, since not only does this give a deeper understanding of 'Sirens', and Joyce's musico-literary construction, it also serves to demonstrate differences and similarities in the musical and literary uses of techniques of counterpoint.

Musical counterpoint does not transpose directly to literary form for reasons of temporality, as critics including Wolf, and Grandt, have commented.[68] However, this 'difference' may paradoxically bring with it, or contain, a 'similarity'. This difference may therefore have a double function, both conscious and unconscious, for counterpoint occurs, as performance, in the imagination of readers. This is a performance which occurs as an effect and enaction of reading, whose technique is unconscious to the performer, to whom it just seems to happen.

A creative reading process in which the reader reads with a conscious and unconscious, overt and subliminal, awareness of the gaps and absences, and presences in the text—at the time and in the lines of reading—does constitute a literary variation of musical counterpoint. This is most obvious, and effective, in 'Sirens' in the simultaneity of characters' actions, set into play by Joyce the writer, not perhaps in the guise of 'implied author' but, more radically, as 'musical form as narrator'. As Bloom is walking along the Ormond Quay, the barmaids are laughing and talking behind the bar to each other; at the same time; Boylan approaches in a carriage and Simon Dedalus walks into the bar.

In its staggered entry of the characters into the bar, and depiction of the characters not in the bar yet; 'Sirens' performs both a literary counterpoint that evokes the staggered entry of voices in polyphonic fugue; and a counterpoint between *parts* or voices. The subject, countersubject, and answers are played by voices in a pattern of absence and presence in the Ormond that continues throughout the exposition and counter-exposition. In this temporal sense, of simultaneity, it constitutes a contrapuntal fugue structure; or rather a literary variation, or interpretation, of such a structural form.

As well as the contrapuntal use of polyphony, another significant form of musicalization in the language of 'Sirens' is recurring motif in Joyce's paronomasiac play on words. Wolf comments on how Joyce's use of motifs creates: 'intense effect of self-referentiality'[69] and adapts recurring leitmotifs and their semantic associations metonymically to stand for characters, such as the multiple significations of the barmaids as 'bronze and gold', and the 'jingle jangling' set of associations signifying, and standing for, Blazes Boylan, in his jaunting car, known as a *jingle*. Further, the references to Martha are semantically linked to Bloom. Structural unity is achieved not only by the formal self-referentiality of motifs but also, as Wolf argues, in the metonymic manner of leitmotif.[70] Narrative unity and the effect of a story unfolding in a fragmented, 'musicalized' pattern is built up by the semantic associations of the motifs, indicated by the recurring motifs which each time they recur, do so in a different variation: 'bronzegold goldbronze'; 'Where bronze from anear? Where gold from afar?'; 'goldbronze'; 'bronzegigglegold'; 'gold', 'Gold pinnacled hair'; 'peepofgold?'; 'Miss bronze'; 'deep bronze laughter'; 'Bronze whiteness', amongst many others.

While disputing evidence for a fugue structure, critics always concurred that 'Sirens' counts as 'musicalized' narrative (Wolf 1999). Scher criticizes vague uses of 'musical' terms by comparative intermedial critics. He discerns three types of critical usage of the term 'musical' in literary criticism: 'the acoustic, the evocative and the structural', arguing that only 'alluding to the [...] artistic arrangement in musiclike sequence' in literary works, seems potentially meaningful'.[71] Although he believes that: 'ideally the adjective "musical" should be left to poets'. he argues that if used in criticism it should be used to denote: 'literary phenomena that relate specifically to music'. Scher further argues that, instead of using terms such as 'musical and musicality' in the 'impressionistic' sense, intermedial critics should instead make reference to:

> acoustic or phonetic quality of poetry or prose...and within this broader acoustic context it may be practicable to distinguish between the euphonious and the cacophonous.[72]

Despite other disagreements, 'Sirens' was read and heard by the critics as a musical episode on the following grounds of its:

1) Setting. The musical bar of the Ormond hotel.
2) Themes. Love and War, expressed through songs and story-telling.
3) Acoustic or phonetic quality of language.

FIGURES OF SPEECH SOUND

In his variation on the structure of 'Homeric' metalanguage, Joyce wrote a narrative using poetic, dialogic language. For Jakobson: 'Only in poetry with its regular reiteration of equivalent units is the time of the speech flow experienced, as it is—to cite another semiotic pattern—with music' (96). This poetic language works in 'Sirens' both in the condensed, metonymic, synecdochical poetic language-time of the 'prelude' and the developments through episodes of the exposition and counter-exposition. For example, the narrative is punctuated, at its end, by the carnivalesque musical expression of wind (Bloom's breaking wind):

> Pwee! Little wind piped wee
> Fff! Oo!
> Rrrpr. Kraa. Kraandl.
> My eppripfftaph. Be pfrwrit (330)

Blazes Boylan is referred to by sounds that are related to 'jingle'. 'Jingle jingle jaunted jingling'. The introduction of words associated with 'jingle', in the exposition signals Boylan's journey to the Ormond, in onomatopoeic phrases 'Jingle (336). 'Jingle jaunty jingle' (337), 'with patience Lenehan waited for Boylan with impatience, for jingle jaunty blazes boy' (339). 'Jingling on supple rubbers it jaunted from the bridge to Ormond quay' (339). The fugue's parts, as in dramatic parts, are referred to synecdochically, focusing on lips and hair (of the Sirens), and metonymically, by the sound association and a sound/colour association: 'Jingle. Bloo' (328). This is followed by the suggestion of dramatic romantic conflict:

> Boomed crashing chords. When love absorbs. War! War!

The word 'Boomed' plays with and echoes the sound of Bloom's name. This technique is seen in a range of synaesthetic, colour-sound associations: 'Blew'. 'Blue bloom'. 'Bloo'. 'Bloom. Old Bloom' (328-330).

'When love absorbs. War! War!' is from the aforementioned song, *Love and War* sung by Simon Dedalus, Ben Dollard and Father Cowley, in the counterexposition as the fugue narrative unfolds. Another level of meaning can be read in the lyric lines of songs sung in the bar, signalled by their inscription in italics, interwoven throughout the fugue. The lines of lyrics are interwoven throughout the dialogic polyphonic narrative of the characters singing. For example over three pages, the words of *Goodbye, Sweetheart, Goodbye*: This last line followed by:

> I'm off, said Boylan with impatience (343)

And he departs, jingling, for his rendezvous with Bloom's wife, 'jingle jaunty jingle', sensed receding by Bloom. Joyce metonymically creates a fugal effect of counterpoint, through counter-posing in the jingling sounds of Boylan's departure, Bloom's equally metonymic and musically sounding, flow of consciousness, sense impressions, perceptions and thoughts in the Ormond Hotel restaurant. Bloom's thoughts on Boylan are juxtaposed, in his imagination, with the sounds of Boylan's passage to Molly:

> Jingle jaunted down the quays. Blazes sprawled on bounding tyres

In Bloom's anxious imagination, Boylan arrives and seduces Molly before he actually does. While Bloom listens to the songs in the bar and to Ritchie Goulding talking, his thought ranges:

> Her wavyavyeavheavyeavyevyevy hair un comb'd.

He imagines Molly's hair tumbling loose and wavy as the sea.

As Bloom continues to sit in the dining room writing to Martha, Boylan arrives at Molly's door:

> Jogjig stopped. Dandy tan shoe of dandy. Boylan socks skyblue clocks came light to earth... (364)

He raps metonymically with onomatopoeia, echoing with significant carnivalesque associations of meaning, signaling infidelity. Here with references to 'jig jog', suggesting Mediterranean and Arabic slang for copulation; and Paul de Kock, a popular novelist of that time, whose book[73] is in the genre that Molly reads:

> One rapped on a door, one tapped with a knock, did he knock Paul de Kock, with a loud proud knocker, with a cock carracarracarra cock.

In poetic language, meaning is inextricably and fundamentally linked by semantic association to sound. Roman Jakobson writes:

> In a sequence, where similarity is superimposed on contiguity, two similar phonemic sequences near to each other are prone to assume a paronomastic function. Words similar in sound are drawn together in meaning.[74]

A paronym is as noted a word cognate with another, or a word formed from a foreign word. 'Sirens' is woven from interlingual, intermedial, intertextual, paronomastic, punning word play. This mode of writing gives ample space for and requires the reader's active, creative, performative interpretation. A distinguishing characteristic of this writing that enacts a fugal modality is articulation and inscription of an intermedial form of literary language in poetic prose through psychological-linguistic association. In the nexus of this association, implying an intermedial nexus in-between the objective structure of language and the subjective psyche of the individual writer/reader, the fugal flight of imagination takes off. Although he went further in *Finnegan's Wake*, Joyce's *Ulysses* is an example of a unique language work where a writer/reader creatively and actively discovers meanings in poetic language enacted through sound-based rhythms. And *Ulysses* retains its communicability for the reader through organizational structure of the narrative enacted through and in the writing process by the implied author, a fictional narrative transfusion of the actual author, 'Joyce,' at a certain point in place and time. Since in reading *Ulysses*, the reader is required to be an active participant in the creation of meaning from the text, becoming a performer—Joyce's text enacts another aspect of fugal becoming. The reader also becomes a detective, making meaning by tracking down the clues of references scattered through the language, inter-textually, in cultural, social and political events of the time, as well as in Joyce's own life.

JOYCE'S FUGAL 'QUINTET' OF MASTER SINGERS

Joyce was part of an art movement, international avant-garde modernism, which sought to find new ways of expression, new forms of language as an alternative to totalitarian impulses represented in the twin poles of objective scientific rationality and the unified irrational language of mythologizing ideology. By extension, writers sought an alternative form of creative articulation and expression, to representation. The significance of Joyce's use of musicalization- in criticism of mythologizing is that music is the only art form that is fully non-representational. Therefore, it can be seen to be potentially the most free form of creative articulation, free from overt ideology and social conditioning—although music has been used for precisely the opposite (as discussed in the next chapter on Paul Celan). Wolf cites 'contextual evidence repeatedly highlighted by critics' of the 'oral comment' made by Joyce to his friend George Borach (mentioned earlier), where he mentions that there is a 'quintet' in his fugue in 'Sirens', 'as in the *Meistersinger*, my favourite Wagner opera'.⁷⁵ Luening reveals that Joyce disliked Wagner's operas which he found 'ripe for ridicule' and Joyce and Luening often did cafe impersonations of the 'Ride of the Valkyries', in Zurich.⁷⁶ Luening adds that *Die Meistersinger* was, indeed, the one he preferred of Wagner's operas, meaning it was the only one he found tolerable, which gives a rather different perspective to the businessman Borach's many times repeated recollection of his conversation with Joyce.⁷⁷

Wolf, who like Brown after him, also queries the depth of Joyce's musical knowledge asks what a quintet might have to do with fugue?'⁷⁸ In my interpretation it is clear the *quintet* comprises the five characters drinking and singing in the bar, and saloon, who are amalgamated into the reference: 'Lid-De-Cow-Ker-Doll'. Joyce subtly, intertextually, and comically alludes to the *Meistersinger* characters through the depiction of the men's characters, and their singing. In German traditional culture, a Meistersinger was a superior 'guilds man' who had a trade, and sang. There were important singing contests, which the dramatic action of the *Meistersinger* is set around. There are evocations of this in a carnivalesque way in the Ormond bar where the singers are men united through culture, professionals, and clergy (Father Cowley) and they sing. They start a singing session, a kind of informal song contest, around the piano in the Ormond.

Years after *Ulysses* was published, *Meistersinger* was one of the works used in Nazi propaganda, and, after this, Paul Celan refers to 'master', and 'meister', in a different way in *Deathfugue*. Joyce's intermedial use of language—and specifically his use of the musical fugue form—was a conscious intentional experiment, invoked within the social and cultural context of modernism, which due to the depths of insight and understanding of his pacifist beliefs wove through his writing, in a radically non-totalitarian, and anti-nationalist, anti-fascist way.

Joyce wrote a revolutionary pacific narrative that reconfigures a classical text of European civilization, and parodies the heroic myth; enacting an anti-violent alternative, that records the details and wonder of everyday life lived by ordinary people. In poetic, fluid, musicalized language Joyce articulated a sense of humor and absurdity, through the sensations of the lived body and the fragmentary impressions of the emotional mind and the deep primal themes that run throughout a person's life, influencing them in many unconscious ways. Experimenting with, and inventing radical techniques of modernist literary art, Joyce, perhaps unconsciously, wrote the ontological, existential, fugal music of being—and nothingness.

Transposing musical sound and form in literary language, is an attempt to free the signifier, and open new kinds of possible readings and interpretations of the sign for the reader; an intermedial mode of language which consciously recognizes and plays on language's multiplicity of sign-interpretation, and enables and also invites readers to be creative interpreters and performers of the spoken text.

All of these meaning can be heard, in the **stretto maestrale** section of 'Sirens'. As I said earlier, a *stretto maestrale* is one in which the subject survives the overlapping of subject and answer. In *Ulysses* this suggests too an allusion to the *Meistersinger*, here parodically the voices of the stretto are sung by the quintet of 'master singers'. Bloom has suffered a *setback* of being cuckolded by Boylan, and is betrayed by Molly. Bloom steels himself to the calls of the singers (rebellion), and women in the form of the barmaids, and Martha who he does not actually visit, and a woman in the laneway as he walks away from the hotel. In the **rovescii antesi**/*retrograde reversal.* His *backhand, answer back*, is in his resistance, though things are *back the front*, with Ireland under colonial rule, and another man off to see his wife, he continues on his way, his dialogue of metaphorical *knitting*, a *backwards purl stitch*, which is somewhat like a fugue in a recursive figurative image, a **tela contrappuntistica**/*contrapuntal web* to which analogies of knitting may apply. Bloom hears the seductive calls of 'sirens on the rocks', as did Ulysses (Odysseus), of rebellion, and romance, and he continues on his way. The subject theme remains intact.

In the cod-*cadence* part of 'Sirens' Joyce displays, again, his musical facility, in likening of the 'master singers' in the Ormond, to notes on a diatonic scale, 'First Lid, De, Cow, Ker, Doll, a fifth'. His nicknames recall the solfege scale (Do, Re, Mi, Far, So, La, Te, Do). Elaborating on the names: 'Lidwell, Si Dedalus, Bob Cowley, Kernan and Big Ben Dollard.' The names are arranged from the Tonic (Scale Degree 1—'Lid' or 'Lidwell'), to the Dominant (Scale Degree 5—'Doll' or 'Big Ben Dollard'): Joyce's quintet.

The narrator then mentions Robert Emmett's last words as 'Seven last words'. Added to the five notes or semitones of Lidwell, Si Dedalus, Bob Cowley, Kernan, and Ben Dollard—Lid-De-Cow-Ker-Coll—the added seven 'syllables' make up twelve-tones of the chromatic scale. *When my country takes her place among.* This succession of tones could be seen as a free interpretation of the term **blocchi d'armonia**/*blocks of harmony*. Followed by the **rovescii antesi**/*retrograde reversal.*

Throughout 'Sirens' Joyce uses chromaticism, in his plays on words.

He reverses the solemnity of the song of the decoy, of the croppy boy, with the carnivalesque 'wind' sounds of farting. Bloom's extended flatulence is the **pedale**/*pedal point* (the sustained tone, in the bass, which begins on a consonance and sustains or repeats in dissonance, which resolves back to a consonance, and which is often found towards the end of fugues, though usually played in a different way). *An unseeing stripling stood in the door* after tapping with his cane through the streets. But he did not see the sirens-barmaids or the chorus of drinkers. He was blind and did not see. This stripling, the blind piano-tuner, come back for his tuning fork, represents the implied author Joyce, who had eyesight problems and used a cane. (He did not really see because he was not there, but he saw in his imagination, a play on the 'real' and 'tonal' answer, in the writer's fugue). He heard, and felt, instead. He heard the words of Emmett, interwoven with the flatulence of Bloom, and boisterous talk of the drinkers, in a poignant comment of desperate irony on his country.

↭ 10

PAUL CELAN
AFTER THE DEATHFUGUE

In focusing on the aesthetic of musicalization, and therefore the language, of literary narratives there is a danger of avoiding the—often painful—ideological content of the literary works and the reasons for their writing which may be interpreted in an analysis which does not focus explicitly on language. Although it is important and useful to consider both aspects, their tensions are perhaps most usefully read as a kind of counterpoint in developing a complex compositional understanding of the work. Aesthetic musical form and ideological, or individual psychological content are most usefully seen to work in counterpoint, in fugal literary narratives, and analyzed on this basis.

To understand the language uses, and the struggles of those who were directly involved in the Holocaust, as victims, and the intergenerational impacts of the trauma of a catastrophe such as the Holocaust, we may consider the fugue poems of Paul Celan, *Todesfuge*, and Sylvia Plath, whose *Little Fugue* is a homage to *Todesfuge*. In these poems, the Holocaust is addressed in terms of language, culture, music, and in the deep affect of the poets.

Sylvia Plath is included in this discussion, for although, of course, her trauma was not of the same kind as Celan's it was less direct, she exemplifies the inter-generational impacts of this horror, and from the family perspective of the German-Austrian peoples, and her life also was impacted by migration. Her work is a highly significant politically, as it shows the struggle of women to speak, to articulate their voices, and inner feelings, in the public cultural realm, which preceded and helped to trigger the movement of second wave feminism, of women writing and making art about and of their own everyday lives. Plath, a mother of two young children, aged three and less than one, had been deserted by her husband, and was living with their infants in a flat in

London, in the coldest winter on record, the pipes froze, she was not able to take a bath (the way she relaxed) and tragically she took her life, putting her head in a gas oven. In the months of depression leading up to her death she wrote some of western feminism's most influential poems, inspiring women to write of the 'pigsties' of personal political experience and their daily life, as Cixous put it, as legitimate material for literature. Her poem *Little Fugue*, published in Ariel, was amongst her last poems.

To understand the language uses of the authors in the cases I have researched, one needs to also research the social and cultural dimensions of the lives of the authors. There is a personal, social and cultural dimension to the process and experience of writing and all dimensions come into effect, experienced in different ways by the writer in the creation of a significant new work. The traumatic themes of loss, and desire for restitution of what has been lost, and the function of the process of writing as a kind of working through of the trauma, or an escape, or even as a form of healing, is seen in these works.

BLACK MILK

Celan was born Paul Antschel in 1920, in Chernivtsi (Czernowitz), to Jewish-Romanian German-speaking parents, just after the dissolution of the Austro-Hungarian empire and formation of Romania. He grew up speaking Romanian and German. At school he spoke Romanian. But at home his mother insisted they speak High German, a language of literature and philosophy. Celan who studied medicine briefly in Paris was studying Romance philology at the University of Czernowitz when Russia invaded Bukovina in 1940. John Felstiner's biography, *Paul Celan: Poet, Survivor, Jew* (1995), documents that when Nazis began to deport Jews two years later, Celan's parents refused to go into hiding despite his efforts to persuade them, and one night were deported to death camps. His father died of typhus and his mother was shot in the back as she was deemed unfit to work. Celan was imprisoned in a forced-labour camp where he had to shovel and build roads; he survived the Holocaust, by escaping the camp, and joining the Red Army.

At the end of the war he moved to Bucharest, and began to publish poems. Celan's first poem was first published, as *Tangoul Mortii* (Tango of Death), in a Romanian translation by his friend Petre Solomon, in the Bucharest magazine, *Contemporanul* in 1947, with an editorial note explaining that it was 'built upon the evocation of a real fact. In Lublin, as in many other 'Nazi death camps', one group of the condemned men were forced to sing nostalgic songs while others dug graves.' Felstiner writes that violinists in the camp were forced to play a new tango with new lyrics called 'Death Tango', during marches, grave diggings, tortures and executions. Before the camp was liquidated by the SS the orchestra was shot.[1]

Celan wrote the poem in German and his original version appeared in his first poetry collection *De Sand au den Urnen* (The Sand from the Urns), published in Vienna in 1948 by A. Sexl. It had a very small print run. The collection was republished as *Mohn und Gedächtnis*, (Poppy and Memory), by Deutsche Verlags-Anstalt, and this included *Todesfuge*. In 1948 he moved in Paris, where he studied German philology and literature. He married the graphic artist Gisele de Lestrange, and they had a son. In 1959 he took up the post of Reader in German Language and Literature at L'Ecole Normal Superieure at the University of Paris, which he held until his death in 1970.

Deathfugue is a poem of mourning. Celan uses musicalized poetic formalization to confront and articulate his sense of loss and sorrow and anger at the devastation of the unspeakable barbarity of the death. His letters show that Celan was haunted by guilt that he was unable to save his parents from deportation by the fascists, although he had warned them, they refused to go into hiding, as they had faith in the city authorities; he was hiding, then he was also sent to a camp. Bearing witness, contained anger, and enormous sadness resound throughout the poem. The repetition and recurring motifs articulate the horror of her silent absence, the unspeakable betrayal by the barbarous representatives of the country his beloved mother associated with learning and culture.

Deathfugue begins with the line, 'Black milk of daybreak we drink it at dusktime'. This line is repeated at the start of four of the poems stanzas, indicating that this is a four-part fugue. The second third and fourth lines alter the melody line to 'Black milk of daybreak we drink you at night'. The metaphorical reference conjures up associations with poisoned breast milk. Felstiner interprets this as an allusion to 'bittersweet' inversions of sustenance 'nullifying the nourishment vital to humankind', and he observes that the motif of 'black milk may not be a metaphor at all but a liquid that camp inmates were given'.[2] The symbolic milk of the 'motherland' may have a wider application in the poem to culture. What was life giving and sustaining has become black and poisonous, the bearer of death not life. 'Black milk' symbolizes the cruel mothertongue of German culture gone mad. The association of drinking with the mouth and with ingesting culture through language is fused in this surrealist image. Black milk can also be associated with the horror of deaths occurring at night; in the actual night, and in the metaphorical nightmare of the Holocaust's systematic insanity. There is also a sense in which the prisoners are being forced to symbolically drink each other in death, to drink in the deaths, to shovel their dead fellows into mass graves in the morning.

> we shovel a grave in the air where you lie not close

This refers to the ovens in which the dead were incinerated.

Celan's poem conjures up images of two women, the two subject lines of the fugue, one German, one Hebrew; their fates horribly intertwined in the unspeakable counterpoint of racial genocide.

He refers to the woman who is spared as the 'golden haired Margarete', 'goldenes Haar Margarete' the complicit female counterpart to Death who is 'a meister aus Deutschland'. In the German, Margarete's 'Haar' sounds like Herr meaning sir or master, a reference to the significance of commanding respect of hair color in the unspeakable racialized hierarchy of death in the mad system of the Nazis. The other symbolic woman referred to has the Hebrew name of Sulamith (from the Biblical *Song of Solomon*) and she has dark hair, ashen hair, symbolizing her death, her hair burning to ashes in the graveyard of the sky. This terrible metaphor signifies, the horrific enormous absence of the losses of the death camps, and the unspeakable pain of Celan's loss of his mother. The poem ends with a counterpoint of subject lines of the hideous *Deathfugue*:

> dein goldenes Haar Margarete
> dein aschenes Haar Sulamith

German and Jewish, were grotesquely interwoven in a totalitarian hierarchy of death. The significance and meaning of these last two lines has been questioned and interpreted differently by critics. Felstner considers the question that there may be some effect of restitution on the counterpoised image of the two women, Aryan and Hebrew. Might this represent a form of reconciliation so that he may continue to use without unbearable pain and guilt the German language of the writers and poets, such as Rilke and Trakl, whom Felstiner says he continued to read after the war. Felstiner rejects this, observing, *Deathfugue*

> ends purely, by doing what Nazism attempted to forbid, naming the other. Archaic, inalienable, truly Sulamith has the last word, not to mention the silence resounding after.[8]

Her 'Haar', whilst flying into the sky as ash, to join the clouds, remains pure and worthy of respect and love.

He continued to use German to write poetry after the war, Celan uses the language to name and immortalize the other, to memorialize the atrocities, madness of orders. In *Motivated Irrationality* (1984) David Pears writes of depersonalized systematic madness as 'motivated irrationality'. By writing about the horror this madness produced in German, Celan performs a reflexive act of catharsis and memorialization (and negative dialectic, allowing change through criticism). This also performs the function of making his poetry accessible to German readers. Felstiner notes that his continued use of German to write his poems was questioned, but it is possible that the debate about Celan's continued usage of the German language, and significance of multiple language use has been distorted. He came from a province where multiple languages are spoken. The main language groups in Romania when he was growing up: Ukrainian, Romanian, German and Polish.

Bukovina is a province in Eastern Europe that had been part of the German Austrian Empire and is now divided between the Ukraine and Romania. During the war it was fought over by Russia and Austria and was ceded to Romania when Austria lost the province (with the dissolution of the German and Austro-Hungarian empires) in the Treaty of St Germain. After the end of World War I in Europe, in the efforts to tackle the 'minorities problem' in the areas of the former German and Austro-Hungarian Empires, the 'stability strategy' of Western powers was focused on the replacement of the former multinational empires with more or less homogenous nation-states. Yet unlike the new states Germany was not required to sign the 'Minority Treaties' designed to safeguard the interests of the minorities in the new nation states.[4]

After the Paris Peace Conference of 1919, there were over 9 million ethnic Germans in Romania, Poland, Yugoslavia and Czechoslovakia. Following the economic and political crisis of 1929 that destroyed the

Weimar Republic, and brought Hitler to power,[5] he pursued a policy of totalitarian German *revanchism* (French 'revancha' meaning revenge, applied to political policy of retaliation in this case to recover 'lost' territory), a form of *irrendentism* (from the Italian 'irrendento' meaning 'unredeemed', refers to political or popular movements intending to reclaim and reoccupy a 'lost' area). It led to Hitler's totalitarian '*Heim ins Reich*' ('Back to the Reich') foreign policy which led to the Holocaust, and World War 2. During the unification of Germany in 1871, 'Greater Germany' (Grossdeutschland) referred to a German nation comprising the German Empire and Austria. 'Lesser Germany' referred to a hypothetical German state without Austria. The terms were from the (now reignited)[6] 19th century debate known as The German Question over the best way to achieve Germany's unification. 'Greater Germany' was later used by some to refer to a hypothetical larger state comprising pre-World War I Germany, Austria and the Sudetenland. The Nazi ideology of the Third Reich developed, after World War 1, from Hitler's *revanchism*, to 'bring home' all Germans outside Germany in an 'all-German Reich'. This led to the Munich Agreement (1938) in which areas of Czechoslovakia inhabited mainly by people born in Germany, were ceded to Germany. This was followed by the Anschluss of 1938, where through political and populist deceptions, and faked telegrams, and invasion, the Nazis annexed Austria. This triggered World War II, with the next expansion, the invasion of Poland in 1939, which caused England and France to join the war.[7]

Hitler's Nazi foreign policy of *Heim ins Reich* included mass uprooting and forced migration both of Germans, and the occupants of the areas whose properties, homes, lands, and businesses were seized for the Germans. At the same time was the concurrent genocide policy of creating 'Judenfrie' areas: which resulted in the genocidal murder of six million Jews (recent research estimates it was far higher), through concentration camps, gassing, mass murder, where local people were co-opted to shoot and bury thousands of Jews and gypsies. Grotesquely, fairgrounds were where gas vans would be used to gas large numbers of mothers and children.[8] In Nazi terminology and propaganda *Heim ins Reich* referred to the former territories of the Holy Roman Empire, a vast multi-ethnic complex of lands in central and western Europe from 800-1806 that included Germany, Burgundy, Italy and Bohemia. The ambitions for expansion were to continue eastwards into Poland,

Baltic states, and the Soviet Union, making a new Germany from the North Sea to the Urals. In 1940 Chernivtsi was occupied by Soviets, but in 1941 the Romanian and German fascists returned, Romania was a fascist regime under General Antonescu, who had just been given a strip of land he renamed Transnistria, in return for support in Hitler's invasion of the Soviet Union.[9]

In 1941 Antonescu deported the Jews from northern Bukovina and capital city Chernivtsi (Czernowitz) in Romania where Celan's family lived. 100,000 (most of the population) were deported from Chernivtsi and killed in labour camps, Celan's parents among them. In 1944 the Red Army of the Soviets invaded again to counter the atrocities and stem the advance of the Nazis. Chernivski was occupied by Soviet troops; at the end of WW2 it was annexed, and is now part of Ukraine.[10]

When Celan was growing up, there was a flexibility regarding educated and vernacular language use in Eastern European countries that made it usual for individuals to learn regional and national languages. Whereas Romanian and Ukrainian were minority languages German was a national language with an extensive literature. When Celan was asked why he chose to use the language of German to write poetry in, the language of the people who murdered his mother, Celan defended his use of the language he grew up speaking, as his 'mother tongue'.[11] In effect his use of German was a form of fugal counterpoint, of answering back.

'DEATH IS A MEISTER FROM GERMANY'

Before analyzing the poem in terms of its fugue form it is necessary to note the significance, and ambiguity, of Celan's use of the word meister in *Deathfugue*'s oft-quoted line, '*Death is ein Meister aus Deutschland*'. In English translations meister has been translated as 'master', for instance in Felstiner's translation (2001). Recently, *meister* is translated as 'gang boss', in Jerome Rothenberg's translation (2005)

Neither translation fully encompasses the ambiguity and subtlety of meaning of the German 'meister'. 'Master' is inadequately dimensioned. In German there is no equivalent term for the English 'master'. A meister in German relates to a craftsman, who has attained a level of high proficiency, and that meaning has entered the English language as 'master craftsman'. The closest translation of *meister* into English is 'gentleman', although in contemporary Germany this usage now has an old fashioned air. Although its general cultural usage has lapsed, it was used in German in relation to groups of men, somewhat ironically or jovially, addressing friends or mates, as 'gentlemen'.[12] The term Meister has fallen from general use and has not been much used for the past fifty years. Celan gave the term, which had been in cultural use before and during the war, a euphemistic dimension that acknowledges the unspeakable depravity unleashed in the concentration of death camps, by 'gentlemen' *aus Deutschland*. Through using 'meister'; in this context Celan introduces the twisted ambiguity in the meaning of the German 'gentleman'. The term might appear to evoke manners and culture, yet that 'gentleman' brings barbaric death with gentlemanly 'mastery'. The use of the term gentleman implies a significant irony of euphemism, in contrast to the interpretation of 'meister' as 'gang-boss' in Rothenburg's translation. Gang-boss straightforwardly implies a thug. This omits the Faustian complexity of Celan's use that implicitly references the devil as 'gentleman'. Celan is therefore making a point of abysmal irony about fascism, its appearance belying its barbarous, murderous cruelty, like the appearance of Goethe's devil in *Faust*.

This line from *Deathfugue* has migrated into the German culture. Although this euphemistic usage may not be widely known in English, '*Death is a gentleman from Germany*', and the term '*German gentleman*' in reference to Nazis or fascists, has, in some instances, unofficially passed into German language use. It has currency, severed from its origins, by language users who may be unaware of Celan's poem. (Conversation with Philip Mann, January 2006).[13] And there is evidence of this use in understood English. For example, in Harold Pinter's 1966 British film *The Quiller Memorandum*, an adaptation of Elleston Trevor's novel, in which a British spy in Berlin attempts to infiltrate a neo-Nazi gang, the gangleader refers to himself euphemistically as a 'German gentleman'. This shows the justification of Rothenburg's translation as 'gang boss' which however reaches but one aspect of its meaning. It is an acknowledgment of the 'ambiguity' cultivated by Nazis who wished to cloak their barbaric motives in a veneer of 'gentlemanly' male camaraderie and mateship. Rothenburg's translation strips away the glamour and mystique of fascism's facade, and depicts the 'meister' as a straightforward thug. We can ask if Celan's use of language in *Todesfuge* including his use of *meister* fulfills the criteria for linguistic elements that Deleuze and Guattari theorize as 'intensives or tensors', expressing:

> inner tensions of language... marking a movement of language toward its extremes, toward a reversible beyond or before...a move towards the limit of a notion or a surpassing of it...master-words, verbs, or prepositions that assume all sort of senses; prenominal or purely intensive verbs as in Hebrew; conjunctions, exclamations, adverbs; and *terms that connote pain.*

These are found in 'accents that are interior to words, their discordant function.' They suggest 'minor literature' develops these tensors or intensives.[14] In Derrida's essay 'Shibboleth for Paul Celan' he argues that Celan's poetry with its polyphonic meanings becomes a cipher, which readers cannot fully understand.[15]

DEATHFUGUE'S STRUCTURE

A transposition of the structure of a musical fugue can be read in *Deathfugue*. The themes are developed through the use of fugal techniques including repetition, thematic variation and recurring motifs. There are two subject themes—Jew and German. The subject themes are developed through counterpoint and are represented by two symbolic women: 'dein goldenes Haar Margarete' (golden haired Margarete); 'dein aschenes Haar Sulamith' (ashen-haired Sulamith). The subject 'voices' are: 'black milk' (which the Jews are forced to drink), 'we-Jews', 'ein meister aus Deutschland', and 'dein goldenes Haar Margarete'. Margarete, is doubled with Sulamith who is also represented by her absence in relation to Margarete. Her name is not stated—signifying the absence, loss through murder of the Jewish woman who is symbolically stands for Celan's mother (and by extension all Jewish women, all Jewish mothers murdered in the genocide). Through each of the poem's stanzas the subject themes of fugue are developed contrapuntally by the voices using fugal techniques of development, including repetition, elaboration, distortion, inversion, mirroring. How does Celan do this? He quite formally follows contrapuntal structure of a musical fugue using fugue techniques of counterpoint, recurring motifs transposed into melodic, rhythmic written language. A fugue begins with a statement of the subject themes. In the development of the fugue, the voices develop the themes contrapuntally in variations on the subject theme, to produce a complex polyphonic counterpoint, ending in a cadence and coda.

How can a fugue work musically in *Deathfugue?* The subject themes are: Jew and German. In the first stanza each voice makes its entry in turn. I list here the voices in some cases in an abbreviation of the form in which they are introduced in the poem (for instance the Black milk is in the poem a two-line voice).[1]

> 1) 'Black milk of daybreak we drink it at evening' (Black milk)
>
> 2) 'we shovel a grave in the air where you lie not close (we Jews)
>
> 3) 'A man lives in the house he plays with his snakes he writes/ he writes when darkness falls over Deutschland *dein goldenes Haar Margarete* (Margarete- the bitch)
>
> ...he writes '*id*' and steps from the House and the stars are all flashing he/ whistles his dogs to come ('meister')

Voices one ('meister' 'black milk') and two ('we'— Jews) represent the Jewish theme. 'Voices' played as three (meister) and four (Margarete) represent the German subject-theme. In each of the stanzas, four voices enter in a different fugal variation. For instance, in the next stanza these become:

> 1) Black milk of daybreak we drink you at night
> 2) *dein aschnenes haar Sulamith* we shovel a grave in the air/ where you lie not close
> 3) A man lives in the house he plays with his snakes he writes
> 4) he writes when darkness falls over Deutschland *dein goldenes Haar/ Margarete*

In the next stanza the voices state:

> 1) Black milk of daybreak we drink you at night
> [Development]: we drink you at midday and morning we drink you at evening
> 2) we drink and drink
> 3) a man lives in the house 4) *dein goldenes Haar Margarete/dein ashenes Haar Sulamith* he plays with his snakes

Here the voices are fugally broken up, shortened and run together in a more emotionally frantic stretto of counterpoint. I should point out that the 'black milk' line is developed in each reference to cover two lines, as I have indicated here, but abbreviating in this analysis to show the specific technique.

1 My translation

In the next stanza, the four voices state:

1) Black milk of daybreak we drink you at night
2) Death is a 'gentleman from Germany' his eye is blue

The voice that Celan most criticises is 'Death is a meister aus Deutschland his eye is blue':

> he shoots you with lead bullets   shoots you strictly on cue
> a man lives in the house *dein goldenes haar Margarete*

Celan reflects on the power of the 'meister' and makes moral allusions that refer to sex and evil in the phrase plays with his snakes:

> he rushes his dogs on us, deems us a grave in the air
> he plays with his snakes and dreams
> der Tod es eine *meister aus Deutschland*

Finally the Jewish 'we' voice enters, pushed out of turn, by the German gang-boss of Death. As the poem proceeds, the 'we' voice of the Jews is literally pushed out of the poem by the voices of the German gang-boss meister Death. In technical terms, the 'we' Jewish voice is replaced by the gang-boss German voice (with reference to the fantasy of 'golden-haired' Margarete). Each of the stanzas opens with the voices. Development occurs, differently in stanzas as the voices elaborate their themes. This builds up the meaning and content of the poem through a rhythmic series of variations. After voices enter they develop variations on the themes:

> He shouts peck deeper into the Dirt-Reich you lot the rest of you sing
> and play act/ he clutches the iron rod on his belt he swings it his eyes
> are so blue

The lines of stanza 7 give this fugal development:

> He calls play sweeter to Death that Death is a *meister* aus
> Deutschland
> he shouts mark darkly your strings you'll rise up in smoke to the sky/
> you'll then have a grave in the clouds where you'll lie not close

This is followed by the next stanza with its last lines:

> he rushes his dogs on us, deems us a grave in the air
> he plays with his snakes and dreams

der Tod es eine *meister aus Deutschland*.

This is followed by the coda of comparison of two women, one pure the other deeply corrupted and corrupt:

> your golden-hair Margarete
> your ashen hair Sulamith

Sulamith enters in the stanzas in counterpoint to Margarete. Her ashen hair indicates that Sulamith is dead. She has been murdered by the meister, who favours golden-haired Margarete, suggesting a Faustian-style pact. Margarete has sold her soul to the devil, in order that her life be spared. Linguistically Sulamith then appears in the stanzas two and three, as an echo, a cloud, like the ashen shadow of conscience, of absence against the living golden-haired Aryan woman. She is dead but she has not disappeared, she exists as a memory, as an absence, which shadows Margarete. Sulamith is absent again in the next stanzas. The next reference to Margarete is singular 'your golden hair Margarete'. But in the coda Sulamith overtakes her, and literally is the last word.

> your golden hair Margarete
> your ashen hair Sulamith

Using this fugal technique of counterpoint of motifs Celan brilliantly manages to speak the unspeakable, to write silence, to make absence presence. He thus evokes the power of memory that holds what is lost as a form of presence. Sulamith will not be forgotten; her memory will not disappear. And in death as in life, in contrast with Margarete, the meister's muse, Sulamith remains uncorrupted.

Fugal musicalization is also evident in the rhythms and varied thematic repetitions of his melody lines. The repetition of the poems images echoes the repetition of shoveling, the shoveling of the grave-diggers, Celan's own forced role in the hell of the slave labor camps. This fugal structure shows very effectively how a literary fugue, like a musical fugue, can juxtapose and articulate voices—in counterpoint, which enacts a complex relationship between the voices, here echoing and suggesting the contrapuntal relationships of life and death.

Celan's use of poetic fugal musicalization, in this poem, is crucial to its effectiveness in articulation of the unspeakable. Leonard Olschner has commented:

> '*Todesfugue* represents an attempt to order the unorderable, to grasp

the perfidy of the murder machinery, and also to define a mode of expression, to exorcise the language—German, the language of his mother and his mother's murderers'.[16]

Whereas words alone cannot ever be adequate to express unspeakable horror, the emotive power of music may give expression and release to repressed emotion. Techniques of musicalization in writing may also assist in the performance of this cathartic function. This supports the Aristotelean observation about the emotionally cathartic function of both music and tragic drama. Aristotle recommended poets use the structure of plot as a way of unifying dramatic narratives.

In *Deathfugue,* Celan imposes the unity of order on the unspeakable horror of his poems content through his techniques of fugal musicalization. Using rhythm, repetition, recurring motifs and counterpoint here gives the poet a way to write about the unspeakable, to give voice to the horror, and convey through the emotive powerful rhythmic and melodic effects of the musical fugue, the unspeakable *Deathfugue* of the death camps of Nazi Germany. The very objectivity of musicalization thereby provides a means of voicing the almost incomprehensible suffering and loss of a subjectivity alienated, displaced and numbed by horror. Yet the reference to the musical fugue also does more than this. It alludes to another act of atrocity practiced by depraved commandants of the death camps. They ordered the musician-prisoners to sing, play musical instruments and dance as they were forced to shovel the dead into the mass graves. In Celan's poem it is the *meister* who has that role. (The meister who is in collusion with golden-haired Margarete to whom he 'writes when its nightfall nach Deutschland your golden hair Margarete').

In the black night the Nazi commander symbolically romanticizes, and writes to the golden haired woman. In the daytime;

> He commands us to play up for the Dance

It is useful to note here, as background to Celan's musical themes, the uses and functions of 'music of the holocaust' that Philip Rosen and Nina Abfelbaum document in *Bearing Witness: A Resource Guide to Literature Poetry, Art, Music and Videos by Holocaust Victims and Survivors* (2002). Accounts of over 800 people in this book show that music is 'deeply intertwined in the religious and cultural aspects of Jewish life'. Throughout the horrors of the holocaust, in the ghettos and the death camps, the Jewish people kept their music alive.

Many prominent musicians and composers were put into concentration camps by the Nazis, including Viktor Ullmann, Gideon Klein, Robert Brok, Egon Ledec, Alice Herz-Sommer, Hans Krása, Rafael Schachter, and Alma Boset (Gustav Mahler's niece). They were taken to the so-called 'Model ghetto' of Theresienstadt, where the SS commanders ordered them to compose operas, concerts and reviews for the International Red Cross. This was a facade, and some of the artists and musicians attempted to send out messages, including paintings. Composers continued to compose and produced works prolifically to be played by the orchestras in the camps, and some saw their time as an opportunity to practice and provide pleasure for the inmates with the beauty of their playing, write Philip Rosen and Nina Abfelbaum.

Compositions created in Theresienstad numbered amongst them fugues, Gideon Klein's *Fantasia and Fugue* for string quartet, and Hans Krása's *Passacaglia and Fugue* for violin, viola and cello. When the Red Cross came to inspect the ghetto, Hans Krása was asked to compose a piece to play. What he performed was the children's opera *Brundibár*, a covert message to the Red Cross to think of the children. As a result, he was deported to Auschwitz and killed, write Rosen and Apfelbaum. Nearly all of these musicians and composers were in 1944 deported to Auschwitz where they were murdered; *Bearing Witness* is a memorial to their spirit.

In the ghettos, people invented new lyrics for traditional melodies, Rosen and Apfelbaum write this was in the Jewish tradition of re-inventing lyrics for well-known melodies to keep up their inner strength and spirit.[17] The ghetto songs documented lives and conditions of those who were interned. Many of these songs and compositions have been recorded including songs written and sung by members of the Jewish Underground in the Vilna Ghetto, and Hirsch Glik of the Vilna Ghetto composed martial music inspired by young people involved in the Warsaw Ghetto Uprising.[18] Amongst the most poignant contributions to this communal elegy are the songs sung and written by Jewish children in the ghettos of Eastern Europe.

In the extermination camps the SS ordered the prisoner-musicians into orchestras and forced them to play as the 'fellow inmates went to work or were marched to the gas chambers'. In Auschwitz-Birkenau there were six orchestras, including an all-women orchestra conducted by Alma Boset until her death, and one with 120 performer–inmates. The authors observe that: 'The suicide rate among the musicians was very high'.[19]

The Nazis attempted to control Jewish musical expression but they could not destroy the songs and music of the Jewish people, who continued to sing and play music together, gaining from this a sense of spiritual and emotional strength, Rosen and Abfellbaum write:

> The compositions, lyrics and music written during the Holocaust show that even under the worst, most horrific conditions, a people's desire to bring humanity and beauty to the world shines through. Hitler failed miserably in his efforts to stifle Jewish musicians from creating and performing their music. Although the victims perished in the gas chambers of Auschwitz and the death pits of Ponary, their legacies live on in the poignant music they produced.[20]

In the book is the poignant story of a heroine of the ghettos, folk and opera singer, Liuba Levitska, in the Vilna Ghetto. She sang her most famous song, *Two Little Doves* (written by Y.L. Cahan) in a ghetto-concert soon after the murder of 1,500 Jews who had been interned there. When the Nazis took her to Ponary, outside Vilna, she sang *Two Little Doves* in the death pits, to the end.[21]

This countered the use of music by Nazi commanders. Celan who was forced to work as a shoveller in a labor camp, had heard of such uses of music by the SS and this is the main structural theme of *Deathfugue*. In the poem, like the commanders who ordered musicians to play to block out the sounds of the screams of people being murdered, the *meister*: 'commands us to play for the dance'. At the same time, the meister orders the prisoners to shovel and dig graves for their fellows,

> he shouts peck deeper into the Dirt-Reich you lot the rest of you sing and play-act
> he clutches the iron rod on his belt he swings it his eyes are so blue
> stick deeper the spades you lot the others play up for the Dance

The dance is death. The meister's sword represents phallic aggression. He commands the prisoner's to sing, play, and dance. The people are also referred to by the meister as 'dogs', a term used by the Nazis with sexual connatations:

> he whistles his dogs to come
> he whistles his Jews to arise

Unbearably, the fugal theme continues, the music does not stop:

> He calls play sweeter to Death that Death is a *meister* aus Deutschland
> he shouts mark darkly your strings you'll rise up in smoke to the sky

This implies the musicians who are playing will be the next to burn. In his reference to playing death sweetly, Celan also alludes to an association in German culture of music with death. This is enacted in works such as Schubert's *Erlkonigm*, Wagner's *Liebestod* and Bach's *Komm Susser Tod* (Come Sweet Death). It is (sacrilegiously) to Bach's work that the commander refers when he barks, 'Spielt susser Tod'. This suggests an implicit reference to Bach's fugues, a cultural achievement from a very different era, evoked in the poem's title.

The poem's rhythms and cadences can be read as Celan's attempt to contain and control through poetic expression his feelings about how his mother died. A further interpretation of fugue in the poem evokes the background silence, the amnesiac state of the German people in relation to the deportation of the Jews whilst it was occurring.

There is another aspect of fugue that can be read into the Celan's *Deathfugue*. In his autobiographical novel *Survival in Auschwitz* Primo Levi has documented the amnesiac sleepwalker state of the occupants of the concentration death camps. They were referred to in Auschwitz slang as *Musselmanner* or 'non-men'. (Oddly translated in Levi's book as 'muslims'). People who were so exhausted by starvation and privation that they became depersonalized and lost all feeling. Levi remembers a haunting image of 'an emaciated man, with head dropped and shoulders curved, on whose face and in whose eyes not a trace of thought is seen'.[22] The terrible challenge facing the camp-prisoners such as Levi, and Celan, was to retain a sense of themselves, their humanity, to not become Musselmanner. They did more than this. Celan escaped and joined the Red Army. Levi has written that he was one of only three survivors of a group of six hundred and fifty. Once freed their survival was confirmed not only (or mainly) through their physical release but by emotional, spiritual and cultural release of their experiences into writing, which created enduring eyewitness testimonials to these horrors.

Nothing could be more shattering than the unimaginable horror of the concentration camps, the demonic apotheosis of depersonalizing trauma. It is in the fugue of art and writing that emerged from these that we are able to know about what happened, the works bear witness. Rosen observes, the only positive side of this unspeakable experience of trauma and horror in the unimaginable dimensions of the holocaust, is enacted in the art and music of the Holocaust which demonstrates the strength of the human spirit to remain human, and, when shattered, to rediscover a sense of self, a new subjectivity through the process of writing —which to some extent may transform and go beyond the primary experience of traumatic shock. (A struggle with the emotionally annihilating forces of depersonalization is echoed in the struggle of all writers who have experienced traumatic shock and are compelled to compulsively write their own experience of fragmentation and alienation). Celan wrote *Deathfugue* when the losses and traumas were still immediately fresh in his experience. For writers who write from experiences of trauma, it may be that the use of musicalization is a form of objectively restoring order to the chaos of emotional devastation, and a way of being able to—consciously or otherwise—approach numbed emotions and reconstitute through language a sense of subjectivity and self—through bearing witness.

The process of writing (and art making) is a way for the traumatized individual of seeking restitution, to reconstitute what has been lost, involving most crucially a lost sense of self. It is the creation of a new sense of subjectivity and self in this process which can make the process of writing about traumatic experiences a cathartic experience for the writer, and also for the reader who in reading poems by Celan, and narratives by Levi, for instance, experiences both an awareness of the atrocities of human cruelty and a reaffirmation of the ability of the human spirit to survive, and in this, what it means to be human.

Conversely, Melanie Klein (1981), Julia Kristeva (1982) and Freud (2003) describe the pathology of they who do not assimilate traumatic experience and whose memories might then recur compulsively in an uncontrollable repetition. Kristeva analyzes the fascination of horror for the subject, in her book *Powers of Horror*. She focuses on the fascination of abjection in terms of an anti-Semitic writer Celine. She sees the importance of attempting to analyze the psychology of fascism and the role universal abjection plays in this. I am more interested in examining the experiences of universal abjection, in the writer's fugue, in relation to writers whose writings stand against totalizing forces including overt manifestations of prejudice and racism which appear in Celine's works. I discuss the works of writers who bear witness to horror, including the cataclysmic horror of the holocaust, through the perspective of the involvement of the 'oppressed'. The writers whose works I have examined in *The Writer's Fugue*, in relation to abjection, have experienced trauma, and have written from their experiences of trauma, developing a subjectivity in the process of their writing which memorializes and testifies to the strength of the individual in resisting totalitarian forces and prejudice, in retaining a sense of humanity despite, and through, the powers of horror.

Walter Benjamin refers to Freud's theories on the effects of trauma on the individual in relation to Baudelaire and the traumatic subjectivity of modernity. Freud's theories on trauma and its effects are also relevant to consider in relation to Celan. In *Beyond the Pleasure Principle* Freud who developed the word-concept, 'traumatic', suggests:

> We may use the term traumatic to describe those excitations from outside that are strong enough to break through the protective barrier; in my view the notion of 'trauma' cries out to be applied to such a case given that the resistance to stimuli is normally so effective. An event such as external trauma will doubtless provide a massive disturbance in the organism's energy system, and mobilize all available defence mechanisms. In the process, however, the pleasure principle is put into abeyance. It is no longer possible to prevent the psychic apparatus from being flooded by large quanta of stimulation; instead a quite different challenge presents itself: to assert control over the stimuli; to physically annex the quanta of stimulation that have burst in, and then proceed to dispose of them.[23]

From another angle, of a writer, this becomes a psychoanalytical of inspiration. The writer flooded by stimuli, in the form of a drive, or partial drive, which may take the form of a mood or be accompanied by a mood, a desire to write, in effect uses the writing process as a way of asserting control over stimuli, to psychically annex the traumatic memories and sensations in the process of writing literary narratives. In an experience of loss associated with trauma, another loss is incurred, the traumatized individual loses their sense of self-identity; they lose awareness of themselves, as Primo Levi has documented.

Taking a Freudian view, Celan's representation of human cruelty and barbarism in *Deathfugue* originated in massive trauma. In writing the poem perhaps, from this perspective, he is seeking to understand and symbolically represent the enormity of the trauma, and articulate his pain and anger. In so doing he rebuilds a sense of subjectivity, from and through his sense of loss, against the numbness of trauma. Writing about trauma is thereby part of the healing process of the overwhelmed psyche. It is part of the process of restoring a balance, or the pleasure principle, in Freudian terms.

Freud suggests, if 'it is a characteristic of drives to restore a prior state, we should not be surprised that so many processes in the psyche take place quite independently of the pleasure principle. This characteristic would automatically be transmitted to each and every partial drive, and in the case of such drives would involve the retrieval of a particular stage of the development process'.[24] The fugal modality of writing literary fugues may then be understood, in this context, as the writer's attempt, through repetition— the repetitive self-based action of writing—to restore a 'prior state', of balance, before traumatic shock led to alienation and displacement. This usage is, perhaps, suggested in Celan's poems through his use of rhythms from lullabies in his allusion to unspeakable horror. The fugal modality of the writing process may thereby be understood as an attempt by the writer to restore the pleasure principal. This idea is evoked in the concept of *jouissance*, in the experience of writing and reading.

Celan understood the redemptive, or at least releasing, function of the fugal modality of writing, but this experience came at great personal cost. Language had fatal significance to Celan. Barbarous citizens of a nation whose literature she had loved murdered his mother who had passionately admired German poetry and writing. The language of the poetry he read and wrote became for Celan forever associated with her loss. A year after he found out about his parents deaths he wrote:

> And can you bear, Mother, as once on a time,
> the gentle, the German, the pain-laden rhyme.

The lines from his poem *Black Flakes*[25] have the soothing rhythm of a lullaby echoing his childhood memories, yet like a Grimm's fairy tale, a lullaby that contained unspeakable horrors. Celan continued to write in German, but the horrifically conflicted legacy of the language of his writing and reading, led him to the belief that language must be set free from history. His work became increasingly experimental, innovative, non representational and deconstructed. He experimented with broken syntax and radical minimalism as he sought to transform silence into words, and convey his fragmented perception of shattering experience of the modern social world. On receiving the Bremen Prize for Literature, in 1958 in his acceptance speech he said:

> Only one thing remained reachable, close and secure amid all losses: language. Yes, language. In spite of everything, it remained secure against loss... But it had to go through its own lack of answers, through terrifying silence, through the thousand darknesses of murderous speech. It went through.[26]

The conflicted fugue of the German and Jewish themes continued through the rest of his life. In 1967 he met the philosopher, Heidegger. As the Rector of Freiburg University Heidegger had spoken in support of, and continued to teach under, Nazi rule. After meeting at a reading Celan gave at the University on July 24 1967, Heidegger invited Celan to visit his home, a hut in Todtnauberg, in the mountains of the Black Forest. This was where Heidegger had run Nazi indoctrination sessions in 1933, writes Pierre Joris, Celan's translator:

> Celan felt uneasy and was not ready to give Heidegger a "Persilschein", a "Persil-passport" i.e. did not want to whitewash the politically compromised philosopher. Celan, at that time, was reading Heidegger's Nietzsche as well as Nietzsche himself, and seems to have thought highly of Heidegger's interpretations.[27]

Despite conflicted feelings, Celan visited Heidegger in his hut. They went for a walk. Celan wrote in Heidegger's guest book. Celan wrote of this in his poem *Todtnauberg*.

> whose name did it record
> before mine?-
> in this book
> the line about
> a hope, today,
> for a thinker's
> urgent word
> to come

Joris suggests that Celan was trying to elicit an apology from Heidegger about his support of the Nazis. Heidegger did not (ever) apologize; and just over two years later, Celan committed suicide, in 1970.

'POETRY AFTER AUSCHWITZ IS BARBARIC'

Adorno later revised his controversial statement, in *Negative Dialectics* he writes: 'Perennial suffering has as much right to expression as a tortured man has to scream; hence it may have been wrong to say that after Auschwitz you could no longer write poems.'[28] He puts this into the context of the guilt of the survivor struggling to find a way to justify living, his survival of a traumatic horror, when others did not. Adorno writes: 'it is not wrong to raise the less cultural question whether after Auschwitz you can go on living- especially one who has escaped by accident, and who by rights should have been killed, may go on living'. He adds: 'His mere survival calls for the coldness, the basic principle of bourgeois subjectivity, without which there could have been no Auschwitz; this is the drastic guilt of him who was spared.[29]

I would respond that we need to change the temperature of acceptable expression of 'bourgeois subjectivity' to be more alive.

Adorno concludes this statement by describing this cold survivor, in post-traumatic shock: 'By way of atonement he will be plagued by dreams such that he is no longer living at all, that he was sent to the ovens in 1944 and his whole existence since has been imaginary...'[30]

Adorno was a survivor of the Holocaust (he was able to escape in time to the U.S.) and many of his friends and community were murdered. Walter Benjamin was one friend and colleague who lost his life, as he was fleeing as an exile with a group from Paris, when the Nazis were searching for him, in 1940 they were stopped on the border of France and Spain, and after being told they could not pass Benjamin swallowed pills he had brought for such a circumstance, to take his own life, rather than be killed, which was in accordance with his philosophy of the heroism of suicide, and suicide as the sign of modernism, and of heroism in a world which oppresses the individual and targets writers, artists, intellectuals, and cultural groups such as in the Shoah. For Benjamin it was a choice between being murdered or committing suicide.

MUSIC AFTER AUSCHWITZ- KLEZMA CHRONOTOPE

Klezmer music, traditional Yiddish folk music which is melody based, and usually played with stringed instruments, violin, cello, mandolin, piano accordion, woodwind, drums, and voice, has passed through the rupture of the Holocaust and is currently undergoing another revival.

As recently as 2015, this is seen in the founding of the Holocaust Survivor Band, comprising two men Saul Dreier, 89, drums, and Reuwen ('Ruby') Sosnowicz, piano accordion; it is based in New York. Mr Dreier, who was interned in three concentration camps, and still bears the tattoo, started the klezmer band inspired by and replaying the klezmer music he grew up with in Poland. They play to large appreciative audiences in nursing homes and public venues, and they have been written about in the media, and have videos on Youtube.[31] In one video Mr Dreier recalls the music in the concentration camps. He talks about being imprisoned with a leading cantor, who would sing, and he would accompany him by banging spoons together. Remembering the camp, he said: "We didn't have nothing to eat, but when we heard music it made us alive." Mr Sosnowicz was a boy during the Holocaust, he was hidden by a Polish farmer and lived with the cows, and had to find food in rubbish bins at night. When the second world war ended he was interned in a displaced persons camps, which is where he began to play accordion. Later he became a professional musician. Music was his recovery. Of music he plays he says: 'The melody makes it sound as if I am living my own life before the Holocaust." In an article in the *New York Times*, accompanying his documentary 'Holocaust Survivor Band', Joshua Z. Weinstein wrote that 'Music has always been a tool of survival for these men.' He described their new klezma music as a "catharsis", and though the band summons up the "bittersweet memories of childhood" it goes beyond that and, as the men say themselves: "it is a celebration of life".

Klezma music is said to have originated in Jewish communities in medieval Eastern Europe. It was popular in Yiddish and Roma communities, as dance music, and played at celebrations such as weddings.

Musical mimesis can be a form of recovery, when all has been lost In the revival of klezma in the 1970s, thirty years or so after the genocide of the holocaust, what many thought had been lost forever, came back. Writing about the klezma revival, Barbara Kirschenblatt-Gimblett likens the music of the klezma revival to chronotope in Bakhtin's use of the concept.[32] That is to say that the music functions in the way that time and space in narratives can function, as a conceptual space and time which the reader, singer, player, listener or dancer can enter and inhabit conceptually in memory and community.

This is a very relevant concept then to peoples from Eastern Europe where the national borders have been redrawn many times displacing entire populations many times over lifetimes. And it is also relevant to migrants, refugees, and exiles, and to Indigenous peoples.

Klezma is relevant to Celan's poetry, and his approach to writing poetry. This is seen in his transformation of fugue music. It is notable in his elliptical minimal approach to creating poetry. He references recognizable lines and titles of ballades and rondeaux, from medieval. poetry. This is most clearly, and cleverly seen in his poem *Eine Gauner-und Ganon*, (Rogue and Gonif's Ditty), which begins with a reference to a poem by the fifteenth-century French lyric poet, Villon, who was in jail on charges of stealing and which he scratched into the wall of his cell awaiting execution, but his life was spared (like Celan) he was exiled, and he disappeared without trace. This punning poem begins by stating the identity (name) and home of Villon. Celan rewrote this poem, giving himself other names/identities, and places to hail from, in letters to friends, before he settled on name and birthplace; showing the struggle to retain identity when the place he came from no longer existed, the maps had been redrawn, as Katjia Garloff discusses in her *Words from Abroad: Trauma and Displacement in Postwar German-Jewish Writers* (2005). In Celan's opening he announces:

> EINE GAUNER-UND GANOVENWEISE (A ROGUES' AND GO-NIFS' DITTY)/GESUNGEN ZU PARIS EMPRES (SUNG AT PARIS NEAR) / PONTOISE/VON PAUL CELAN (BY PAUL CELAN)/AUS CZERNOWITZ BEI/SADOGOA/(FROM CZERNOWITZ NEAR SADAGORA)

The opening appropriation is followed by a quotation from Heinrich Heine's poem *An Edom*, (To Edom). The remainder of the poem interweaves fragments from a sixteenth-century German folk lansquenet song Garloff comments that it is unclear as to whether in his references, and quotations, the lansquenets are being depicted as victims or perpetrators. Is this of relevance to one shade of possible meaning in a word that Celan repeats, *mandelbaum* (almond tree) and varies with invented words, *mandeltraum* (almond dream)? Amongst the words that Celan makes a play on is 'Mandelbaum', or almond tree. Another, in code is *chandelbaum*. Chandel means candle or light in 'Rotwelsch', secret language of thieves and vagabonds, and suggests a menorah, or candelabra, which resembles a tree, comments Garloff. Might this also be a reference to the Mandelbaum Gate in Jerusalem? A former checkpoint between Israeli and Jordanian sectors of Jerusalem, and which between 1948 and 1967 was the only border crossing between the two areas of the divided city, it became a symbol of conflict, and violent contestation, and it was blown up in 1948, before Celan published the poem. It was in the form of a house, the former residence of a Rabbi Mandelbaum, and family, who had to leave when it was taken over as a military checkpoint. Is the reference to 'mandelbaum', a part of a contrapuntal response to reverse the role of Jew as victim to perpetrator? Or was he merely commenting on this (or was this shade of meaning unintended by Celan?)

Celan was the first translator into German of the Russian poet Osip Mandelstam, and given Celan's penchant for playing with sounds, in allusions, it is not too far-fetched to deduce another reference here, as there were certain similarities between the poets, in that Mandelstam was, like Celan, persecuted, and imprisoned.

Affirmed in a last line of the poem, Garloff suggests the word plague 'pest' is a defiant reference to the metaphor, of plague, for fascism in Camus's novel, *The Plague (Le Peste*, in French), as well as the plague of the time that Villon was writing.

Several have commented that given the weight placed by Western literary tradition on originality that the charges of plagiarism against Celan increased his feeling of being persecuted, which was amplified by the criticism of his use of German, at the same time as there was a resurgence of antisemitism that showed the 'tenacity of the antisemitic stereotypes of unproductive, thieving, or parasitic Jews in German culture' as Garloff has pointed out.[33] In *Eine Gauner*, he answered back by calling up the multi-lingual heterogeneity of pre-Holocaust Eastern Europe, in carnivalesque borrowing and quotation, and reinvention[34] of words, which shows how songs and music are shared, learned and passed down, yet sung and played in different ways by the voices, as in a fugue—and in klezma.

This though does not mean that such works that individual authors and poets create are not inventive and original in their own new ways; neither does it imply that they are plagiarized, but that they are forms of language and culture used by individual authors in different ways, like ballads, rondeaux, myths, legends, fairy tales and nursery rhymes.

↪ 11

SYLVIA PLATH
LITTLE FUGUE

Sylvia Plath (1932-1963) was born in Boston to a second-generation American mother, Aurelia Schober Plath, of Austrian descent, and a German father, Otto Plath an entomologist and professor of biology at Boston University; her mother had been his student. He was according to the accounts, a strict authoritarian and his character and death when she was eight (of complications of diabetes) had a profound impact on Sylvia as conjectured in her relationships, and in her poetry. She wrote her first published poem at age eight and a half, on nature, and said in an interview, with Peter Orr, that she wrote from when she was quite small: 'I guess I liked nursery rhymes and I guess I thought I could do the same thing'.[1] She did well academically. She won an internship to work at *Mademoiselle* magazine in New York; but returned to her first breakdown, suicide attempt, and the nightmarish therapy, which she wrote about in her prose and her poems... She recovered, went to Smith, and won a Fulbright scholarship to study at Cambridge, where she taught, and where she met her husband poet Ted Hughes. They had two children; he left her with them, for another woman. In deep depression, after the publication of the semi-autobiographical novel, *The Bell Jar*, she took her life. The poems published in *Ariel* were written in her last nine months.

Sylvia Plath's poem *Little Fugue* evokes implicit symbolic reference to Celan's *Deathfugue*. This is particularly evident in her use of the adjective black, the metaphor of the black yew tree as a metaphor for holocaust barbarity, 'black statements', and death: 'Death opened, like a yew tree, blackly'. Some motifs of Celan's *Deathfugue* echo in *Little Fugue* which makes references to Beethoven's *Grosse Fuge*, as an evocation of an authoritative male figure (Name-of-the-Father) whom she describes as 'Gothic and barbarous, pure German', symbolized as death, echoing Celan's 'meister aus Deutschland'; 'Gothic and barbarous' recalls Rousseau's words of criticism of (new) 'harmony' in his *Complete Dictionary*.[2] Plath's poem was written from a personal distance from the events she references in her imagery, and inverted emotional articulation. Her identification was imaginary, and neurotic; as her father was German, her mother of German-speaking Austrian family, and she was a child growing up in America whilst the Second World War stormed through Europe. In *Deathfugue*, Plath's poems (cf. *Daddy*) continue the interrogation of the themes of the terrible losses and trauma experienced in the camps where Celan and his parents were interned. Plath uses these themes in relation to her troubled relationship with the memory of her father, the shock of whose death, and of her association of him through race, with the Holocaust, when she found out, had impacts which recurred in her life. *Little Fugue* enacts a neurotic melancholic mourning for her father, and for victims of the holocaust, interwoven, in an emotional counterpoint in the (psychologically-charged) symbolic associations in the poem. How does Plath reference *Todesfuge*? I shall briefly discuss this in the context of questions of authenticity, appropriation, and genuine expressiveness, which Plath's use of the fugue form might raise, as it is based on variations on a theme, and these were questions that Celan's *Deathfugue* provoked, as previously discussed in the accusations of plagiarism and legitimacy that were made against him, and proved to be unfounded.

As did Celan, though for different reasons, Plath incurred criticism, though in her case it was posthumous, over the grounds of her 'legitimacy' in writing on the Holocaust.

Little Fugue enacts a fugue through use of contrapuntal imagery of monotones: black (the yew is a symbol of death) and white (clouds). Echoing Celan's use of golden and ashen hair in relation to the symbolic Margarete and Sulamith in his *Deathfugue*, Plath's counterpoint is colour–coded, and references music. It develops through allusions to the piano's white and black keys, suggesting harmonies and dissonant allusions reflexively also through her references to the *Grosse Fuge*, its German spelling suggesting the Name-of-the-Father, with which she, the 'little fugue', his child, is contrapuntally (genetically) interwoven. The subjects of the fugue are therefore Sylvia Plath and her father, or the narrator's memories of a father (suggesting Lacan's symbolic Law of the Father). There is another echo of *Deathfugue* in the underlying mourning motives in Plath's poem. Celan's fugue mourns his mother.

Plath's poem is an elegy, of savage biting irony, mourning the loss of a symbolic benevolent and caring father, in the 'Fatherland'. Allusions to *Todesfuge* in *Little Fugue* include reference to the Death-meister's 'blue eye', an image of incinerated dead prisoners as white (ash) clouds in the sky, and music. Celan uses *Deathfugue* as his title and alludes to a piece of music in his reference to the title of Bach's *Come Sweet Death*. Plath refers to Beethoven's romantic work *Grosse Fuge*, far more emotional in range than fugues are generally thought of, which likely influenced Plath's choice of this particular fugue, or it might have been the title, and the allusion to German high culture.

The two subjects lines, the narrator and the dead father, are developed by a number of voices. The narrator's father is portrayed as the 'Death meister' through recurring motifs, of images developed from the image of the 'black yew', such as: black, white, yew hedge, fugue music, in: blind pianist, Beethoven, tumult of keys, you (father's) voice, orders, silence (inversion of music).

Little Fugue's narrator's fingers identify with the 'blind pianist'. She is the blind pianist, with the blind smile who can hear Beethoven, who says 'I envy the big noises, /the yew hedge of the Grosse Fuge.'

A coda occurs in the last two stanzas. The fugue is circular and in the last stanza the symbolic allusions from the beginning, developed throughout the fugue, are drawn together and their symbolic meaning is made clear in their associative relationship as perceived in the narrator's emotional psychology. The clouds are white, this suggests the ash of the ovens referred to in Celan's poems, where the ash of clouds, forms the graveyard in the sky. The narrator sees her dead father as a yew tree (symbolic of death in Europe, and the trees found in graveyards) beneath the white clouds. Both are 'senseless' in their own ways.

There are things that the poem's narrative voice does not want to know. That she is covering up in her surface descriptions of 'featurelessness'. This refers to the fact that the clouds of ashes emitting from the Nazi ovens, literally indicated dead who had no features, they had been burnt to ash; their bodies incinerated and 'featureless'. 'The eye of the blind pianist' is a cipher for herself. She is acknowledging her complicity—helplessly—whitewashing, due to the unbearable subject she cannot avoid, her father's nationality: the holocaust.

Her image of the piano keys sets up a contrapuntal relationship of interwoven fates enacting the Nazis and the Jews, which neurotically out of horror, abjection, the poem's narrator replaces or interpolates with her relationship with the symbolic (or dead) father. 'Black yew, white cloud'. In the next line, she acknowledges, 'The horrific complications.' She relates this to the black and white piano keys, the contrapuntal fate of Nazi-Germans and Jews inseparable in the keyboard on which the Grosse Fuge and the little fugue, the fugue of the holocaust and its aftermath in her imagination are played. 'Finger-traps—a tumult of keys'. These melodies trap fingers; they are dangerous.

Yet in her role as white cloud, featureless, she is:

> Empty and silly as plates/ So the blind smile'

This refers to helplessness, vulnerability of the victimized. It also acknowledges perhaps her distanced position in relation to the prisoners in the camps. Yet, from this perspective the narrator exclaims in a risky complicity that she envies 'big noises', 'yew' hedge of the gross Fuge.

Little Fugue's narrator is (masochistically) here admitting—or willfully pretending—very dangerous desires, she is flirting with danger, flirting with death. On the other hand her exclamation has the willed defiant petulance reminiscent of a child, who when told that something is bad for her, doesn't care. Yet it might also symbolically represent an attempt to avoid the conflicted legacy of her father's background. How can the poem's narrator love him if, perhaps, if he had stayed in Germany he may have been the Nazi? This is a 'senseless' question. It requires loss of sense. She acknowledges this deafness, an imagined Nazi meister, deaf to the cries of the Jews. Imagining a father, of course plays with the term *fuhrer*, leader, also father, of Death (the black yew tree) she synaesthetically continues.

Dead men cry from the yew hedge. They cry from death. They are the restless dead who will not sleep. These are the silenced voices that haunt the living, in intergenerational trauma that arises from the collective memorialized memories of the murdered masses.

> I am guilty of nothing.

Here the narrator asserts her innocence. Yet she has stated her complicit envy for the meister, for his fascist strength. This is a statement of denial, and confession. The territory of Kristeva's abject. It suggests that Father-Death, is sin in denial. That death is a denial—of life.

But in the next stanza she asks if he is 'tortured'. How can the meister not be self-tortured if he commits such atrocity, genocide? She turns to interrogate a man in her memory now, evoking German-Austrian immigrants, during the 'Great War', in a delicatessen in California:

> Lopping the sausages!

These sausages, with symbolic evocations of barbarity, butchery, the werst, colour the narrator's nightmares, they colour her sleep, with the hysterical red of 'cut necks'.

> There was a silence!

This indicates that the narrator's sleep is numb, too depersonalized, or dissociated for dreams. It is a sleep of the Musselmanner, an abject realm of horror, of a unspeakable silence.

This again evokes, in a contrapuntal inversion, music of the Grosse Fuge. Within the symbolic Grosse Fuge, Plath implies there is a great silence, a whiting out.

> I was seven, I knew nothing

Again. The narrator depicts a wrestle of moral conscience, she was a child, she did not know. She knew nothing—then—of the concentration camps, the holocaust, the war in Germany which was occurring when she was living in America with her German father and Austrian mother. As a young child, life was complex but simple. As well as her father she mourns her lost innocence. What happened, she found out was that 'The world occurred'.

She found out things she didn't want to know. And her father?

> You had one leg, and a Prussian mind
>
> ...
>
> I am lame in the memory

Plath's father lost his leg in the silence of the past, which was never able to be discussed by them because he died, in the absence of his loss she interrogates his memory. Hopelessly against his loss, she is reduced in her (neurotic) imagination to being a victim of the Holocaust. She personifies the Father as Death. But this is also Death in the sense that he is dead. Against a literal, childlike association, then, she has psychologically positioned herself as helpless—when she wishes to talk to him he is not there to listen. He is dead, he is death, and he is as cruel as Death as he will ignore her wish for warmth, love and comfort.

He will ignore her needs for love, compassion, for a good father. He is not a good father, because he is dead, he is death, and he is associated in *Little Fugue* narrator's mind with the imagined Nazi *meister*, as the second world war was raging when she was growing up. Debate about the Holocaust continued through her life. The loss of her father left an absence to fill, or deny, with abject fear and desire. *Little Fugue*'s narrator acknowledges that this death, and its associations has made her metaphorically 'lame'. But now, at the end of the fugue, she makes an attempt to acknowledge that he was a man after all not just a symbolic figure in her black and white memory:

>I remember a blue eye

The Aryan image also references the meister in *Todesfuge* who has a blue eye.

>A briefcase of tangerines

She tries to add more colour and warmth to the picture but it is too late.

>This was a man, then!

This is an ironic Shakespearean reference, which in its irony negates rather than affirms. Because in the next line this 'man' is eclipsed by something much darker and more lasting:

>Death opened, like a black tree, blackly.

The black yew tree (suggesting 'you') has continued throughout the fugue, fatally interwoven, counterpoised with her whiteness.

Wherein the two-stanza coda, the last, is devoted to white, to her. This is a bleak stanza in which she references affinity once again with the *Musselmanner*, numbed by contact with the *meister*.

It evokes not so much survival but its endangerment; it implies her survival is temporary. As if the death of the Grosse Fuge, the yew tree, may be opening like a black tree, blackly, for her. This also brings up dark themes of incest and the challenging symbolic breaking of the incest taboo. *Little Fugue* is, then, a transgression, it's about transgressions of the most unspeakable kind that passes description, desire to be complicit with a meister of darkness; to overcome its terror. As if to exorcise the demons, of the past, the narrator is literally imagining the worst things that she could.

Contemplating a marriage... morning, she is arranging her 'mourning', planning for her marriage with the meister. She is the white cloud to come, the ashes in the future air, the white keys on the fateful keyboard. From the graveyard of the yew tree and the cloud, the deadly meister is calling and deeply she understands: 'The clouds are a marriage dress, of that pallor'.

This use of the preposition 'that', its finality, indicates she has made up her own arrangement of associations of images and emotions in her black and white world, on the fugal keyboard of her life and death, and within this fatal irrational 'logic' she understands the imperatives of an imagined meister. Although she was not interned in a concentration camp, out of a misplaced guilt she has imagined the abjection that has achieved a symbolic reality. And so the *Little Fugue* comes to a traumatic close. In the contrapuntal coda, stanza twelve iterates themes of Black Death and the *grosse fuge*, interweaving stanza thirteen's line of white helplessness, the narrator's victimhood at the hands of death. She succumbed to the *Grosse Fuge*, yew tree, in a marriage dress, of that pallor, the pallor of death camp clouds. There is no stanza 14.

In *Little Fugue* Plath symbolically interweaves her fugue with the memory of her absent father and what 'he' represents to her through associations. It would perhaps take what is known to psychoanalysts as a circuit-breaker (Kristeva 1982) to significantly rearrange these associations to form a less self-destructive pattern. But relief and cure were not brought by electroconvulsive therapy (electric shock treatment, or ECT) she was subjected to for depression as a young woman, that she condemns in her story *Johnny Panic and the Bible of Dreams*, and her novel, *The Bell Jar*, as well as in many of her poems.

Plath's work was criticized by some critics who question her right to use the Holocaust as part of the imagery of her poetry in an act of personal mourning, when she had no involvement (though her father was German and her mother was Austrian); a critical interpretation of her work Gubar documents in *Poetry After Auschwitz*: 'Plath's non-Jewishness as well as her lack of a personal stake in the disaster made her speaking on behalf of the victims appear a desecration'.[3] But Plath's usage of the holocaust imagery should not be seen as gratuitous. Her drive to use this symbolic imagery reveals a traumatic and troubled subjectivity articulated in the process of writing powerful and emotive modern poetry, which also constitutes a tragically harrowing expression of a writer's fugue.

Not only did Plath have legitimate reasons to write about the Holocaust to do with her family background but, crucially to the theory of a fugal modality of writing, in Little Fugue, for several reasons which I have mentioned, Plath can be seen in her life and art to be enacting an individualistic writer's fugue, the tensions of which, whilst giving rise to the powerful poetry of Ariel, became insurmountable and ended in her suicide.

Plath also implicitly suggested in one of her powerful prose works, written shortly before her death that she was thinking about traumatic shocks in her early life. There was the birth of her brother: 'A baby. I hated babies. I who for two and a half years had been the centre of a tender universe...My beautiful fusion with the world was over...'(120). Far worse, the death of her father when she was eight.

> And this is how it stiffens, my vision of that seaside childhood. My father died. We moved inland. Whereupon those nine first years of my life sealed themselves off like a ship in a bottle—beautiful, inaccessible, obsolete, a fine, white flying myth. (124)

She recalled these early traumas in *Ocean 1212-W*, one of the last prose pieces that she wrote in 1962, collected and published by Hughes, in *Johnny Panic and the Bible of Dreams and other prose writings*, in his selection of his deceased wife's writings that he labelled: '*Part 1: The most successful short stories and prose pieces.*' (There are four parts). Some tentative comparisons can be drawn between the fugues of Plath and Celan. Plath's fugue was enacted in language, in writing and was played out in her relation to languages. At home Sylvia Plath's father reportedly spoke German. She attempted suicide when she was teenager. The internal psychological conflicts she experienced fugally focused on and in her writing. This is a pattern of abjection in writers, which Kristeva has observed. Yet her abjection centered very much on being a female and being a writer (this perhaps, to her mind, echoed Celan's experience of being a Jew writing in German, she was a woman writing poetry, on powerful repressed themes, both were outsiders, or taboo-breakers, in the mainstream literary culture of the language in which they wrote). The tensions in Plath's life as writer produced a conflict between being a writer and poet, in the role-playing phases of womanhood: a daughter, wife and mother. Plath was a young woman in the 1950s, just years before second wave feminism effected significant cultural and social changes, which partly emancipated women of her class from exclusively household roles. And it was Sylvia's suicide, and posthumously her emergent stature as a writer, which helped to propel this movement for change. It seems that her inner tensions that led to her suicide, were triggered by being abandoned by her husband, following her primary experience in childhood of her father's death, which may have exacerbated conflicts of expectations about her identity as a writer and poet. Whereas, as Ted Hughes records,[4] she wrote copiously and continuously and produced a large volume of writing; there is a disparity between the kinds of writing she did. It was in the last few months of her life that she produced the poems of contained genius in *Ariel*, in the time after Hughes had left her with their children in his homeland, England. It was as if in the writing of these poems, all the social trappings fell away. She went into her inner world, and the words she wrote come straight from the mythically perceived heart of profound social observation and uncompromising emotion. Many were trapped in the 1950s, in the roles of social expectation. In Sylvia Plath the social and cultural inner tensions broke into the fugue of her poetry. When she was writing in the 1950s it was not considered socially acceptable for a woman to be a poet or genius. And driven by anxiety, suicide attempts, damage by electroconvulsive therapy, a lacerating perception, and desire to write, Sylvia Plath had as much need as any other woman and mother of social normality. Although all her life she wrote that she did not fit in. In one of the last prose pieces she wrote, in 1963, *America! America!*, she reflected: '

> Somehow it didn't take—this initiation into the nihil of belonging. Maybe I was just too weird to begin with. What did these picked buds of American womanhood do at their sorority meetings? They ate cake; ate cake and catted about the Saturday night date.[5]

She wrote in the social voice of self-conscious, conventionally crafted stories, driven by the desire, and need, to support herself through her writing, and the 'mythic' power of the uncompromising self-less voice of her poetry. She wrote in different 'voices' yet her writing was always self-based; her different tones reflected the publications and audiences she was aiming for. She wrote poetry, prose, journalism, memoir, a play, and journals, letters, and critical writing. Her *Little Fugue* is written in a minor key. Her consciousness of this, her social position as a writer, is shown in its title. It recalls her practice of drafting her poems on the back of sheets of paper her husband wrote his poems on, she was placing herself in a relational position, however in *The Other Ariel* Lynda K. Bundtzen writes that she burned many of Ted Hughes papers, including his poems, when she suspected him of having an affair. And she wrote responses in her poems to his, on the back of his, such as her poem 'Burning the Letters' on the back of his draft of his poem 'Toll of Air Raids'. Anne Stevenson, Plath's biographer, comments on Plath's 'desecrations' (of burning Hughes's papers and book) Buntzen adds this 'suggests that Plath's crime was directed not only at her husband, but also at culture',[6] which could mean many things.

There is a growing understanding of the dangers for everyone in relationships in adult life, of unconsciously repeating self-destructive patterns (emotional needs and responses) from (flawed) primary relationships in childhood with parents or caregivers. To not examine and become aware of such experiences and responses is to remain prey to destructive drives. Plath's work can be read in this light, as cultural testimonial to the struggle of the individual writer as woman and mother to bring what is usually 'unsaid' to consciousness, to write of the real themes of women's lives that are often silenced, and to work through them. Tragically she became overwhelmed.

The fugue poems were driven by experiences of loss, and a desire for restitution, and a moral conscience, manifesting as a vocation to write, which enabled not only a cathartic release of the writing experience for the poets but also significantly for the release of the materialized objects of their poems which live on as cultural testimonials: memorials to devastating effects on individuals and communities of the horror of atrocities perpetrated in the twentieth century by the fascist state and felt for generations. Their poems enable the world to remember, to know, and learn from, the individual's traumas and losses, and pain which Sylvia Plath inscribed with enduring power.

12

THE WRITERS' FUGUE IN REVIEW

CRAB CANON

In music, crab canon is defined by its self-reflexivity. Evoking self-reflexive elements of crab canon, the modern writer's fugue signifies a state of writing un/consciousness that is subjective and objective, that goes both 'inwards' in the writer's introspective semiotic creative processes, and 'outwards' in the linguistic symbolic form of the text.

In a deterritorialized 'flight' of writing, the individual writer transforms subjective conceptual experiences and sense-based perceptions, derived from and driven by traumatic shock, life writing in its most symbolic sense, into the objective form of language and the material form of the text, thus articulating and inscribing an experience of 'subjectivity' in materialized, cultural form. The self-release of writing has been identified and defined as *jouissance* by French writers including Barthes and writers of *écriture feminine*. This has a resonance with Rousseau's experience of the joy of losing oneself in the communal performance of music in a public place.

When language is seen and heard symbolically as a 'public place' this has a *de re* modal analogy in the fugal concept of losing awareness of one's own identity in the process of writing as creative art. In this fugal modality of writing, this releasing loss of awareness of identity is an un/conscious semiotic response to traumatic experience. It is balanced by rigorous self-discipline needed by the composer of a fugue to maintain the polyphonic melodic structure of the fugue, from its intentional inception as a melodic line of notes, through its development via many polyphonic variations, to the self-referential closure of its coda.

WRITING SUBJECTIVITY

In this investigation I have used the pluralistic cultural figure of the fugue as a heuristic device to explore questions concerning the uses and functions of language and its role in constructing the identity of the 'subject' and subjectivity in the literature, culture and society of modernity. The study, in drawing upon an extensive body of cultural theory literature develops a distinctive theoretical position (the writer's fugue) from which to analyze major literary texts of modernism. The literary fugue studies I have brought together for this analysis constitute innovative intermedial literary works in which the formalization of musicalization is—perhaps paradoxically—a core constituent in the construction of the individual identity of the subject-writer in the process of writing as creative art. The articulation of subjectivity in these individualistic experimental works is linked to innovation in language, which is also closely linked to the articulation of affect based on the traumatic experience of the writing subject, the writing self. The construction of individualistic works of art from self-based writing derived from inner compulsion born of trauma is often at a great cost to the author. This 'subjective' individualistic writing is compulsive, driven—not necessarily consciously—by the trauma of the individual subject/writer's experience within the social, cultural, political, and ideological context of his or her life in modernity. The individual identity of the writing subject is transformed into the dualistic affective subjectivity and material objectivity of the text—through the use of formalized objective techniques of musicalization in polyphonic fugue narratives in the literature of modernity. Each author, including the two poets, illustrate this transformation but in unique ways.

The investigation has been conducted via the analogous modality of five broad conceptual themes, which together form the title of this project. These themes chromatically (but not literally) echo the five traditional canons of Greek Rhetoric as codified by the Roman writer Quintilian: *Writer's Fugue*—Invention; *Musicalization*—Arrangement; *Trauma*—Style; *Subjectivity*—Memory; *Literature of Modernity*—Delivery. This research investigation has performatively, self-reflexively, and fugally, 'rewritten' these rhetorical categories in a metaphorical adaptation of the terms in which they originated. Here, I summarize the findings of my research in relation to the five broad themes of the investigation.

INVENTION

Consistent with the traditional rhetorical concept of 'Inventio', I gathered together diverse bodies of 'evidence'. These I developed into a methodological strategy of inquiry and analysis: the Writer's Fugue. I investigated various rhetorical and symbolic ways or tropes used by significant modern authors in the articulation of literary works derived from self-based trauma. The writing of these creative artists is driven by and articulated in an affective self-based imperative that I call the fugal modality of writing. I have argued that each of these creative artists un/consciously seeks a mode of release and conversion of the involuntary memories of trauma. While this motivation may be unconscious and subliminal, its affects are manifest in the sublimated affects of trauma in their literary works which readers can uncover by literary means, since the release they seek is activated and articulated in the individualistic invention of their literary writing. This form of writing is compulsively driven in a process of creative practice which is (mildly) dissociative and involves elements of incommensurability: the unconscious, the irrational and the unintentional.

I began investigation with the intention of exploring the concept of the 'construction' of the subject in language and the construction of subjectivity in the literature of modernity. As a verb (to fugue) 'to construct' is to fit together, frame or build—something. As a grammatical term, to combine words syntactically, draw or delineate especially according to given conditions. As a noun, a construct is a thing constructed, especially by the mind; in psychology, a construct is an object of perception or thought constructed by combining sense-impressions. In linguistics, it means a group of words in a phrase. As a noun, a 'construction' is an act or mode of constructing and the thing constructed; a syntactical connection. All of these meanings find a place in the fugal analysis.

Here *writer's fugue* and the *fugal modality of writing* are used synonymously. As a verb, the writer's *fugue*—to fugue—operates as flight and a construct: to both fly and to fit together, frame, build. The concepts of the writer's fugue and the fugal modality of writing have been used to take flight, and fit together, frame and build this investigation into the construction of the subject and subjectivity in the literature of modernity. The writer's fugue/fugal modality of writing combines words syntactically to draw and delineate according to given conditions the process of a certain form of innovative writing which self-reflexively becomes (writing). The writers' fugal modality of writing self-reflexively becomes itself in the process of writing, thereby becoming itself as a noun.

The writer's fugue as a noun is a thing constructed notably by the mind, and writing tools. Psychologically it is an object of perception or thought, constructed by combining sense-impressions. The way that the writer's fugue and fugal modality of writing operate constitutes a notion of intentionality and *de re* thought that I have derived from Brentano's phenomenology, according to which there are no empty acts of consciousness. Accordingly, the writer's fugue and fugal modality of writing describe, and enact, the process of intentionality through which a writing subject's mind tends in a mental act (such as desiring or fearing) towards an object of thought (such as Albertine; Saint-Loup; the Ormond Bar or De Quincey's dead sister) in the performative process of writing. This is a modality of *de re* thought—of objects of thoughts. This reflects the distinction in Ferdinand de Saussure's differentiation between language as opaque and language as transparent.[1] It does not necessarily have any bearing on an external reality beyond the signs of the proposition itself. On Saussure's theory of structural linguistics, language is a system of signs in which signs relate to signifiers and signifieds (other signs) rather than to any external reality beyond the sign. This was foreshadowed by Brentano's *de re* theory of intentionality in which intentional thoughts are of objects of thought that are articulated in the thinker's propositional conception, in the modality of their thought processes; in the case of writing this occurs in the duration of the writing process.

The practice of musicalized writing is an intentional act of language use in which, in the 'notional world' of the writer's writing-conceptualization, in that process, signifiers relate to signifieds in a *de re* relation. This notional world involves all of the writer's psychological and linguistic resources, it involves consciousness and the unconscious and subconscious, rationality, irrationality, emotion and affect, memory voluntary and involuntary. The fugal modality of writing is driven by association. Psycho-linguistic association is, in a sense, melodic. It constitutes—and generates—variations on a theme, its ultimate effect or form depends on the modality of the individual writer. Figuratively speaking writer's fugue is a special kind of waking dream. It involves a contrapuntal relation of *logos* and *chora* scarcely—if at all—discernible in its operation to the writing subject as she, or he, is immersed, focused, fugally, in the performative process—the process of writing as self-based creation driven by a compulsive or inspired, need, derived from known, or possibly unknown or unacknowledged, trauma.

ARRANGEMENT

I have argued and sought to demonstrate that the use of fugue musicalization in literary writing constitutes a compositional arrangement which articulates conscious and unconscious messages of the writer's motivation in choosing to use a fugal musicalized structure. In her research into the poetry of death camp inmates in the Holocaust, Gubar (2003; 2004) observed the importance of the use of formalization in the writing of and about trauma. The use of musicalization and intermediality allows the 'safe' keeping of a distance from traumatic material. Musicalization is a process of semiotic conversion, condensation and displacement that makes it possible for writers to write, and readers to read, of profoundly traumatic events and displaced conversions derived from or reconstructing traumatic experience. As discussed in the chapter De Quincey, there are associations between the notion of incommensurability, accidents, and the term accidence, which all resonate in the arrangements of fugal compositions, which articulate and reflect the impacts of the author's experiences, and memories of traumatic accidents. A deeper meaning, of subliminal double-voiced discourse emerges from the etymology of two concepts that structure this piece of textual writing. The first is to do with the concept of *accident*, which De Quincey uses as a symbol to structure *The English Mail Coach*. The noun, *accidence*, is a part of grammar dealing with the variable form of words. Its etymology has roots in medieval Latin, and *accidentia*, in Greek, *parepomena*; and it is the plural of *accidens* as folly.

Accident: means an event that is without apparent cause or unexpected. A chapter of accidents: a sequence of misfortunes. Another meaning is irregularity of structure, a property of quantity not essential to conception of a substance; or a mere accessory. The world is not designed according to plan, there is an irregularity, incommensurability; humans are not here by design, but by accident.

Accidental: A related meaning is 'accidental', used as an adverb or noun meaning happening by chance, undesignedly, or unexpectedly, a thing not essential to a conception, occasional. In Music, it means a note, not in a key signature, in sharp, flat or natural key.

This etymological sketch reveals some interesting associations and connections between musical language, literary language, and incommensurability of events—accidents—that cause trauma. Connections were made in Greek mythology and tragedy between incommensurability, the unknown and unconscious (that which characters are not aware of, for example when Oedipus kills his father and marries his mother) and accidents causing trauma. In Greek tragedy, musical language and literary or dramatic language were also inseparably linked.

From this perspective, the *Dream-Fugue* is read as commenting on the changes that were occurring in society as it became increasingly secular, with the progress of modernization. *Dream-Fugue* makes the powerful point that this progress, symbolized by the mail coach, can lead to accidents. It was telling that it not an actual accident that occurs but that it is conceptualized in terms of psychological impact on the narrator/implied author—and that it is psychological affect of trauma and post traumatic stress that defines the event in terms of 'accident'. There is a more symbolic semiotic meaning in the use of accidental in relation to the use of the musical term accidental. This has significance in relation to the development of the fugue form and to the use of the form of fugue in literary compositions.

TRAUMA: STYLE

The writer's fugue is characterized by a musicalized style of writing which both exhibits and conceals its origins in traumatic experience. The affects of trauma are connected to and manifest in ways in which the traumatized individual constructs their self-identity in language. It is significant that in the case of the psychogenic fugue the affects of trauma manifest in a temporary loss of awareness of the individual's identity as this is socially and culturally constructed in language. This was particularly pronounced in the case of the German fugueur F.F. who literally forgot how to speak his native language German, yet who remembered how to speak English.[2] This suggests that the fugueur was trying to flee his identity and 'being' in Germany; he flew to America where he 'came to his senses', and significantly booked himself into a hospital. It is symbolically significant that at least some of the people in fugues in the psychogenic studies seek help from 'the authorities' representing 'the law' (firefighters and police) and medical authority (hospitals) once they have 'come around'. This indicates the depth of their disorientation and the authenticity of their loss of awareness of their social and cultural identity—and also their residual faith in the authority and power of social language to help them. Help was slow to arrive for Cornelia Rau, and only came due to the strenuous continuous efforts of first, asylum seekers alerting advocates, and then the tireless work of individuals and advocacy organizations, and a media report, as discussed in Chapter 4.

Accounts on the dissociative fugue by those who have researched or self-reported this experience, indicate the desire of people who have experienced fugue first hand to find out more about what happened to them; and some were as puzzled as the researchers. What emerges in the medical, media, and legal government reports is that the psychogenic fugue follows a pattern. It has definite discernible causes: trauma due to the stressors of major traumatic life events. Medical researchers suggest that, in some cases, that once an individual has suffered from a 'minor' head injury their brain remembers the 'escape' of loss of consciousness, and that under stress this might provide a learnt mode of response, to 'flee' into temporary unconsciousness of oneself, and one's usual surroundings (that are causing the stress).

It is difficult and intellectually risky to process trauma. Yet somehow it seems as if the emergence of the individual writer in modernity has coincided with and is congruent with the experience of trauma (symbolized in the split of faith and reason). This emergence has occurred in the process of writing which has a connection to the individual subject's processing of trauma.

The psychogenic or dissociative fugue might seem to be exemplary of (un/consciously) self-motivated deconstruction. This is not to be confused with self destruction. Fugue is a 'flight' response of self-survival. On the level of unconscious drives, and semiosis the individual 'self-deconstructs' or forgets self. In a state of altered consciousness, that gives him, or her, the freedom to move, and journey away from the social and cultural environment, away from their symbolic 'home', and the perceived threat. And concurrently the fugueur journeys away from their usual self identity, away, that is, from the 'subjectivity' that is their social identity, a product of social and cultural environment. The significance of objective external factors of social, cultural and political institutions and ideology has been emphasized by numerous theorists researched in this investigation. Language itself is one of these institutional contexts. Freud referred to the shadowy hegemonic forces of language as *instanz*. It is to flee the determinism of language institutions—and to assert her or his free will—that the fugueur literally loses her capacity to speak *that* language.

This is a psychological dissociative phenomenon that is seen in the cases of dissociative fugues that were discussed in Chapter 4. It is symbolized in the desperate journeys of those seeking asylum, and exiled writers. That many such writers and refugees are becoming entrapped in prisons run by the country in which they sought sanctuary, lawfully, is a matter of ongoing contestation in Australia.

This inquiry has attempted to explore the construction —including 'deconstruction' and reconstruction—of the subject in language, and 'subjectivity' in literature of modernity as a frame for analysis of the process of writing as creative art. As studies, I have focused on a certain kind of poetic fugue writing in ground-breaking, original and culturally significant literary fugue narratives of Romanticism and Modernism. The understanding of subjectivity explored is contextualized within post-Saussurean linguistic structuralist and poststructuralist discourse relating to problems of the 'subject', and parallel problems associated with the construction of subjectivity in literary language in modernity. The concept of subjectivity investigated in relation to the process of writing as creative art, is dualistic and dichotomous. It has made use of a construction based on a dichotomy identified by Louis Althusser.

Althusser's theory of subjectivity was influenced by Jacques Lacan's theories concerning the construction of the subject in language. Subjectivity begins when an infant utters the first words and enters the symbolic order of language, which Lacan held is governed by the 'Law of the Father'. Althusser identified a duality implicit in the concept of the construction of the subject in language. The first function is signified by the use of 'subject' as in, for instance, the active principle of a sentence. The second function is signified by the use of 'subject' as in, for instance, the subject as subject to the laws of society—the symbolic structure of language. In his research paper 'Three Notes on the Theory of Discourses' Althusser writes:

> The structure requires Trager [tracing]: ideological discourse recruits them for it by interpellating individuals as subjects to assume the functions of Trager. The conscription carried out by the structure is blank, abstract, anonymous: the structure does not care to know who will assume the functions of Trager. Ideological discourse provides the who: it interpellates individuals in the general form of the interpellation of subjects.[3]

Althusser proposes there is an element of choice in this: 'ideological' discourse will only permeate at the level of the unconscious of an individual who feels affinity with that ideological discourse. He proposes that disciplines have distinctive 'discourses', and that an individual will be drawn to a certain ideological discourse. He writes:

> Ideological discourse 'sets out'...from the premises that subjects exist- or, rather, it is that which makes these subjects exist, consenting only to one operation, which is, it must be said essential to its economy: guaranteeing this existence for the subjects established by a Subject Who [sic] interpellates them and simultaneously summons them before the bar of His judgement.[4]

The (capitalized) Subject is the discipline, or the ideological discourse. Althusser makes a comment that has relevance to the case studies of dissociative fugue and the forgetting of individual identity:

> Only a 'subject presumed to exist' is ever interpellated—provided with his identity papers so that he can prove that he is indeed the subject who has been interpellated. Ideology functions, in the true sense of the word, the way the police function. It interpellates. and provides the interpellated subject with/asks the interpellated subject for his identity papers, without providing its identity papers in return, for it is in the Subject-uniform which is its very identity.[5]

For Althusser the second use of subject is always and inextricably associated with ideology which is outside the individual by which she or he is 'interpellated'. On this view, we are 'hailed' or interpellated by ideology, thereby resulting in a dual-construction of the subject who is both an active principle in her life, yet also un/consciously connected to and interpellated by ideologically inflected language structures that symbolically constitute the social, political and cultural institutions of modernity. A paradox implied in dual-constructions of the subject in language raises the question: how do we write new language? (Or does language write us?) This is a question with relevance in relation to the writing of subjectivity in literary language as creative art. Questions that we may ask in relation to theories of the duality of subject construction in the creative process of writing are: Is a theory of language use and subject construction that involves, or revolves around such a duality self-contradictory? Is there, after all, a 'deeper' truth or meaning that exists to be found outside, beneath or beyond language and what might this be? It would seem, emphatically, yes. Is music a subject discipline which also provides a means of individual expression'? Again, yes. And, what is the wider social significance of this?

The musicalized writing I have investigated is characterized by a search for deeper truths through artistic linguistic invention, whereby the writer has originated and developed original, affective musico-literary language. This inquiry investigated language use and word-play in literary narratives where the writer has in their writing created new conceptual terms for writing language, that emerged from their own writing, in the structuring of their works, for instance, in 'Sirens' in *Ulysses*, where Joyce developed an original set of critical style terms, which he applied and used in his *fuga per canonem*: **tela contrappuntistica**/*contrapuntal web*, **blocchi d'armonia**/*blocks of harmony* and **rovescii antesi**/*retrograde reversal*—in the works of De Quincey who subverted the five canons of Greek rhetoric to create his own *literature of power* and *impassioned prose*; in Proust's term *involuntary memory*, and Celan's title for his poem *Todesfuge*, and Plath's *Little Fugue* and its metaphors.

DELIVERY

Modernity is not, or even principally, a historical era; it signifies or expresses a significant change in the conditions of life that have refigured the psychological structures of the human being into an individual alienated in urban modernity. In France, Baudrillard reminds us that the French Revolution of 1789 'established the modern, centralized and democratic bourgeois State, the nation with its constitutional system, its political and bureaucratic organization.'[6] This brought changes that profoundly affected the individual subject, or person.

On Baudrillard's definition: 'Changes of political, economic, technological, and psychological structures' of 'objective historical factors of modernity' do not in themselves constitute modernity. Instead, it is an awareness of these: an 'aware denial of these structural changes,' or their reinterpretation through mentality, cultural style, everydayness and way of life, that instead is what defines 'modernity':

> Modernity is neither the rationality nor the autonomy of individual consciousness, which however found it. It is after the phase of the triumphant ascension of liberties and individual rights, the reactionary exaltation of a subjectivity threatened everywhere by the homogenization of social life.[7]

In contemporary discourse, ways of understanding writing as creative 'authorship' have focused on ideological issues concerning the uses and functions of language, and the relationship of the individual to the institutional disciplinary laws of society that are inscribed, articulated, and learnt, and countered in other uses, in the freedom of expression of individuals, in language. If, as Althusser suggests, subjectivity comprises in part the effects of interpellation by ideological discourse how can and does a 'subject' to write an original language work? And what about affect? The realm of affect in which we experience emotions of trauma and *jouissance* (amongst the full range of emotions) is also the realm of subjectivity, of language uses. How can the writer as creative artist articulate 'genuine' affect if the only language available to her, or him, is not her own, it is the language of the Law of the Father? Joyce responded to his concern about the limitations of language when he determined to invent a new language of his own to articulate perceptions and experience that were not given words or expressive form in conventional or available social uses of English. It follows then, on Althusser's model, that if the discourse that is interpellated is the discourse of freedom of expression, then the writing subject who practices this, is one who works and writes, freely, in this context.

Postmodernism in the creative arts is associated with the rejection of the idea that there is a hidden or deep truth to be found beyond the style of objective discourse. Gutting has written that postmodernism 'combines the structuralist style of objective, technical and even formal discourse about the human world with a rejection of the structuralist claim that there is any deep or final truth that such discourse can uncover.'[8] Romantic and Modernist authors were criticized for supposedly attempting what is 'impossible'—in the classical rhetorical meaning of Impossibility. In this particular instance, impossibility is signified by the aim to articulate in language a 'deep' meaning beyond language. In *'La Mort de l'auteur'*, Barthes deployed a celebrated attack on (his perception of) the conventional bourgeois conception of the individual 'personne' that he configured in a fictitious character he termed 'l'auteur-dieu' (author-God). This sovereign ruler was a bourgeois epitomizing the worst excesses and complacencies of capitalism. In a renowned passage, Barthes wrote:

> The author is a modern figure, a product of our society insofar as, emerging from the Middle Ages with English empiricism, French rationalism and the personal faith of the Reformation, it discovered the prestige of the individual, of, as it is more nobly put, the 'human person.'[9]

Barthes argued that it is logical that 'in literature it should be this positivism, the epitome and culmination of capitalist ideology, which has attached the greatest importance to the 'person' of the author.'[10] Barthes re-conceptualized the 'person' as the subject (sujet); literature as 'writing' (écriture); the 'Author' as the scriptor (scripteur).[11] Now, Barthes declared, linguistically, 'l'auteur n'est jamais rien de plus que celui qui écrit, tout comme je n'est autre que celui qui dit je' (the author is never more than the instance [celui] writing, just as I is nothing other than the instance [celui] saying I'). Barthes insists: 'language knows a 'subject', not a 'person', and this subject, empty outside of the very enunciation which defines it, suffices to make language 'hold together', suffices, that is to say, to exhaust it'.[12]

Is this a devastating critique of the concept of the modern 'author' or does it merely privilege the linguistic aspects of literature? Barthes critique privileges a textual concept of text over the (authored) literary work, 'c'est le langage qui parle, ce n'est pas l'auteur' (it is language which speaks, not the author).[13] Barthes elaborates:

> Succeeding the Author, the scriptor no longer bears within him passions, humours, feelings, impressions, but rather this immense dictionary from which he draws a writing that can never halt: life never does more than imitate the book, and the book itself is only a tissue of signs, an imitation that is lost, infinitely deferred.[14]

Barthes reference to a tissue of signs, *le texte est un tissu de citations*, opens a multi-layered paronomasiac play on the translated linguistic ambiguity in meaning between sign and citation suggesting all writing is a composite of citations.

Barthes does not say the 'immense dictionary' does not contain affect. Yet 'Death of the Author' is indicative of a crisis and a rupture that revolves around changing perceptions and understanding of the construction of the subject and subjectivity in language in modernity. It reconceptualized the writer as creative artist, 'person' and 'genius', into the 'scriptor' as linguistic subject—a 'writer' not an 'author'. This arose in the mid-late twentieth century and in retrospect, was a manifestation of millennial anxieties.

The subtext of Barthes' reconceptualization of the Author was an ideological critique of a hegemonic cultural form of literature that is believed to uphold the status quo of bourgeois capitalist society.

The reconceptualization of authorship and the writing process symbolized by the trope of 'La mort de l'auteur' may have signified the end of a contested concept of the author as self-based creative genius (at least in contemporary discourse). But it is an idea of the cultural redundancy of the role of the writer as creative artist, that is alluded to by Jean-Yves Tadié in his biography *Marcel Proust*. Tadié positions this crisis historically as the end of autobiography. He bases his argument on the fact that Proust wrote in the genre of the 'portrait of the artist'. A genre that, like the traditional concept of the Author is he claimed dead. 'We must therefore be aware that Proust was inheriting a legacy that was a thousand years old, and that he would be one of the last to do so'.[15] From a late twentieth-century perspective, Tadié perceived a 'triangular structure' in literary practice and aesthetic understanding that stretches from antiquity to Modernism. This triangular structure comprises 'appearance, the essence or the idea, and the artist'. Although in recent years, this has been refuted with the rise of the new author publishing movement which includes a resurgence of autobiographies and memoirs, and many other forms of literature.

This investigation has explored the drama identified by Tadié from the perspective of 'the third corner of the triangle' in theory, the forgotten third, the supposedly doomed but, as it turns out in the end, resilient protagonist of the self-based life narrative, the modern writer as artist—in the contested context of 'subjectivity,' writing of what they witnessed, that we learn from.

Notes

PRELUDE

1 David Hamlyn, 1987, p.18.
2 Ibid.
3 Ibid.

INTRODUCTION

1 Mikhail Bakhtin, 1981, p. 269.
2 Ibid., p. 273.
3 Ibid.
4 Michael Holquist, trans. and ed. 'Glossary', *The Dialogic Imagination*, p.426.
5 Ibid., p. 427.
6 Ibid.
7 Immanuel Kant, 1787, *Critique of Pure Reason*, B 34, p. 65. (Critique A and B).
8 See George Lukács, 1963.
9 *These Heathen Dreams: The Life of a Cultural Bolshevik*, 2014, by filmmaker Anne Tsoulis.
10 Brian Cooper, 2003. Also see: Kendell RE. *The Classification of Depressive Illnesses* (Maudsley Monograph 18) London: Oxford University Press, 1968; Bhrolchain N.M., Brown G.W., Harris T.O. 'Psychotic and neurotic depression 2. Clinical characteristics'. *British Journal of Psychiatry*, 1979; 134 (1); pp. 94-107; Brown G.W, Bhrolchain N.M. Harris T.O, 'Psychotic and Neurotic depression 3. Aetiological and background factors', *Journal of Affective Disorders* 1979; 1, pp. 195-211; Akiskal H.S., McKinney W.T. 'Overview of recent research in depression. Integration of ten conceptual models into a comprehensive clinical frame'. *Archives General Psychiatry* 1975 (32), pp. 285-305
11 'Cultural project has sights on Indigenous suicide', *Bunbury Mail* 19/7/2016. 'Indigenous Suicide –White Comfort Politics and Survivorship', *The Stringer* 15/1/2016 15/1/2016; www.CreativeSpirits.info, Aboriginal culture-People-Aboriginal-sucide-rate
12 See Frantz Fanon, *Black Skin, White Masks* (1962).
13 C. Bunt's memoir of her mother: *A Blossoming*, 2015.
14 R. Skilbeck, *Australian Fugue The Antipode Room* (2014).
15 Australian Border Force Act 2015-Section 42-Secrecy www.austlii.edu.au
16 The Australian media has been covering refugee human rights issues.
17 Helen Davidson, 'Teachers, social workers demand right to talk about offshore detention centres.' *The Guardian*, 21/10/2016; Paul Karp, 'Absolutely inappropriate': Malcolm Turnbull blasts teachers' refugee protest.' *The Guardian*, 8/12/2016.
18 See Paul Karp, 'Malcolm Turnbull says Amnesty criticism of Nauru detention

'absolutely false', *The Guardian*, 18/10/2016. Ben Doherty, 'Australia' refugee policy is one of deliberate harm. And there's no claiming 'we didn't know,'" *Guardian*, 18/12/16.
19 Bridie Jabour and Daniel Hurst, 'Nauru to increase visa cost for journalists from $200 to $8,000', *The Guardian*, 9/1/2014.
20 M. Isaacs, 2014.
21 J. Queripel, 2016.
22 R. Skilbeck, *Sydney Morning Herald*, 17/7/15.

CHAPTER 1 EXILED WRITERS' HUMAN RIGHTS

1 Australian Human Rights Commission, http://www.hreoc.gov.au/
2 E. W. Said, *Culture and Imperialism* (New York: Vintage Books, 1993); and *Musical Elaborations* (London: Chatto and Windus, 1991).
3 Paul Karp, 'Submissions on 18c cite laws that pose "greater risk" to free speech.' *The Guardian*. 21/1/2017.
4 R. Skilbeck, 3/5/2009; 3/2/2008.
5 *The Daily Fugue*. The articles begin with: 'Why I am Boycotting the Sydney Biennale' (Feb 8, 2014), ruthskilbeck.com.
6 Rosie Scott interview with the author, 2007. Rosie Scott received the inaugural Sydney PEN Award in 2006 (http://www.pen.org.au).
7 There have been two incarnations of the Pacific Solution, which are discussed here.
8 H. Babacan, 2010.
9 R. Skilbeck, "Art Journalism and the Impacts of "Globalisation": New Fugal Modalities of Story-telling in Austral-Asian Writing," *PJR*, 14 (2008): 141-61.
10 See Edward Said, *Culture and Imperialism*.
11 Mikhail Bakhtin, "Discourse in the Novel," in *The Dialogic Imagination: Four Essays* ed. Michael Holquist, trans. Carl Emerson and Michael Holquist, 1981.
12 Homi Bhabha, *The Location of Culture* (Abingdon: Routledge, 1994).
13 R. Skilbeck, "Re-viewing Feminist Influences in Transnational Art: A Multimodal, Fugal Analysis of Mary Kelly's Texts of 'Maternal Desire.'"*International Journal of the Arts in Society*, Vol. 4, Issue 5, 2010: 18-28. 'Ruth Skilbeck in Conversation with Mary Kelly and Kelly Barrie', *The M Word: Real Mothers in Contemporary Art*, eds Myrel Chernick and Jenny Klein, York University, Toronto: Demeter Press, 2011.
14 See L. M. Tesser 2015.
15 Jeffrey C. Alexander et al., *Cultural Trauma and Collective Identity*, 2004. Also see: Cathy Caruth, 1996; and C. Caruth, ed, 1995.
16 Michel Foucault, *Discipline and Punish: The Birth of the Prison*, 1973.
17 D.W. Hamlyn, *History of Western Philosophy*, pp. 217-242.
18 D.W. Hamlyn, p. 233.
19 D.W. Hamlyn, p.222.
20 Ibid., p.222.
21 Ibid., p. 222.

22 C. Bunt, 2015, p. 102.
23 E. Taylor, 2009.
24 The "Manus Offshore Processing Centre" is situated on Lombrum Naval Base, on Los Negros Island, 'although the Centre's location is commonly described as Manus Island'. Cornall Review, p. 20. "Nauru Offshore Processing Centre" is on Nauru island.
25 Helen Davidson, 'Teachers, social workers demand right to talk about offshore detention centres' *The Guardian*, 21 October 2016.
26 Julia Kristeva, *Revolution in Poetic Language* 1974/1984.
27 See Refugee Council of Australia Timeline, http://www.refugeecouncil.org.au
28 1951 Refugee Convention. UN Human Rights Office of the High Commissioner's website, and the UNHCR website. http://www.unhcr.orgen-au/1951.
29 Australian Human Rights Commission, Submission to Senate, 2009. AHRC website.www.humanrights.gov.au.
30 AHRC. Asylum seekers, refugees and human rights, report, 2013.
31 Frank Brennan, *Tampering with Asylum*, 2003.
32 Refugee Council of Australia [RCA] Timeline, http://www.refugeecouncil.org.
33 Frank Brennan, 2003; and Refugee Council of Australia website.
34 *A Last Resort? National Inquiry into Children in Immigration Detention*, report. April 2014. www.humanrights.gov.au.
35 Rosie Scott interview with the author, October 2007.
36 Steven Biddulph, "LOVE is Stronger than Fear. The SIEV X Memorial," *Acting from the Heart: Australian Advocates for Asylum Seekers Tell Their Stories*, eds. Sarah Mares and Louise Newman, 2007, 182.
37 *Human Rights and Equal Opportunity Commission, A Last Resort? National Inquiry into Children in Immigration Detention*, April 2004: 442-3 HREOC was renamed Australian Human Rights Commission.
38 Mohsen Soltany Zand interview with the author, October 2007.
39 Cheikh Kone interview with the author, April 2008, Sydney.
40 M. Foucault, *Les mots et les choses* (1966) (*The Order of Things*, 1973); *Surveiller et punir* (1975) (*Discipline and Punish)*, trans by Alan Sheridan (1977).
41 Immigration (Detention Reform) Bill 220 Submitted by the Australian Human Rights Commission to the Senate, July 31, 2009, www.humanrights.gov.au/
42 Sharon Pickering, 2001, p.169.
43 AHRC Immigration (Detention Reform) Bill 220 Submitted by the Australian Human Rights Commission to Senate, July 31, 2009, AHRC www.humanrights.gov.au/legal-research-and-resources.
44 Mohsen Soltany Zand, CDs: *Mohsen* and *Australian Dream*, Stickylabel.
45 Mohsen Soltany Zand interviews with the author, 2008.
46 R. Skilbeck 'Make Art Not War'. *Homepage Daily* 3/2/2008
47 Sydney PEN website.
48 Sydney PEN website.

49 R. Skilbeck 'Refugee Writers Beyond Detention' *Homepage Daily* 3/2/2009.
50 Cheikh Kone interview with the author, April 12, 2008, Sydney.
51 Sydney PEN website
52 Australian Commission for Human Rights website
53 Refugee Council of Australia Timeline http://www.refugeecouncil.org.au
54 Refugee Council of Australia Media release, September 8, 2009
55 Ibid.
56 Sydney PEN website.
57 Amnesty International, *Island of Despair: Australia's "Processing" of Refugees on Nauru* https://static.amnesty.org.au/wp-content/uploads/2016/10.
58 Primo Levi, *The Drowned and the Saved*, 19 p. 47.
59 B. Doherty, H. Davidson & P. Karp, 'Papua New Guinea court rules detention of asylum seekers on Manus Island is illegal', *The Guardian*, 26 April, 2016.
60 Amnesty International, *Island of Despair: Australia's "Processing" of Refugees on Nauru*, p.11
61 Ibid.
62 Imram Mohammad, 'The torture in my country is transparent, in Australia it is not obvious.' January 12, 2017; Amnesty International report, *Island of Despair*, 2016.
63 Amnesty International, *Island of Despair*. London, 2016, p. 11.
64 Audit: *Offshore Processing Centres in Nauru and Papua New Guinea: Procurement of Garrison Support and Welfare Services* (Sept 13, 2016). Australian National Audit Organisation. www.anao.gov.au/work/performance-audit. No page numbers.
65 References to the audit are from the ANAO. Audit on the website, details above.
66 Audit as above. All the Audit references are from this same source.
67 Biennale of Sydney information from Biennale of Sydney website. Retrieved January 27, 2017.
68 See articles on the 2014 Sydney Biennale artists' boycott protest, www.ruthskilbeck.com.
69 Tom Dusevic, 'Transfield's Luca Belgiorno-Nettis branches into information technology', *The Australian*, May 15, 2015.
70 Franco Belgiorno-Nettis interviewer Robin Hughes, in 10 Tapes, recorded 3/29/1993. Australian Biography: www.australianbiography.gov.au/subjects/belgiorno/interview. ABC *Dynasties* Episode 6. 15/12/2003 www.abc.net.au/dynasties/series.
71 1951 Convention Relating to the Status of Refugees and its 1967 Protocol. UNHCR Refugee Agency website: http://www.unhcr.org/en-au/1951-refugee-convention.html
72 Mark Aarons and John Loftus, *Unholy Trinity: The Vatican, The Nazis, and The Swiss Banks*. 1992. New York: St Martins. 1998, second edition.
73 M. Aarons, *War Criminals Welcome: Australia, A Sanctuary for War Criminals since 1945*, Black Inc. 2001.
74 See: 'Two days of remembrance of a dark chapter of human history,' Britac (*The British Serb Magazine*). Retrieved January 29 2017
75 M. Aarons, 2001; Barry Lituchy 2006.
76 Gideon Boas and Pascale Chifflet, 'Suspected War Criminals in Australia: Law and Policy',

Melbourne University Law Review, Vol. 40:46, 2016.

77 Robert Manne, *The Petrov Affair: Politics and Espionage*, Pergamon Press, Sydney, 1987.
78 'Explosive Letter on Santamaria Labour Movement Abused says M.L.A.' *The Sun-Herald*, Sydney, 31 October, 1954, p. 5.
79 "Quit Moscow" Move Tonight: Breach Over Petrov Case', *The Sun-Herald*. Sydney. 25 April, 1954. p.1.
80 *Persons of Interest*, 2014. Director: Haydn Keenan; Producer: Gai Steele. Smart Street Films. www.smartstreetfilms.com.au.
81 See Horner, 2014, pp. 279-80. 82.
82 Horner 2014, pp 279-80 and P. Edwards, 2015.
83 For example, see George Morgan, 'Dangers lurk in the march towards a post-modern career', *Sydney Morning Herald*, October 18, 2016.
84 Ibid.
85 P. Edwards, ' In from the cold: the official history of ASIO', *The Australian*, January 10, 2015.
86 See Cathy Alexander, 'What ASIO might know about you- and how to find out for sure.' *Crikey*, May 27, 2014.
87 Mark McKenna, 'ASIO surveillance in 'Persons of Interest', *The Monthly*, Feb 2014.
88 Ibid.
89 R. Skilbeck, 'A response from an Author-Publisher to the Intellectual Property Arrangements Issue paper' Submission DR457. http://www.pc.gov.au/__data/assets/pdf_file/0015/201174/sub dr457-intellectual-property.pdf. 2016.
90 'Snowy Mountains Scheme: Birthplace of multiculturalism in Australia'. http://www.racismnowaycom.au/teaching-resources/factsheets/37.html
91 L. Egan, 'A symbol of Australian multiculturalism: Snowy Mountains Hydro-Electric Scheme declared a National Heritage Place.', *Il Globo*, 10/16/2016, http://ilglobo.com.au/news.
92 M. Aarons, 'Ardent Nazi leader took Liberal to extremes', *Sydney Morning Herald*, May 4, 2006.
93 Ibid
94 Ibid. See Jonathan Pearlman, 'Nazi propagandist and Liberal hard man dies after 30 powerful years', *Sydney Morning Herald*, Feb 24, 2006.
95 M. Aarons 2006 and J. Pearlman 2006.
96 Ibid.
97 Cornall Review, p. 75. Cornall quotes a G4S security risk assessment.
98 Nauru Files, *The Guardian*. 2016.
99 Gideon Boas and Pascale Chifflet, 'Suspected War Criminals in Australia: Law and Policy', *Melbourne University Law Review*, Vol. 40:46, 2016.
100 Royal Commission website: https://www.childabuseroyalcommission.gov.au.
101 Ibid.
102 Ibid.
103 Louise Milligan, 'George Pell failed to care for young abuse victims, royal commission told. ABC News, Updated 31 Oct 2016.

104 June Lee, 'Royal Commission told cardinal George Pell tried to buy victim's silence about abuse,' *Sydney Morning Herald*, May 26, 2015.

105 Kieran Tapsell, 'Catholic church's 'pontifical secret' stops disclosure of sex abuse allegations, expert says', *Sydney Morning Herald*, 9 February 2017.

106 February 2017. *Analysis of Claims of Child Sexual Abuse Made With Respect to Catholic Church Institutions in Australia,* Sydney: Commonwealth of Australia.

107 Ibid, also see media report AAP, 'Christian Brother paedophile Robert Best's hypocrisy was 'gobsmacking', judge says' 20/2/17.

108 February 2017. *Analysis of Claims of Child Sexual Abuse Made With Respect to Catholic Church Institutions in Australia,* Sydney: Commonwealth of Australia.

109 Ibid.

110 February 2017. *Analysis of Claims of Child Sexual Abuse Made With Respect to Catholic Church Institutions in Australia,* Sydney: Commonwealth of Australia.

111 See Michale Phayer, *The Catholic Church and the Holocaust, 1930-1965.* Bloomington, Indiana: Indiana University Press, 2000, p. 34, 237. Also: Miroslav Filipovic wikipedia entry.

112 Lituchy, Barry M, ed. *Jasenovac and the Holocaust in Yugoslavia: analyses and survivor testimonies/ edited with an introduction by Barry M. Lituchy; with the editorial assistance of Milo Yelesiyevich.* International Conference and Exhibit on the Jasenovac Concentration Camps. New York: Jasenovac Research Institute, 2006.

113 Ibid.

114 Ibid.

115 International Holocaust Day, Art Exhibition 'Jasenovac- the Right to remembrance'/Embassy of the republic of Serbia in Washington, D.C. 1/31/2017.

116 *Crikey*. ' Oops. Coonan attends neo-Nazi celebration...' April 27, 2007. www.crikey/com/au/2007/04/27; and *Jewish News*, 26 April 2007.

117 M. Aarons, 'Ardent Nazi took Liberal to extremes'. *Sydney Morning Herald*, 3/2/2006.

118 See *Crikey*, ' Oops. Coonan attends neo-Nazi celebration...' April 27, 2007. www.crikey/com/au/2007/04/27; *Jewish News*, 26 April 2007. J-Wire, 'BDS Hammered in NSW Legislative Council', 9/16/2011;

119 *Crikey*, ' Oops. Coonan attends neo-Nazi celebration...' April 27, 2007.

120 See J-Wire, 'BDS Hammered in NSW Legislative Council', 9/16/2011.

121 Ibid.

122 *Crikey*, ' Oops. Coonan attends neo-Nazi celebration...' April 27, 2007.

123 *InSerbia News*, 'Australian Prime minister congratulates Croats NDH day' April 17, 2014.

124 Ibid.

125 Binoy Kampmark, 'Tony Abbott, the NDH and Australia's Fascist Affair', *Counterpunch*, April 21, 2014.

126 Ibid.

127 SBC TV news: 'Croatia summons Australia's ambassador over M.P's speech', April 22, 2014, updated April 24, 2014. SBS. http://www.sbs.com.au/news/article/2014/04/22/

128 Ibid.

129 SBS: 'MP sparks Croatia-Australia diplomatic spat', 23 April, 2014.
130 Ibid.
131 See D. Horner, *The Spy-Catchers*, 2014
132 M. Aarons, *War Criminals Welcome*, 2001; D. Horner: *The Spy-Catchers*, 2014.
133 George Morgan, 'Dangers lurk in the march towards a post-modern career', *Sydney Morning Herald*, October 19, 2016; Gary Newman, 'When a casual affair turns sour,' *SMH*, April 17, 2012.
134 Cornall Review, 23 May 2014, p. 7 and see pp. 66-69.
135 Cornall Review, p. 69, and p. 8.
136 Cornall Review, p 8; 66-69.
137 Cornall Review, pages 26, 28, 56.
138 Cornall Review, pp. 63-66.
139 Cornall Review, p. 63.
140 Cornall Review, p. 63.
141 Cornall Review, p. 64.
142 Ibid.
143 Ibid.
144 Ibid.
145 Ibid., p. 66.
146 Ibid.
147 Ibid.
148 Ibid.
149 'Statement of Withdrawal from 19th Biennale of Sydney.' *#19 BoS Working Group* http://19boswg.blogspot.com.au/2014/02/statement-of-withdrawal-from-19th.
150 Ibid.
151 *#19BoS Working Group* blog. http://19boswg.blogspot.com.au.
152 Ibid.
153 Ibid.
154 Michael Safi and Paul Farrell, 'Sydney Biennale chairman quits over company's link to detention centres', *The Guardian*, 7 March, 2014.
155 R. Skilbeck, 'Biennale Breakthrough', *Daily Fugue.* 2014/03.
156 Josh Taylor 'Immigration spies on Facebook pages to weed out 'false hope' for asylum seekers,' *Crikey*, September 20, 2016.
157 *The Forgotten Children: National Inquiry into Children in Immigration Detention* (2014)., Australian Human Rights Commission, 2014; *Review into recent allegations relating to conditions and circumstances at the Regional Processing Centre in Nauru, February*, 2015. www.border.gov.au/ReportsandPublications/Documents/reviews-and-inquiries/review-conditions- circumstances-nauru.pdf ('Moss Review').
158 Moss Review, 'Executive Summary', pp. 3-6.
159 Moss Review, p. 43 (3.142).
160 Ibid, p. 70.
161 N. Hasham, 'New York Times attacks Prime Minister Tony Abbott over 'stop

the boats' policy', *Sydney Morning Herald*, September 4, 2015; Anna Shea, 'Stopping the boats doesn't save lives-it puts them in danger,' *The Drum*, 10. 29. 2015 (www.abc. net.news).

162   E. Tiozek, 'Manus Island detention centre staff failing to respect PNG law, flying out to escape questioning, police say.' ABC news, 28 Sept 2015 www.abc.net.au

163   Mark Isaacs, *The Undesirables*, Hardie Grant Books, Melbourne, 2017.

164   Ibid.

165   MEAA. *Criminalising the Truth, Suppressing the Right to Know: Media and Entertainment Arts Alliance Press Freedom* report, May 2016. Also see: Amnesty International *Islands of Despair: Australia's "Processing" of Refugees on Nauru*, Oct 17, 2016.

166   See Behrouz Boochani, 'For refugees kidnapped and exiled to the Manus prison, hope is our secret weapon.' *The Guardian*, 3 Oct, 2016; Josh Taylor 'Immigration spies on Facebook pages to weed out 'false hope' for asylum seekers'. *Crikey*, 20/9/ 2016.

167   'The Nauru files: cache of 2000 leaked reports reveal scale of abuse of children in Australian offshore detention'. *The Guardian*, 10 August, 2015. www.theguardian.com/australia-news/2016/aug/10/the-nauru-files-2000-leaked-reports-reveal-scale-of-abuse-of-children-in-australian-offshore-detention.

'Speaking before the publication of the Nauru files, Prof Louise Newman, a former member of the Immigration Health Advisory Group, says such attacks have continued. She speaks "on a nightly basis" to women on Nauru who have been sexually assaulted.' 'The Nauru Files,' *The Guardian*, 10 August 2016.

168   PEN International, *Resolution on Australia* pdf, 2016. www.pen-international.org/wp-content/uploads/2016/10.

169   *Offshore processing centres in Nauru and Papua New Guinea: Procurement of Garrison Support and Welfare Services*, September 13 2016. www.anao.gov.au/

170   Audit: Australian National Audit Organisation report, https://www.anao.gov.

171   See: R. Skilbeck, 'An Ethical' Future for the Biennale of Sydney? 'Boycott' Artists to Draft New Corporate Social Responsibility Policy.' *Daily Fugue*, 19/3/14. *The Guardian*'s 'Malcolm Turnbull slams 'vicious ingratitude', 10/3/2014; *Sydney Morning Herald*: 'Malcolm Turnbull denounces 'vicious ingratitude' of Biennale artists after Transfield withdraws as sponsor,' 11/3/14; R. Skilbeck, 'An Ethical' Future for the Biennale of Sydney? 'Boycott' Artists to Draft New Corporate Social Responsibility Policy.' *Daily Fugue*, 19/3/14.

172   *#19 BoS Working Group*: 'Statement of Withdrawal from 19th Biennale of Sydney. http://19boswg.blogspot.com.au, February 21, 2014.

173   'An Ethical' Future for the Biennale of Sydney?' *The Daily Fugue*, 19/3/2014

174   Ibid, and statements:www.19boswg.blogspot.com.au #19BoS Working Group 19boswg.blogspot.com.

175   L. Cochrane, 'Australia engages second agency for sole refugee in Cambodia', ABC 11/2/2016.

176   Steve Dow, 'Arts companies hit hard by Australia Council funding cuts'. *The Saturday Paper*, May 21, 2016. www.thesaturdaypaper.com.au/news.

177 Ben Doherty, 'Day of the Imprisoned Writer: Behrouz Boochani- detained on Manus Island'. *The Guardian*, November 15, 2015.
178 'Manus Island refugee who had breakdown found 'hungry and homeless'. *The Guardian*, January 10, 2017 (reporting by Behrouz Boochani).
179 *Christopher Barnett. Interview with Ruth Skilbeck*, Arts Features International, 1/2/2013.
180 S. Freud, 2003.
181 Nigel Scullion, 'Indigenous-run services for families affected by suicide to be introduced nationwide'. *The Guardian*, 23 January 2017.
182 'Northern Territory Emergency Response-"The Intervention"'. *Creative Spirits.* www.creativespirits.info/aboriginalculture/politics.
183 'Kylie Sambo on income management and Aboriginal Youth in the NT, https://www.youtube.com/watch?v=YH4wWumwRhc video, April 11. 2013. Uploaded by IRAG Alice Springs. Also on *Creative Spirits* website.
184 Bev Manton, 'Shopping with the Basics Card is Utterly Useless'. *Creative Spirits* website. 'Northern Territory Emergency Response; (NTER). www.creativespirits.info; and in 'Perpetuating neglect', *Koori Mail*, 481, p. 57.
185 Ali Cobby Eckerman 'Deadly Voices: An Intervention,' Sydney Writers Festival, event 240, 23/5/2010.
186 Research by Monash University, *Creative Spirits* website.
187 Eva Cox, 'It's time to harness angry feminist energy and inject it into welfare policy.' *The Guardian*, 15 January 2017.
188 National Union of Journalists (UK) (2004/08) *Reporting Asylum and Refugee Issues*, http:// www.mediawise.org.uk.

CHAPTER 2   TAKING FLIGHT INTO WRITING

1 Steven Paul Scher, 485.
2 S.P. Scher, 2004.
3 E. W. Said, 1991, p. xii.
4 S.P. Scher 2004.
5 Roger Fowler quoted in Scher 2004: 475.
6 See *Thought and Object: Essays on Intentionality*, A. Woodfield, ed. 1982.
7 Thomas de Quincey, 1897b.
8 Edmund Husserl, 1931/1982.
9 Ibid., 156-157.
10 D. W. Hamlyn, 1987, p. 321.
11 L. Kramer, 1990, p. 267.
12 Ibid., p. 267.
13 Ibid., pp. 269-270.
14 R. Barthes, 1977, p. 155.
15 Ibid., p. 155.

16 Ibid., p. 156.
17 W. Benjamin, 1940/2003.
18 S. Freud, 1917.
19 J. Lacan 1973.
20 Melanie Klein, 1930, pp. 335-336.
21 Ibid., p. 308.
22 D. Kiberd, 2000, p. xlix.
23 J. Kristeva, 1982, pp. 23-24.
24 Linda Hutcheon, Narcissistic Narratives, 1984.
25 J. Kristeva, 1974 (French)/English trans. 1984, p. 6.
26 Ibid., p. 7.
27 Ibid., p. 8.
28 Ibid., p. 9.
29 M. Bradbury and J. McFarlane, 1978, p. 71.
30 Ibid.
31 C. Baudelaire, 1859/2006, p. 402.
32 Ibid., p. 403.
33 M. Proust, Swann's Way, pp. 57-58.
34 W. Benjamin, 1940/2003, p. 315.
35 W. Benjamin 2006, pp. 315-316.
36 J. Kristeva, 1982, p. 38.
37 J. Lacan, 1973.
38 J. Kristeva 1982, p.45.34
39 Ibid., p. 23.
40 Ibid., p. 23.
41 J. Kristeva, 1984, p. 88.
42 J. Lacan 1972, p.289.
43 G. Deleuze and F. Guattari, 1980.
44 K. Mullin, 2004.
45 M. Foucault, 1975.
46 J. Derrida, 1976, p. 86; p. 105.
47 J. Derrida, 1976, p. 86; p. 105.

CHAPTER 3 THE FUGUE IN MUSIC

1 J.-J. Rousseau, trans. William Waring, *A Complete Dictionary of Music*, 1779.
2 From: *Rivista Musica Italia LIII*, 1951, quoted in Alfred Mann, 1958/1987, p. 7.
3 A. Mann, 1958/1987; Imogen Horsley, 1966; Paul Mark Walker, 2000.
4 T. Service, 2005.
5 Charles Rosen, 1972, p. 23.
6 Ibid., p. 25.

7   Ibid., p. 25.
8   Ibid., p. 25.
9   I. Horsley, 1966.
10 Ibid., p. 10.
11 A. Mann, 1987, p. 6.
12 J.-J. Rousseau, *Essay on the Origins of Language*, 1966, p. 66.
13 J.-J. Rousseau, *Dictionary*, p. 191.
14 Ibid.
15 A. Mann 1987 p. 11.
16 A. Mann 1987.
17 I. Horsley 1966.
18 A. Mann 1987, p. 5.
19 P.M. Walker 2000.
20 A. Mann 1987, pp, 5-6.
21 Giambattista Martini, from *Esemplare*, in A. Mann, 1987, Part 2.
22 A. Mann 1987, p. 7.
23 Manfred Bukofzer, *Music in the Baroque Era*, 1947, p. 671.
24 D.F. Tovey, 'Fugue', in *The Forms of Music*, 1975, p. 36.
25 J.-J. Rousseau, Essay, p. 51.
26 I. Horsely 1966, p. 7.
27 Ibid.
28 A. Mann 1987, p. 3.
29 Ibid.
30 A. Mann 1987, p. 4
31 Ibid.
32 See Max Weber, 1958; and A. Mann, 1987.
33 I. Horsley 1966, p. 8.
34 Ibid.
35 J.-J. Rousseau, Oeuvres Complètes, Volume V, 1995, p. 115.
36 Ibid, Letter, p. 116.
37 Ibid., p. 107.
38 P. M. Walker, 2000, p. 2.
39 Ibid., p. 3.
40 Ibid.
41 Ibid.
42 Ibid.
43 D. Alighieri, *The Divine Comedy*, Milano, 1820. Lines 118-120.
44 *The Divine Comedy*, Part 2: Purgatorio, trans. Dorothy L. Sayers, 1955, p. 169.
45 John Milton, 1909.
46 C. Wolff, 2000, p. 422.
47 John Butt, 1997b, p. 60.

48 Cynthia Verba, 1993.
49 Ibid.
50 Ibid., p.1.
51 J.-J. Rousseau, *The Confessions*. 1781/1995, p. 358 *Le Parlement de Paris.
52 Ibid., pp.-336-338.
53 Ibid., pp. 353-335.
54 Ibid., pp. 358-359.
55 Ibid., p. 375.
56 Jean-Philippe Rameau, *Traité de l'harmonie*, Paris: Ballard, 1722.
57 Max Weber, *The Rational and Social Foundations of Music*, 1958.

CHAPTER 4 IDENTITY SHIFTS, FUGAL RECURSION

1 T. W. Adorno, 1967, 'Cultural Criticism and Society', *Prism*s, trans. S. and S. Weber, 1997.
2 T. W. Adorno, *Negative Dialectics*, p. 362-363.
3 S. Gubar, 2004, p. 444.
4 Ibid.
5 J. Felstiner, 1995.
6 S. Friedlander, 2001, p. 4.
7 S. Friedlander, 1995, p. 5.
8 P. Levi, 1986/1988.
9 H. Arendt, 1963.
10 J. Felstiner, 2005, p. 46.
11 John Banville, in *Magnum Ireland*, 2005.
12 J. Kristeva, 1986, p. 17.
13 H. Cixous 1984: 147-158.
14 H. Cixous, 1975.
15 S. Freud, 2003, p. 24.
16 H. Cixous, 1998; R. Barthes, 1977.
17 J. Felstiner, 1995a.
18 D. Hofstadter, 1980, p.130.
19 H. Hesse, *The Glass Bead Game*, pp. 30-31.

CHAPTER 5 STATELESS: THE DISSOCIATIVE FUGUE

1 E. Glisky et al., 2004, p.1132.
2 H. Markowitsch, 1999, p. 561.
3 M.D. Kopelman et al., 1994, p. 2000.
4 E. Glisky et al. 2004, pp. 1135-1136.
5 Ibid.
6 Ibid.
7 E. Glisky et al. 2004, p. 1138.

8   Ibid.
9   Ibid.
10 Ibid.
11 E. Glisky et al. 2004, p. 1138.
12 Ibid.
13 M.D. Kopelman et al., 1994, p. 676.
14 Ibid.
15 Ibid.
16 M.D. Kopelman et al, 1994, p. 675.
17 Ibid.
18 Ibid.
19 A.D. Macleod 1999.
20 I. Hacking, 1998.
21 M.D. Kopelman, 2000.
22 Jean-Paul Sartre, 1972.
23 M.D. Kopelman, 2000, p. 587.
24 H. Markowitsch et al., 1999, p.120.
25 Ibid.
26 Ibid.
27 Ibid., p. 123
28 H. Markowitsch et al., 1999, p.125.
29 M.D. Kopelman et al., 1994 p. 688.
30 C. Rycroft, 1986.
31 Ibid.
32 Ibid., p. 197.
33 *Diagnostic and Statistical Manual of Mental Disorders-5*, 2013.
34 I. Hacking, 1968, p. 1.
35 P. Tissié, 1887. My translation.
36 I. Hacking, 1998.
37 See J.-Y. Tadié 1996/2000; M. Murphy, 2005.
38 M. Bradbury and J. McFarlane, 1978/83.
39 See I. Hacking, 1998, p.1.
40 Ibid, pp. 1-2.
41 M.D. Kopelman et al. 1994, pp. 675-691.
42 Ibid., p. 690.
43 *Inquiry into the Circumstances of the Immigration Detention of Cornelia Rau*: report/https://www.border.gov.au/ReportsandPublications/Documents/reviews-and-inquiries/palmer-report.pdf, 2005.
44 Robert Manne, 'The Unknown Story of Cornelia Rau, *The Monthly*, September, 2005, https://www.themonthly.com.au.
45 Ibid., and Beyond Our Ken, www.beyondourken.com.au.

46 *Beyond Our Ken* documentary website.
47 Ibid.
48 Review of Beyond Our Ken on http://www.beyondourken.com.au/wp-content/uploads/2016/02/Empire-Review-of-Beyond-our-Ken.pdf
49 J. Schembri, *The Age*. http://blogs.theage.com.au.au/2008/09/beyond_
50 Ibid.
51 R. Manne, 2005.
52 A. Tibbit, "Abuse case: staff asked to lie." *Sydney Morning Herald*, 26/7/2008.
53 Ibid.
54 *The Age*. http://blogs.theage.com.au.au/schembri/archives/2008/09/beyond_
55 Ibid.
56 See *Beyond Our Ken* website,
57 A. Tibbitts, Abuse case: staff asked to lie." *Sydney Morning Herald*, 26/7/2008.
58 See Urban Cinefile, 'Beyond Our Ken' http://www.urbancinefile.com.au
59 See R. Manne, 2005 (online article p. 2/26).
60 Ibid., p. 2/26.
61 Ibid., p. 3/26.
62 Robert Wainwright, *The Age*, 12/2/2005.
63 R. Manne, 2005, p. 4.
64 R. Manne, 2005 p. 3/25.
65 Ibid., p. 5/26.
66 R. Manne, 2005, p. 6/24.
67 Palmer Report 2005.
68 R. Manne, 2005, p. 6/24.
69 Palmer Report, p. 10.
70 Ibid.
71 Ibid.
72 Palmer Report, 2005, p. 10.
73 Ibid., pp 11-12.
74 R. Manne, 2005, pp. 10-11/24.
75 Palmer Report, p. 40.
76 R. Manne, 2005, p. 12/24.
77 Palmer Report, p. 15.
78 R. Skilbeck 2008, and R. Skilbeck 2010.
79 Palmer Report, p. 88.
80 Ibid., p. 80.
81 Palmer Report, p. 81; and ABC timeline, www.abc.net.au/4corners 04/04/2005.
82 Ibid.
83 Palmer Report, p. 20.
84 B. Williamson, 'Inside Glenside' ABC website, 2011.
85 See M. Foucault, 1975.

86 B. Williamson, 2011.
87 Christine Rau, 'My Sister Lost her Mind and Australia Lost its Heart'. *Sydney Morning Herald*, Feb 2, 2005.
88 Ibid.
89 Christine Rau, 2005.
90 R. Skilbeck, 2015.
91 'Cornelia Rau' Wikipedia entry
92 M. D. Kopelman, 2000, p. 612.
93 Ibid.
94 M. Kopelman, 2000, p. 612.
95 C. Rycroft 1987, p. 197.
96 S. Freud, 2003, pp 93-94.
97 Ibid., p. 94.
98 V. A. Conley, p. 70.
99 H. Cixous, 1990, p. 102.
100 Ibid., p. 102.
101 H. Cixous, 1984.
102 H. Cixous, 1991, p. 26.
103 Ibid.
104 H. Cixous, 1981.
105 L. Althusser, 2006, p. 281.
106 W. Benjamin, 1940/2003.
107 I. Hacking, 1998.
108 M. Foucault, 1977.
109 Ibid., p. 116.
110 Ibid., p. 123.
111 Ibid., p. 124.
112 Ibid., pp. 124-125.
113 G. Deleuze and F. Guattari, 1986, p. 6.
114 G. Deleuze, 1992, 3-7.
115 W. Benjamin, 2003, p. 32.
116 Edmund Burke. Published in English, and French translation.
117 E. Burke, ' A Letter to a Noble Lord', in *The Works*,1834, p.264.
118 G. Deleuze and F. Guattari. 1986, p.19.

CHAPTER 7 THOMAS DE QUINCEY'S *DREAM-FUGUE*

1 D. Masson, 'Introduction', in T. de Quincey, 1897, p. 270.
2 Thomas de Quincey, 1879, p. 192.
3 T. de Quincey in Japp 1981: 326-7.
4 G. Lindop, 1981.

5   J. Barrell 1991, p. 32.
6   Charles Baudelaire, 1860/2000.
7   Lindop, 1981, p. 11.
8   S. Freud, 1940/2003.
9   W. Benjamin 1969/1989, p. 115.
10 Werner Wolf, 1999, p. 23.
11 Julian North 1997, p. 86-7.
12 Calvin S. Brown, 1938, p. 160.
13 W. Wolf, 1999, p.113.
14 Ibid., p. 114.
15 Ibid.
16 Ibid.
17 Aldous Huxley, 1928/2001. p. 293.
18 W. Wolf, 1999, p. 2.
19 Ibid., p. 16.
20 Ibid.
21 Daniel O'Quinn, 2004, p. 1.
22 Virginia Woolfe, 1932/1953.
23 Alina Clej, 1995, p. xi.
24 J. Barrell, 1991, p. 44.
25 A. Clej, 1995, p. xi.

CHAPTER 8   MARCEL PROUST'S FUGUE OF *LOST TIME*

1   W. Benjamin 1969/1989, p. 113.
2   Cf. R. Hayman, 1990, p. 366.
3   Ibid.
4   R. Hayman, 1990, p. 369.
5   Cf. V. Nabokov, 1980/1983; G. Brée, 1956.
6   G. Deleuze, 1964/2000, p. 3.
7   Ibid.
8   V. Nabokov, 1980, p.208.
9   Ibid.
10 R. Hayman, 1990.
11 J.-Y. Tadié, 1996/2000, p. 50.
12 G.M. Beard, 1874, p. 2.
13 A. Proust and G. Ballet, 1897.
14 J.-Y. Tadié pp. 64-65.
15 Cf. J.-Y. Tadié, 1996/2000; and R. Hayman, 1990.
16 J.-Y. Tadié 2000.
17 R. Hayman, 1990.

18 M. Blanchot, 1981, p. 9.
19 V. Nabokov 1980/1983, p. 228.
20 J.-Y. Tadié 1996/2000, p. 82.
21 V. Nabokov 1980/1983, p. 231.
22 M. Blanchot 1943/1981, p. 99.
23 J.-Y. Tadié 2000, pp. 128-129.
24 Ibid., p. 127.
25 M. Proust quoted in R. Hayman, 1990, p. 79.
26 J.-Y. Tadié 2000, p. 717.
27 J.-Y. Tadié 2000, p. 128.
28 D. Hamlyn, 1986 p. 286-287. William James, 1890.
29 William James, 1890.
30 W. Benjamin, 1940/2003, p. 315.
31 Ibid.
32 H. Bergson quoted in: J.-Y. Tadié 2000, p. 129.
33 H. Bergson, *Time and Free Will: An Essay on the Immediate Data of Consciousness*, 1889, trans. F.L. Pogson. London: Allen and Unwin, 1910.
34 V. Nabokov, 1980, p. 208.
35 H. Bergson 1896/1988, p. 221.
36 V. Nabokov 1980, p. 208.
37 H. Bergson 1896/1988, p. 116.
38 V. Nabokov, 1980, p. 207.
39 Ibid., p. 287.
40 W.G. Leibniz, 1898/1925.
41 M. Kundera, 1986/93, p. 26.
42 W. Carter, 2006.
43 G. Deleuze and F. Guattari 1987, pp. 318-319.
44 I.C. Wimmers 2003, p. 167.
45 Ibid.
46 G. Deleuze 2000, p. 3.
47 R. Ashton, 1997, p. 105; Coleridge, *The Complete Poetical Works*, 1912/2001.
48 C. Dahlhaus 1967/1982, p.79.
49 Ibid., p.80.
50 Ibid.
51 C. Dahlhaus 1967/1982, p. 81.
52 Ibid.
53 J. Kristeva, 1974/1984.
54 G. Broadbent, 1991, p. 88.
55 G. Deleuze, 1964, pp. 101-116.
56 D.W. Hamlyn, pp. 19-20; p. 39; p. 48.
57 G. Bataille, 1991, p. 95.

58 J. Kristeva, 1986, p. 113.
59 G. Deleuze and F. Guattari, 1987, p. 296.
60 Ibid.
61 J. Kristeva 1980/1982, p.5.
62 G. Deleuze, 1964/2000, p. 110.
63 V. Nabokov, 1980, pp. 208-209.
64 G. Deleuze, 2000, p. 108.

CHAPTER 9 JAMES JOYCE *SIRENS'* FUGUE

1 G. Borach 1979, p. 72.
2 W. Wolf 1999.
3 G. Lukács, 1972, p. 36.
4 M. Bradbury and J. McFarlane, 1978, p. 197.
5 R. Ellman, p. 1982.
6 *Ulysses*, p. 42.
7 L. Chrisman, 2004, p. 184-5; F. Fanon, 2001; D. Kiberd, 2000.
8 L. Chrisman, 2004, p. 185.
9 Homer, The Odyssey, p. 23.
10 D. Kiberd, 2000, p. xiv.
11 V. Nabokov, 1980, p. 287
12 V. Nabokov, 1980, p. 287.
13 Ibid., p. 287.
14 D. Kiberd, 2000, p. xvi.
15 Ibid.
16 J. Kristeva, 1986, p. 52; M. Bakhtin, 1965.
17 V. Nabokov, 1980, p. 8.
18 D. Kiberd, 1992, p. xxiii.
19 James Joyce, Selected Letters, p. 129.
20 Quoted in G. Budde, 1995, p. 199.
21 See, S.S. Brown 2013; M. Witen 2010; D. Ferrer 2001; M. Groden 2001.
22 W. Wolf, 1999, p. 130.
23 See, S.S. Brown, p.2013; and M. Witen, 2010.
24 L. Levin, 1965, p. 12.
25 S. S. Brown, 2013.
26 S. D. G. Knowles, 2001, p. 167.
27 S. S. Brown, 2013, p. 177.
28 M. Boyd, 1983, p. 193.
29 S.S. Brown, p. 178.
30 James Joyce Archive 13: 32-56.
31 S. Brown 2007.

32 S. S. Brown (2013); D. Ferrer, 2001; and M. Groden, 2001.
33 S. Gilbert 1955, p. 248.
34 Quoted in S.S. Brown 2013, p. 175.
35 D. Ferrer quoted in S. S. Brown 2013, p. 176.
36 S. S. Brown, 2013, p. 176.
37 Ibid.
38 Cf. D.F. Tovey, *The Forms of Music*, p. 37.
39 S. S. Brown, 2013, p. 177.
40 Cf. Ebenezer Prout, *Fugue*, 1891, Greenwood Press, New York, 1969.
41 A. Gédalge, 1901, p. 8.
42 Cf. I. Horsley, 1966, p. 108.
43 G. Antheil, 1945, p. 153-54.
44 O. Luening, 1980.
45 T. Martin and R. Bauerle, 1990, p. 43.
46 Eight-Part Fugue by Giambattista Martini in Mann's *The Study of Fugue*, p. 305.
47 M. Witen, 2010.
48 Cf. S. Brown, 2007.
49 D. Hofstadter, 1979, pp. 8-10.
50 Ibid., p. 9.
51 D. Gifford, 1988.
52 K. Mullin, 2004.
53 D. Gifford 1988.
54 D. Kiberd, 1992/2000, p. xxii.
55 Ibid., p.xxii.
56 D. Gifford 1989, p. 290.
57 Cf. C. Burney, 1753, p. viii.
58 T. Martin and R. Bauerle, 1990, p. 42.
59 D. Gifford, 1989, p. 290.
60 D. Gifford, 1974/1988.
61 Ibid.
62 D. Gifford, 1974/1988.
63 D. Gifford, 1988.
64 Ibid.
65 D. Kiberd, 1992.
66 Ibid., p. xi.
67 G. Lukács 1963; also see Andrea Fabry 'A Comparative View of Modernism in Central European Literature' in *Comparative Central European Culture*, ed Steven Tötösy de Zepetnek (Purdue, 2002).
68 W. Wolf, 1999; J. Grandt 2003.
69 W. Wolf, 1999, p. 139.
70 W. Wolf, 1999.

71 S.P. Scher, 2004, p. 199.
72 S.P. Scher, 2004, p. 19.
73 D. Gifford 1988.
74 R. Jakobson, 1972a, p. 112.
75 G. Budde quoted in W. Wolf 1999, p. 129.
76 T. Martin and R. Bauerle, 1990, p. 42.
77 Ibid.
78 W. Wolf, 1999, p. 129.

CHAPTER 10 PAUL CELAN AFTER THE *DEATHFUGUE*

1 J. Felstiner 1995, p. 28.
2 Ibid., p. 33.
3 J. Felstiner 2001, p. 254.
4 See Alan Sharp, 2nd edition, 2008; and cf. Manfried Rauchensteiner, 2nd ed. 2013
5 A. Sharp, 2008.
6 See Hans Kundani 'The Return of the German Question', Social Europe, 1/27, 2015; Roger Cohen, 'The German Question Redux', *New York Times*, July 13, 2015.
7 See A. Sharp, *The Versailles Settlement*, 2008.; and L. M. Tesser, 2015.
8 See Raphael Israeli, 2013; Barry M. Lituchy, 2006, p.xxxiii..
9 See Birgit Gortz, 'The Forgotten Holocaust in Transnistria'. D.W. 1/ 27/ 2014. www.dw.com/; Keno Verseck, 'Romania's Forgotten Holocaust: Filmmaker Confronts Leaders Over Silence, Spiegel Online, 11/15/2012, www.speigel.de.
10 Ibid.
11 J. Felstiner 1995.
12 Conversations (2003-2007) with author, Philip Mann.
13 Ibid.
14 G. Deleuze and F. Guattari, 1986, pp. 22-23
15 J. Derrida, 1994.
16 L. Olscher quoted in J. Friedlander 2001, p. 80.
17 P. Rosen, and N. Abfelbaum 2001, pp. 173-174.
18 Ibid., p. 166.
19 Ibid.
20 P. Rosen and N. Abfelbaum 2001, pp. 174-175.
21 Ibid., p. 175.
22 P. Levi, 1961, p. 90.
23 S. Freud, 2003, pp. 68-69.
24 S. Freud 2003, p. 100.
25 P. Celan, *Selected Poems and Prose*, p. 11.
26 Celan quoted in: Felstiner 2001, p. 114-5.
27 Pierre Joris, 1988.
28 T. W. Adorno, *Negative Dialectics*, p. 363.

29 Ibid., p. 363.
30 Ibid.
31 'Holocaust Survivor Band' video documentary and *New York Times* article by Joshua Z. Weinstein. https://www.nytimes.com/video/opinion.
32 B. Kirschenblatt-Gimblett, 'Sounds of Sensibility,' *Judaism*. Issue no. 185, vol. 47, no. 1
33 Katjia Garloff, 2005, p. 132.
34 Ibid., p. 143.

CHAPTER 11   SYLVIA PLATH *LITTLE FUGUE*

1 S. Plath and P. Orr, 1966.
2 J.-J. Rousseau, *Complete Dictionary of Music*, p. 191.
3 S. Gubar, 2003 p. 178.
4 T. Hughes, 'Introduction' in Sylvia Plath, *Johnny Panic*, 1979, p. 11-13.
5 S. Plath, 'America! America!', *Johnny Panic*,. 1963/1979 p. 37.
6 L. Bundtzen, 2001/2005, pp 77-78.

CHAPTER 12   THE WRITERS' FUGUE IN REVIEW

1 F. de Saussure, 1916/1983.
2 E. Glisky et al. 2004.
3 L. Althusser 2003, p. 55.
4 Ibid.
5 Ibid.
6 J. Baudrillard, 1985, p. 425.
7 J. Baudrillard, 1982, p. 29.
8 G. Gutting 2001, p. 250.
9 R. Barthes, 1984, pp. 61-62.
10 R. Barthes, 1978b, p. 143.
11 Ibid., pp. 146-7.
12 Ibid., p. 145.
13 R. Barthes, 1984, p. 63.
14 R. Barthes, 1977b, p. 147.
15 J.-Y. Tadié, 1996, p. 346.

Works Consulted

Adorno, Theodor W. *Introduction to the Sociology of Music*, trans. E.B. Ashton. New York: The Seabury Press, 1976.
— — "Cultural Criticism and Society", 1967, *Prisms*, trans. Samuel and Shierry Weber. Cambridge: MIT Press, 1997.
— — "Reconciliation Under Duress."*Aesthetics and Politics: The Key Texts in the Classic Debate within German Marxism*, ed. Ernst Bloch. 1977. London: Verso, 2002.
— — "Lyric Poetry and Society." *The Adorno Reader.* Brian O'Connor, ed. Oxford: Blackwell Publishers, 2000.
— — *Negative Dialectics*, 1966, trans. E.B. Ashton. New York: The Seabury Press-Continuum, 1973.
— — *Minima Moralia: Reflections from Damaged Life*, 1951, trans. E.F.N. Jephcott. London: New Left Books, 1974.
— — *Philosophy of Modern Music*, trans. Anne G. Mitchell and Wesley V. Blomster. New York: The Seabury Press, 1973.
— — *Prisms*, trans. Samuel and Shierry Weber. Cambridge: MIT Press, 1997
Adorno, Theodor W. and Horkheimer, M. *Dialectic of Enlightenment*, trans. John Cumming. London: Verso, 1997.
Alexander, Jeffrey C., et al. *Cultural Trauma and Collective Identity*. California: University of California Press, 2004.
Alighieri, Dante. *La Divina Commedia di Dante Alighieri col comento Di G. Biagioli, Volume Secondo.* Milan, 1820.
— — *The Divine Comedy. 2. Purgatory. 1308-1321*, trans. Dorothy L. Sayers. London: Penguin Books 1955
Althusser, Louis. *Philosophy of the Encounter: Later Writings, 1978-1987*, ed. O. Corpet and F. Matheron, trans. G.M. Goshgarian. London: Verso, 2006.
— — *The Humanist Controversy and Other Writings*. F. Matheron, ed. trans. and intro by G.M Goshgarian. London: Verso, 2003.
— — *Writings on Psychoanalysis: Freud and Lacan*, ed. O. Corpet and F. Matheron, trans. J. Mehlman. New York: Columbia University Press, 1996.
Anderson, Benedict. *Imagined Communities: Reflections on the Origin and Spread of Nationalism.* London: Verso, 1991.
Antheil, George. *Bad Boy of Music.* New York: Doubleday, 1945.
Arendt, Hannah. 'Eichmann in Jersusalem: A Report on the Banality of Evil-1', *The New Yorker*, New York, 1963, http://www.newyorker.com/magazine/1963/02/16/eichmann-in-jerusalem-
— — *Eichmann in Jersusalem: A Report on the Banality of Evil*, 1963. New York: Viking 1968

Aristotle. *Poetics,* trans. Malcolm Heath. London: Penguin Books, 1996.
Aronson, Alex. *Music and the Novel: A Study in Twentieth-Century Fiction.* Totowa, New Jersey: Rowman and Littlefield, 1980.
Ashton, Rosemary. *The Life of Samuel Taylor Coleridge: A Critical Biography.* Oxford: Basil Blackwell, 1997.
Attridge, Derek. *Peculiar Language: Literature as Difference from the Renaissance to James Joyce.* London: Routlege, 2004.
Australian Human Rights Commission. *Immigration (Detention Reform) Bill 220.* Submitted to the Senate, July 31, 2009. Australian Human Rights Commission website <http://hreoc.gov.au>
Australian Human Rights Commission/ Triggs, Gillian, D. *The Forgotten Children: National Inquiry into Children in Immigration Detention.* Sydney, NSW: Australian Human Rights Commission, 2014.
Bach, Johanne Sebastian. *Die Kunst der Fuge. 1745-50. BWV 1080.* CD-ROM. Jordi Savall, conductor. Le Concert des Nations. Alia Vox. Audio CD: Oct. 9, 2001.
— — *Das Wohltemperierte Klavier. 1 und 2.846-869 und 870-893.* Sviatoslav Richter, artist. Sony-BMG. RCA Red Seal. Oct. 12, 2004.
— — *Musikalisches Opfer. 1747.BWV 1079.* CD-ROM. Savall, conductor. Le Concert des Nations. Alia Vox. Audio CD: Oct. 9, 2001.
— — *The Art of the Fugue and A Musical Offering.* Alfred Dörffel and Wolfgang Graeser. New York: Dover Publications, 1992.
Bach, Ken. "*De Re* Belief and Methodological Solipsism," *Thought and Object: Essays on Intentionality,* ed. Andrew Woodfield, Oxford, 1982.
Bakhtin, Mikhail. *Rabelais and His World,* 1965, trans. Hélène Iswolsky. Bloomington: Indiana University Press, 1993.
— — *The Dialogic Imagination: Four Essays,* ed. Michael Holquist, trans. Carl Emerson and Michael Holquist. Austin and London: University of Texas Press, 1981.
Banville, John, ed. *Magnum Ireland.* London: Thames and Hudson, 2005.
Babacan, Hurriyet. "300 Days: Social Inclusion and the Rudd Government", *Rights, Reconciliation, Respect, Responsibility: Planning for a Socially Inclusive Future for Australia Conference,* University of Technology, Sydney, October 2, 2008.
Barnett, Christopher. *When they came/for you elegies/of resistance/* Kent Town: Wakefield Press, 2013.
Barrell, John. *The Infection of Thomas De Quincey: A Psychopathology of Imperialism.* USA: Yale University Press, 1991.
Barthes, Roland. "La Mort de l'auteur," in *Le Bruissement de la langue,* 1968. Paris: Seuil. 61-67, 1984.
— — "The Death of the Author," 1968, *Image, Music, Text,* trans. S. Heath. New York: Hill and Wang, 1978a.
— — *A Lover's Discourse,* trans. Richard Howard. London: Penguin, 1990.

— — *Elements of Semiology*, 1968, trans. Annette Lavers and Colin Smith. New York: Hill and Wang, 1978c.
— — "From Work to Text," in *Image, Music, Text*, 1977, trans. S. Heath. New York: Hill and Wang, 1978b.
— — *Le Degré zéro de l'écriture*. Paris: Seuil, 1972.
— — *Le Plaisir du texte*. Paris: Seuil, 1973.
Bataille, George. *The Impossible*, 1962, trans. M. Hurley. San Francisco: City Lights Books, 1991.
Baudelaire, Charles. *Selected Writings on Art and Literature*, trans. P.E. Charvet. London: Penguin, 2006.
— — *Artificial Paradise*, 1860, trans. Patricia Roseberry. London: Broadwater House, 2000.
— — *Baudelaire: Selected Poems*, trans. Joanna Richardson. London: Penguin, 1976.
Baudelaire, Charles. *Les Paradis Artificiels suivis des Journaux Intimes. Éclaircissements et Notes de Blaise Allan*. Lausanne: La Guilde du Livre, n.d.
Benjamin, Walter. *Selected Writings, Volume 4: 1938–1940*, ed. Michael W. Jennings and Howard Eiland. Cambridge: Harvard University Press, 2003.
— — *The Origin of German Tragic Drama*, trans. John Osbourne. London: Verso, 1998.
— — *Charles Baudelaire: Ein Lyriker im Zeitalter des Hochkapitalismus* (nachw. R. Tiedemann). Frankfurt am Main: Suhrkampf, 1955.
— — *Charles Baudelaire: A Lyric Poet in the Era of High Capitalism*, 1969, trans. H. Zohn, London: Verso, 1989.
Bergson, Henri. *Essai sur les données immédiates de la conscience*. Paris: Presses Universitaires de France, 2003.
— — *L'Evoltion créatrice*. Paris: Presses Universitaires de France, 1941.
— — *Matière et mémoire*, 1896, Paris: Presses Universitaires de France, 2004.
— *Matter and Memory*, 1896, trans. N.M. Paul and W.S. Palmer. New York: Zone Books, 1988.
— — *Time and Free Will: An Essay on the Immediate Data of Consciousness*, 1889, trans. F.L. Pogson. London: Allen and Unwin, 1910.
Beard, George Miller. *Cases of Hysteria, Neurasthenic, Spinal Irritations, and Allied Afflictions; With Remarks*. Chicago: Spalding, 1894.
Berman, Marshall. "All That is Solid Melts into Air": the Experience of Modernity', 1983, *The Postmodern Reader*, ed. Michel Drolet. London: Routledge, 2004.
Bernhart, Walter, Steven Paul Scher and Werner Wolf, eds. *Word and Music Studies Defining the Field: Proceedings of the First International Conference on Word and Music Studies at Graz 1997*. Amsterdam: Rodopi, 1999.
Bhabha, Homi. *The Location of Culture*. London: Routledge, 1994.
Biddulph, Steve. "LOVE is Stronger than Fear. The SIEV X Memorial,"

in *Acting from the Heart: Australian Advocates for Asylum Seekers Tell their Stories,* eds. Sarah Mares and Louise Newman. Sydney: Finch Publishing, 2007.

Blake, William. *Songs of Innocence and Experience (The Illuminated Books of William Blake Vol. 2),* 1794. Princeton University Press, 1991.

Blanchot, Maurice. *The Gaze of Orpheus and Other Literary Essays,* 1943, trans. Lydia Davies and ed. P. Adams Sitney. New York: Station Hill Press, 1981.

Borach, Georges. "Conversations with James Joyce." *Portraits of the Artist in Exile: Recollections of James Joyce by Europeans,* ed. Willard Potts. San Diego: Harcourt Brace Jovanovich Publishers, 1979.

Boulanger, A. "Influence or Confluence: Joyce, Eliot, Cohen and the Case for Comparative Studies." *Comparative Literature Studies,* Vol. 39, No. 1. 2002. 18-47.

Boulez, Pierre. *Orientations.* New York: Harvard University Press, 1986.

Bowen, Zack. *Bloom's Old Sweet Song: Essays on Joyce and Music.* Gainesville: University Press of Florida, 1995.

Boyd, Malcolm. *Bach*.1983. Oxford: Oxford University Press, 2000.

Bradbury, Malcolm and James McFarlane, eds. *Modernism.* 1978. Harmondsworth: Penguin, 1983.

Brée, Germaine. *Marcel Proust and Deliverance from Time,* trans. C.J Richards and A.D. Truitt. London: Chatto and Windus, 1956.

Brennan, Frank. *Tampering with Asylum.* St Lucia: University of Queensland Press, 2003.

Brentano, Franz. *Psychology from an Empirical Standpoint. Vol. 1-11,* ed. Linda L. McAlister and trans. Antos C. Rancurello, D.B. Terrell and Linda L. McAlister. New York: Humanities Press, 1973.

— — *Psychologie vom empirischen Standpunkte. Vols 1-11,* 1874. 2nd ed. Leipzig: Duncker and Humblot, 1974.

— — *Psychology from an Empirical Standpoint. Vol. 111: Sensory and Noetic Consciousness.* 1928, ed. Oskar Kraus. English edition, ed. Linda L. McAlister, and trans. Margarete Schättle and Linda McAlister. London: Routledge and Kegan Paul, 1981.

— — *Psychology From an Empirical Standpoint. Realism and the Background of Phenomenology,* ed. and trans. R. Chisholm. New York: The Free Press, 1960.

Brown, Susan. "The Mystery of the Fuga Per Canonem Solved." *Genetic Joyce Studies,* no. 7 (Spring 2007).

Brown, Susan Sutliff. "The Mystery of the Fuga Per Canonem Solved." *Joycean Unions.* 2013. 173-179.

Brown, Calvin S. *Music and Literature: A Comparison of the Arts.* Athens: Ga, 1948.

— — "The Musical Structure of De Quincey's 'Dream-Fugue.'" *The Musical Quarterly,* 24 (1938): 341-350.

Budde, Gudrun. "Fuge als literarische Form? Zum Sirenen-Kapitel aus "Ulysses' von James Joyce." *Musik und Literatur: komparatistiche*

Studien zur Strukturverwandtschaft, ed. Albert Gier and Gerold W. Gruber. Frankfurt-am-Main: Peter Lang, 1995: 195-213.

Bundtzen, Lynda K. *The Other Ariel.* Stroud: Sutton Publishing, 2005.

Bunt, Charlie. *A Blossoming: A Memoir of Australian Artist Joan A. Holt.* Charlie Bunt, 2015.

Burke, Edmund. *Reflections on the Revolution in France.* London: James Dodsley, 1790.

— — "A Letter to a Noble Lord", *The Works of the Right Hon. Edmund Burke With a Biographical and Critical Introduction and Portrait after Sir Joshua Reynolds,* London: Holdsworth and Ball, 1834.

Burney, Charles. *The present state of music in France and Italy: or, the journal of a tour through those countries, undertaken to collect materials for a general history of music.* London: T. Becket and Co, 1773.

Burwick, Frederick. *Thomas De Quincey: Knowledge and Power.* London: Palgrave, 2001.

Burwick, Frederick, ed. *The Works of Thomas De Quincey. Vol. 15. Articles from Blackwood's Edinburgh Magazine and Tait's Edinburgh Magazine 1844-6,* general ed. G. Lindop, London: Pickering and Chatto, 2003.

Butt, John. "A Mind Unconscious that it is Calculating? Bach's Creative Character and the Rationalist Philosophy of Woolf, Leibniz and Spinoza." John Butt, ed. Cambridge Companion to Bach. Cambridge: Cambridge University Press, 1997.

Caruth, Cathy, *Unclaimed Experience: Trauma, Narrative, and History.* Baltimore: John Hopkins University Press, 1996.

Caruth, Cathy, ed. *Trauma: Explorations in Memory.* Baltimore: John Hopkins University Press, 1995.

Campbell, Jan. "Hysteria, mimesis and the phenomenological imaginary." *Textual Practice* 19 (3) (2005): 331-351.

Carter, William, W. *Proust in Love.* New Haven and London: Yale University Press, 2006.

Celan, Paul. *Selected Poems and Prose of Paul Celan,* trans. John Felstiner. New York, W.W. Norton, 2001.

— — *Paul Celan Selections,* eds. Pierre Joris and Jerome Rothenberg. California: University of California Press, 2005.

— — *Breathturn,* trans. Pierre Joris. Los Angeles: Sun and Moon, 1995.

— — 'Reply to a Questionnaire from the Flinker Bookstore, Paris, 1958', in *Collected Prose,* trans. Rosemarie Waldrop. New York: Sheep Meadow Press, 1986.

Cermak, Laird S., ed. "Memory and its Disorders," Francoise Boller and Jordan Grafman, series eds. *Handbook of Neuropsychology* 2nd edition, Vol. 2. Amsterdam: Elsevier Science, 2000.

Chabut, Marie-Hélène."The Role of Corporeality in the Shaping of Early Modern European Culture and Epistemology." *Eighteenth Century Studies* 38 (2) (2005): 323-328.

Chaucer, Geoffrey. *The Canterbury Tales*, 1308-1321, trans. David Wright. 1986. Oxford: Oxford University Press (World's Classics), 2011.
Chisholm, Roderick, M. *Brentano and Intrinsic Value*. Cambridge: Cambridge University Press, 1986.
— — "On the Simplicity of the Soul." *Philosophical Perspectives*. 5 (1991): 167-181.
— — "The Objects of Sensation: A Brentano Study." *Topoi*. 8 (1989): 3-8.
Chisholm, Roderick, M., ed. *Realism and the Background of Phenomenology*. New York: The Free Press, 1960.
Chrisman, L. "Nationalism and Postcolonial Studies" in (ed.) N. Lazarus, *Postcolonial Literary Studies*. Cambridge: Cambridge University Press, 2004.
Christensen, Thomas. *Rameau and Musical Thought in the Enlightenment*. Cambridge: Cambridge University Press, 1993.
Cixous, Hélène. "Writing and the Law: Blanchot, Joyce, Kafka and Lispector," in *Readings: The Poetics of Blanchot, Joyce, Kafka, Lispector, Tsvetaeva*, trans. Verena Conley. Minneapolis: University of Minnesota Press, 1991.
— — *Coming to Writing and Other Essays*, trans and ed. Deborah Jenson,. Cambridge, Mass.: Harvard University Press, 1991b.
— — *First Days of the Year*. Trans. with a preface by Catherine MacGillivray. Minneapolis: University of Minnesota Press, 1998.
— — "Le Rire de la Méduse." (1975). Maïté Albisture and Daniel Armogathe, eds. "La Greif des femmes," Vol. 2. *Anthologie de texts féministe du second empire à nos jours*. (1978):307-313. Paris: Éditions Hier and Demain.
— — 'The Laugh of the Medusa'. *New French Feminisms*. Trans. Keith Cohen and Paula Cohen, eds. Elaine Marks and Isabelle de Courtivron. New York: Schoken, 1981.
— — "[La jeune née] The Newly Born Woman." *Theory and History of Literature*, Vol. 2. 1975, trans. Betsy Wing. Minneapolis, University of Minnesota, 1986.
— — "'Le roman aujord-hui' entretien avec Henri-Quéré." *Fabula*. No. 3 (1984): 147-158.
Cixous, Hélène; Leclerc, Annie; Gagnon, Madeleine. *La venue a l'écriture*. Paris: Union générale d'éditions. (1977): 10-18.
Clej, Alina. *A Genealogy of the Modern Self: Thomas De Quincey and the Intoxication of Writing*. California: Stanford University Press, 1995.
— — "The Debt of the Translator: an Essay on Translation and Modernism." *Symploke* 5.1 (1997) 7-26.
— — "Introduction." *The Works of Thomas De Quincey. Vol. 10. Articles from Tait's Edinburgh Magazine 1834-8*. Alina Clej, ed. Grevel Lindop, general ed. London: Pickering and Chatto, 2000.
Coleridge, Samuel Taylor. *The Complete Poetical Works of Samuel Taylor*

Coleridge Including Poems and Versions of poems now Published for the First Time. 1912, ed. E, H. Coleridge. Oxford: OUP, 2001.

Conley, Verena Andermatt. *Hélène Cixous: Writing the Feminine.* Lincoln: University of Nebraska Press, 1991.

Cooper, Brian. 'Sylvia Plath and the depression continuum', *Journal of the Royal Society of Medicine.* 2003, Jun; 96(6) pp. 296-301.

Dahlhaus, Carl. *Esthetics of Music.* 1967, trans. William Austin. Cambridge: Cambridge University Press, 1982.

DeGeorge, R. and F., eds. *The Structuralists from Marx to Levi-Strauss.* New York: Doubleday, 1972.

Deleuze, Gilles. *Difference and Repetition.* 1964. Trans. Paul Patton. London: The Athlone Press, 1994.

— — *Proust and Signs.* 1964, trans. Richard Howard. London: Athlone Press, 2000.

— — "Postscript on the Societies of Control." 1992. *October*, 59: 3-7.

Deleuze, Gilles and Guattari, Felix. *Mille Plateaux.* Paris: Les Editions de Minuit, 1980.

— — *One Thousand Plateaus: Capitalism and Schizophrenia.* 1980. Trans. Brian Massumi. Manchester : University of Manchester Press, 1987.

— — *Kafka: Towards a Minor Literature.* Theory and History of Literature, Vol., 30. Minneapolis: University of Minnesota Press, 1986.

Dennett, Daniel. "Beyond Belief," *Thought and Object: Essays on Intentionality*, ed. Andrew Woodfield. Oxford: Clarendon Press, 1982.

Derrida, Jacques. *Of Grammatology*, trans. Gayatri Chakravorty Spivak, 1976. Baltimore: John Hopkins University Press, 1997.

— — *L'écriture et la différence.* Paris: Éditions du Seuil, 1967.

— — *Writing and Difference,* trans. Alan Bass. London: Routledge and Kegan Paul, 1978.

— — *Glas,* trans. J.P. Leavey Jr and R. Rand. Nebraska: University of Nebraska Press, 1990.

— — *The Postcard: from Socrates to Freud and Beyond,* trans. A. Bass. Chicago: University of Chicago Press, 1987.

— — "Shibboleth for Paul Celan". *Word Traces: Readings of Paul Celan,* ed. Aris Fioretos. Baltimore: John Hopkins University Press, 1994.

Descartes, Rene. *Meditations on First Philosophy in which the Existence of God and the Distinction of the Soul from the Body are Demonstrated,* 1641, trans. D. Cress. USA: Hackett Publishing Company, 1979.

— — *Discourse on Method and the Meditation,* trans. F. E. Sutcliffe. Harmondsworth: Penguin Books, 1998.

De Quincey, Thomas. *The Collected Writings of Thomas De Quincey Vol.1 Autobiography from 1785-1803,* ed. David Masson. Soho Square, London: A. and C. Black, 1896.

— — *The Collected Writings of Thomas De Quincey Vol. Xlll. Tales and Prose Phantasies*, ed. David Masson. Soho Square, London: A. and C. Black, 1897a.

— — *The Collected Writings of Thomas De Quincey Vol. X. Literary Theory and Criticism*, ed. David Masson. Soho Square, London: A. and C. Black, 1897b.

— — *The Autobiography of an Opium Eater by Thomas De Quincey*. Boston: Ticknor, Reed and Fields, n.d.

— — *Suspiria De Profundis With Other Essays Critical, Historical, Biographical, Philosophical, Imaginative and Humorous by Thomas De Quincey*. Vol. 1., ed., with Introduction and Notes by Alexander H. Japp. London: William Heinemann, 1891.

— — *Thomas De Quincey. His Life and Writings With Unpublished Correspondence*. Vol. 1. Second edition. H.A. Page, ed. London: John Higg and Co, 1879.

— — *The Works of De Quincey, Vol. 1. Writings, 1820*. Barry Symonds, ed.; Grevel Lindop, general edir London: Pickering and Chatto, 2000a.

— — *The Works of De Quincey, Vol. 2. Confessions of an English Opium-Eater. 1821-1856*. Grevel Lindop, ed. London: Pickering and Chatto, 2000b.

— — *The Works of Thomas De Quincey. Vol. 10. Articles from Tait's Edinburgh Magazine 1834-8*. Alina Clej, ed.; Grevel Lindop, general ed. London: Pickering and Chatto, 2003a.

— — *The Works of Thomas De Quincey. Vol. 15. Articles from Blackwood's Edinburgh Magazine and Tait's Edinburgh Magazine1844-6*. Frederick Burwick, ed.; Grevel Lindop, general ed. London: Pickering and Chatto, 2003b.

— — *The Works of Thomas De Quincey. Vol. 16. Articles from Tait's Edinburgh Magazine, MacPhail's Edinburgh Ecclesiastical Journal, The Glasgow Athenaeum Album, the North British Review, and Blackwood's Edinburgh Magazine 1847-9*. Robert Morrison, ed.; Grevel Lindop, general ed. London: Pickering and Chatto, 2003c.

Diagnostic and Statistical Manual of Mental Disorders-Fifth Edition, *American Psychiatric Publishing*, U.S.A. 2013

Diagnostic and Statistical Manual of Mental Disorders-Fourth Edition, *American Psychiatric Publishing*, U.S.A. 2000

Doblhofer, Ernst. *Voices in Stone: the Decipherment of Ancient Scripts and Writings*.1957, trans. Mervyn Savill. London: Souvenir Press, 1961.

Ellmann, R. *James Joyce: New and Revised Edition*. Oxford: Oxford University Press, 1982.

Fairclough, Norman. "Discourse, social theory, and social research: The discourse of welfare reform." *Journal of Sociolinguistics*. Vol. 4, No. 2 (2000): 163-195.

Fanon, F. *The Wretched of the Earth*. London: Penguin, 2001.

Farrell, P., N. Evershed and H. Davidson, 'The Nauru Files', *The Guardian*, 10 August 2016.

Felstiner, John. *Paul Celan: Poet, Survivor, Jew*. New Haven and London: Yale University Press, 1995..

Ferrer, Daniel. "What Song the Sirens Sang... Is No Longer Beyond All Conjecture: A Preliminary Description of the New 'Proteus' and 'Sirens' Manuscripts." *James Joyce Quarterly*, 39/1 (Fall 2001): 53-68.

Flew, Antony. *A Dictionary of Philosophy*, 1979. London: The Macmillan Press, 1981.

Foucault, Michel. "Qu'est-ce qu'un auteur?" in *Dits et écrits*. Vol. 1 1954-1975. 1969. Paris: Gallimard, 1994.

— — "What is an Author", 1969, *Language, Counter-Memory, Practice, Selected Essays and Interviews*, trans. Donald F. Bouchard. New York: Cornell University Press, 1980.

— — *Language, Counter-Memory, Practice, Selected Essays and Interviews*. 1977, trans. Donald F. Bouchard. New York: Cornell University Press, 1980.

— — *The Archaeology of Knowledge*, 1969, trans. A.M. Sheridan Smith. London: Routledge, 2004.

— — *The Order of Things: an archaeology of the human sciences*, 1966, trans. A.M. Sheridan Smith. London: Routledge, 2002.

— — *Discipline and Punish: The Birth of the Prison*. London: Allen Lane, 1975.

Foster. Hal. ed. *Postmodern Culture*. London: Pluto, 1985.

Fowler, Roger. *A Dictionary of Modern Critical Terms*. London: Routledge and Kegan Paul, 1981.

Freud, Sigmund. *Collected Papers, Vol. 4*, trans. Joan Riviere. New York: Nasic Books, 1959.

— — "Mourning and Melancholia", 1917, *On Metapsychology: The Theory of Psychoanalysis*. 1917. The Freud Pelican Library. Vol. 11. Trans. James Strachey. Harmondsworth: Penguin. 91-178.

— — "Creative Writers and Day-Dreaming", 1908, *Collected Papers Vol 4*. Trans. Joan Riviere. New York: Basic Books, 1959.

— — "Leonardo da Vinci and a Memory of His Childhood". 1919. *The Freud Reader*, ed. Peter Gay. New York: W.W. Norton and Co., 1995.

— — *Eine Kindheitserinnerung des Leonardo da Vinci. (Schriften zur angewandten Seelenkunde, 7. Heft.)* Zweite Auflage. Leipzig und Wien 1919.

— — *The Essentials of Psycho-Analysis*. Intro. Anna Freud, trans. James Strachey. London: Penguin, 1991.

— — *Jenseits des Lustprinzips. (II. Beiheft der Internationalen Zeitschrift für Psychoanalyse.)* Zweite Auflage. Leipzig, Wien und Zürich 1921.

— — *Beyond the Pleasure Principal and Other Writings*, 1940, trans. John

Reddick. London: Penguin, 2003.
— — *The Interpretation of Dreams*, 1899, trans. James Strachey. New York: Avon Books, 1965.
— — *Introductory Lectures on Psycho-Analysis*, trans. Joan Riviere, 1922, London: Allen and Unwin, 1949.
— — *Civilization and Its Discontents*, 1930, trans. David McLintock. London: Penguin, 2002
Fischer, Andreas. "Strange Words, Strange Music: The Verbal Music of "Sirens."" *Bronze by Gold: The Music of Joyce*, ed. Sebastian D. G. Knowles. New York and London: Garland Publishing, 1999: 245-262
Friedlander, Saul, ed. *Probing the Limits of Representation: Nazism and the Final Solution.* Cambridge Mass./London: Harvard University Press, 1992.
Fry, Northrop. "The Archetypes of Literature." *Twentieth Century Literary Criticism.* David Lodge, ed. London: Longmans, 1951.
— — "Milton's Lydias." *Twentieth Century Literary Criticism,* 1959. David Lodge, ed. London: Longmans. 1972.
Garloff, Katjia. *Words from Abroad: Trauma and Displacement in Postwar German Jewish Writers.* US: Wayne State University Press, 2005.
Gédalge, André. *Traité de la fugue.* Paris: Enoch and Co, 1901.
Gifford, Don. *Ulysses Annotated.* 1988. London: University of California Press, 1989.
Gilbert, Stuart. *James Joyce's Ulysses: A Study.* London: Faber and Faber Limited, 1952.
Gilbert, S. and Gubar, S. *No Man's Land: The Place of the Woman Writer in the Twentieth Century. Vol. Three. Letters from the Front.* New Haven, USA: Yale University Press, 1994.
Girard, Rene. *Deceit, Desire and the Novel: Self and Other in Literary Structure,* trans. Yvonne Freccero. Baltimore: John Hopkins University Press, 1976.
Glisky, Elizabeth, et al. "A Case of Psychogenic Fugue: I understand, aber ich verstehe nichts." *Neuropsychologia.* Vol. 42, Issue 8, (2004): 1132-1147.
Glover, J., ed. *The Philosophy of Mind.* Oxford: Oxford University Press, 1986.
Gordon, Michael, 'Australia's forgotten detention centre: the peculiar torture of Christmas Island's asylum seekers locked up with hardened criminals'. *Sydney Morning Herald*, Sept 17, 2016.
Grandt, Jürgen, E. "Might be what you like, till you hear the words': Joyce in Zurich and the Contrapuntal Language of *Ulysses*." *Joyce Studies Annual.* Vol. 14, Summer (2003): 74-91.
Groden, Michael. "The National Library of Ireland's New Joyce Manuscripts: A Statement and Document Descriptions." *James Joyce Quarterly,* 39/1 (Fall 2001): 29-51.
Gubar, Susan. *Poetry After Auschwitz: Remembering What One Never Knew.*

USA: Indiana University Press, 2003.
— — "The Long and the Short of Holocaust Verse." *New Literary History*. Vol. 35, No. 3 (2004): 443-468.
Gutting, Gary. *French Philosophy in the Twenty-First Century*. Cambridge: Cambridge University Press, 2001.
Hacking, Ian. *Mad Travellers: Reflections of the Reality of Transient Mental Illnesses*. Virginia: The University Press of Virginia, 1998.
— — "Les Aliénés voyageurs: how fugue became a medical entity." *History of Psychiatry, 1996 Sept 7 (27 pt 3), 425-49*.
Hale, John K. "Milton's Greek, 1644-1645: Two Notes." *Milton Quarterly*. Vol. 34, No. 1(2000): 13-16.
Hamlyn, David. *A History of Western Philosophy*. London: Penguin, 1987.
Hardy, Frank. *But the Dead are Many*. London: The Bodley Head, 1975.
Hawkins, Sir John. *A General History of the Science and Practice of Music*. London: T. Payne and Son, 1776.
Hayman, Ronald. *Proust*. London: William Heinemann, 1990.
Heidegger, Martin. *Being and Time*, trans. J. Macquarie and E. Robinson. San Francisco: Harper, 1962.
Herman, David. "'Sirens' after Schönberg." *James Joyce Quarterly*, 31/4 (Summer 1994): 473-94.
Herman, P. C. "Warring Chains of Signifiers: Metaphoric Ambivalence and the Politics of Paradise Lost." *Texas Studies in Literature and Language*. Vol. 40, Issue 3 (1998): 268-293.
Hesse, Hermann. *The Glass Bead Game*, 1943, trans. Richard and Clara Winston. London: Vintage, 2000.
Hoffman, John. *The Gramscian Challenge: Coercion and Consent in Marxist Political Theory*. Oxford: Basil Blackwell, 1984.
Hofstadter, Douglas, R. *Gödel, Escher, Bach: An Eternal Golden Braid–A Metaphorical Fugue on Minds and Machines in the Spirit of Lewis Carroll*. 1979. London: Penguin 1980.
Homer. *The Odyssey*, trans. E.V. Rieu. G.B: Penguin, 1967.
Hopkins, Robert. "De Quincey on War and the Pastoral Design of The English Mail-Coach." *Studies in Romanticism* 6. (1967). 129-151.
Horsley, Imogen. *Fugue: History and Practice*. New York: Collin-Macmillan, 1966.
Hughes, Ted. 'Introduction', Plath, Sylvia. *Johnny Panic and the Bible of Dreams*. London: Faber and Faber, 1979.
Hulme, T.E. "Romanticism and Classicism." 1924. *Twentieth Century Literary Criticism*. David Lodge, ed. London: Longmans, 1972.
Human Rights and Equal Opportunity Commission. *A Last Resort? National Inquiry into Children in Immigration Detention*. Australian Commission for Human Rights website, www.hreoc.gov.au, 2004.
Husserl, Edmund. *The Phenomenology of Internal Time Consciousness*, ed. M. Heidegger, trans. James S. Churchill. The Hague: Martinus Nijhoff Publishers, 1964.

— — *Cartesian Meditations: an Introduction to Phenomenology*, trans. Dorion Cairns. The Hague: Martinus Nijhoff Publishers, 1982.

Hutcheon, Linda. *Narcissistic Narrative: the Metafictional Paradox*. London: Methuen, 1984.

Huxley, Aldous. *Point Counter Point*. London: Penguin, 1928.

Inquiry into the Circumstances of the Immigration Detention of Cornelia Rau. *Inquiry into the Circumstances of the Immigration Detention of Cornelia Rau: report/[Mick Palmer]*. Canberra, A.C.T. Department of Immigration and Multicultural and Indigenous Affairs, 2005.

Irigaray, Luce. *Ce sexe qui n'en pas un*. Paris: Éditions de Minuit, 1977.

Isaacs, Mark. *The Undesireables: Inside Nauru*. Melbourne and London, Hardie Grant Books, 2014.

Raphael Israeli, *The Death Camps of Croatia: Visions and Revisions, 1941-1945*. New Brunswick: Transaction Publishers, 2013

Jackson, Andra. "Mystery woman at Baxter may be ill." *The Sydney Morning Herald* and *The Age*, 31 January 2005.

Jakobson, Roman. "Linguistics and Poetics." R. and F. Fernande de George, eds. *The Structuralists from Marx to Levi-Strauss*, New York: Doubleday (Anchor), 1972a.

— — "Problems in the Study of Language and Literature." R. and F. Fernande de George, eds. *The Structuralists from Marx to Levi-Strauss*, New York: Doubleday (Anchor), 1972b.

James, William. *The Principles of Psychology* (two volumes), New York: Henry Holt and Co, 1890.

— — *A Pluralistic Universe: Hibbert Lectures at Manchester College on the Present Situation in Philosophy* New York: Longmans, Green and Co., 1909.

Janet, Pierre. *Lautomatisme psychologique. Essai de psychologie expérimentale sur les formes inférieures de lactivité humaine*. Paris: F. Alcan, 1889.

Jameson, Frederic. "Beyond the Cave: Demystifying the Ideology of Modernisms" 1975, in *Contemporary Marxist Literary Criticism*, Francis Mulhern, ed. New York and Abingdon, Oxon., Routledge, 2013.

Jameson, Frederic. *Postmodernism or The Cultural Logic of Late Capitalism*. 1991. USA: Duke University Press, 2003.

Japp, Alexander, H. "Introduction." *Suspiria De Profundis With Other Essays Critical, Historical, Biographical, Philosophical, Imaginative and Humorous by Thomas De Quincey. Vol. 1. Edited from the Original MSS., with Introduction and Notes by Alexander H. Japp* London: William Heinemann, 1891.

Johnson, Patricia Cannon."The Neoplatonists and the Mystery Schools of the Mediterranean." *The Library of Alexandria: Centre of Learning in the Ancient World*, ed. Roy Macleod, London: Palgrave MacMillan, 2004.

Johnstone, Kenneth. *The Hidden Wordsworth: Poet, Lover, Rebel, Spy*. New

York: WW. Norton and Co, 1998.
Joris, Pierre. 1988. *Celan/Heidegger: Translation at the Mountain of Death*. http://wings.buffalo.edu/epc/authors/joris/todtnauberg.html.
Joyce, James. *Ulysses*. 1922. London: Penguin, 2000.
— — *Portrait of the Artist as a Young Man*, 1916, Harmondsworth: Penguin, 1991.
— — *Letters of James Joyce*, ed. Gilbert, Stuart (vol 1); Ellmann, Richard (vol 2 and 3). New York: Viking; London: Faber, 1966.
Kant, Immanuel. *Immanuel Kant's Critique of Pure Reason*. 1787. Trans. Norman Kemp Smith. 1929. Houndsmills: Macmillan, 1986.
Kiberd, Declan. "Introduction", *Ulysses*, James Joyce. London: Penguin, 2000.
Kierkegaard, Sorel. *Either/Or*, 1842, trans. George L. Stengren. New York: Harper and Row, 1986.
Kintzler, Catherine. *Poetique de L'opera francais de Corneille et Rousseau*. Paris. Minerve, 1991.
Kirschenblatt-Gimblett, Barbara, "Sounds of Sensibility", *Judaism: A Quarterly Journal of Jewish Life and Thought*, Issue no. 185, vol. 47, no. 1 (winter 1998), pp. 49-788.
Klein, Melanie. *Love, Guilt and Reparation and Other Works 1921- 1945 by Melanie Klein*. London: The Hogarth Press, 1975.
— — 'Love, Guilt and Reparation' in *Love Guilt and Reparation and Other Works*. 1930, London: The Hogarth Press, 1975.
Knowles, Sebastian D. G. *Dublin Helix*. Gainesville: University of Florida P, 2001.
Kopelman, Michael, D. et al. "The Great Escape: A Neuropsychological Study of Psychogenic Amnesia." *Neuropsychologica*. Vol. 32, No. 6 (1994): 675-691.
Kopelman, Michael, D. "Focal Retrograde Amnesia and the Attribution of Causality: An Exceptionally Critical Review." *Cognitive Neuropsychology*, Vol. 17, No. 7 (2000): 585-621.
Kraemer, Eric, R. "Divine Omniscience and Criteria of Intentionality." *Philosophy and Phenomenological Research*. Vol. 45, No. 1. Sept, (1984): 131- 135.
Kramer, Lawrence. 'Culture and Musical Hermeneutics: The Salome Complex'. *Cambridge Opera Journal*. Vol. 2. No. 3 (Nov., 1990): 269-294.
— — *Classical Music and Postmodern Knowledge*. USA: The University of California Press, 1995.
— — *Musical Meaning: Towards a Critical History*. USA: The University of California Press, 2001.
— — *After the Lovedeath: Sexual Violence and the Making of Culture*. USA: The University of California, 1997.
Kress, Gunther and Theo Van Leeuwen. *Multimodal Discourse: The Modes and Media of Contemporary Communication*. London: Edward Arnold, 2002.

Kristeva, Julia. *La révolution du langage poétique.* Paris: Éditions du Seuil, 1974.
— — *Revolution in Poetic Language.* New York: Columbia University Press, 1984.
— — *Pouvoirs de l'horreur.* Paris: Éditions du Seuil, 1980.
— — *Powers of Horror: An Essay on Abjection,* trans. Leon S. Roudiez. New York: Columbia University Press, 1982.
— — *The Kristeva Reader,* trans., ed. and intro. by Toril Moi. Oxford: Blackwell, 1986.
Kundera, Milan. *The Art of the Novel,* trans. Linda Asher. New York: HarperCollins, 1993.
Lacan, Jacques. *Écrits.* Paris: Éditions du Seuil, 1966.
— — *The Four Fundamental Concepts of Psychoanalysis.*1973.Trans. Alan Sheridan. USA: W.W. Norton and Company, 1981.
— — "The Insistence of the Letter in the Unconscious." 1957. Eds. Richard and Fernande DeGeorge. *The Structuralists From Marx to Levi-Strauss.* New York: Doubleday Anchor, 1972.
Lant, Kathleen Margaret. 'The Big Strip Tease: Female Bodies and Male Power in the Poetry of Sylvia Plath'. *Contemporary Literature* 44.4 (Winter 1993), 620-670.
Leibniz, G. W. *The Monadology and Other Philosophical Writings,* trans. and ed. Robert Latta. Oxford: Oxford University Press, 1925.
Lerner, Fred. *The Story of Libraries from the Invention of Writing to the Computer Age.* New York: The Continuum Publishing Company, 1999.
Levi, Primo. *Survival in Auschwitz.* 1961. New York: Simon and Schuster, 1996.
— — *The Drowned and the Saved.* 1986, trans. Raymond Rosenthal. London: Michael Joseph, 1988.
— — *If This is a Man,* trans. Stuart Wolf and Paul Bailey. London: Abacus, 1987.
Levin, Harry. *James Joyce: A Critical Introduction.* London: Faber and Faber, 1941.
Levin, Lawrence L. "The Sirens Episode as Music: Joyce's Experiment in Prose Polyphony", *James Joyce Quarterly,* 3/1 (Fall 1965): 12-24.
Lindop, Grevel. *The Opium Eater, A Life of Thomas De Quincey.* London: J.M. Dent and Sons Ltd, 1981.
— — "General Introduction". *The Works of De Quincey, Vol. 1. Writings, 1799-820.* Grevel Lindop, general ed. London: Pickering and Chatto, 2000
— — "Introduction". *The Works of De Quincey, Vol. 2. Confessions of an English Opium-Eater.* 1821-1856, ed. Grevel Lindop. London: Pickering and Chatto.
Lituchy, Barry M, ed. *Jasenovac and the Holocaust in Yugoslavia: analyses and survivor testimonies/ edited with an introduction by Barry M.*

Lituchy; with the editorial assistance of Milo Yelesiyevich. International Conference and Exhibit on the Jasenovac Concentration Camps. New York: Jasenovac Research Institute, 2006

Lodge, David. *The Art of Fiction*. London: Penguin, 1992.

— — *Twentieth Century Literary Criticism*. London: Longmans, 1972.

— — "The Language of Modernist Fiction: Metaphor and Metonymy." *Modernism*, eds. M. Bradbury and J. McFarlane. Harmondsworth: Penguin, 1983.

Lucie-Smith, Edward, ed. *Primer of Experimental Poetry 1 1870-1922*. London: Rapp and Whiting (Andre Deutsch), 1971.

Lukács, Georg. *The Meaning of Contemporary Realism*. Trans. John and Necke Mande. London: Merlin, 1963.

— — 'Lukács on his Life and Work.' *New Left Review*, 1/68, 1971, 49-58.

Macleod, A.D. "Posttraumatic Stress Disorder, Dissociative Fugue and a Locator Beacon." *Australian and New Zealand Journal of Psychiatry*. 33 (1999): 102-104.

Manguel, Alberto. *A History of Reading*. New York: Viking, 1995.

Mann, Philip, *The Dandy at Dusk*, London: Paris Paysan Press, 2016.

Mann, Alfred. *The Study of Fugue*. 1958. New York: W.W. Norton and Co, 1965.

Mann, Thomas. *Death in Venice*, 1912, trans. H.T. Lowe-Porter. Harmondsworth: Penguin, 1957.

Manne, Robert. "The Unknown Story of Cornelia Rau." *The Monthly*, September 2005.

Markowitsch, Hans J. "Functional Neuroimaging Correlates of Functional Amnesia." *Memory*, 7 (516) (1999): 561-583.

Markowitsch, Hans J., ed. *Transient Global Amnesia and Related Disorders*. Toronto: Hogrefe and Huber, 1990.

Markowitsch, Hans J., et al. "Impaired episodic memory retrieval in a case of probable psychogenic amnesia." *Psychiatry Research: Neuroimaging Section*. 74 (1997) 119-126.

Martin, C. Gimelli. *The Ruins of Allegory: Paradise Lost and the Metamorphosis of Epic Convention*. Durham: Duke University Press, 1998.

Martin, Timothy. *Joyce and Wagner – A Study of Influence*. Cambridge:- Cambridge University Press, 1999.

Martin, Timothy, and Ruth Bauerle. "The Voice from the Prompt Box: Otto Luening Remembers James Joyce in Zurich." *Journal of Modern Literature* 17/1 (Summer 1990): 34-48.

Masson, David. 'Introduction'. 'The English Mail-Coach', *The Collected Writings of Thomas De Quincey Vol. X111, Tales and Prose Phantasies*, ed. David Masson. London: A and C. Black, 1897.

Mathews, David. *Landscape into Sound*. St Albans: Claridge Press, 1992.

McClary, Susan. *Feminine Endings: Music, Gender and Sexuality*. 1991. Second edition. Minneapolis: University of Minnesota Press, 2002.

McLuhan, Marshall. *The Gutenberg Galaxy: The Making of Typographic*

Man. Toronto: University of Toronto Press, 1962.
Melbourne, Jane. "The Narrator as Chorus in 'Paradise Lost.'" *Studies in English Literature, 1500-1900.* Vol. 33, (1993): 149-162.
Menuhin, Yehudi, *The Music of Man,* ed. Curtis W. Davis. New York: Methuen, 1979.
Micale, Mark, S., ed. *The Mind of Modernism: Medicine, Psychology and the Cultural Arts in Europe and America 1880-1940.* Stanford, California: Stanford University Press, 2004.
Milton, John. *The Complete Poems of John Milton,* ed. Charles W. Eliot, New York; P.F. Collier and Son, 1909.
— — *Paradise Lost. Books 1 and 11.* Intro. Rev. J.C. Scrimgeour, London: Macmillan and Co, 1915.
Moore, Susanna. *In the Cut.* New York: Picador, 1995.
Moretti, Franco. *Signs Taken for Wonders: Essays in the Sociology of Literary Forms,* trans. Susan Fischer et al. London: Verso, 1988.
Morrison, Robert. "Introduction". *The Works of Thomas De Quincey. Vol. 16. Articles from Tait's Edinburgh Magazine, MacPhail's Edinburgh Ecclesiastical Journal, The Glasgow Athenaeum Album, the North British Review, and Blackwood's Edinburgh Magazine 1847-9,* Robert Morrison, ed. Grevel Lindop, general ed. London: Pickering and Chatto, 2000.
Moss, Philip/Department of Immigration and Border Protection. *Review into recent allegations relating to conditions and circumstances at the Regional Processing Centre at Nauru/Philip Moss Review.* Canberra, Australian Capital Territory: Department of Immigration and Border Protection, 2015.
Mozart, Wolfgang Amadeus. *Symphony No. 41, KV 551 "Jupiter."* 1788. Leonard Bernstein, conductor. Vienna Philharmonic Orchestra. Deutsche Grammophon. Audio CD: Sept 19, 1995.
Mulhearn, Francis, ed. *Contemporary Marxist Literary Criticism.* New York and Abingdon, Oxon. Routledge, 2013.
Mullin, Kathryn."'The essence of vulgarity': The Barmaid Controversy in the 'Sirens' episode of James Joyce's *Ulysses.*"*Textual Practice* 18. 4. 2004: 475-495.
Murphy, Michael. "À bout de souffle: Marcel Proust's American Nervousness and the roman d'Albertine." *Women: a Cultural Review,* Vol. 16, No. 2 2005: 164-188.
Nabokov, Vladimir. *Lectures on Literature.* London: Picador, 1980.
National Union of Journalists. *Reporting Asylum and Refugee Issues,* 2004. <http://www.mediawise.org.uk >. Retried 5/1/2008
Nietzsche, Frederich. *The Birth of Tragedy,* 1872, trans. Douglas Smith. Oxford: Oxford University Press, 2000.
— — *Die Geburt der Tragödie aus dem Geiste der Musik,* 1872, Berlin: Deutschen Taschenbuch Verlag. Walter de Gruyter, 1988.
— — *The Birth of Tragedy,* 1872, trans. Shaun Whiteside. London: Penguin, 2003.

— — *The Birth of Tragedy and the Case of Wagner*, trans. Walter Kaufmann. New York: Vintage Books, 1966.

— — *The Case of Wagner, Nietzsche contra Wagner, and selected Aphorisms*, trans. Anthony M. Ludovici. Edinburgh: T.N. Foulis, 1911.

North, Julian. 'Review of *De Quincey Reviewed: Thomas De Quincey's Critical Reception, 1821-1994*'. *Romanticism on the Net.* https://www.erudit.org/revue/ron/1999/v/n13/005845ar.html.

Ordway, Scott J. "A Dominant Boylan: Music, meaning, and Sonata Form in the 'Sirens' Episode of *Ulysses*." *James Joyce Quarterly*, 45/ I (Fall 2007): 85-96.

Oosterling, Henk. "Sens(a)ble Intermediality and Interesse, Towards an Ontology of the In-Between." *Intermedialities*, no. 1. printemps Spring 2003. CRI Montreal: 29-46.

O'Quinn, Daniel. "Ravishment Twice Weekly: De Quincey's Opera Pleasures." *Romanticism on the Net.* Issue 34, 2004: 1-18.

Page, H.A., ed. "Introduction." *Thomas De Quincey. His Life and Writings With Unpublished Correspondence.* Vol 1. 2nd ed London: 1879.

Painter, George, D. *Marcel Proust, a Biography* Vol. I. London: Chatto and Windus, 1959.

Painter, George, D. *Marcel Proust, a Biography* Vol. II. London: Chatto and Windus, 1959.

Perloff, Marjorie, 'Sound Scraps, Vision Scraps,' *Reading for Form*, eds. Susan J. Wolfson and Marshall Brown. Seattle: University of Washington Press, 2006.

Pears, David. *Motivated Irrationality*. Oxford: Oxford University Press, 1984.

Pickering, Sharon. "Common Sense and Original Deviancy: News Discourses and Asylum Seekers in Australia". *Journal of Refugee Studies* 14 (2001): 169-89.

Pierrot, Jean. *The Decadent Imagination*, trans. Derek Coltman. Chicago: The University of Chicago Press, 1981.

Plath, Sylvia. *Ariel.* 1965. London: Faber and Faber. 1979.

— — *Johnny Panic and the Bible of Dreams and other prose writings with an Introduction by Ted Hughes.* London: Faber and Faber, 1977.

— — *Three Women.* 1960. London: Faber and Faber, 1976.

— — *The Colossus.* 1960. London: Faber and Faber, 1967.

— — *Winter Trees.* London: Faber and Faber, 1971.

— — *Crossing the Water.* London: Faber and Faber. 1971.

— — *The Bell Jar.* 1963. London: Faber and Faber, 1977.

Plath, Sylvia and P. Orr. "A 1962 Sylvia Plath Interview with Peter Orr". *The Poet Speaks: Interviews with Contemporary Poets Conducted by Hilary Morrish, Peter Orr, John Press, and Ian Scott-Kilvery.* London: Routledge, 1966.

Plato. *The Dialogues of Plato. Vol. 3. The Republic, Timaeus, Critias*, trans. B. Jowett. London: Oxford University Press, 1892.

— — *The Republic.* Trans. Desmond Lee. London: Penguin, 1983.

Poli, Roberto. "At the Origins of Analytic Philosophy." *Aletheia* 6 (1994): 218-231.
Porter, Roger, J. "The Demon-Past: De Quincey and the Autobiographer's Dilemma." *Studies in English Literature* 20, 1980. 591-609.
Power, Arthur. "The Joyce I Knew." *James Joyce: Interviews and Recollections*, ed. E. H. Mikhail. London: Macmillan Press Ltd., 1990. 81-84
Price, Larkin B., ed. *Marcel Proust: A Critical Panorama*. USA: University of Illinois Press, 1973.
Proust, Adrien and G. Ballet. *L'hygiène du neurasthénique*. Paris: Masson, 1897.
Proust, Marcel, *Remembrance of Things Past*. Volume 1. *Swann's Way*. (1922), trans. C.K. Scott Moncrieff. London: Chatto and Windus, 1960.
— — Volume 1. *Swann's Way*.(1922), trans. C.K. Scott Moncrieff and Terence Kilmartin. London: Chatto and Windus, 1996.
— — *In Search of Lost Time*. Volume 2. *Within a Budding Grove*, trans. C.K. Scott Moncrieff and Terence Kilmartin. London: Vintage-Chatto and Windus, 1996a.
— — *In Search of Lost Time*. Volume 3. *The Guermantes Way*, trans. C.K. Scott Moncrieff and Terence Kilmartin. London: Vintage-Chatto and Windus, 1996a
— — *In Search of Lost Time*. Volume 3. *The Guermantes Way*, trans. C.K. Scott Moncrieff and Terence Kilmartin. London: Vintage-Chatto and Windus, 1996b.
— — *In Search of Lost Time*. Volume 4. *Sodom and Gomorrah*, trans. C.K. Scott Moncrieff and Terence Kilmartin. London: Vintage-Chatto and Windus, 1996c.
— — *In Search of Lost Time*. Volume 5. *The Captive; The Fugitive*, trans. C.K Scott Moncrieff and Terence Kilmartin. London: Vintage-Chatto and Windus, 1996d.
— — *In Search of Lost Time*. Volume 6. *Time Regained*, trans. C.K Scott Moncrieff and Terence Kilmartin. London: Vintage-Chatto and Windus, 1996e.
— — *Jean Santeuil, precede de Les Plairs et les Jours. Pierre Clarac et Yves Sandre*, ed. 4. Paris : Collection Pleiade. Gallimard, 1971.
— — *Pleasures and Regrets*, trans. Louise Varese. London: Peter Owen, 1986..
— — *Against Saint-Beauve and Other Essays*, trans. John Sturrock. London: Penguin Books, 1988.
Queripel, John. *Bonhoeffer: Prophet and Martyr*, Eugene: Wipf and Stock, 2016
Quintilianus, Marcus Fabius. *Institutio Oratoria*, trans. H.E. Butler. Loeb Classical Library. Cambridge: Harvard University Press, 1920.
Rameau, Jean-Philippe. *Erreurs sur la Musique dans l'Encyclopédie*. Paris: Sébastien Jorry, 1755.

— — *Suite des erreurs sur la Musique dans l'Encyclopédie*. Paris: 1756.
— — *Traité de l'harmonie réduite à ses principes naturels*. Paris: Ballard, 1722.
— — *Treatise on Harmony*, trans. Philip Gossett. New York: Dover, 1971.
— — *Musique raisonnée*. C. Kintzler and J.C. Malgroire, eds. Paris: Stock, 1980.
Rauchensteiner, Manfred. *The First World War and the End of the Habsburg Monarchy 1914-1918*, 1993, 2nd ed. Wien: Böhlau Verlag, 2013.
Refugee Council. *Media release*. Sydney, September 8, 2009.
Richardson, Joanna. "Introduction." *Baudelaire: Selected Poems*, trans. Joanna Richardson. G.B: Penguin, 1976.
Riley, Denise. *The Words of Selves: Identification, Solidarity, Irony*. Stanford: Stanford University Press, 2000.
Rimbaud, Arthur. *Rimbaud: Complete works, Selected Letters*, trans. Wallace Fowlie. London: University of Chicago Press, 1966.
Roberts, Daniel Sanjiv. "Not 'Forsworn with Pink Ribbons': Hannah More, Thomas De Quincey, and the Literature of Power." *Romanticism on the Net*. Issue 17 (2002). 1-11.
Roe, Nicholas. *Wordsworth and Coleridge: The Radical Years*. Oxford: Clarendon Press, 1988.
Rogers, Margaret. "Decoding the Fugue in 'Sirens." *James Joyce Literary Supplement* 4.1. (1990) 15-20.
Rosen, Philip and Nina Abfelbaum, *Bearing Witness: A Resource Guide to Literature, Poetry, Art, Music and Videos by Holocaust Victims and Survivors*. Westport USA: Greenwood Publishing Group, 2001.
Rosen, Charles. *The Romantic Generation*. Cambridge, Mass: Harvard University Press, 1975.
— — *The Classical Style: Hayden, Mozart, Beethoven*. New York: W. W. Norton and Co.,1972.
Rousseau Jean-Jacques. *A Complete Dictionary of Music Consisting of a copious Explanation of all the Words necessary to a true Knowledge and Understanding of Music*, trans. William Wearing, second edition. London, Fleet-Street and Dublin. 1779.
— — *Essai sur l'origine des langues*, ed. Catherine Kintzler. Paris: Flammarion, 1993.
— — *Essay on the Origin of Language*, trans. Jogn H. Moran and Alexander Gode. Chicago: University of Chicago Press,1966.
— — *Oeuvres Completes. Vol. V. Écrits sur la musique, le langage, et la théâtre y compris notamment: la Lettre à D'Alembert; Dictionnaire de musique; Essai sur l'origine des langues*. B. Gagnebin and M. Raymond, eds. Paris. Éditions Gallimard, 1995.
— — "Letter to M. d'Alembert", 1758, *Politics and the Arts*, trans. Allan Bloom. Ithaca, NY: Cornell University Press, 1960.
— — *The Confessions*, 1781, trans. J.M. Cohen. London: Penguin.1953.
— — *The Social Contract*, 1762, trans. Maurice Cranston. London:

Penguin, 2004.
—— *Essay on the Origin of Languages* in *On the Origin of Languages*, trans. J.H. Moran and A. Gode. Chicago: University of Chicago Press, 1986.
Rousseau, Jean-Jacques and Herder Johann Gottfried. *On the Origin of Language*. 1966, trans. John H. Moran and Alexander Gode. Chicago: The University of Chicago Press, 1986.
Ruskin, John. *Sesame and Lilies*. London: George Allen, 1905.
Russett, Margaret. *De Quincey's Romanticism: Canonical Minority and the Forms of Transmission*. Cambridge: Cambridge University Press, 1997.
Rycroft, Charles. "Dissociation of the Personality." *Oxford Companion to the Mind*, ed. Richard L. Gregory. Oxford: OUP, 1987.
—— *Anxiety and Neurosis*. London: Maresfield, 1988.
Sackville-West, Edward. *A Flame in Sunlight: Life and Work of Thomas De Quincey*. London: Cassell and Co.,1936.
Said, Edward, W. *Musical Elaborations*. London: Chatto and Windus, 1991.
Said, Edward, W. *Culture and Imperialism*. 1993. New York: Vintage,1994.
Sartre, Jean-Paul. *Being and Nothingness: An Essay on Phenomenological Ontology*. 1943. Trans. Hazel E. Barnes. London: Methuen. 1972.
Savio, Antonio Fonda and Letizia Fonda. "James Joyce: Two Reminiscences." *James Joyce: Interviews and Recollections*, ed. E. H. Mikhail. London: Macmillan Press Ltd., 1990. 48-50
Saussure, Ferdinand de. *Course in General Linguistics*, trans. Wade Baskin. London: Duckworth, 1983.
Scher, Steven Paul. *Essays on Music and Literature by Steven Paul Scher 1967-2004*. (Word and Music Studies 5), eds. Walter Bernhart and Werner Wolf. The Netherlands: Rodopi, 2004.
Schmidt, Dennis, J. "Black Milk and Blue: Celan and Heidegger on Pain and Language". *Word Traces: Readings of Paul Celan*, ed. Aris Fioretos. Baltimore: The John Hopkins University Press, 1994.
Scholes, Percy, ed. *The Oxford Companion to Music*. Oxford: Oxford University Press, 1993.
Scholes, Robert and Robert Kellog. *The Nature of Narrative*. Oxford: Oxford University Press, 1966.
Scott, Rosie. *Faith Singer*. Sydney: Hachette, 2003.
Scott, Rosie and Keneally, Tom, eds. *Another Country: Writers in Detention*. Sydney: Halstead Press, 2004.
Scott, Rosie and Keneally, Tom, eds. *A Country Too Far: Writings on Asylum Seekers*. Sydney: Penguin, 2013.
Schrader, Leo. "Bach: the Conflict Between the Sacred and the Secular." *Journal of the History of Ideas*, VII, no. 2, 1946.
Sharp, Alan. *The Versailles Settlement: Peacemaking After the First World War 1919-1923*, London: Palgrave Macmillan, 2nd ed., 2008.
Shilstone, Frederick W. "Autobiography as 'Involute': De Quincey on

the Therapies of Memory." *South Atlantic Review* 48 (1) 1983: 20-34

Shockley, Alan. *Music in the Words: Musical Form and Counterpoint in the Twentieth Century Novel.* Farnham: Ashgate, 2009.

Skilbeck, Ruth. *Australian Fugue: The Antipode Room.* Newcastle: Postmistress Press, 2014.

— — *Missing* (Australian Fugue). Newcastle: PostMistress Press, 2015.

— — "Through the 'I's' if Lost Time: Proust's Performative Fugue of Temps Perdu." *Time, Transcendence, Performance Conference proceedings.* Melbourne: Monash University, October 1, 2009.

— — "Emotional trauma steals memories and lives." *Sydney Morning Herald,* Sydney, July 18, 2015.

— — "Exiled Writers, Human Rights and Social Advocacy Movements in Australia: a Critical Fugal Analysis. *Cultural Studies of Rights: Critical Articulations,* ed. John Nguyet Erni. Abingdon, Oxon; New York, Routledge, 2011; 2014.

— — "First Things: Reflections on Single-Lens Digital Reflex Photography with a Wide Angle Lens." *The International Journal of the Image,* Vol.3, Issue 4. 2013: 55-67.

— — "Remembering Australia's Forgotten Mothers: Reclaiming Lost Identity in Colonial History." *Journal of the Motherhood Initiative for Research and Community Involvement,* Vol. 3, Issue 2. 2012. 163-177.

— — "Gazing Boldly Back and Forward: Urban Aboriginal Women Artists and New Global Feminisms in Transnational Art." *International Journal of the Arts in Society,* Vol.5, Issue 6: 2011, 261-276.

— — "Re-viewing Feminist Influences in Transnational Art: A Multimodal, Fugal Analysis of Mary Kelly's Texts of 'Maternal Desire.'"*International Journal of the Arts in Society,* Vol. 4, Issue 5, 2010: 18-28.

— — "Art Journalism and the Impact of 'Globalisation': New Fugal Modalities of Storytelling in Austral-Asian Writing." *Pacific Journalism Review,* Vol. 14, No. 2, 2008: 141-161.

— — "War Drums Beat Over Beckett", *The Irish Times,* January 18, 2003.

— — "Australian Contemporary Art Comes of Age." *Australian Art Collector,* Issue 25, July-Sept 2003, pp. 75-96.

— — 'Tracey Moffatt'. *POL Oxygen: Design, Art, Architecture.* Special Collectors Issue 8, 2004, 44-52.

— — 'French Resistance.' *(Not Only)Black + White.* Issue 47, pp. 20-21.

Skilbeck, Ruth, Mary Kelly and Kelly Barry, "Ruth Skilbeck in Conversation with Mary Kelly and Kelly Barrie", *The M Word: Real Mothers in Contemporary Art,* eds Myrel Chernick and Jenny Klein, Toronto: Demeter Press, 2011.

Smith, Don Noel. "Musical Form and Principles in the Scheme of Ulysses." *Twentieth Century Literature,* 18/1 (April 1972): 79-92

Sontag, Susan. *Illness as Metaphor; Aids and its Metaphors*. 1978. London: Penguin, 1991.
Spender, Lady Natasha. "Psychology of Music." *The Oxford Companion to the Mind*, ed. Richard L. Gregory, Oxford: OUP, 1987.
Squires, Judith. *The New Politics of Gender Equality*. London: Palgrave/Macmillan, 2007.
Stein, Gertrude. "Bee Time Vine" *Primer of Experimental Poetry*, ed. E. Lucie-Smith London: Rapp and Whiting/André Deutsch, 1971.
Stevenson, Anne. *Bitter Fame: A Life of Sylvia Plath (BF)*. Boston: Houghton-Mifflin, 1989.
Subotnik, Rose. "Whose Magic Flute? Intimations of Reality at the Gates of the Enlightenment." *19th-Century Music*. 15 Fall 1991: 132-50
Sultan, Stanley. "The Sirens at the Ormond Bar: *Ulysses*." *University of Kansas City Review*, 26/1 (December 1959): 83-92.
Sydney PEN. 'President's Letter', *Sydney PEN Magazine*. 2016: 2.
Sydney PEN. *Sydney PEN Award*. <http://www.pen.org.au. >2006
Sykes-Davies, Hugh. *Thomas De Quincey*. British Book News. Bibliographical Series of Supplements, *Writers and their Work*, no. 167. London: Longmann, 1964.
Sztompka, Piotr. "The Trauma of Social Change: A Case of Postcommunist Societies" in *Cultural Trauma and Collective Identity*, ed. Jeffrey C. Alexander. California: University of California Press, 2004.
Tabermer, Stuart. *German Literature in the Age of Globalisation*. London: A and C Black, 2004.
Tadié, Jean-Yves. *Marcel Proust*, 1996, trans. Euan Cameron. London: Penguin Books-Viking, 2000.
Taylor, Eugene. *The Mystery of Personality: A History of Psycho-dynamic Theories*. New York: Springer-Verlag, 2009.
Tennant, Emma. *Sylvia and Ted*. London: Harper Collins. 2001.
Tesser, Lyn M. 'Europe's pivotal peace projects: Ethnic separation and European integration. *European Policy Analysi*s, March Issue, 2015.
Tissié, Philippe Auguste. *Les aliénés voyageurs : essai médico-physiologique thèse de médecine de Bordeaux n° 29*, 1887. Paris: Doin, 1887.
Todorov, Tzvetan. *The Poetics of Prose*, trans. Richard Howard. New York: Cornell University Press, 1977.
Tulving, Endel, ed. *Memory, Consciousness and the Brain: The Tallinn Conference*. New York: The Psychology Press, 1999.
Turkus, Joan, A. "Introduction to Dissociation." *Dissociation in the UK* website. Retrieved March 15, 2005.
Verba, Cynthia. *Music and the French Enlightenment: Reconstruction of a Dialogue 1750-1764*. Oxford: Clarendon Press, 1993.
Walker, Paul Mark. *Theories of Fugue from the Age of Josquin to the Age of Bach*. New York: University of Rochester Press, 2000.

Watson, Gary, ed. *Free Will*. Oxford: Oxford University Press, 1982.
Weaver, Jack W. *Joyce's Music and Noise – Theme and Variation in His Writings*. Gainesville: University Press of Florida, 1998.
Weber, Max. *The Rational and Social Foundations of Music*. 1921, trans. Don Martindale. Carbondale: Southern Illinois University Press, 1958.
— — *The Protestant Ethic and the Spirit of Capitalism*. 1905. London: George Allen and Unwin, 1930.
Williams, Ralph Vaughan. "Fugue" *Grove's Music Dictionary of Music and Musicians. Vol II*, ed. J.A. Fuller Maitland. Boston: The Macmillan Company, 1906. 114-121.
Wimmers, Inge Crosman. *Proust and Emotion: The Importance of Affect in "À la recherché du temps perdu"*. Toronto: University of Toronto Press, 2003.
Wimsatt, W.K Jnr. and Monroe C. Beardsley. 1946. "The Intentional Fallacy." *Twentieth Century Literary Criticism*, ed. David Lodge. London: Longmans, 1972.
— — "The Affective Fallacy." 1949. *Twentieth Century Literary Criticism*, ed. David Lodge. London: Longmans, 1972.
Wittgenstein, Ludwig. *Philosophical Investigations*, 1953, trans. G.E.M. Anscombe. Oxford: Basil Blackwell, 1981.
Wokler, Robert. *Rousseau on Society, Politics, Music and Language: An Historical Interpretation of his Early Writings*. New York and London: Garland Publishing, 1987.
Wolf, Werner. *The Musicalization of Fiction. A Study in the Theory and History of Intermediality*. The Netherlands: Rodopi, 1999.
Wolff, Christoph. *Johann Sebastian Bach: The Learned Musician*. USA: Norton, 2000.
Woolf, Virginia. *The Common Reader: Second Series*. London: The Hogarth Press, 1932.
Wordsworth, William and Samuel Coleridge. *Lyrical Ballads*, 1798, eds, R.L. Brett and A.R. Jones. London: Methuen, 1965.
Wordsworth, Jonathan and Wordsworth, Jessica, eds. *The New Penguin Book of Romantic Poetry*. London: Penguin, 2003.
Yeats, William Butler. *Selected Poetry*. London: Pan Macmillan, 1979.
Young, Robert. *Postcolonialism*. Oxford: Blackwell, 2001.
Young, Robert, M. and Ian Pitchford, eds. "Freud's Theory of Creativity." *Psychoanalytic Aesthetics of the British School*. Retrieved March 8, 2006.
Zimmerman, Nadya. "Musical Form as Narrator: The Fugue of the Sirens in James Joyce's Ulysses." *Journal of Modern Literature*, 26/1 (Fall 2002): 108-18.

www.ingramcontent.com/pod-product-compliance
Lightning Source LLC
Chambersburg PA
CBHW021114300426
44113CB00006B/140